The Whitehall reader

The Whitehall reader

The UK's administrative machine in action

Edited by Peter Barberis

Open University Press
Buckingham · Philadelphia

Open University Press
Celtic Court
22 Ballmoor
Buckingham
MK18 1XW

and
1900 Frost Road, Suite 101
Bristol, PA 19007, USA

First Published 1996

A catalogue record of this book is available from the British Library

ISBN 0 335 19311 0 (pb)   0 335 19312 9 (hb)

Library of Congress Cataloging-in-Publication Data
Barberis, Peter, 1948–
     The Whitehall reader / Peter Barberis.
        p.   cm.
     Includes bibliographical references and index.
     ISBN 0-335-19311-0 (pbk.).   ISBN 0-335-19312-9 (hbk.)
        1. Administrative agencies—Great Britain. 2. Executive departments—Great
     Britain. 3. Great Britain—Politics and government—1945-   I. Title.
JN318.B37 1996
354.41'01—dc20   95-24921
                                                                                CIP

Typeset by Type Study, Scarborough
Printed in Great Britain by St Edmundsbury Press, Bury St Edmunds, Suffolk

Contents

Introduction and acknowledgements

The title of this volume – *The Whitehall Reader* – should convey its character. A word or two of explanation may nevertheless be useful. The subject area is Whitehall. Strictly, this includes the political executive as well as the permanent bureaucracy of senior civil servants. In focusing mainly, though not exclusively, on the latter this collection of readings follows the common usage of the term 'Whitehall'. As a collection of readings it also follows a pattern now familiar – at least in the social sciences. It features extracts from a multiplicity of different sources, given shape by a series of brief commentaries.

The aim is to provide ready access for students (and tutors) to a range of writings that together give a fair flavour of the main activities in and around Whitehall in recent years. There has been a deliberate emphasis upon official documents, occasional papers, quality newspaper articles and other miscellaneous source material. So the selections do not purport to be quite a representative sample of the literature. This is justified in the cause of making available to students material that exists (usually) in published form but that may not be easily accessible. There is nevertheless a leavening of extracts from books and (especially) from some of the more familiar academic journals. With this, it is hoped, there is a reasonable balance between the authoritative, the seminal and the more derivative but equally informative contributions; between the well-known and the less familiar; between the polemical, the agenda-setting and the analytical approaches. No apology is made for bringing together the contributions of politicians, civil servants, academics and other informed observers. The aim is not to sell any particular 'line' about Whitehall but to provide the vehicle for others, many of whom have lines to sell. By letting the various protagonists, critics and commentators speak in their own words this book should give students a more vivid impression of the issues involved than is usually possible even from the most accomplished detached commentary. In conjunction with lectures, wider reading and due time for reflection, this collection will, it is hoped, enhance students' understanding and help to enliven seminar discussions.

A difficulty for the compiler is to judge the likely shelf-life of the selections. Choices are made in the hope that they and the issues they reflect will hold their place at least for a reasonable period. This is a hostage to fortune. The world is a rapidly changing place. The curse of the ephemeral is ever-present. Initiatives make their appearance and spark the scene. Then, at a blink, they have been outshone by the glister of the latest model. Buzz words come and they go, drowned by the hum of new ones. The all-consuming passions of one day may become the still, misty, reminiscences of the next. Much can be lost, gained or transfigured in the warp and weft of a Parliamentary session, to say nothing about the convulsions of the fever-charged mass media. Until tomorrow and the day after we cannot know for sure whether the concerns of the moment will continue to claim our attention. Some will wither on the vine. Others will assume their place as permanent fixtures, beyond serious dispute and therefore little discussed, though baring a proud edge from time-to-time. Others will remain matters of more conspicuous significance and contention. But which ones?

In spite of all this, most of the selections in this reader are from the past ten years or so. There are exceptions, but not many. Each reading is organized into one of six chapters. These chapters reflect issues and arguments that have been central to the academic study and public debate about Whitehall during this period, some being of longer standing. They are likely so to remain for some time to come, because they continue and will continue the process of implementation and further development; or because they are at the apex of political, ideological or philosophical conflict; or simply because, for complex social or technical reasons, they will be difficult to resolve. Each chapter has a short prologue, setting the scene and introducing the chosen readings. All this is preceded by an introductory essay (Chapter 1) outlining the main developments in Whitehall since the Fulton Report of 1968.

The second chapter introduces the series of readings and focuses upon the structure and workings of the Whitehall machine. The third deals with civil servants, their relationships with ministers and their involvement in decision-making. This is a hardy perennial, and the readings reflect the fact. But the immediate context seems to have changed in recent years. The readings reflect this too. The next chapter concerns questions of loyalty and responsibility. There are both practical and more philosophical dimensions to this knot of puzzles, some of which have provoked fierce controversy. No less controversial have been Whitehall's managerial reforms. Chapter 5 is devoted to a description and exposition of the main recent reforms and of the intentions associated with their introduction. There is thus an emphasis upon government and other official sources. This emphasis is reversed in Chapter 6. Here the critics have their say. Some are opposed in principle to many if not all the major initiatives of the 1980s and 1990s. Others are more favourably disposed but frustrated at the pace or vigour of implementation. Chapter 7 looks at Whitehall, Parliament and the public. It touches upon civil servants and the select committees, including the controversial Osmotherly Rules. It covers the question of open government, much discussed now and down the years. The volume concludes with an annotated bibliography, directing the reader to further sources. Many of these are directly connected to the subject matter of the readings but the net has also been cast wider to encourage further lines of enquiry.

As with *Desert Island Discs*, everyone will have his or her own favourites or preferred selections from the vast available literature. Here, unlike for the imaginary castaway, choices must necessarily reflect factors other than idealized self-gratification. This makes things no easier. Fortunately, I had guidance from some of the leading lights within the Joint University Council Public Administration Committee. Specifically, I should like to record my thanks to Professors Richard Chapman (University of Durham), John Greenwood (De Montfort, Leicester) and Grant Jordan (Aberdeen), and to Drs Barry O'Toole (University of Glasgow) and Rick Wilford (Queen's, Belfast). I am grateful to Liz Rutherford and Alison Hill, who word-processed my own contributions to this volume, and to the Open University Press, who handled the project through its various stages. Pam Beckley at HMSO deserves special mention for helping to pilot through the procedural minefield my request for Crown copyright clearances. Needless to say, the final responsibility is mine and mine alone for the selections made in this volume and for the way they have been organized and presented.

The editor and publishers are grateful to the following for permission to reproduce material. Reed Consumer Books and Sheil Land Associates for Reading 2.1. Blackwell Publishers for Readings 2.2, 2.5, 3.6, 3.7, 4.3 and 6.5. Macmillan Press Ltd for Reading 2.3. The Joint University Council for Reading 2.4. Times Newspapers Ltd and the Rt Hon. Baroness Castle of Blackburn for Reading 3.1. Peters Fraser & Dunlop Group Ltd for Reading 3.2. Guardian Newspapers Ltd for Reading 3.3. HMSO (following guidelines for the reproduction of Crown and Parliamentary Copyright) for Readings 3.4, 4.2, 4.4, 7.2, 7.3 and 7.8. Wroxton College for Reading 3.5. Cambridge University Press and Professor Anthony King for Reading 3.8. Cambridge University Press and Professor Richard Rose for Reading 3.9. The Controller of HMSO for Readings 4.1, 5.2, 5.3, 5.4, 7.1 and 7.6. The Department of Government, University of Essex for Reading 4.5. Touche Ross and Co., Shell UK Ltd and Peter Jay for Reading 4.6. The Joint University Council and Sir Robin Butler for Readings 5.1 and 5.6. Addison-Wesley Publishing Company Inc. for Reading 5.5. Conservative Political Centre for Reading 5.7. IDPM, University of Manchester for Reading 6.1. Times Newspapers Ltd and Professor Fred Inglis for Reading 6.2. Times Newspapers Ltd and Vernon Bogdanor for Reading 6.3. Open University Press for Reading 6.4. The Social Market Foundation for Reading 6.6. The European Policy Forum for Reading 6.7. Frank Cass Publishers for Reading 7.4. The BBC for Reading 7.5. Charter 88 Trust for Reading 7.7.

1

Introductory essay: Whitehall since the Fulton Report

The purpose of this introductory essay is to chronicle the main developments over the past thirty years and to note their significance for the way in which the senior civil service operates. This is no easy task. For one thing, so much has happened. For another thing, the wheel is still in spin, so to speak. It is as yet too early to say exactly where some of the more recent developments will ultimately lead. Particular initiatives sometimes assume a new significance when the dust has settled. They can seem different, too, from an alternative ideological perspective. What to one may be no more than a common-sense attempt to improve efficiency may, to another, have deeper implications that strike at the very soul of the civil service tradition. Even where there is common ground as to what is at stake, there may be profound disagreement as to whether it is good or bad.

In a brief survey such as this, only the broadest outline can be presented. The first section deals with the Fulton Report and its immediate aftermath. This is followed, in the second section, by an account of the 'new managerialism' of the 1980s and 1990s. The third section considers some of the implications of recent developments for the shape, structure and role of the Whitehall bureaucracy. The fourth and final section highlights some of the recent and current concerns about what has been happening in Whitehall, drawing attention to some of the alternative and conflicting interpretations.

Fulton and its aftermath

The Fulton Committee was appointed in 1966. It reported in June 1968. The Fulton Report is often and rightly seen as a landmark in the modern history of the civil service. Yet it is necessary, for three reasons, to qualify its importance. First, it was by no means the first major report on the civil service. From the famous Northcote-Trevelyan Report (1854) onwards there had been at least one substantial enquiry each generation. The most notable of these were the Playfair Commission (1875), the Ridley Royal Commission (four reports, 1887–90), the MacDonnell Royal Commission (six reports, 1912–15), the Tomlin Royal Commission (1929–31) and the Priestley Royal Commission (1953–5). In the years immediately prior to Fulton the then Estimates Committee had conducted enquiries into Treasury control of expenditure (1957–8) and recruitment (1964–5). The Plowden Committee (HM Treasury 1961) had examined the control of public expenditure, highlighting much about the way Whitehall worked. Fulton, then, was one in a long line of official enquiries into the civil service.

Second, and in part the consequence of this, Fulton said little that was truly original. This is no surprise. Not only was there a well worn trail of official enquiries but also, and more to the point, Fulton was the product of a wider contemporary mileau. It reflected an increasingly critical mood among commentators. Of course, criticism of the civil service was nothing new. Throughout the twentieth century there had been periodic assaults, mainly, though not exclusively, from academic and radical quarters (Lowell 1908; Demetriadi 1921a, b; Robson 1937; Laski 1938; Mallalieu 1942; Greaves 1947). Such critics had remained in a minority, though. Their efforts had little purchase upon the sway of events. By the late 1950s and 1960s this had begun to change. Britain had long been a nation in relative economic decline. Now the reality had become the common perception. There ensued a game of heroes and villains. The top mandarins of Whitehall, hitherto the heroes, were now cast as the villains. They were at the centre of affairs: they must therefore take their share of the blame. A train of consistently hostile accounts highlighted their shortcomings (Balogh 1959; Chapman 1963; Rees 1963; Fabian Society 1964; Nicholson 1967). In the light of all this it would have been difficult for Fulton to have said much in a reformist vein that was worth saying and had not already been said.

The third qualification to the importance of the Fulton Report is more contentious. There has been a serious debate as to the precise influence exerted by the Report, both in the immediate aftermath and in the longer term (see Fry 1993). Such debate is as yet unresolved. Without taking sides, it would clearly be a violation of truth to suggest that the Fulton Report carried the day in the months and years following its publication, or that everything that has since happened in the civil service has its roots in Fulton.

Why, then, is it still right to see Fulton as an important landmark? First, among all the official reports on the civil service, it was the most critical yet. Second, it did articulate a prevailing mood – at least among contemporary reformers and even if their apparent ascendancy was to prove illusory. Third, Fulton provided, if not a blueprint, then at least a focus and an inspiration for those who subsequently sought to challenge the status quo. Indeed, it became the point of reference for many years to come, for both followers and dissenters alike.

Fulton launched a full-blooded attack. It opened with these famous words: 'The Home Civil Service is still fundamentally the product of the nineteenth century philosophy of the Northcote–Trevelyan Report. The tasks it faces are those of the second half of the twentieth century' (Fulton 1968: 9, para. 1). The very success of the nineteenth-century reforms, alleged Fulton, rendered the civil service incapable of adapting to meet the needs of a later age. It issued a litany of complaints. Specifically, it claimed that:

- there was too much emphasis at senior levels upon 'the cult of the generalist';
- specialist knowledge was usually (not always) available but was not brought fully to bear at policy-making level, because the rigid grading system, based upon classes, inhibited the recognition and deployment of talent;
- thus the service was too elitist, with middle and upper-middle class 'Oxbridge' people filling most of the senior positions;
- it was insular, remote and insensitive to the public it served, yet without the full benefit that might otherwise accrue from a cohesive elite;
- this was partly because there was too much mobility between departments (a reflection of the generalist philosophy) and too little planned career development;
- this in turn was partly because the Treasury was not able satisfactorily to manage both the economy and the civil service;
- there was a lack of systematic training, a further reflection of the British philosophy of administration (i.e. learning from experience, not from abstract theory);
- this last feature was linked with an excessive emphasis upon advising ministers, so that senior officials were giving too little attention to the efficient management of their departments;
- there was a lack of clearly defined responsibility and accountability located among individual civil servants within the hierarchy.

To deal with these alleged shortcomings, Fulton made 158 specific recommendations. Among the more important were the calls for:

- much less deference to the notion of the 'gifted all-rounder' or generalist, with correspondingly greater emphasis upon the role of the specialist, with greater utilization of talent at all levels;
- a classless service, all posts to be graded within a single, unified hierarchy, giving more equitable opportunities;
- the recruitment of graduates from a broader range and having regard to the nature and relevance of applicants' qualifications;
- at all times and at all levels an emphasis on the need to 'look at the job' and then find the most suitable people, rather than recruit a pool of entrants and then fit them into whatever posts happened to be vacant;
- the civil service to remain predominantly a career service;
- its insularity to be overcome by a programme of (two-way) secondments with local government, industry and other organizations;
- excessive mobility between departments within Whitehall was to be tempered by more coherent career planning, with careers revolving around *either* the economic/finance *or* the social service functions, with only exceptional transfers between these broad areas (similar to Northcote-Trevelyan's notion of transfers between 'cognate' areas);

- the creation of a Civil Service Department, taking away from the Treasury all responsibilities for personnel management and staffing;
- the establishment of a Civil Service College, to give a boost and necessary emphasis to post-entry training at all levels, partly to achieve greater attention to the management of their departments by senior civil servants whose near-monopoly of policy advice to ministers would be tempered by the enhanced role for specialists;
- the creation within each department of policy units, or 'think tanks';
- 'accountable management', with individual civil servants at various levels in the hierarchy being given clearly defined responsibilities for areas of work for which they would be held accountable within if not outside Whitehall;
- the 'hiving off' of certain functions within each ministry to semi-independent bodies or agencies.

At the heart of the Fulton Report was a desire to make Whitehall more efficient, more managerially minded. It was laced with egalitarian implications. For these reasons and for the reasons mentioned above it seemed to be swimming with the tide. The Wilson Government swiftly endorsed the principles embodied in the Report. In November 1968 the Civil Service Department (CSD) was created. Its Permanent Secretary, Sir William Armstrong, was also the Head of the Home Civil Service. The latter designation had until then been attached to the permanent headship of the Treasury. Previously the Treasury's supremacy in Whitehall over finance and economics had been challenged by the creation in 1964 of the Department of Economic Affairs (DEA). Now it lost to the CSD most of its responsibilities for staffing and personnel in the civil service. It was the Treasury's nadir. Moreover, the Civil Service College (CSC), established in 1970, was in effect to replace the Treasury Centre for Administrative Studies (CAS). The CAS had provided training for newly recruited high flyers – too little training and inadequately at that, according to Fulton. The CSC stepped in to provide a wider range of post-entry training. Meanwhile the Treasury retired to a neutral corner, so to speak, bruised but not defeated. It was later to return triumphantly, helping to deliver the knock-out blow to both the DEA and the CSD, recovering much of the ground it had lost.

Other changes followed. In 1971 the Administrative Class (the mandarin elite) was technically merged with the Executive Class and the Clerical Class to form a new Administration Group. An Administrative Trainee Scheme was launched, ostensibly providing a more broadly based entry route. This was followed by the introduction in January 1972 of an 'open structure'. Posts at and above under-secretary (later assistant secretary) level would no longer belong formally to any discrete group.

These reforms are, it will be noted, structural in character. But Fulton was at least as much about attitudinal changes. This was going to be more difficult to accomplish. As time passed, two things began to happen. On the one hand, critics of the system began to get more agitated as their expectations remained unfulfilled. Culprits were sought and duly found. On the other hand, defenders of the tradition so roundly condemned by Fulton began to make themselves heard again.

For many of the critics, the pace of change was too slow. There was little sustained impetus from the political level. Harold Wilson himself broadly supported Fulton (Pimlott 1992: 515–18). So did some of his cabinet colleagues. But others were lukewarm or hostile. Wilson was not prepared to invest political capital. Nor did he wish to upset the bureaucracy. Besides, his government was beset with other and more pressing matters. To this extent, the bureaucracy was left to reform itself – the quintessential self-regulation. In the view of many of the critics, the mandarins simply emasculated the proposed reforms. Among the more trenchant critics were Peter Kellner and Lord Crowther-Hunt (1980), the latter a member of the Fulton Committee. They argued (pp. 59–77) that the reforms ostensibly introduced were merely cosmetic, designed to give the appearance of change while warding off anything that would make the senior mandarins more 'professional' and accountable. Their villain was Sir William Armstrong. Others looked further. The terms of reference given to the Fulton Committee precluded it from examining the constitutional position of civil servants. For this the more radical critics took the government to task. One commentator observed that 'No amount of improved personnel management on the shop floor would achieve anything unless something were done about the old . . . boiler' (Robertson 1971: 4). Others again were more inclined to blame Fulton. This cut two ways. Some thought Fulton could have gone further in spite of the terms of reference (Garrett 1980: 20–3). Others chided the Committee for failing to take full cognizance of the parameters imposed. Enter (or re-enter) the defenders of the civil service tradition.

Fulton made many proposals which, in the opinion of some, were inappropriate and misconceived, having regard to the constitutional role of the civil service (RIPA 1968; Parris 1969: 284–316; Sisson 1971). Two examples may be cited, both of which have a continuing resonance. First, Fulton wanted civil servants to be less anonymous and more directly accountable. Here the traditionalists (and others) claimed that Fulton had given insufficient consideration as to how this could be squared with the convention of ministerial responsibility. Ministers, because they are members of an elected government, are answerable and accountable to Parliament. Civil servants should remain anonymous – or at least should appear in public only as their ministers' emissaries when discussing policy issues. Even by the Fulton era such a clear role distinction was becoming difficult to maintain. Few then thought the convention wholly satisfactory. Fewer think it so today. But no other formal doctrine has taken its place. As one observer noted, 'The House of Commons has not yet found a way of making anybody other than ministers accountable to it' (Chester 1979: 54).

In another of its observations Fulton invited a traditionalist riposte. Quite apart from its charges of amateurism, Fulton objected that senior civil servants spent too much time propping up their ministers and too little time managing their departments. In reply it was argued that 'analytical procedures' now dignified with the term management had always taken place; that Fulton was guilty of a great 'management hoax' (Sisson 1971). In any case, it was the job of senior officials to work to their ministers. This was what most ministers wanted. In so doing mandarins were making a vital contribution to democratic government. A fusion between politics and administration lay at the heart of the British system (Thomas 1978: 33–7). Top civil servants were permanent politicians (but not party politicians) as well as minders of large organizations. To suppose otherwise was naive, either in its ignorance of this reality or in its assumption that the separation of policy from administration (or management) could be effected without recasting the whole system of government.

In other ways, too, Fulton left itself open to counter-attack. It gave insufficient credit for changes that had already taken place. Lord Simey, a member of the Committee, issued a note of dissent. He agreed that the foundations of the modern civil service were laid in the nineteenth century. But he insisted that subsequent events had produced 'a very different and more positive-minded Administrative Class over the years' (Fulton 1968: 101). The main report gave grudging acknowledgement that certain changes had taken place, only to disregard these in its final analysis. The tone of the Fulton Report was certainly intemperate. This was both a weakness and a strength. It was a weakness in that it allowed traditionalists to claim that the picture presented by Fulton contained more caricature than reality. It did little to mollify the leading lights of Whitehall. Sir William Armstrong may not have been Fulton's most vigorous ally, but nor was he quite the arch-opponent portrayed by Kellner and Crowther-Hunt. He probably did have a desire to modernize the Whitehall machine. He had a difficult job persuading many of his colleagues. The tone of the Fulton Report did not help him in this task. On the other hand, the stridency of the Report was also a strength. It may well have been necessary to 'bend the stick' in order to correct an existing imbalance. Besides, if Fulton violated the canons of strict accuracy there were many nuggets of truth in the analysis. It presented artistic rather than literal truths. As such, it could remain an inspiration even if some of its detailed proposals fell by the wayside or were deemed unattainable. And if Kellner and Crowther-Hunt's lampooning was unfair, then many agreed in 1980 with their verdict that the essence of reform seemed to have been lost. A few years earlier the English Committee had engaged in a wide-ranging review of the civil service (Expenditure Committee 1977). It was, in some ways, a post-Fulton audit. Members of the Committee were deeply divided among themselves. A minority of Labour members, most notably Brian Sedgemore, recorded their dissent. Whether for good or ill, there was nevertheless broad agreement that Whitehall had yet to embrace the spirit of Fulton. But the history of earlier movements for reform, such as those which had found expression in the famous Northcote-Trevelyan Report, offered two lessons: first, that worthwhile reforms can take a generation or more to come to fruition; second, that by the time reforms have worked their way into the fabric of the system circumstances have changed and other movements are already in train, often the product of new and different impulses. In short, the path of change is a messy and uncertain one.

The new managerialism: policy initiatives of the 1980s and 1990s

In 1980, then, it seemed that the immediate post-Fulton momentum had been lost. Yet already events were unfolding that would point to a different verdict.

By the late 1980s and certainly by the early 1990s there was widespread talk about Whitehall's managerial revolution. A succession of initiatives had been unleashed. To describe them in more or less chronological order is not to imply a coherent, preplanned sequence in which each package was a consciously designed building block for the next instalment. Nor is it to suggest that the reforms of the 1980s and 1990s were part of a predetermined and specifically Conservative blueprint. Apart from reducing the size of the bureaucracy and a general commitment to value for money (see next section), the Conservative election manifesto in 1979 made no specific mention of the civil service. On the other hand, Margaret Thatcher's sustained resolve provided the 'flywheel' that stimulated the drive for reform.

Margaret Thatcher can certainly be accorded credit (or blame) for reintroducing to Whitehall Sir Derek (Lord) Rayner. Rayner was Chairman of Marks and Spencer. He had been an adviser to the Heath Government and had operated at permanent secretary level in the Ministry of Defence before returning to Marks and Spencer. Now he was back in Whitehall, this time as Thatcher's adviser on efficiency. He was supported by a newly created Efficiency Unit, a small group later to come under the umbrella of the Cabinet Office. Rayner and his team launched a series of scrutinies. Their immediate purpose was to herald savings by identifying tasks and procedures that could be either abolished or streamlined. He wanted to work with departments, not against them. He allowed departments to choose areas for scrutiny. In this he had a bigger game plan: to develop a culture in which departments internalized efficiency-consciousness rather than responding to 'alien' promptings. Against this ambitious objective early results were inauspicious (Metcalfe and Richards 1984). Rayner left Whitehall in 1983, and was succeeded by Sir Robin Ibbs. The Efficiency Unit continued, its work gradually changing in focus.

Meanwhile, in the Department of the Environment Michael Heseltine, during his first spell there as Secretary of State (1979–83), had introduced Management Information Systems for Ministers (MINIS). In a passage reproduced in this volume (Reading 3.2) Heseltine describes the background. MINIS was a mechanism by which he, as minister, could monitor what was going on in the department. It involved the systematic collation of information, regularly updated. This was apparently something of an innovation in Whitehall. Heseltine's enthusiasm was not shared by all his cabinet colleagues. Nor were there many converts among senior officials. Some wondered whether it was really the job of a minister to get involved in the workings of a department in quite this way. Few departments followed the DoE example. Some adopted paler versions of MINIS; others remained aloof.

More wide-ranging was the Financial Management Initiative (FMI). It was launched in 1982 and its intention was to assign to individuals and groups of civil servants a more transparent responsibility for particular areas of work. Designated people would, in effect, be in charge of 'cost centres'. They would work to predetermined targets or objectives. Performance would be measured against these targets and in the context of more finely calibrated budget heads. This implied a disaggregation and greater delegation as the location of responsibilities was pushed further down the line. Managers (as they came increasingly to be called) would account upwards for their block of the budget, but not for the micro-elements over which they would be given greater autonomy. Senior officials would adopt a more strategic and less detailed style of control. This, at least, was the theory. FMI would embrace all departments. This it did. Not surprisingly, progress was uneven and in some areas distinctly modest (PAC 1987; Richards 1987). There were various technical difficulties; for example, in setting specific objectives and developing satisfactory perform-ance measures. More importantly, there were, and are, matters of principle; for example, whether civil servants should see themselves as managers and whether those at senior levels should be strategic overseers. Many of the doubts expressed about these notions echoed the more critical responses that had attended Fulton's proposals for more accountable management. Never-theless, in his valedictory, the Head of the Home Civil Service described FMI as the most important development in the previous eighteen years (Armstrong 1988: 12).

No sooner had these words been spoken than a new initiative was to be launched – one which was to stir the passions more violently. In February 1988 the Efficiency Unit published *Improving Management in Government: the Next Steps. Report to the Prime Minister*. It was jointly authored by Kate Jenkins, Karen Caines and Andrew Jackson. These three were members of the Efficiency Unit, now headed by Sir Robin Ibbs. It therefore became known as the Ibbs Report. The Ibbs Report was brief, critical and prescriptive. In these respects it invited comparison with the famous Northcote-Trevelyan Report of the 1850s. It has been claimed by some as an equally significant landmark (Massey 1993: 51). It covered some of the ground trampled over by Fulton. Specifically, it identified a managerial deficit. Senior officials were still spending too much time wet-nursing ministers and too little time managing their departments. This tendency was perpetuated by a system of promotions which rewarded policy work rather than managerial competence. Like Fulton, Ibbs's solution was to separate policy from administration, or management. This was to be achieved by the creation of executive agencies operating at arm's length from the main departments. The latter would be left free to concentrate upon strategic matters. In another echo of Fulton and in furtherance of FMI principles, Ibbs wanted extensive delegation of responsibilities for their respective operations. This could mean greater freedom to manage personnel, including more flexible, and hence varied, conditions of service. In a signal departure from Fulton, Ibbs called into question the notion of a life-long career in a unified civil service.

Many of the critics have seen in this last comment clear evidence (or confirmation) of an attempt to unwind certain of the principles underpinning the Northcote-Trevelyan reforms. These principles included, among other things, common, open and competitive entry organized through an indepen-dent Civil Service Commission and into a service characterized by common grading and other centrally determined conditions of service. In 1991 the government abolished the Civil Service Commission. The commissioners would remain, served by a small team to oversee the conduct of recruitment. From the 1960s (and before Fulton) departments had slowly but steadily played a greater role in recruitment. Now they were given responsibility for all save the Fast Stream, recruitment to which would remain centralized.

Departments would be at liberty to employ (or not to employ) the services of a newly created executive agency, Recruitment and Assessment Services (RAS). The majority of departments decided to use and, at the time of writing, continue to use RAS. Further delegation to departments and executive agencies in matters of recruitment and in the setting of pay and other conditions of service were announced in the White Paper of July 1994, *The Civil Service: Continuity and Change* (Cabinet Office 1994). Other documents, published simultaneously, proposed further areas of financial delegation (HM Treasury 1994) and the removal of certain residual recruitment functions from the civil service commissioners (OPSS 1994a). The commissioners would be the custodians of probity and integrity: but they would do no recruiting themselves.

The pace of change was frantic. Whitehall was and continues to be in a state of permanent revolution. Five years after the Ibbs Report some 97 executive agencies had been created (Cabinet Office 1994: 13, para. 2.21). Together they accounted for nearly two-thirds of the total civil service manpower. More were promised. Quite what this meant was slightly more difficult to measure. Each executive agency has a framework document. Among other things these framework documents specify or lay ground-rules for the specification of targets against which performance can be assessed. This has provided fertile ground for warring protagonists, not least because the pay bonuses of chief executives (and others) are determined in part by performance measures. Some agencies have met their targets; others have missed by anything from a mile to a mite. But what does it all mean? If a target is exceeded, then perhaps the target was not sufficiently challenging. If there is a performance deficit, then perhaps the target was too stringent. If it is just met or just missed, then maybe the target had been just right – or just wrong! And what if an area of work is simply not measurable as an output? Is it better to invent some indirect indicator than to do without? Otherwise activities that yield only 'soft outputs' could become marginalized. To some this is the face of rigorous but sensitive management. To others, it is management gone mad.

Who would have the vital say in determining performance targets and, in a more general sense, the terms of reference for each of these executive agencies? Here there would be interaction between the 'iron triangle' of ministers, agency chief executives and senior officials in what now came to be known as 'core departments' (i.e. in Whitehall). Much would depend upon the extent to which the core and central departments (i.e. the Treasury) were prepared to let go. An investigation headed by Sir Angus Fraser, who had succeeded Sir Robin Ibbs, found that delegation was being impeded (Efficiency Unit 1991). Fraser wanted to see a reduction of 25 per cent in the staffing of central services (e.g. finance, personnel) within the core departments as responsibilities were devolved down to the executive agencies. But these were still early days, little more than three years after Ibbs. Another three years on and things seemed to be loosening up, though the picture remains a mixed one (Trosa 1994).

Is not variety the very essence of delegation? Such had been the fear of Sir Peter Middleton, Permanent Secretary to the Treasury between 1983 and 1991. Middleton was lukewarm about the implications of Ibbs. He resisted the proposal that agency chief executives should become accounting officers. In this capacity they would be directly accountable to the Committee of Public Accounts, alongside the permanent secretaries in their respective departments, for whom previously this had been a sovereign function. Middleton feared fragmentation and ultimate loss of financial control. He lost his battle. The government, too, was keen to maintain financial control. It pitched its faith in a lower centre of gravity by giving chief executives a specific public responsibility as accounting officers for their agencies. They would, the government hoped, become custodians of the public purse rather than pressure points for profligacy. Sir Terry Burns, Middleton's successor, is a disciple of the new thinking. In 1994 he announced a reduction in the number of mid-ranking and senior Treasury officials. More significantly, there was to be a change in the relationship between the Treasury and the spending departments. The Treasury would engage in less detailed supervision, developing instead a more strategic role.

All this is part of a more general philosophy of delegation: of control through systems rather than constant 'flesh pumping'; and of maximizing outputs against given (and more sparing) inputs. In particular it has been characterized by an attempt to separate policy work from operations. This has been seen clearly in the creation of executive agencies. It has been seen equally clearly with the launch of market testing and contracting out (see Reading 5.4). The idea here is to expose government bureaucracy to external competition. No longer can they assume that their services will be required. The government would first consider whether or not a particular function was still necessary. If so, it would then decide whether it would be better performed within the embrace of the main department or by an executive agency operating at arm's length. Such was supposed to be the line of reasoning by which executive agencies were established. The government had remained reticent as critics asked whether there was to be a further stage – the contracting out of functions to the private sector where this seemed (to the government) an even better bet than executive agencies. The critics' fears seemed to have been borne out. But how far would the government go? And upon what basis would it test the market? Would it be guided by empiricism or was it to be propelled by ideology? In this connection a further element of controversy arose from the fact that, in some cases, the government did not allow in-house bids, thus ensuring that certain tasks would be handed over to private contractors. By October 1994 some £2.1 billion worth of activities had been 'examined'. The government claimed a reduction of 26,900 posts and annual savings of £410 million (*Next Steps Briefing Note*, April 1995). A few executive agencies had been privatized and a few more were earmarked for privatization. Private contractors were being employed to perform certain tasks, among the more controversial being the use of Group 4 Security to transport prisoners.

Meanwhile, in July 1991, the Citizen's Charter had been launched (see Reading 5.3). With this, attention turned towards the quality of services, within budgetary limits. It promised to empower the citizen to obtain better public services. It would ultimately require all public agencies to demonstrate that they were providing satisfactory levels of service. If standards fell below stipulated levels, then the citizen would be able to claim compensation, if not redress. This would require greater transparency. For this and other reasons there was issued a White Paper on open government (see Reading 7.6). This was not the first official document on this sensitive topic. It followed long and careful deliberation. Whitehall was and is now more open, though not to the extent that many of the critics would wish.

Open government goes much wider than the 'new' or any other managerialism. It has profound implications for the constitution and for the character of British democracy. Management within Whitehall has been and continues to be a central and important fact. So, too, are other things, some of which will be touched upon below. Many of them have been affected by the new managerialism, but this does not mean that everything is management or that management is everything. Explanation can easily give the appearance of justification. It is necessary to explain the thinking behind the succession of initiatives launched during the 1980s and 1990s so that they may be better understood. To an extent this means setting out the 'official' position. But the above account also hints at certain of the criticisms. These are fleshed out in the final section of this introductory essay. Before that, though, a few words need to be said about the changing shape, structure and role of the Whitehall bureaucracy.

The changing shape, structure and role of the civil service

One of the more notable changes since the Fulton era – or, to be more precise, since 1979 – has been in the number of civil servants. Figure 1 shows the magnitude of the reduction in total numbers, some 27 per cent since 1979. The necessities of the Second World War had swollen the numbers, especially of industrial civil servants. After the war, numbers remained high by peacetime standards. Such were the consequences of the Welfare State and the managed economy and of all that this implied for the role of government. Not until the mid-1950s did numbers fall decisively below three-quarters of a million. But they were still pretty close to this mark, albeit falling slightly, when the Thatcher Government assumed office in May 1979.

The two most explicit initial objectives of the Thatcher Government towards the civil service were to reduce numbers and to deprivilege what it saw as an unjustifiably protected group of employees, in the broader context of better value for money. The reduction in numbers has been sustained, albeit with one or two slight and temporary reversals in the trend. It has been achieved partly by changing the status of certain bodies (latterly including contracting out) whose employees are no longer classified as civil servants, partly by substantive reductions in the numbers of people engaged in given areas of work. Most of these reductions have been at lower levels and outside Whitehall itself, especially among industrial civil servants (see Figure 1). But the senior echelons have by no means escaped unscathed. Numbers in the senior open structure (grades 1–3: permanent, deputy and under secretaries and their equivalents) fell from 814 in 1979 to 627 in 1994, a reduction of 23 per cent. Among all at grade 5 (assistant secretary or equivalent) and above numbers fell from 3,387 in 1979 to 2,516 in 1994, a reduction of almost 26 per cent (*Civil Service Statistics*). It is still worth noting, though, that the numbers of

Figure 1   Number of civil servants 1945–1994
Source: *Civil Service Statistics*

non-industrial civil servants were greater in 1994 than they had been at any time between 1946 and 1969.

The advent of the Major Government has seen no weakening of the resolve to reduce numbers. The White Paper of July 1994 expressed the wish that numbers should fall 'significantly below 500,000' before the end of the decade (Cabinet Office 1994: 30, para. 3.33). As mentioned above, the majority of civil servants now work in executive agencies. Most of them have been granted agency status under the Major Government, though the impetus emanated from the Thatcher years.

It was during the Thatcher years – especially the first half of the 1980s – that the policy of 'deprivileging' was high on the agenda. This policy took a number of forms, apart from the sheer reduction in numbers. It was Thatcher's wish to abandon the index-linking of civil servants' pensions. Index-linking had been formally introduced in the early 1970s as part of a broader strategy of regularizing various forms of earnings, downwards as well as upwards, within the parameters of inflation. It had been agreed by Edward Heath, a fact which did not endear the policy to Margaret Thatcher. It afforded to civil servants a more generous deal than was enjoyed by most in the private sector. But Thatcher failed in this particular assault. Civil servants' pensions remain index-linked and non-contributory.

Thatcher was more successful in matters of pay, union membership and collective bargaining. There were a number of confrontations, including a particularly bitter strike in the early 1980s. In a high-profile skirmish in the mid-1980s at the Government Communication Headquarters (GCHQ) in Cheltenham employees were forced to renounce their membership of a trade union. The pay of *senior* civil servants was and remains a tricky issue. Significant increases cost relatively little, given the relatively low numbers of people involved. But they can be symbolic. Thatcher and some of her ministers believed that many of those who had spent all their lives in the 'Whitehall womb' were unworthy of higher salaries. If they were any good they would have got out into the private sector to do 'real work for real money'. On the other hand, if salaries and other conditions, including job satisfaction or whatever motivates people, bore unduly unfavourable comparison then there could be an exodus of the best, leaving only the worst. A Top Salaries Review Body had been established in 1970. It was retained, with modification, under Thatcher and still exists, now known as the Senior Salaries Review Body. It recommends salary levels for the most senior civil servants (grade 3 and above) as well as for judges, top military personnel and other public figures. Governments have usually accepted its recommendations. At other levels, the Whitley system remains. This is the system, established after the First World War, in which pay and conditions of service are determined in effect by a process of regulated bargaining between employers and unions (Parris 1973). Senior officials are represented by the Association of First Division Civil Servants (FDA), so called because the First Division was the forerunner of the Administrative Class. Under Thatcher and Major, Whitleyism has survived, though diminished to the extent that the trade unions are less powerful and that collective bargaining has been increasingly supplemented by more fragmented structures and practices. Most senior and mid-ranking officials are eligible for some sort of bonus payment. Increasingly, special conditions are written into individual employment contracts, in particular those of agency chief executives.

Under Thatcher – and for that matter Major – there have been relatively few upheavals in Whitehall's departmental structure. Perhaps the most significant was the abolition in November 1981 of the Civil Service Department (CSD) (Chapman 1983). Thatcher had clashed with Sir Ian (now Lord) Bancroft, Head of the Home Civil Service and Permanent Secretary of the CSD. Long before that the CSD had been under a cloud. It had enjoyed a period of ascendancy under its first head, Sir William Armstrong. But Armstrong had himself fallen under a cloud, having become publicly associated with policies that were perceived to have failed, most visibly during the miners' strike of 1973–4. His department also suffered a loss of authority in Whitehall.

Armstrong's successors, Sir Douglas Allen (Lord Croham) and then Bancroft, had an uphill task. The Treasury and the Cabinet Office were waiting in the wings. The English Committee (1976–7) was uncertain about the future of the CSD. The Callaghan Government was uncertain too. Thatcher's abolition of the CSD was therefore not a matter of purely personal whim. The Treasury took back some of the functions it had lost after Fulton. Others went to a newly created Management and Personnel Office (MPO) in the Cabinet Office. For about eighteen months there were now two joint heads of the home civil service: one, Sir Douglas Wass, Permanent Secretary to the Treasury; the other, Sir Robert Armstrong (no relation to Sir William), Secretary of the Cabinet. When Wass retired in 1983, Armstrong became the sole Head of the Home Civil Service, while remaining Cabinet Secretary. Sir Robin Butler succeeded Armstrong in this dual role from January 1988. Meanwhile, the MPO underwent reorganization to form the nucleus of the Office of the Minister for the Civil Service (OMCS). Still operating under the wing of the Cabinet Office, it became, in 1992, the Office for Public Service and Science (OPSS). From July 1995 it was renamed the Office of Public Service (OPS), responsibility for science being transferred to the Department of Trade and Industry. As such it retains overall responsibility and/or a significant role in many areas, including the Next Steps Programme, the Citizen's Charter, the Efficiency Unit, open government, recruitment and training, management development, senior appointments and the machinery of government. It is a moot point as to whether or not, with this accretion of functions, the OPS will begin to fill the role of the CSD.

A few other organizational changes during the 1980s and 1990s are worthy of note. In 1983, the Department of Trade and Industry (DTI) was reconstituted by the merger of the separate departments of trade and of industry, DTI mark 1 having been created in 1970 but split up four years later. The break up of the DTI in 1974 had brought the creation of the Department of Energy. This was partly in the context of a world oil crisis. The Department of Energy continued in existence until the mini reorganization following the 1992 general election. This same reorganization brought the Department of National Heritage. And in July 1995 the Department of Employment was abolished, some of its functions being given to the DTI, others to the Department of the Environment and the remainder forming part of a new Department for Education and Employment. Not a department but rather an efficiency device launched in 1970, Programme Analysis and Review (PAR) was formally abandoned in 1979. It had been intended as a systematic and critical internal review of departmental and inter-departmental programmes. But by the late 1970s it had lost most of what bite it had ever had (Gray and Jenkins 1982). Similarly, in 1983, the Central Policy Review Staff, or think tank, was abolished. Its abolition was, again, not a piece of pure Thatcherism. Even under Wilson and Callaghan it had failed to sustain the position it had been given under Heath when it had been created in 1970 (Blackstone and Plowden 1988). Thatcher in particular felt no need for advice from a resident body that comprised a mixture of career and temporary officials. To an extent the CPRS was a complement and a counterweight to the existing Whitehall machine. But its abolition did not signal Thatcher's satisfaction with the normal channels of official advice. On the contrary. She, more than other premiers, turned to other sources – not, as some have implied, to the exclusion of permanent officials but certainly to whatever extent was necessary in order to avoid being imprisoned by the regular Whitehall machine. One of these other sources was the Policy Unit, set up by Harold Wilson and now strengthened under Thatcher (and Major). Another was the Centre for Policy Studies, an independent think tank set up in 1974 by Thatcher's mentor, Sir Keith (Lord) Joseph. This and other right-wing think tanks were to be quite influential at times during the 1980s (Cockett 1994). Within departments, temporary special advisers assumed greater significance. There had been long-standing precedent for the employment by ministers of personal advisers. But they did not become either a significant or a normal feature until Wilson led Labour to office in 1964. The 'regulars' were highly suspicious. Not until the 1970s and perhaps even the 1980s did the 'specials' really establish their position. Even today their numbers are limited (two per minister). But they almost certainly have more clout than during the Wilson years.

All this has meant a change of role for the permanent mandarins. Previously ministers had appeared to be cocooned within the embrace of what Richard Crossman described as a 'padded cell'. They could go only as far as civil servants were prepared to let them go. Behind the facade of ministerial supremacy it was the officials who really ran the show. Such, at least, was the belief that inspired the highly successful television series *Yes, Minister* and *Yes, Prime Minister*. The belief was nourished by the frustrations expressed by a number of ministers – a few Conservatives, but mainly Labour ministers such as Tony Benn, Richard Crossman and Barbara Castle. Castle's 'mandarin power' article is included in abridged form in this volume (Reading 3.1).

In the 1970s it was widely thought that officials had become too powerful. How to tackle the 'problem of the bureaucracy' was the topic of many a seminar discussion. Thatcher provided a partial answer. Some now believe that she went too far. Where once the bureaucracy was seen as an obstacle to democratic government, it is now seen by some as too compliant with the impulses of ministers. There has been a kind of pincer movement. The changes described earlier in this chapter have driven many senior officials towards a more managerial role. At the same time they no longer have a near-exclusive monopoly over policy advice to ministers. Thatcher did not politicize the civil service in the sense of appointing to permanent posts people with known Conservative sympathies. But she did take a keen interest in top appointments and wanted to secure the promotion of 'doers' rather than 'thinkers' (RIPA 1987; Richards 1993). Her lengthy tenure in Number 10 Downing Street and sustained sense of policy direction allowed her to leave a deep impression on Whitehall. It seems to have carried forward into the Major Government. This, together with the implications of the new managerialism, has given rise to a number of concerns and items (new and old) on the agenda for debate about the way Whitehall works.

Recent and current issues

There is no evidence whatsoever that Thatcher packed the most senior permanent positions with Conservative sympathizers. It has nevertheless been alleged that the Whitehall bureaucracy has become politicized in another sense. This, it is said, is the consequence of a bureaucracy serving without interruption one particular party in office for almost a generation. The argument is expressed by former Labour premier Lord Callaghan (Reading 3.4). Some have gone further, arguing that it may be difficult, without corrective action, for the bureaucracy to serve with equal loyalty a government of different political colour. Such corrective action could include a much greater influence for special advisers or even the placing of known sympathizers into permanent positions. The latter, though, would imply the very politicization that many still believe to be undesirable. It would be undesirable because the civil service would no longer even pretend to offer the independent, impartial, professional advice that is supposed to be one of its classic strengths. If this independence has been in any way compromised the solution, they say, is to restore the traditional impartiality, not to destroy it altogether.

Others, though, deny that there is a real problem. They point to the sheer professionalism of senior mandarins and their time-honoured adaptability to whoever happens to be in government. But some even among this group of commentators have wondered whether the traditional independent impartiality of the civil service has been compromised in recent years. It is one thing to say that loyalties are transferable; it is another thing to assume a proper balance between those loyalties to the government of the day and the loyalties to traditional canons of impartiality. The British system works on the assumption that civil servants offer to ministers the best advice they can. This may not always be the advice ministers want to hear. The minister should listen but is not bound to act upon the advice received. If the minister decides upon a different or contrary course of action, then the officials must follow the minister's line. Two broad questions arise. First, to what extent is it legitimate for the official to keep up the argument, perhaps mobilizing other forces in the process; or, alternatively, to anticipate the course of events and give the minister (in the name of loyalty) only the advice that is likely to be politically acceptable? Second, if the minister insists on pursuing his or her chosen line, are civil servants bound to follow to the exclusion of every other consideration, their only escape resting in the contractual right of resignation, and then still accompanied by the requirement forever to uphold confidences to which they have been privy? Questions of loyalty are the subject of some of the readings in Chapter 4. Few would doubt that, in the normal course of events, senior civil servants owe their primary loyalty to ministers. But are there circumstances in which a higher loyalty comes into play? If so, then to whom and in what circumstances?

Clive Ponting believed that he had a higher duty (Reading 4.2). As an assistant secretary in the Ministry of Defence he deliberately leaked information concerning the sinking in 1982 of the Argentine warship *General Belgrano* during the Falklands War. He felt justified in exposing what he believed to have been a misleading explanation given to Parliament by the minister. He was prosecuted under the Official Secrets Act, but acquitted by the jury despite heavy pressure from the judge. The judge had said that the duty of civil servants was in effect unconditionally to the government of the day. The Armstrong Memorandum, issued in the wake of the Ponting trial, reinforced this pronouncement. It specified that the civil service has no 'personality' other than through the government of the day. The critics were not assuaged. Did this mean that civil servants were to do whatever their ministers wanted, even if it meant behaving dishonestly or misleading Parliament? These questions had in any case come into sharper focus with the setting up in 1979–80 of the new select committees. Select committees were certainly not invented in 1979. There was ample precedent stretching back over two centuries of officials giving evidence to Parliamentary committees. But the sheer range of the new committees – one for each department – would increase the exposure of civil servants. Whitehall girded its loins. Edward Osmotherly, an official in the CSD, revised a code of guidance for civil servants who were called to give evidence to select committees. The Osmotherly Rules, as they came to be known, were held by critics to have the effect of inhibiting officials from giving full and frank testimony, though most select committee members seem to have been reasonably satisfied (see Readings 7.2 and 7.3). The Osmotherly Rules have now been redrafted and reissued as Departmental Evidence and Response to Select Committees (Reading 7.1). But the Osmotherly principles have been retained. Critics still feel that there should be some way of 'splitting the seam' between civil servants and ministers when something very serious, or even crooked or dishonest, has been going on. The hub of the matter is how this can be done without breaking the bond of confidence between minister and official that is widely (not universally) held to be essential to a productive day-to-day relationship.

A number of *causes célèbres* have occurred or come to light in the 1990s. These include the Pergau Dam project, the Matrix-Churchill case and the arms to Iraq affair. All involve allegations of a lack of integrity of one sort or another among ministers and officials. The Scott Report on the sale of arms to Iraq is yet to be published at the time of writing. But the Nolan Committee on standards of conduct in public life has already laid down a number of markers. This committee was set up in October 1994 following a number of apparent misdemeanours including and additional to those mentioned above, the result of which was a collective blight upon the integrity of the 'governing classes'. There may or may not have been a deterioration in standards of conduct. Much depends upon the chronological point of comparison. But there has in recent years been a weakening of public confidence. Of this the Nolan Committee (1995: 107) found clear evidence. In its first report, published in May 1995, it reflected the emphasis at least of the informed public, with its focus upon procedures for appointments to quasi-autonomous non-governmental organizations (QUANGOs) and upon the conduct of ministers and other MPs. Nolan did not think that politicians had habitually abused their positions. Nor did the committee wish to prevent MPs in general either from articulating the views of outside interests or from receiving payments. But it did want stronger and more closely supervised procedures to ensure the declaration of all remunerative associations. Ministers are, of course, prohibited from maintaining any such connections while they remain in office. Nolan, however, was also concerned with the acceptance of certain paid appointments by ministers upon leaving office. There had been similar concerns in the 1970s when an uncommonly high number of senior civil servants had, upon retirement or resignation, taken up appointments with companies directly or indirectly connected with their previous positions in Whitehall. Such concerns had stimulated the creation of an Advisory Committee on Business Interests. Senior civil servants are required to seek the approval of the Advisory Committee before taking up any paid appointment within two years of their leaving Whitehall. The Advisory Committee may recommend a deferral of up to two years in the taking up of any such appointment, or the imposition of special conditions (e.g. restricting contact with the former department) where the proposed appointment seems to have a bearing on the official's previous position in Whitehall. In the case of permanent secretaries, there is an automatic three-month moratorium, a condition which Nolan sought to extend to Cabinet ministers along with a general requirement that all government ministers and special advisers should seek the approval of the Advisory Committee along the lines laid down for senior permanent officials.

The Nolan Committee also turned its attention to the civil service. While believing that standards of behaviour among civil servants remained generally very high, Nolan echoed an earlier report of the Public Accounts Committee in expressing the view that the greater emphasis upon delegation and the movement of personnel in and out of the service should not lead to undue 'corner-cutting' and consequent undermining of core values (Nolan 1995: 57–8, paras 43–7). In particular, it wanted to ensure that the new performance-linked pay arrangements should not compromise the political impartiality of the civil service (p. 58, para. 48). The worry here is that civil servants may be tempted to focus upon the specific and politically inspired performance targets set by ministers to the exclusion of other and wider considerations. This, it is feared, may happen when pay is linked to the achievement of specific targets.

These concerns are part of the wider agenda of proprieties attending the relationship between ministers and civil servants. There are things which ministers can and cannot reasonably expect civil servants to do. The need to lay bare and to distinguish more clearly between the acceptable and the unacceptable is part of the case for a code of conduct. So, too, is the need to protect civil servants from being pressurized by ministers to engage in activities of dubious propriety or legality. The FDA began campaigning for a code of ethics in the mid-1980s in the light of the Ponting Trial. In November 1994 the Treasury and Civil Service Committee agreed, offering a prototype code (see Reading 4.4). With a few minor amendments, the government accepted this code (Cabinet Office 1995: 46–53). Initially sceptical, it found a certain attraction in the brevity of the TCSC version compared with the much longer and more detailed document proposed by the FDA. It does not specify what, in concrete terms, is acceptable or unacceptable. But it establishes broad ground rules and creates procedures to protect civil servants. It provides a right of appeal to the First Civil Service Commissioner who, in turn, is to be granted a greater measure of independence. At the same time Nolan also wanted a parallel code for ministers with strong prime ministerial supervision. *Questions of Procedure for Ministers* was thought by Nolan to be inadequate. First published in 1992 but existing in various forms since the 1940s, it says little about dealings with civil servants and its status is unclear. It will be interesting to see whether all this helps to clarify the position of civil servants: whether it will help those who feel themselves placed in a professional and/or moral dilemma; or whether it will make little difference; or whether, as Sir Geoffrey Chipperfield fears (Reading 4.5), it will discourage the individual civil servant from setting and living by his or her own standards. It is not in any case yet clear that there will be a code for ministers, though the code for civil servants will certainly come into effect in due course. But the Major Government continues to resist as unnecessary calls to underpin the code with legislation. For some of the critics this is a cardinal weakness likely to undermine its effectiveness and a reflection of the British aversion to giving statutory form to its governmental procedures.

The broader context to all this is that Britain does not have a written constitution. The role of the civil service as an organ of state has never been committed to text and enshrined in any document carrying the authority of law. The historical reasons for this and the arguments about whether Britain should have a written constitution lie beyond the scope of this volume. Much continues to rest upon convention. One of these conventions is that of ministerial responsibility. In strict terms this means that ministers alone are publicly answerable and accountable to Parliament. Civil servants are accountable in private to their ministers but not directly to the public. Officials appear before Parliamentary committees in effect as representatives of their ministers, certainly where questions of policy arise. If things go wrong, the minister faces the music in public, while remaining at liberty to take internal action if there has been culpability in the department. But over the past two or three decades the practice has slowly shifted. As noted above, Fulton's proposal for more accountable management fell on fallow ground. It was thought, among other things, to strike at the foundation of the doctrine of individual ministerial responsibility. By the 1980s and 1990s ministers seemed less overwhelmed with the solemn joys of such responsibility! When a number of prisoners escaped from high-security jails in 1994 and 1995 Home Secretary Michael Howard told the House of Commons that his responsibility was for overall policy and for the operations emanating from broad policy. He would answer but not accept culpability for operational malfunctioning. This was the job of the respective prison governor and of the Prison Service, now an executive agency. He further denied that the distinction he was making between policy and operations had emerged simply with the creation of executive agencies. He had a point: there had developed over a long period of time the convention that ministers should not be brought to book for everything. Nevertheless, the creation of executive agencies seems to have signalled a more brutal distinction between policy and operations than many had thought possible or desirable. At the same time, what had fallen foul in the 1960s had, by the 1990s, become the reality, even if by no means the uncontested reality.

This brief survey has shown how in this, as in many other ways, the civil service has changed since Fulton. How much and in exactly what ways it has changed are themselves matters of contention. So, too, is the question as to whether change has been for good or ill; and, if in some respects for good, then whether at the cost of detriment in other respects. Many of Whitehall's more radical critics at the time of Fulton wanted a greater emphasis upon management. Some still do. Others were never keen. Others again wanted more management but now feel that this has been bought at too high a price. It has been accompanied, they say, by a diminution of some of the traditional values such as impartiality, independence and integrity. The Government says it still believes in these things, and indeed it does. But critics wonder whether it is willing or even able to hold the line in a tight corner. Moreover, the Government no longer retains faith in central recruitment, common pay scales and other service-wide conditions. Nor does it uphold with the same strength of conviction as did former governments the principle of the civil service as a life-long career, although it does assume that this will remain the reality for most of its employees.

It is a moot point as to whether, say, unified pay scales are necessary to uphold other values, such as impartiality. Then again, some would say that a rather less independent Whitehall bureaucracy is more sensitive to the wishes of an elected government. But does a more democratically sensitive bureaucracy help to produce 'better' government? And so it goes on.

The Whitehall machine: structure and process

Whitehall is the hub of British central government. Geographically it assumes a relatively small area within Westminster, near the Houses of Parliament. In and around Whitehall are located the headquarters of all the main departments of state – the Treasury, the Cabinet Office, the Foreign and Commonwealth Office, the Ministry of Defence, the Department of Health and the Department of Social Security. The Ministry of Agriculture, Fisheries and Food, the Home Office and the Departments of the Environment, Education and Employment, National Heritage, Transport and Trade and Industry are all in quite close proximity. The Scottish Office, the Welsh Office and the Northern Ireland Office also have central offices in Whitehall as well as in their respective capitals. There is a separate (though closely related) civil service for Northern Ireland, with its own official head. Only a small proportion of all civil servants work in Whitehall – just a few thousand among a total of some half a million. But these include most of the 'important' people, despite movements towards decentralization, delegation and the dispersal of staff away from London. These, then, are the senior civil servants who help to shape and give direction to policies and who maintain on behalf of ministers a general oversight of the operation and conduct of those policies, increasingly through the medium of executive agencies.

The way in which central government has been organized to perform these functions has changed over time. Reading 2.1 is a very short excerpt from Peter Hennessy's *Whitehall*. Hennessy divides departments into seven categories. Other and equally plausible categories could be devised but these seven illustrate the range and broad nature of government functions. The listing of departments as shown in Reading 2.1 incorporates certain changes introduced since Hennessy's book went to press for its first publication early in 1989. Patrick Dunleavy's focus in Reading 2.2 is not only upon the structure of Whitehall but also upon the behaviour of officials in different types of government agency. He presents, among other things, a counterweight to the view that bureaucrats are rational, self-serving, self-inflating agents. Such views have been associated with public choice theorists of the New Right, often accompanied by proposals designed to deflate and disaggregate traditional structures. Dunleavy's bureau-shaping model suggests a different type of rationality – or rather a rationality with different and more variable effects than those postulated by public choice theorists.

The medium through which Dunleavy's bureau-shaping model operates is the budget. One of the classic accounts of the way in which Whitehall mandarins make public spending decisions is Heclo and Wildavsky's *Private Government of Public Money*. In a book first published in 1974, with a second edition seven years later, these two Americans laid heavy emphasis upon the unwritten rules of engagement between the Treasury and the spending departments. They highlighted the shared values, the unspoken assumptions and the common understandings that were said to underpin the process of bargaining about the disposition of the nation's purse. In Reading 2.3 they describe the 'Whitehall village'. Many believe that Whitehall has retained its village character. Yet in certain respects things have changed. Thain and Wright (Reading 2.4) indicate that there may now exist a less accommodating and more conflictual pattern of relationships between actors from different quarters in Whitehall. With this and a number of other hypotheses they set an agenda for enquiry – a programme of research whose product is, at the time of writing, about to be published as a major treatise on the Treasury and Whitehall (Thain and Wright 1995).

Among the concepts employed in many studies of policy-making are those of policy community and policy network. In Reading 2.5 Maurice Wright explains the meaning of each and shows how they can assist in the study of public policy – the process and product of the Whitehall machine and of the context in which it operates.

| *Peter Hennessy*

The structure and organization of Whitehall

> The first thing to be noted about the central government of this country is that it is a federation of departments.
>
> (Sir William Armstrong 1970[1])

> What is often underestimated is the extent to which departments have characteristics and, indeed, even characters. Departments are to a very great extent coloured in their attitudes by the last major reform that they undertook.
>
> (Shirley Williams 1980[2])

In the first of his legendary Ford Lectures on 'the Troublemakers' at Oxford in 1956, A.J.P. Taylor began by emphasizing a truth which must never be allowed to sink beneath the gaze of any observer of government. 'We may remind ourselves over and over again', he told his capacity audience,[3] 'that the foreign policy of a country is made by a few experts and a few rather less expert politicians . . . We write "the British" when we mean "the few members of the Foreign Office who happened to concern themselves with this question".'[4] Taylor's Law, at a slight risk of oversimplification, can be applied to virtually every area of policy-making in which the state plays a role sufficiently substantial to have it institutionally enshrined in the stone, brick or plate glass of a central government department. Departments matter. They lead lives of their own. As Shirley Williams put it, they have banners to defend on which the departmental traditions and orthodoxy are emblazoned like fading regimental colours in a cathedral – and these are defended against all-comers whether they be pressure-groups, select committees, international organizations or other ministries. Among the other departments the 'auldest enemies' can often be found. The Treasury is the 'auldest' of them all. I can remember over lunch one under secretary with a vivid imagination likening his Treasury colleagues to sentries on the ramparts at night gazing down on the fires around which huddled their assortment of departmental foes waiting for the dawn assault upon their walls.

Any book on Whitehall needs a Baedeker guide to the banners and the battlements of the departmental satrapies. For most of them I have drawn up, with the help of Andrea Jones of Sussex University, a departmental chart. No tabulation can be perfect as functions can overlap (the Department of the Environment, for example, is both an economic and a social ministry and the Treasury is both a central and an economic department). But, for the sake of convenience, I have divided the departments up as follows:

Central
Prime Minister's Office
Cabinet Office (including Office of Public Service)
Treasury

Overseas and defence
Foreign and Commonwealth Office
Overseas Development Administration
Ministry of Defence

Social
Department of Health
Department for Education and Employment
Department of Social Security
Department of National Heritage

Economic
Department of Trade and Industry
Department of the Environment
Ministry of Agriculture, Fisheries and Food
Department of Transport

Territorial
Home Office
Scottish Office
Welsh Office
Northern Ireland Office

Secret
Security Service, MI5
Secret Intelligence Service, MI6
Government Communications Headquarters

Money-raising
Board of Inland Revenue
Board of Customs and Excise

The geography of Whitehall is never static. But the geomorphology of its 1980s bedrock would be recognizable to any set of post-war ministers and officials who had lived their careers atop of it. Even if substantial swathes of executive functions were hived off, the current departmental boundaries would most likely remain with their in-house functions largely reduced to policy-making and regulation.

References

1 Sir William Armstrong (1970) 'The civil service and its tasks', *O and M Bulletin*, Vol. 25, No. 2, HMSO, pp. 63–79.
2 Shirley Williams (1980) 'The decision makers', in *Policy and Practice: the Experience of Government*, Royal Institute of Public Administration, p. 92.
3 A.J.P. Taylor (1983) *A Personal History*, Hamish Hamilton, p. 210.
4 A.J.P. Taylor (1957) *The Troublemakers: Dissent over Foreign Policy 1792–1939*, Hamish Hamilton, p. 11.

| *Patrick Dunleavy*

The architecture of the British central state

The bureau-shaping model

The approach adopted here grounds empirical analysis in an explicit theoretical position, the 'bureau-shaping' model which was initially developed in opposition to public choice accounts of government organizations. The most influential economic accounts of bureaucracies see them as tightly hierarchical Weberian line agencies run by rationally self-interested actors who are consequently committed to maximizing their budgets (Niskanen 1971, 1973, 1975, 1978; for unconvincing variants of bureaucrats' maximization see also Breton and Wintrobe 1982; Migue and Berlanger 1972; Noll and Fiorina 1979). Against such views, the bureau-shaping model argues that top bureaucrats' instrumental rationality would not be well served by the risky and low pay-off collective strategy of inflating their agency's overall budget (Dunleavy 1985). Instead they should try to reshape their departments as small staff agencies, removed from line responsibilities and hence more insulated from adverse impacts in the event of overall spending reductions in their policy area. This model neatly explains the strongly marked institutional tendency in most liberal democracies for welfare state expansion to create a complex decentralized network of sub-central agencies. In contrast new right models must predict the continued growth of large-budget, centrally run line agencies. Similarly, budget-maximizing accounts imply that contracting-out forms of privatization will be strongly opposed by top managers. But the bureau-shaping model argues that such developments will positively foster agency remodelling in line with top bureaucrats' preferences, and hence will generally be welcomed and pushed ahead by managers (Dunleavy 1986; and see Ascher 1987 for relevant empirical research).

At the heart of the bureau-shaping model lies the recognition common to much recent organizational analysis from different perspectives (such as

Kaufman *et al.* 1987; Hanf and Scharpf 1978; Rhodes 1981) that modern administrative systems are highly articulated and differentiated. The simplified conception of isolated line bureaucracies in traditional organization theory and public choice accounts of bureaucracy is inadequate. There are still some policy areas where national-level government departments directly implement policy with their own personnel. But many contemporary administrative systems are multi-organizational and inherently less hierarchical in their operations than classical accounts assume. Where policy responsibilities are fragmented between tiers of government or deconcentrated to diverse quasi-governmental agencies, then apparently simple concepts – such as that of an agency's 'budget' – suddenly begin to look complex.

In any differentiated administrative system it is possible to distinguish four possible meanings of 'budget' (Dunleavy 1985: 306–9, 315–20):

1 An agency's *core* budget consists of its running costs for personnel and goods directly consumed by its own operations plus any capital expenditure on equipment or buildings directly needed for its basic functions.
2 The *bureau budget* includes the core budget items above, plus any moneys which the agency directly pays out to the private sector, for example, by awarding contracts to private firms or by making transfer payments to individuals.
3 An agency's *programme* budget includes its bureau budget plus any moneys which the agency passes on to other public sector bureaux for them to spend. Inter-organizational transfers of this last kind can only be included in an agency's programme budget total if it exercises some hierarchical control or supervision over the ways in which the funding is spent.
4 The *super-programme* budget consists of an agency's programme budget plus any spending by other bureaux from their own resources over which the agency none the less either exercises some policy responsibilities, or which it can limit or expand in planning terms, or for which it can wholly or partially claim political credit.

The concept of a super-programme budget is a new element added to the bureau-shaping model in this paper. In policy fields like education, housing, social services or local transport, Whitehall departments have extensive supervisory controls over how local councils deliver services, irrespective of whether the expenditures concerned are financed from central government specific grants, the Exchequer block grant to local authorities, or councils' own local income sources (such as property or poll taxes and capital receipts). The whole development of the block grant system as a means of containing central state commitments to local services was premised upon Whitehall ministries' ability to exercise effective policy controls unlinked from any direct tie-in to specific grants (Martlew 1983; Page 1981). The key mechanisms for achieving this aim include regulations, circulars, inspectorates, and government influence over professional ideas of 'good practice'.

From 1965, when the Public Expenditure Survey (PES) process was introduced, there have been annual battles between spending departments and the Treasury over policy sector planning totals, some of which are quite largely funded by councils' resources. The vigour with which spending departments press their case, and the items and priorities which they highlight in doing so, again indirectly influence how much local authorities can spend from their own resources. The introduction of cash limits on Whitehall's block grant to local government in the mid-1970s, plus the creation of comprehensive DoE controls on individual local authorities' spending totals in the 1980s, have extended central departments' ability to structure councils' allocations of their supposedly autonomous resources (Dunleavy and Rhodes 1986). The White Paper which issues from each PES round is a fascinating example of Whitehall departments claiming credit for programmes which they only partially finance (see Treasury 1987). Even if local authorities' own-sourced spending is excluded from public expenditure totals in the future (1988), central departments will maintain a battery of controls over such spending, and selective credit-claiming by ministers is unlikely to diminish.

The relative size of the four budget levels distinguished above will vary widely from one type of agency to another. The bureau-shaping model uses these variations to distinguish five main analytic types of agency (Dunleavy 1985: 309–15).

(a)   *Delivery agencies* are the classic line bureaucracies of Weberian theory. They directly deliver services to citizens or enterprises, using their own employed manpower to carry out most policy implementation. Their functions are usually labour-intensive. Consequently they have large core budgets, which absorb a very high proportion of their bureau and programme budgets.

(b)   *Regulatory agencies* are concerned with limiting or controlling the behaviour of individuals, enterprises or other public sector agencies. They normally externalize many of the costs of their activities onto those people or organizations being regulated, and hence appear relatively cheap to run in tax-funding or public expenditure terms. Since they are primarily inspecting and paper-moving organizations, their core budgets absorb a high proportion of their bureau or programme budgets, like delivery agencies. However, regulatory agencies have much smaller programme budgets than delivery agencies, because their man-power needs are much less and they externalize costs.

(c)   *Transfer agencies* handle payments of some form of subsidy or entitlement by government to private individuals or firms. They are above all money-moving organizations. Since subsidy payments are easily systematized within centrally administered and computerized administrations, in any national government there is likely to be at least one transfer agency with a large staff. None the less the administration costs of transfer payments are characteristically quite small in relation to the subsidies paid out, so that the core budget absorbs only a fraction of the bureau budget. Transfer agencies do not pass on much money to other public sector bodies, unless a decentralized implementing tier is required for a particular benefit. So the bureau budget usually absorbs almost all of a transfer agency's programme budget.

(d)   *Contracts agencies* are concerned with developing service specifications or capital projects for tendering, and then letting contracts to private sector firms (or to commercially run public sector agencies such as public corporations). Contracts agency staff are primarily employed in research and development into projects, drawing up equipment or service specifications, liaising with companies, contract management and compliance, etc. The actual implementation of the projects or services, the ordering of plant and materials, the employment of most of the staff, and the production of physical outputs are all carried out by the contractors. Consequently contracts agencies' core budgets typically absorb only a modest share of their bureau budget, although more than would be the case for transfer agencies. Bureau budgets of course absorb almost all of contracts agencies' programme budgets.

(e) *Control agencies'* primary task is to channel funding to other public sector bureaux in the form of grants, and to supervise how these other state organizations spend the money and implement policy. Again the administration costs involved will typically comprise only a fraction of the sums transferred, but this time the bureau budget will also be a small part of the programme budget. Control agencies are the main type of organization where super-programme budgets are likely to show a significant increase on programme budget levels.

In addition to these basic agency types, three additional categories need to be distinguished to create an exhaustive typology for this analysis.

(f) *Taxing agencies* closely resemble regulatory agencies in externalizing costs onto individuals, enterprises or other bureaux, and in being primarily labour-intensive paper-moving organizations. Their administration costs tend to be small in relation to the yield of taxes gathered, accounting for less than 4 per cent of the money raised by the Inland Revenue, and 1 per cent of the taxes collected by Customs and Excise. However, there has been a strong tendency in Western Europe for governments to raise revenues from fewer but more general taxes, such as income tax and VAT (Rose 1981: 94–127; Rose and Karran 1987). As tax structures have been regularized and generalized, governments have increasingly sought to integrate subsidy and transfer payments systems into the tax collection apparatus. The growth of tax expenditures, and their contemporary significance in government policy-making, means of course that all estimations of the distribution of public spending across policy fields are badly flawed, a problem which remains unaddressed in this paper as in virtually all other official and academic analyses (see Heald 1983: 20–2, 176, 292–3). But the increasing use of tax expenditures as a politically acceptable substitute for direct public spending may also imply that additional policy formulation and implementation functions fall on specialized tax collection agencies. For example, because of tax exemptions, the Inland Revenue in Britain has a 'stake' in many issues, including the encouragement of home ownership, company cars and company-assisted motoring, company-assisted health care and life assurance. As a consequence of all these trends, taxing agencies are now much larger organizations with greater running costs than regulatory agencies. Their core budgets absorb almost all their bureau and programme budgets.

(g) *Trading agencies* are full governmental organizations directly controlled by political appointees (without the intermediary board found with public corporations). They either operate directly in economic markets in a fully or quasi-commercial mode, or they deliver services to other organizations in the public sector but fully charge them for the costs involved. These agencies' core budgets normally absorb a large part of their bureau budgets, although the ratio is less where the agency is delivering a service with attached materials or equipment costs compared with a situation where it is primarily charging for expertise and paperwork. Bureau budgets and programme budgets will be identical.

(h)   *Servicing agencies* provide facilities or services to other governmental bodies, but on a basis which cannot be easily or sensibly broken down or recharged. Their outputs are collective benefits for a set of agencies or a whole tier of government. Although their outputs are not priced, in other respects they closely resemble trading agencies.

Once we recognize the distinct meanings which are attached to the term 'budget', the claim that bureaucracies maximize their budgets clearly becomes ambiguous. Which particular budget should rationally self-interested officials seek to increase? The only consistent answer for a public choice account would seem to be that officials will maximize their agency's core budget, followed in some cases by the bureau budget. The benefits from budget maximization flowing to bottom- and middle-level officials are clearly linked to core budgets, while those flowing to top officials are somewhat more attached to the bureau budget (Dunleavy 1985: 307–9). Top officials may want to boost bureau budgets primarily as an insurance strategy, allowing them to insulate their core budgets from possible challenge. But no rational official would seem to have much motivation to push for increases in funding that will simply be passed on to very fragmented private sector recipients of transfer payments, or to other public sector agencies. Still less would they have any reason to care about the super-programme budget. To worry about such totals central officials would have to make a fetish of a particular budget aggregate, or be mission-committed, or be afflicted by some form of altruism. And, of course, when public choice accounts begin to ascribe mixed self-interested and other-regarding motivations to individuals they almost immediately become non-substantive and unfalsifiable (Dunleavy 1984; see, for example, Downs 1967).

The bureau-shaping model argues that to the extent that rational bureaucrats are primarily concerned to maximize their core budgets (and perhaps their bureau budgets), this incentive is strongest in delivery agencies since they have the largest core budgets and staffs. It will also be important in taxing, regulatory and other smaller agencies where the core budget absorbs most or all of the programme budget. Self-interested officials in some kinds of contract and transfer agencies also have a strong specific incentive to maximize their bureau budgets, over and above their core budgets, when:

- the scale of single decisions about contracts or transfers is large;
- final decisions about allocation are discretionary and made at top policy levels;
- the recipients of contracts or transfers are a few large organizations; and
- these recipients can organize a flowback of benefits in return for officials' exercising patronage on their behalf.

For example, officials in procurement agencies have strong reasons to maximize their bureau budgets, since defence and other contracts often confer tremendous patronage potential. There are many opportunities for the corporations involved in tendering to organize substantial reciprocal benefits for their official contacts (such as side-deals which help boost promotion, lucrative *pantouflage* opportunities, post-retirement directorships for 'helpful' senior officials). Top officials in contracts agencies and in transfer agencies dealing with organized, corporate 'clients' also retain considerable resources in a 'control maximization' game, whether or not they are able to convert this control into personally advantageous side-payments. In these circumstances it would be rational to push up bureau budgets, even though the extra moneys involved mainly flow outside the agency in question. But it is hard to see any reason why policy-level staff at, say, a welfare benefits agency should want to push up payments to the unemployed or to old age pensioners, since none of the conditions specified above would be met. In general, for contract and transfer agencies, the incentives for bureau budget maximization will be much stronger for those agencies which transfer subsidies or allocate contracts to large corporations or to a meso-corporatist interest grouping, than for those agencies dealing with such highly fragmented 'clients' as the recipients of state welfare payments.

. . .

The bureau-shaping model set out here has no difficulty in accommodating sweeping institutional changes. Focusing on a central state defined in terms of effective ministerial control means that superficial changes in the nomenclature or status of component organizations within this apparatus do not materially alter the scope of analysis. And using analytically specified agencies as the basic foci of attention means that the bureau-shaping model already incorporates separate reference to many of the agencies likely to result from the implementation of the Next Steps proposals. The differentiated focus on core, bureau and programme budgets ensures that even extensive organizational changes can be effectively accommodated. For example, where a ministerial department supervises an executive agency which is then privatized, three things happen in the bureau-shaping framework. (i) The subordinate agency disappears from the central state. But (ii) its funding is transferred from the programme to the bureau budget of the ministerial department. And (iii) the department itself may change bureau-type from a control to a contracts agency (depending on the significance of the privatized subordinate agency to the department's programme budget and on whether other subordinate public agencies are being funded). Thus the Next Steps reforms will just make possible a finer grain delineation of analytically defined agencies without any alteration of the fundamental intellectual basis for academic study.

. . .

The whole thrust of the bureau-shaping model is to predict and explain exactly the kinds of administrative developments which the Next Steps proposals entail. Originally formulated in 1983, over five years before any public hint of Whitehall reorganization appeared, the model strongly predicts that policy-level officials will favour hiving off in terms of their demand-and-supply calculation for budgetary increases. In Figure 2, the horizontal axis shows the level of an agency's programme budget, and the vertical axis shows the costs and benefits to senior officials of advocating a budgetary increase (see

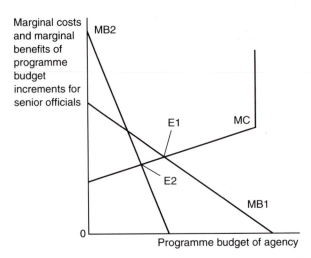

Figure 2   The marginal costs and benefits of hiving-off reorganizations for senior
officials in central departments

Key: MC curve shows the marginal costs of advocating a programme budget increment
       MB curves show the marginal benefits of programme budget increments
       MB1 = curve for delivery agency configuration
       MB2 = curve for control or contracts agency configuration
       E1 and E2 are the equilibrium programme budget points with MB1 and MB2
       respectively

Dunleavy 1985: 318–20). The line labelled MC (for marginal cost) shows the
costs to senior officials of advocating a further marginal expansion of their
department's programme budget. I assume that these costs (in terms of the
time and effort taken justifying a budgetary increment to sponsors, and the
political and administrative risks attached) rise as the agency's existing budget
gets larger (with a constant set of administrative functions). At some
environmentally determined point, no further budgetary increases are feasible
and the MC curve becomes vertical.

The line MB1 shows the benefits which senior officials initially derive from a
marginal increase in the programme budget flowing through their department
when it is set up as a delivery agency. I assume that these benefits will fall away
as the programme budget level goes up. Within delivery agencies this decline
will be a gradual tapering, for senior officials' welfare will be quite directly
linked to high levels of programme budget. But if the department is transformed via hiving off from a delivery agency into a control agency (or a contracts agency where hived off sections are privatized) then the marginal benefit
curve for senior officials will shift radically to the configuration MB2. In the
new slimmed down central department senior officials will safeguard their
own welfare at much lower levels of the programme budget. Since most of
their programme budget flows outside to other agencies or to contractors their
incentives to advocate further programme budget increases are reduced.
Hence the MB2 curve (showing their welfare gain from increments) falls much
more steeply.

The diagram also illustrates why the Next Steps reorganization is likely to proceed, since it provides strong incentives for both senior officials and government ministers anxious to constrain public spending. The equilibrium points E1 and E2 indicate the optimum levels of programme budget for the senior officials of the central department in its delivery agency and control agency configurations respectively. If the department's actual programme budget level lies to the left of the optimum then senior officials will advocate programme budget increases, whereas if the programme budget level is to the right of the optimum they will not advocate further increases. The shift from MB1 to MB2 involves a clockwise rotation of senior officials' marginal benefit curve which *reduces* their optimum programme budget level. In a control (or contracts) agency configuration, Whitehall administrators will find that their personal welfare is less and less involved with the level of funding going to implementing agencies, and hence will reduce their advocacy of budgetary increases. This shift explains why government ministers opposed to public spending growth should favour the Next Steps reorganization.

At the same time, senior officials' welfare levels can be visualized as the area of the graph lying above the MC curve but under the MB1 and MB2 curves respectively, and to the left of the optimum programme budget levels E1 and E2. It should be clear from Figure 2 as I have drawn it here that this area is larger in the control (or contracts) agency configuration than in the delivery agency configuration. In practice, the graph could be drawn differently – to show the area under MB2 as equal to or even smaller than that under MB1 – because there is no *a priori* way of establishing what the welfare implications of a rotating marginal benefit curve will be for senior officials. The key point to note here, in contrast to budget-maximizing models of bureaucracy, is that there are no grounds for believing that the hiving off of large parts of the civil service into separate agencies will automatically reduce the welfare of policy-level officials who control the Whitehall departments. Indeed, such a reorganization may well deliver enhanced personal welfare levels to senior bureaucrats, by insulating them from responsibility for routine tasks, control of implementation, mistakes in administration, management of labour relations with hostile unions, control of demand-sensitive running costs, etc. The new central departments acting as sponsors to executive agencies and sub-national governments are also likely to accord much better with senior officials' preferences for working in small, élite, high status, and collegial staff organizations close to political power centres and in metropolitan locations (see Dunleavy 1985: 320–4) . . .

References

Ascher, K. (1987) *The Politics of Privatization: Contracting out in the NHS and Local Authorities*, London, Macmillan.

Breton, A. and Wintrobe, D. (1982) *The Logic of Bureaucratic Conduct: an Economic Analysis of Competition, Exchange and Efficiency in Private and Public Organizations*, Cambridge, Cambridge University Press.

Downs, A. (1967) *Inside Bureaucracy*, New York, Little, Brown.

Dunleavy, P. (1984) 'Bureaucrats, budgets and the growth of the state. Part I, existing public choice approaches', Unpublished paper, London School of Economics (available from the author).

Dunleavy, P. (1985) 'Bureaucrats, budgets and the growth of the state: reconstructing an instrumental model', *British Journal of Political Science*, 15, 299–328.

Dunleavy, P. (1986) 'Explaining the privatization boom: public choice versus radical approaches', *Public Administration*, 64, 13–34.

Dunleavy, P. and Rhodes, R.A.W. (1986) 'Government beyond Whitehall', in H. Drucker *et al.* (eds) *Developments in British Politics 2*, London, Macmillan, 107–48.

Hanf, K. and Scharpf, F. (eds) (1978) *Interorganizational Policy Making*, London, Sage.

Heald, D. (1983) *Public Expenditure*, Oxford, Martin Robertson.

Kaufman, F., Majone, G. and Ostrom, V. (eds) (1987) *Guidance, Control and Evaluation in the Public Sector*, Berlin, de Gruyter.

Martlew, C. (1983) 'The state and local government finance', *Public Administration*, 61, 127–47.

Migue, J. and Berlanger, G. (1972) 'Towards a general theory of managerial discretion', *Public Choice*, 17, 27–43.

Niskanen, W. (1971) *Bureaucracy and Representative Government*, New York, Aldine Atherton.

Niskanen, W. (1973) *Bureaucracy: Servant or Master?*, London, Institute of Economic Affairs.

Niskanen, W. (1975) 'Bureaucrats and politicians', *Journal of Law and Economics*, 18, 617–43.

Niskanen, W. (1978) 'Competition among government bureaus', in J.M. Buchanan (ed.) *The Economics of Politics*, London, Institute for Economic Affairs.

Noll, R.G. and Fiorina, M.P. (1979) 'Voters, bureaucrats and legislators: a rational perspective on the growth of bureaucracy', *Journal of Public Economics*, 9, 239–54.

Page, E. (1981) 'Grant consolidation and the development of inter-governmental relations in the United States and United Kingdom', *Politics*, 1(1), 19–24.

Rhodes, R.A.W. (1981) *Control and Power in Central–Local Relations*, Farnborough, Gower.

Rhodes, R.A.W. (1986) *The National World of Local Government*, London, Allen and Unwin.

Rose, R. (1981) *Big Government: the Programme Approach*, London, Sage.

Rose, R. (1987) *Ministers and Ministries: a Functional Analysis*, Oxford, Clarendon Press.

Rose, R. and Karran, T. (1987) *Taxation by Public Inertia: Financing the Growth of Government*, London, Allen and Unwin.

Treasury (1987) *The Government's Expenditure Plans, 1987–88*, Cm 56, Vol. II, London, HMSO.

Abridged from P. Dunleavy (1989) 'The architecture of the British central state. Part I: framework for analysis', *Public Administration*, Vol. 67, pp. 249–76. Reproduced with the permission of Blackwell Publishers.

Hugh Heclo and Aaron Wildavsky

The Whitehall village

Political life at the centre of British government seems a highly interrelated whole, yet words can be written and read only one at a time in strict sequential order. Analysis must subdivide reality to make it manageable. One way of allaying this difficulty is to use concepts which retain at least some flavour of the essential unity amid diversity. Rather than set ministers against civil servants or weigh divided chunks of power among institutions we prefer to speak of political administrators and their community relationships. When we speak of family life in the Treasury or village life in Whitehall we are talking about people united by coherent patterns of praxis, the shared experiences that facilitate learning.

But we are also speaking of people whose common kinship and culture separates them from outsiders. Coherence among British political adminis-trators is expressed through exclusiveness. Their interactions are sequestered within the executive. Apart from the final decisions reached, their behaviour is neither known nor intended to be known beyond government circles. Insiders are overwhelming; outsiders are overwhelmed. In a word, governing public money is a private affair.

This privacy at the political centre can best be introduced in terms of four central features in British government. None is absolutely unique to Britain, but there are probably few nations where all four can be found to the same extent or in such powerful combination. The structure of government community sets the basic outline for distinguishing insiders from outsiders. Mutual trust is a pervasive bond expressing an awareness of how to deal with members of one's own group and, by extension, strangers. Common calcu-lations help political administrators deal with a complex world but also separate them from the layman, who finds it difficult to see why government cannot simply decide on the right policy and execute it. Political climate often gathers force outside government but blows this way and that largely through insiders' concentration on their own reactions and assessments. Community, confidence, calculations and climate are variations on the theme of a shared, exclusive group life in British government.

Because much is shared, much is disputable. Men of common kinship know they can continually bargain and fight for what they want from each other, not in a once-and-for-all massacre, but in the marketplace exchange of an agreed culture, day after day and year after year. The market is political. The medium of exchange is repute. The bargaining counters are public moneys. The signals are bids to allocate more to this and less to that governmental programme. Channels of communication are opened by the willingness of participants to listen and to take part in the market: both activities require trust. The kinsmen must speak in common idioms or they will have difficulty in communicating. They must refine the technical apparatus or they will not be able to distinguish their own messages from the confusion of a world filled with static. To interpret messages properly, they need to know who are the senders and receivers, how they relate to one another and what the rules of broadcasting allow them to do. The medium is government and the message is public money. To know who gets what, we must begin with the communal relationships that structure the process of expenditure.

The government community

Few people are directly involved. When we speak of political administrators in British central government, we mean the assemblage of ministers and senior civil servants who preside over the work of Cabinets and departments. At the margins of government are a number of important backbench MPs, journalists and interest group leaders, altogether only a few hundred people.

. . .

The small numbers at the centre in Britain mean (apart from the obvious overwork) that the cooperation of operating departments is essential. 'There are so few people that there's no chance of the Treasury taking things over', a high official explained. 'It is utterly dependent on the departments to do most of what has to be done.' The task of the Treasury . . . is to work with, through, and around departments. Participants may disagree or be disagreeable, but the system will not work unless they get together. The Treasury itself might do a study here or there, but for most things it must co-opt or coerce or contract with departments . . . The smallness at the centre also explains why the Cabinet Office, a handful of top calibre civil servants, is crucial to the conduct of government business. To survive, the Cabinet – like any committee or elementary sea creature – requires a constant and manageable circulation of material through its body. Without the Cabinet Office to direct the mass of department requests, highlight major issues and pace the flow of papers, the Cabinet works would become irretrievably clogged.

British political administration is concentrated spatially as well as numerically . . . Basically, if you are not in (or within easy reach of) London, you are politically nowhere. Success in political administration depends on the judgements of your fellows and to be judged you must get to London. In a hundred different ways, the provincial can reveal that he is not intimately acquainted with current wisdom. He is likely to be written off, for an important part of merit in the eyes of the judges is an awareness of current modes, even phrases of thought, that are the special preserve of those 'in the know'.

Within London itself, the vital political living space is highly compact. Government departments may be huge but their top political and civil service leadership is likely to be concentrated within a thousand yards of Whitehall. No wide Washingtonian avenues string out the leadership of the great departments of State. The office of one's opposite number is probably only a few minutes' walk away. Lunch can be taken within five hundred yards at one of the clubs in Pall Mall or, more convenient still, at the Cabinet Office mess, where ministers do not come, membership is by invitation only, and attendance is a sign of acceptance into the upper reaches of the Civil Service.

. . .

The crucial fact about all this is that British political administrators invariably know or know about each other. Life at the top in Britain may not be warm-hearted chumminess, but it does demonstrate a coherence and continuity unknown in the United States. If coordination means the degree to which different participants take each other into account (if only to disagree), then British political administration is extraordinarily well coordinated. Whereas in Washington the men who know each other are likely to be connected through common concern with a single area of policy, in London they know each other, period. Just as it would be unthinkable for a Prime Minister not to know personally his Cabinet appointees, so everyone who is anyone has got to have extensive personal contacts.

. . .

Mutual confidence

. . .

The number of people involved is at most a few hundred, and they change but slowly. They all know or have heard about each other, and they all enjoy rating one another. Ministers are likely to be aware of not only each others' political performance, but the exact university degree (first, second or third) that colleagues won and where. There is no permanent secretary who is not prepared to rate the leadership abilities of ministers under whom he has served. No Treasury official of any experience hesitates to judge the incisiveness and reliability of his opposite numbers in the departments. No departmental finance officer worth considering is unaware of the extent to which Treasury supply officials know the substantive merits of the proposals he sends them. The ratings work by slow accretion. It is difficult to get a high rating and equally difficult to lose one. But over the years events reveal to colleagues that some men are bright and others dull; some strong, others weak; some trustworthy and others not.

The one inescapable theme in virtually every interview we conducted is the vital importance participants place on personal trust for each other. By trust one is speaking of personal dependability, 'soundness', a feeling that here is a person in whom one can reliably place confidence and confidences. Mutual trust is considered paramount by officials who know they will have to continue doing business with each other year after year on issue after issue; they believe that, if professionalism means anything, it means knowing how to treat members of one's own group. Trust is vital between ministers and civil servants, each of whom must fight the other's battles, one behind Cabinet doors and in the public arena, the other among the mass of departmental expertise and official encounters. Mutual reliance is important, though as we shall see less operational, among ministers of the government who survive by hanging together against the other party's crowd and an intractable world. Since everyone's prospects for power over policy and authority over decisions depend on the judgement of colleagues, reputation in general is always likely to be more important to participants than is any issue in particular.

From this central place of personal trust, much else follows. The desire to create and maintain trust explains the great dread of being caught by surprise that prevails among both ministers and civil servants. To be surprised is no sin, but to be seen to be surprised decreases confidence and nurtures distrust among colleagues. Avoiding embarrassment to ministers in public, and particularly in the House of Commons, is one of the driving forces throughout British government. Many failings of a minister may be overlooked, but misjudgement and error is far less damaging than to be seen as unsure, surprised and out of touch with important events. The same motive force operates even more forcefully within the executive itself; ministerial embarrassment and civil servant loss of face are two sides of the same coin. Avoiding a decline in reputation among their peers is a matter of utmost concern to officials who still hope to go further and to do more than they have done. Ministers and civil servants who refuse information to Parliament are not dissembling when they lay great stress on the 'embarrassment' that this would cause.[1] Sharing information widely is thought to reduce the scope for ministers and officials to deal with each other in mutual confidence. For those with eyes to see, it is clear which personal working relationships count to these men.

. . .

How is trust established? The shortest answer by a department finance officer was 'I must be honest'. Another added that 'apart from being frank with the Treasury you must be seen to be frank'. This means, according to a third, that 'you must set out the weaknesses of your case as well as the strengths. The minister, of course, often says he does not want all the arguments put to the Treasury but you do it anyway and argue that your strengths outweigh the weaknesses.' Why, we asked, is it necessary to be so frank? 'Because just as I tell the minister, they [the Treasury] will find out anyway; they are no fools. And if the Treasury have to find out for themselves they will think, without any question, that the weaknesses they have found are more important than any strengths you have presented in isolation.' The idea, as a permanent secretary put it, that 'the Treasury will always catch up with you in the end', is well entrenched. Quite apart from and overriding any of the financial and personnel sanctions at the Treasury's command, there is the sense that such frankness is the way of dealing with someone in one's own group.

Trust is also established by showing the Treasury that the department is well able to look after itself. A permanent secretary, who had come from the Treasury, 'knew you had to show the Treasury that you had a rigorous internal expenditure control system in your own department'. Demonstrating good internal controls fosters confidence and makes the department's life easier. 'Conversely', observed a Treasury under secretary, 'if the department has blotted its copybook, the Treasury is suspicious, awkward, and, failing to persuade us, the department has no alternative but to go to the minister'.

Departments are tempted to increase Treasury confidence by overconsulting them so as to avoid any suggestion that things might be going on they did not know about. The Treasury may be brought in at the very first stages and made aware of the pressures 'so they can see we are doing the best we can right from the very outset. This shows them that you are not bullying or rushing your way through the project.' Occasionally, a Treasury man will even be invited to visit field sites and installations, 'so that when later we say we have to replace a boiler house they'll have some idea what it's all about'.

But confidence is more than a question of frankness, consultation and internal controls. Treasury people do not like to trust men who are not able. Getting competent work done in departments is one way they have to protect their reputation and learn who to trust. Since they cannot observe the work directly they must take the department official's ability to discuss and defend it as a surrogate of his competence. 'You know that if the person can't answer questions or probes', said a Treasury Assistant Secretary, 'then he is not a person with whom you can deal on a confidential basis'. A man who can cope with Treasury scepticism earns – and deserves – respect. There is, however, one way a finance officer can still maintain Treasury respect for a poor case. First he must acknowledge that it does not make a great deal of sense; after that password it is permissible for him to say that 'there may be holes, I know, but the minister wants it and thinks it is politically important'. Then both civil servants can address the question like the insiders they are.

Mutual confidence, particularly at higher levels, is created not only by talk but by action. When a Treasury man speaks of trust, one thing he wants to know is whether the department official can keep his side of the bargain. When they agree that 'as between ourselves, this is the line we will take with our ministers', the Treasury man expects that the minister will be briefed accordingly, with a straight face and with noticeable impact. Or as one Treasury undersecretary put it, 'Can my opposite number deliver his master or not?'

. . .

Civil service cosiness is reined by their need for ministerial support. Personal trust between officials is unlikely to produce significant results without a complementary confidence between officials and their ministers. Ministers are expected, in the British phrase, to defend their corner. Extracting money from the Exchequer to support the great interests of his department is one of the prime ways in which the reputation and career of a minister is built. Ministers know that colleagues in the Cabinet and officials within the department are watching their behaviour and will tell others whether they are considered competent people.

Reference

1 See, for example, HC 549 (1970–1), pp. 34, 36, 46.

The private government of public money revisited

Since 1945 public expenditure has played a key role in economic policy. In the heyday of the Keynesian consensus, adjustments to the total of public spending and specific changes to key items within that total (for example public sector investment) formed an integral part of an active fiscal policy. When the economy was depressed the pump was primed; when the balance of payments or sterling gave policy-makers cause for concern, or when the economy was 'overheating', spending programmes were pared back. Similarly, when governments became concerned about growth and the need to 'plan' the economy, public spending was to take the lead in encouraging the private sector to increase output. In political terms too, levels of spending became highly significant. Party competition in the 1950s and 1960s centred upon the issue of who could 'deliver' the most in terms of welfare spending. The ability of government to 'touch the accelerator' through public expenditure increases led to academic interest in the 'political-business' cycle as general elections coincided with higher real income. The Thatcher years were no exception to this; expenditure plans were boosted prior to both the 1983 and 1987 elections.

The period after 1976 saw changes in the economic and political role of spending. After 1975 public expenditure totals were not predicated upon assumptions about the achievement of full employment: containment actually became a goal of policy despite rising levels of unemployment and falling output. The advent of the first Thatcher administration consolidated this change: public spending was seen as an economic evil, reductions in its level would lead to lower inflation and financial stability. The Medium-Term Financial Strategy unveiled in 1980 codified its new place in the order of things: medium-term reductions in total spending were deemed necessary for the achievement of a whole set of objectives, including reductions in monetary growth (Thain 1985). It was not that public expenditure ceased to be economically important, but that it was no longer to have the lead-part in macro-economic policy; rather it was to be in the supporting cast helping to assure more important monetarist goals. The Thatcher years also show how extraordinarily difficult it was to cut the real level of spending. Despite political resolve, strong leadership and seeming public support for action against the 'bureaucracy' of government, total spending has carried on rising. Of equal significance, the elections of 1979, 1983 and 1987 highlighted how much of a constraint public support of the NHS and other key aspects of the welfare state had become on a government of the radical right.

Both policies for growth and restraint have been frustrated by the tendency for expenditure to rise faster than intended or anticipated: it appears to have a momentum independent of declared policy. In seeking the explanation for this phenomenon there are many diverse and complex elements. Besides the aims and constraints (and opportunities) provided by an international economic system, which since the early 1970s has brought the economies of the industrialized countries into a state of increasing interdependence, besides the familiar politics of expenditure opportunism and expediency, there emerged in the mid-1970s the less familiar politics of cuts and squeezes, elevated to ideology and doctrine in the 'new right' politics of the Conservative governments after 1979. In turn, the supporters of these ideas were confronted and challenged by ingrained societal attitudes and expectations nurtured by more than two decades of growth-politics, and articulated through elected representative bodies and their bureaucracies, and organized groups representing special and general interests and clientele. The resultant compound of the mix of these multiple, diverse, changing and conflicting elements − 'public expenditure politics' − emerged from policy processes which themselves were subject to change, and which reflected a political/administrative culture affected by and affecting those elements.

While all of these contradictory factors need to be analysed, our main concern is with the policy processes and culture through which policies for public expenditure are mediated and finally determined. Some may still argue that this ground was well-worked by Heclo and Wildavsky (1974, 1981) and that further research will add little to their classic account. To that we would reply that it relates to the period of the early 1970s, roughly 1970–2, and that in the past fifteen years there have been such changes in economic and political doctrines, in 'ideas-in-good-currency', as well as in the institutions and processes of public policy-making, that their interpretation of 'private government' stands in need of substantial modification. Besides, that interpretation was a singular one; from the lack of competing knowledge it has remained largely unchallenged. Even at the time of writing it paid little attention to the 'economics' of public spending. In its concern with 'idylls of the constitution', the study aspired to a general critique of the centre of British government, boldly extrapolating from the particularities of Treasury–departmental spending relationships evidence for the weakness of collective decision-making.

. . .

The effects of cash limits and cash planning

What have been the effects of cash limits and cash planning? There are two main kinds, and they are interrelated. First, the effects on public expenditure;

second, the effects on the system for planning and controlling that expenditure. Both also raise issues about effectiveness, but these are dealt with more explicitly in the next section.

Looking first at the system, the main effect has been to emphasize the primacy of short-term cash control in the budgetary processes. Planning has been subordinated to control. A consequent effect is the shifting of the location and burden of decision-making further towards the centre, and hence the strengthening of the Treasury's position *vis-à-vis* the departments. The more powerful position of the centre has been strengthened by a number of institutional changes. The abolition of the Civil Service Department (CSD) in November 1981 restored to the Treasury its former responsibilities for the pay and conditions of the Civil Service. This was a deliberate attempt to tighten central control by concentrating in the Treasury the responsibility for the central allocation of all resources. The rump of the CSD, with residual responsibility for management and personnel, was returned to the Treasury in 1987 from the Cabinet Office. By this time the Treasury had resumed responsibility for Civil Service manpower, pay, superannuation and allowances, conditions of service, and management and efficiency.

This reconcentration of authority in the Treasury has been used by it primarily to attempt to achieve tighter control of the aggregates of public spending. It has been accompanied by a decentralization of authority for managing allocations and spending cash. While decisions about how much to allocate (and cut) are made increasingly at the centre, in particular local authority expenditure, decisions about how those allocations are to be managed (and cuts implemented) are made increasingly at the periphery. Where cash limits have produced cuts and squeezes, responsibility for what is cut and where has tended to be delegated. However, the decentralization of managerial authority within departments, and between them and their clients, is not only the result of the conditions created by cut-back and squeeze following the introduction of cash limits and cash planning. The Conservative governments' concern with the efficiency and effectiveness of public expenditure, and attempts to improve managerial performance, have also contributed.

The introduction of the Financial Management Initiative (FMI) in 1982, the reduction of civil service manpower, the Rayner and other VFM exercises, the work of the Efficiency Unit, have all contributed to a changed environment which has affected the expenditure process, both in the way bids are formulated in departments (for example, the gradual integration in some departments of activity and resource management data – objectives, targets, performance indicators – with Public Expenditure Survey Committee (PESC) returns), and more especially the way allocated resources are used by programme managers. Any squeeze imposed by cash limits, intended or otherwise, has obliged spending authorities to seek economies in the use of resources, and to pay more attention to the measurement of performance. Any assessment of the effects and effectiveness of cash limits has therefore to be made within the broader context of attempts to provide for 'better management'.

While the Treasury has used its enhanced authority to attempt to control public expenditure more effectively, and has taken some pains to be seen to be so doing (Likierman 1986), it is by no means clear how successful it has been. It is not demonstrably the case that surveys in cash have provided more certainty in predicting the outturn of planned expenditure than volume plans. Likierman has shown how great are the problems of calculating public expenditure plans. Whether control in the sense of avoidable under- or over-spending in the total of public expenditure, and in individual pro-grammes, has improved as a result of cash limits and cash planning is difficult to assess. Likierman (1986: 299–302) argues that changes in classification, and the switch from volume-planning to cash-planning, have made it difficult to provide a reliable database to compare expenditure totals, which in any case have been affected by factors beyond the control of governments. Walshe (1987: 79–80), while acknowledging such factors, concludes that there has been a 'general upward drift of the cash figures' since the introduction of cash planning. Whether departmental budgetary systems have performed better or worse, measured by avoidable under- or over-spending, is even more difficult to answer. Likierman and others have argued that it is impossible to isolate those circumstances within the control of departments from the effects of Budget changes, policy decisions and so on.

The effectiveness of cash limits and cash planning

Any assessment of the effectiveness of cash limits and cash planning at this early stage in the research would be premature. Here we point to some of the difficulties in making an assessment and explore some of the issues which arise.

The first problem is to identify the aims and objectives of the key players, and how these have been articulated in the policy processes. Here we shall try to distinguish the ostensible and publicly stated aims from those which have been pursued in practice. By so doing we hope to be able to compare what has happened, the observed effects of cash limits and cash planning, with both the seeming and real aims of the Treasury, departments' Principal Finance Officers (PFOs), line managers and of course governments. On this basis we can check who has won or lost since 1976 (or, perhaps, test the hidden notion that the only success possible is to remain 'playing the game' ready to fight next year's battle). We have already drawn attention to the difficulties of establishing what has happened to public expenditure over time, both in aggregate and programme by programme, but the use of qualitative and quantitative data should enable us at the very least to establish what the participants perceive or believe to have happened, and whether they perceive or believe they have won or lost. Such perceptions and beliefs of course are determinants of behaviour and help to guide and shape strategy.

Another measure of effectiveness is a comparison of the operation of the current system for planning and controlling public expenditure with the principles laid down in the Plowden Report (1961). Else and Marshall (1979) conducted one such exercise for the 1970s. Such comparison will afford the means to establish whether, and, if so, how far and why the Treasury has departed from those principles in the last decade.

Discussion of the effectiveness of the system has tended to focus on the question of whether it has become more or less rational as a result of the introduction of cash limits and cash planning. Such discussion begs the question of whose rationality is considered. In our analysis we shall try to distinguish and compare the different perceptions of rationality: the rationality of the 'strategic coordinator', the Treasury; the rationality of the programme manager in a spending department; the rationality of the 'professionals' in delivery systems; the rationality of politicians; and the rationality of consumers. Our main concern will be the perceived rationality of the system by Treasury expenditure controllers and financial controllers and line managers in spending departments, and with political rationality as perceived at the centre of government.

It is hypothesized (*pace* Glennerster, 1981) that in times of growth a *modus vivendi* between different types of expectation about rationality is possible in the budgetary processes. But in a period of restraint there is the potential for increasing conflict about how to allocate resources, and the consequences of those allocations, and the growing incompatibilities among different forms of rationality. For example, the decision to abandon volume planning in 1982 and to opt for cash-planning rather than cost-planning could be justified in terms of its rationality as perceived by the strategic coordinator, the Treasury, and by the Conservative government of the day (both of whom perhaps shared the real aim of wanting to reduce the level of public expenditure). That perception might not be shared by departmental PFOs and programme managers who foresaw only greater uncertainty introduced into the process of planning and managing their programmes. They might be more inclined to agree with those, like Pliatzky (1983: 326), who have asserted that 'PESC is not cash *planning* but an extension of short-term cash control'. While the former was the declared and publicly stated aim, the latter might be construed from its conduct in 1981–2 and subsequently to have been its real aim.

If this hypothesis is proved well-founded, we might expect to find great potential for conflict between the Treasury and spending departments. The relationships characterized by Heclo and Wildavsky in the early 1970s as cooperative and accommodating might in the 1980s have become more conflictual. On the other hand, it is possible that despite their different perceptions of rationality, departments might have become habituated to the greater uncertainties generated by cash limits and cash planning, and to the hard times of cuts and squeezes. Their relationships with the Treasury might have changed little.

If departments have curbed their bids, made cuts and absorbed squeezes, this may result less from the Treasury's skill in exploiting its enhanced resources of authority, information and expertise: it may be due rather more to the changes in the politico-administrative culture engendered by the search for greater efficiency and effectiveness described above.

The policy processes

Our primary concern is with the relationships between the Treasury expenditure divisions and departmental finance (and policy) divisions. Using the concepts of policy community and policy network (Wilks and Wright 1987), the structures and characteristics of those interdependencies will be examined.

The analysis will also reveal and explain the norms of behaviour and 'rules-of-the-game' by which expenditure politics are conducted. We are concerned too with the relationships within the Treasury, between members of the spending divisions and between them and other parts of the Treasury. Those relationships, it is hypothesized, have become more important as the politico-economic context of public expenditure has become the major determinant of the 'expenditure judgement', the aggregate total of planning expenditure.

Heclo and Wildavsky provide an obvious starting point. However, life in the village community described by them *circa* 1970–2 is unlikely to be the same in all essentials in the very different economic and political environment of the 1980s. In any case, the introduction of cash limits in 1976 marked a turning point in the expenditure politics of the previous fifteen years, and a sharp break with the steady evolution of PESC along the lines prescribed in the Plowden Report, and eulogized by Heclo and Wildavsky. Nevertheless, their interpretation of the policy processes, and in particular the relationships between the Treasury and spending departments within these processes, provides a firm starting point. Mutual trust between the members of the policy community was the key element in these policy processes; it provided for both the cohesiveness of the community and for the cooperation between its members.

Since the mid-1970s the 'game' has been played in a different economic and political context. The objectives of governments have changed, and their priorities; PESC has changed. We hypothesize that the strategies of the key players have changed as a consequence, and that the 'rules-of-the-game' governing their discretionary behaviour in their relationships will have changed too. We should expect the expenditure community to be less cohesive, and its members less cooperative. Mutual trust may have been replaced by mutual suspicion. The Treasury may have assumed 'hegemonic leadership' in relationships which are less symmetrical than those described by Heclo and Wildavsky.

They contended that the control of the Treasury was primarily one of the effective management of people, about the evaluations and constant re-evaluations of reputations and reliability in the community. While we accept their implicit conceptualization of power as organizational inter-dependence and the exchange of resources in relationships, the *distribution* of those resources of money, authority, information and expertise is liable to change. We argue that the distribution has changed since the mid-1970s: resources of money and authority have been increasingly centralized in the Treasury as the financing of public expenditure has assumed a greater significance economically and politically. For example, the Treasury acted to impose both cash limits and cash planning, to formulate the MTFS, to initiate FMI, to abolish the Civil Service Pay Research Unit and to engender a more hostile climate to public expenditure. Changes in the distribution of resources between the members of the expenditure community may well have influenced consequential changes in the structures of those relationships, in the 'rules-of-the-game' and the strategies of the key players.

While the testing of Heclo and Wildavsky's model of the policy processes and the political/administrative culture which sustains it provides a useful starting point for studying the expenditure community and its behaviour, we must be careful not to assume that their interpretation was necessarily valid even for the period of their study. With the benefit of hindsight (but even on publication of their first edition in 1974), it appears panglossian. They seem dazzled by the putative benefits and efficacy of PESC, and by the ability of Treasury controllers. They applaud just those characteristics which many commentators and critics had questioned then, and were to continue to question throughout the decade.

Shortly after the publication of their book, the inadequacies of PESC were cruelly and expensively exposed by the effects of high and rising rates of inflation and the incurable and unwarranted optimism of ministers about the growth of the economy. It took a substantial crisis to provide sufficient impetus for the introduction of tighter control procedures, although the in-built tendency of PESC to 'grow' programmes had been apparent some time before. If, as Heclo and Wildavsky claim, the Treasury was always so hostile to public expenditure growth, why did it not cut sooner? There is little hint of the potential for crisis in Sir Samuel Goldman's valedictory essay on PESC published in 1973 (Goldman 1973). If the cause of the crisis was irresponsible politicians, and the Treasury was helpless to avert it, as some have alleged (and the Treasury hinted in its evidence at the time to the Expenditure Select Committee), then Treasury power (and the authority of the Chancellor) was not as great as Heclo and Wildavsky asserted: the relationships of mutual trust and cooperation worked adversely for the Treasury – the Treasury 'lost'.

Heclo and Wildavsky's criticisms are directed not at PESC – 'the best in the world' – nor at the character and quality of the relationships between the Treasury and the departments: they criticize the under-developed capacity at the centre of government to provide competing and challenging policy analysis to that conducted by the Treasury. Their concern is with an improvement to PAR and the CPRS to complement or challenge the Treasury's own analysis – or rather lack of analysis.

The financial management initiative (FMI)

While both PAR and the CPRS have long since disappeared, concern with economic, efficient and effective performance has characterized Conservative administrations from the outset. The climate within Whitehall has changed since the mid-1970s. Not only have the policy processes been affected by the introduction and operation of tight cash limits, and the development of cash planning, the 'mood' has been affected by manpower cuts, a continuing squeeze on civil service pay, by value-for-money exercises like the Rayner scrutinies and the investigations of the revitalised National Audit Office, and the emphasis on the need to improve the capacity and performance of line managers. The introduction and development of techniques and disciplines from the private sector have been epitomized by the FMI introduced into Whitehall in 1982. Our concern is less with its 'mechanics', department by department, than with the effects of FMI and the changed 'managerial mood' which it partly represents and promotes in the policy processes through which decisions are made about programme allocations. We shall need to consider the Treasury's role in the future in the promotion of FMI, and any effects that this may have for the work of the expenditure controllers and their relations with departments.

Conclusions

In this article we have attempted to show why we think it is timely and necessary to re-examine the politics of public expenditure in the Whitehall community. We have emphasized the need to integrate analysis of the mechanics of expenditure planning, monitoring and control with a far broader assessment of what has happened to the aims and instruments of economic policy, and the relationships within the policy processes. We are under no illusions about the size and difficulty of the task. The justification for attempting it is a simple one: public expenditure is both the heart and the stuff of politics, and 'the expenditure process is an immense window into the reality of British political administration' (Heclo and Wildavsky 1981: lxii).

References

Else, P.K. and Marshall, G.P. (1979) *The Management of Public Expenditure*, London, Policy Studies Institute.

Glennerster, H. (1981) 'Social services spending in a hostile environment', in C. Hood and M. Wright (eds) *Big Government in Hard Times*, Oxford, Martin Robertson, 174–96.

Goldman, S. (1973) *The Developing System of Public Expenditure Management and Control*, Civil Service College Studies 2, London, HMSO.

Heald, D. (1983) *Public Expenditure*, Oxford, Martin Robertson.

Heclo, H. and Wildavsky, A. (1974) *The Private Government of Public Money*, London, Macmillan (1981 edition).

Likierman, A. (1986) 'Squaring the circle: reconciling predictive uncertainty with the control of public expenditure in the UK', *Policy and Politics*, 14(3), 285–307.

Pliatzky, L. (1983) 'Have volumes gone underground?', *Public Administration*, 61(3), 323–30.

Plowden, E. (Chairman) (1961) *Control of Public Expenditure*, Cmnd 1432, London, HMSO.

Thain, C. (1985) 'The education of the Treasury: the Medium-term Financial Strategy, 1980–84', *Public Administration*, 63(3), 261–85.

Walshe, G. (1987) *Planning Public Spending in the UK*, Basingstoke, Macmillan.

Wilks, S. and Wright, M. (eds) (1987) *Comparative Government–Industry Relations*, Oxford, Oxford University Press.

Abridged from C. Thain and M. Wright (1988) 'Public expenditure in the UK since 1976: still the "Private Government of Public Money"?', *Public Policy and Administration*, Vol. 3, No. 1, pp. 1–18. Reproduced with the permission of the Joint University Council.

Maurice Wright

Policy community and policy network

Unpacking the concepts

The assumption is that 'politics' within sub-systems or policy areas, such as industry, education and health, are different. In order to test that hypothesis, it is necessary first to be clear what we mean by policy, policy area, sector and sub-sector, and government. All of these concepts are conventionally used in general terms. In the case of policy, we must distinguish two necessary types of disaggregation: level and function (or process). Policy functions are familiar enough. They comprise a variety of different activities or processes engaged in by those who participate in the making or carrying out of policy. The politics of each of these processes may differ for a given defined set of policy issues or a programme. The participants' powers, roles and functions will vary with process. Indeed the number and type of participants will vary. Analysis of policy within a sector must therefore be concerned with identifying and differentiating the politics of the different processes.

Another necessary preliminary is the identification of the level or 'arena' at which the politics are being conducted. While some policy is originated and made at the level of the whole sector, education or industry or 'the economy', for example, it is a rather rare occurrence. Policy cannot of course be carried out at that level, for education, industry or the economy are merely abstractions. Policy is carried out by governmental and non-governmental organizations at lower levels, sub-sectorally. If we take the example of industry, even at the sub-sectoral level – manufacturing, services, construction – it is fairly rare for policy to be made for that level, even to be initiated by players operating in that wide arena, but it can happen. In Britain, National Insurance Surcharge was introduced for the whole of manufacturing industry, as was Corporation Tax, while in the 1985 Regional Industrial Development Act, regional development grants were extended to the whole of the services sub-sector. But even at this level we are still dealing with an abstraction. Much more commonly, 'industrial policy' is initiated, made and *always* carried out at lower levels, at the level of the firm and group of firms. It is here that most issues or problems arise, are articulated and are brought to the attention of public policy-makers. It is here, at the level of the firm or corporation, that policy is carried out – or evaded.

The politics of industry policy or education policy may be played in different arenas at different levels, but 'industry' or 'education' are terms describing only general phenomena. Clearly it would be more accurate to speak of an industry *policies* sector, an education *policies* sector, because it is rare for a policy issue or problem to arise which embraces the whole of a sector. Even where that happens, it is the case that an issue is handled by separate groups (or communities) of participants. If we 'unpack' education even roughly, it is obvious that there are separate groups of issues, problems and programmes for higher education, further education, secondary education, primary education and nursery education. Within these broad 'packs' there are separate policies and policy processes, such as universities on the one hand . . . and other institutions of higher education on the other. While it is true that some policy issues will be common or transcend those categories and they may come together in broad policy strategies, the handling of those issues, the politics in the policy processes, may be quite different, reflecting different sets of participants with different resources and different strategies.

. . .

Like the concept of industry, 'government' is an abstraction. Government is neither monolithic nor homogeneous although it is frequently discussed and treated as though it were. Ministries, departments, commissions and councils – governmental and quasi-governmental – differ not only in type of function – deliberative, regulatory, adjudicatory, entrepreneurial – but have different, multiple objectives and pursue different strategies which often collide and conflict with each other. They possess different kinds of resources and deploy them differently according to the perceived objectives and strategy of dominant coalitions within them. More narrowly still, individual governmental organizations are neither monolithic nor homogeneous. Divisions, branches and sections within such organizations may equally be differentiated by functions and resources, and by their ability and willingness to use them in particular ways to pursue particular strategies. Confrontations between the Scottish Department and the Department of Trade and Industry (DTI) over the rescue of Chrysler; DTI and the Ministry of Defence over Westland helicopters; the Department of the Environment (DoE) and Ministry of Agriculture, Fisheries and Food (MAFF) over the deregulation of agricultural land; and the DoE and DTI over inner cities, serve to illustrate the phenomena of particular departmental interests, rivalries and philosophies, and uncoordinated policy-making in the UK. What is perhaps less well known, and more surprising, is the accumulation of evidence which points to the fragmentation of the French state apparatus for making and carrying out industrial policy, and the differences and fissures between and within public sector organizations.[1] Reviewing this evidence Hayward argues the lack of an overall, coherent and consistent industrial policy and emphasizes the plurality of different policy communities.[2] Even in Japan, differences and disagreements within the politico-bureaucratic-business nexus occasionally break the surface and reveal similar underlying tensions. The 'telecom wars' of 1981–5 over the privatiz-ation of Nippon Telephone and Telegraph precipitated a bitter power struggle between the Ministry of International Trade and Industry and the Ministry of Posts and Telecommunications.[3]

. . .

Policy community and policy network

The disaggregation of 'policy area' suggests that within discrete areas there are governmental and non-governmental organizations sharing a common con-cern with sets of policy issues and problems. Their common purpose is to achieve what each may separately perceive as a satisfactory outcome to those issues and problems within the policy processes. The outcomes depend upon the management by each participating organization of its relationships with others similarly engaged. The management of those relationships is the policy-maker's function, partly 'balancing' and partly 'optimizing'.

> He must maintain those relationships between inflow and outflow of resources on which every dynamic system depends; he must adjust all the controllable variables, internal and external, so as to optimise the values of the resulting relations, as valued by him, or by those to whom he is accountable.[4]

The priority accorded to balancing and optimizing in any particular situation will vary with the policy-maker's judgements of reality and value – his 'appreciative system'.

Rhodes has identified five key resources – and has shown how and why organizations may seek to use such resources to exploit their room for decisional manoeuvre. It is not necessary here to rehearse the detail of his power-dependent framework for the analysis of organizational relationships, merely to indicate that a crucial part of it – the concept of policy community – appears to be a useful way of conducting sectoral analysis, and making comparisons between sectors and countries.[5] The analysis which follows departs in one important particular from Rhodes's definition and use of policy community. He treats it as one type of policy network, whereas it is argued here that community and network are better defined for the comparative analysis of policy sectors as two separate (though related) phenomena.

Policy community

Community is not the same as network, although they are frequently used synonymously in the literature. The concept of community, in the sense of political or social unity, qualities in common, agreement, identity, has been employed frequently in writing about policy-making and the policy process, although its use has been mainly as a metaphor for a policy sub-system, rather than as a tool of analysis. Repeatedly in the literature we find references to an 'education policy community', a 'transport policy community', a 'health services policy community'. This designation is helpful only at a very simple level of categorization to distinguish one broad sub-system from another. The members of such communities are rarely identified, although Hayward has done so for the French economic policy community.[6]

The use of community in this very broad sense is of very little help in the analysis of the policy process. The hidden complexity of the term 'industry' has already been referred to and it has been shown to be no more than convenient shorthand for a variety of different activities divided by product, service, technology, market, employment, ownership and size. If we use the term 'industrial policy community' it needs to embrace all those who own, manage, finance and work in companies, firms, corporations and enterprises, together with those whose interests are affected by the activities (or non-activity) of those units – consumers and clients, for example – and those individuals whose organizations have a direct interest in, or responsibility for, the activities of those units and their customers and clients; that is to say, governmental and quasi-governmental agencies of all kinds, at the supra-national, national and sub-national levels. This population of actors and potential actors in the industrial policy community is a large one. It can be extended still further by the inclusion of those organizations which have or take an interest in the activities of the industrial units and governmental and quasi-governmental organizations, such as Parliament and its committees, political parties, the media, analysts and commentators.

While this population of actors and potential actors shares a common interest in industrial policy (as opposed to education policy), and may contribute to one or more of the stages of the policy process on a regular or irregular basis, it is suggested here that it would be more helpful in analysis to reserve the term 'community' for use at a lower level of the disaggregated policy sub-system. If this injunction is followed, the population of actors and potential actors described in general terms can be distinguished from those in other policy sectors by using the term 'universe'. We can then identify, describe and compare, for example, an 'industrial policy universe', an 'economic policy universe', and an 'education policy universe'. While this is a helpful first step in comparative analysis, cross-sectorally and cross-nationally, we need to identify which actors play what roles and how they relate to each other in the policy process.

If we now use our disaggregated categories of government, industry and community, we can identify discrete policy communities at the industrial sector and industrial sub-sectoral levels. The membership of each community is defined by a common identity or interest – for example, product, service, technology, market, firm size, ownership and 'size of batch'. Members share a direct or indirect, actual or potential, interest in the public policy issues and problems which arise or may arise for their community. They possess resources of authority, money, information, expertise and organization, with the potentiality for their use at some stage in the policy processes.

Policy network

Policy community identifies those actors and potential actors drawn from the policy universe who share a common identity or interest. Those actors will 'transact' with each other, exchanging resources in order to balance and optimize their mutual relationships. Network is the linking process, the outcome of those exchanges, within a policy community or between a number of policy communities. A policy network is a 'complex of organizations connected to each other by resource dependencies and distinguished from other complexes by breaks in the structure of resource dependencies'. A policy network may evolve or be constituted around a discrete policy issue or problem, a set of related issues (for example, takeovers and mergers,[7] investment protection, export promotion, health and safety) or around a policy process, such as budgeting, auditing or planning. The members of a network may be drawn from one policy community or several. A policy network describes the general properties of the processes by which some of the members of one or more policy communities interact in a structure of dependent relationships. *Policy issues and problems* (and policy functions) provide the occasion for a policy network.

The analytical advantages of treating community and network as separate phenomena should now be apparent. There are four other advantages. First, while policy sub-systems *always* generate policy communities, community does not necessarily entail network: not all policy communities will generate policy networks. Relationships between members of a community in general, or in terms of a particular policy issue, may be so inchoate and unstructured that no stable network of resource dependencies is discernible. Analysis of such conditions, their causes and effects, is as valid as those in which networks are identifiable. Secondly, it enables us to identify those members of a policy community who are excluded from stable and continuing policy networks. Thirdly, as all policy issues and problems, and policy processes in a sub-sector, are not necessarily handled by one policy network, we can compare the membership, functions and characteristics of networks whose membership is drawn from the same policy community. Fourthly, the distinction between community and network admits of the possibility that members of a policy network may be drawn from different policy communities within the same policy area (for example, basic chemicals and agri-chemicals) or even from different policy areas (such as industry *and* education in industrial training programmes).

In comparing and classifying policy networks, this analysis follows Rhodes,[8] who suggests that their structures will vary along five key dimensions: the interests of the members of the network, the membership, the extent of members' interdependence, the extent to which the network is isolated from other networks and the variations in the distribution of resources between the members. The structures of policy networks can then be compared according to the level of their integration. On a simple 'high–low' scale, those which are highly integrated are characterized by the stability of the relationships of their members; the continuity of a highly restrictive membership; the interdependence within the network, based on the members' shared responsibility for initiating and making policy, or for the delivery of a service, and the insulation from other networks. Those network structures which are weakly integrated tend to have a much larger number of members with a limited degree of organizational interdependence; they are loose, atomistic and often inchoate structures. The level of integration is also influenced by the role played by 'professionals' within the network. Where that role is a pre-eminent and dominating one, Rhodes uses the term 'professional network' to distinguish it from other types.[9]

How the concepts of community and network might be used to analyse and compare different industrial policy sectors is demonstrated by the results of some recent empirical research.[10] For example, Grant, Paterson and Whitston have distinguished at least five policy communities in the UK chemicals industry.[11] Besides a core policy community, organized around the production of basic industrial chemicals, there are separate policy communities for pharmaceuticals, agri-chemicals, paints, and soap and toiletries preparations. In the UK foundries industry, there is a still larger number of policy communities, reflecting sharp differences in product, technology and market.[12] The companies which comprise the industry have very little in common, apart from the process or technique of metal casting. By contrast, the West German foundries industry is much more cohesive, integrated, and tightly structured organizationally. There is one policy community for the whole industry.

The members of these and other policy communities are often joined in several different structures of dependent relationships or policy networks. Some are highly integrated, like those in the pharmaceuticals industry,[13] which handle in separate networks the policy issues of drug-licensing, price regulation and cost-containment; others, as in the foundries industry, are weakly integrated. In those policy networks with a high level of integration, memberships tend to be exclusive, closed rather than open, and continuous. Some members of the policy community will be excluded. The evidence, so far, suggests that access to a policy network is normally controlled by the dominant government agency, although the exclusion of certain categories of participants may be the condition of another's participation. In the industrial policy sectors studied, trade unions are rarely represented. Parliament and its committees and non-industrial groups are invariably excluded. The absence of stable policy networks in the UK foundries industry is partly the result of the number, fragmentation and competition of the representative associations which comprise the several policy communities. There are six major trade associations, four research associations and nine trade unions. By comparison, the West German foundries industry has two trade associations, which work closely together, one research association and one trade union.

Policy networks also vary with the type and substance of the policy issue. The issues of drug-licensing and drug costs are handled by two separate networks in the UK, although some members are common to both. In the chemical industry, there are separate networks for health and safety issues and for R&D. The scope of the policy agenda of a network is a critical factor. While government agencies have greater resources with which to influence the agenda of policy issues – the threat of coercive action, for example – the evolution and the continued stable existence of a network is determined, to a great extent, by the skill with which other key members are able to manipulate and control the agenda of policy issues. What is kept off the agenda may be as important as what is handled by the network. The Association of the British

Pharmaceutical Industry, historically with a monopoly representation of manufacturers' interests, has been conspicuously successful in its control of the policy agenda by deflecting attention away from the controversial and divisive issue of the therapeutic efficacy of drugs and towards the less contentious issue of clinical trials. The mode and manner of the articulation of an issue is also important in agenda control. The issue of the regulation of the prices of individual drugs has been kept off the agenda by the articulation of that issue as one of regulating the level of company profits, through return on investment, rather than the prices of products. In West Germany, cost-cutting proposals have been kept off the agenda, delayed, or marginalized, less by the manipulative skills of the pharmaceutical industry or its representative associations, than by fragmentation of the health-care community and the exploitation of its political resources by a key governmental player, the Free Democratic Party.

Policy networks can also be distinguished by the degree of their insulation from each other. Different parts of the same government agency may belong to separate networks. A trade association or professional organization may be a member of one network within the community but not another. Policy networks also differ in the extent of the stability of the structure of dependent relationships. As patterns of social networks are 'constantly subject to the possibility of structural transformation', policy networks will change over time. In periods of 'policy turbulence' they will be subject to short-term 'catastrophic discontinuities' such as that initiated by the issue of the 'limited list' or the revocation of drug licences without consultation.

Policy network: 'rules of the game'

To understand how and why a policy network operates, it is necessary to understand the 'unwritten constitution' which guides the behaviour of the actors towards each other and influences the strategic deployment of their resources. Their relationships are regulated by rules of the game which set approximate limits to their discretionary behaviour when they exploit and deploy their resources of authority, money, information and expertise in the pursuit of a strategy appropriate to the circumstances of a particular issue, problem or event. Some of the rules can be distinguished by what members say or write or believe the rules to be. Other rules can be inferred from their conduct to each other. In his study of the UK national community of local government associations, Rhodes lists eleven rules of the game, among them: pragmatism, consensus, fairness, accommodation, secrecy, trust, the 'de-politicization of issues' and the 'right to govern' of the central government.[14] Some of these are common to other studies of UK sectoral networks. Cross-sectoral and cross-national comparisons of a number of industrial policy areas show not only similarities of rules of the game but important differences too. The examples which follow are derived from the preliminary results of comparative research on industrial sectors in the UK, West Germany and France.

One important rule of the game is mutuality. Members of networks accept and expect that mutual advantages and benefits will result from their participation in the network. Policy issues are handled within the policy network, on the basis of trust and a respect for confidence. Undertakings given by members of the network or commitments entered into informally are customarily honoured. The social memory of the network exercises a self-discipline. Secondly, there is not only a willingness to consult informally, but an expectation of consultation. On this basis and that of a respect for confidence, members of a network are prepared to exchange ideas or discuss future policies or make available to each other information which would be regarded as sensitive or even damaging in the public domain. The importance of this rule is most obviously demonstrated when it has been broken; when, for example, the Department of Health and Social Security (DHSS) introduces the limited list without prior consultation. Thirdly, there is an emphasis on informality. This is, perhaps, more characteristic of the UK policy sectors studied so far and may reflect a difference in legal and administrative culture. In a different legal tradition – in West Germany, for example – the conduct of an industrial policy network may be much more formally determined. Fourthly, there are rules about the articulation of policy issues in an acceptable mode and language. Fifthly, there are rules about the use of legal remedy. For example, compare the policy networks for handling the licensing of drugs in the UK and West Germany. In the former, pharmaceutical companies eschew legal challenge in the courts, while in West Germany the legal and administrative culture encourages an adversarial approach. Legal challenge to the licensing authority is customary and part of the process by which policy is shaped and implemented. There are also rules about the legitimacy of state action: what members of a network consider acceptable or unacceptable use of the legitimate authority possessed by governmental agencies. Thus, a network may be constituted on the basis of the mutual acceptance of tacit limits to the use of constitutional coercive authority. Its use in an unacceptable way may provoke a 'catastrophic discontinuity'. For example, while members of the UK policy network for handling the issue of company profits in the pharmaceutical industry could not deny the government's constitutional authority to regulate the prices of drugs, the rule of the game governing the behaviour of the members of the network to each other was that the DHSS did not attempt to do this. There was a 'reluctance to exercise legal controls at the level of the individual firm or product as long as industry's overall performance seemed reasonable.'[15]

As Rhodes notes in his study of intergovernmental relations, such rules of the game set only approximate limits to the discretionary behaviour of the participants in policy networks.[16] Rules are not immutable; some may be discarded and replaced by others. Further research at the sectoral level and comparison with other countries should reveal the existence or absence of such rules; how they have evolved and are evolving; to what extent they are observed and in what circumstances and why they are broken or discarded. It may also tell us whether rules of the game are affected by changes in government and different political ideologies.

This illustration of the concept of rules of the game has not distinguished clearly between those rules which relate to policy-in-operation and those which are behavioural; most of the examples are of the latter kind. A deeper level of analysis would reveal what kinds of policy issues are handled by a network and those which are excluded. It would reveal what was on the policy agenda and what was kept off, as well as the extent to which policy issues or problems were redefined by a network to make them more 'manageable'. It would also seek to explain how policy issues were handled within a policy community where there was no stable structure of network resource dependencies.

. . .

References

1 M. Bauer and E. Cohen, *Qui Gouverne les Groupes Industriels?* (Paris, Editions du France, 1981); A. Cawson, P. Holmes and A. Stevens, 'The interaction between firms and the state in France: the telecommunications and consumer electronics sectors', in S. Wilks and M. Wright (eds) *Comparative Government–Industry Relations* (Oxford, Clarendon Press, 1987).

2 J. Hayward, *The State and the Market Economy* (Brighton, Wheatsheaf, 1986).

3 C. Johnson, *MITI, MPT and the Telecom Wars* (Berkeley, CA, Berkeley Board on the International Economy, Working Paper No. 21, 1987) (edited by J. Zysman).

4 Sir Geoffrey Vickers, *The Art of Judgement* (London, Chapman and Hall, 1965), p. 195.

5 R.A.W. Rhodes, *The National World of Local Government* (London, Macmillan, 1987).

6 Hayward, *The State and the Market Economy*, Ch. 2.

7 See, for example, Maurice Wright, 'City rules OK? Policy community, policy network and takeover bids', *Manchester Papers in Politics*, no. 4 (Sept. 1987).

8 Rhodes, *The National World of Local Government*.

9 See also, P. Dunleavy, 'Professions and policy changes: notes towards a model of ecological corporatism', *Public Administration Bulletin*, 36 (1981), 3–16; R.A.W. Rhodes, 'Power dependence, policy communities and intergovernmental networks', *Public Administration Bulletin*, 49 (1985), 4–29.

10 The Economic and Social Research Council's programme of comparative research into government–industry relations began in 1984. Phase I includes the UK, France and West Germany, Phase II the UK, Japan and the USA.

11 W. Grant, W. Paterson and C. Whitston, 'Government–industry relations in the chemical industry: an Anglo-German comparison', in S. Wilks and M. Wright (eds), *Comparative Government–Industry Relations* (Oxford, Clarendon Press, 1987); W. Grant, W. Paterson and C. Whitston, *International Industry, National Governments and the European Community: a Comparative Study of the Chemical Industry in Britain and West Germany* (Oxford, Clarendon Press, 1988).

12 C. Appleby and J. Bessant, 'Adapting to decline: organisational structures and government policy in the UK and West German foundry sectors', in S. Wilks and M. Wright (eds), *Comparative Government–Industry Relations* (Oxford, Clarendon Press, 1987).

13 K. Macmillan and I. Turner, 'The cost containment issue: a study of government–industry relations in the pharmaceutical sectors of the UK and West Germany', and L. Hancher and M. Ruete, 'Legal culture, product licensing and the drug industry', both in S. Wilks and M. Wright (eds) *Comparative Government–Industry Relations* (Oxford, Clarendon Press, 1987).

14 Rhodes, *The National World of Local Government*, pp. 391–2.

15 L. Hancher and M. Ruete, 'Legal administration cultures as policy determinants'

(paper presented at the ESRC conference on government–industry relations, Cambridge, December 1985), p. 22.

16 Rhodes, *The National World of Local Government*, p. 19.

Abridged from M. Wright (1988) 'Policy community, policy network and comparative industrial policies', *Political Studies*, Vol. 36, pp. 593–612. Reproduced with the permission of Blackwell Publishers.

3

Civil servants and ministers: power, influence and public policy

Barbara (now Baroness) Castle's 'Mandarin power' (Reading 3.1) sums up many of the tribulations of a minister inhibited by what she considered to be the stultifying power of the bureaucracy. She had held three portfolios during Harold Wilson's first period of office between 1964 and 1970: at Overseas Development, Transport and Employment. She would hold one more Cabinet position under Wilson, at the DHSS (1974–6). She was neither the first nor the last to vent frustrations. Here she expresses her grievances in the form of an open letter addressed to the top civil servants. Note how she rejects the notion of the civil service as the custodian of the long term and wider public interest. Her championing of the short term as a political counterweight to the bureaucracy is food for thought today in an age when short-termism is often held responsible for the ills of public policy, the only serious discussion being about whom precisely to blame. She balks, too, at the assumption, quite widely held then as now, that Whitehall's performance could be enhanced by the import of greater numbers of business people.

If Castle felt overwhelmed by the bureaucracy, then among informed observers at least a different complaint had become fashionable well before the end of the Thatcher era. Ministers, allegedly, had been riding roughshod over the bureaucracy. Michael Heseltine (Reading 3.2) explains how he fought and won some of his early battles. Heseltine has had a high regard for most of his officials, if not always for the system in which they operate. Officials have usually found him a stimulating minister, perpetually active with ideas and enthusiasm. Not all civil servants have enjoyed such positive experiences with their ministers. Some ministers have been unwilling to listen, let alone to follow the advice of their permanent officials. Such, at least, is the substance of certain press reports – usually denied with equal avidity by Whitehall's top echelons. If true, though, the result may be a poorer quality of public policy. This is the message of a former civil servant, David Faulkner (Reading 3.3). In effect, he offers a case study of policy-making on crime and criminal justice. He is more guarded and oblique than some of the press coverage that fed upon his comments. But he does say that policies of the early 1990s seemed to have been 'hastily conceived and precarious in their application'. He makes the wider and more controversial point that the issues involved in this policy area are too complex for the political or Parliamentary processes. What, one wonders, does Baroness Castle think about that?

If ministers have been accused from time to time of rough-handling the bureaucracy in recent years, the more frequently heard complaint is a rather different one. It is that civil servants have unduly trimmed their advice in self-imposed anticipation of ministerial preferences. This is the burden of former Labour premier Lord (James) Callaghan's evidence to the Treasury and Civil Service Committee (Reading 3.4). He has talked about the bureaucracy having become part of a ministerial 'private fiefdom'. In his posthumously published memoirs, Sir Antony Part (1990: 107) acknowledged that the top mandarins must 'take on in some degree the coloration of the party in power'. Part was Permanent Secretary at the Department of Industry during the 1970s. Perhaps the coloration assumes a deeper shade the longer one party remains in office.

Two further top civil servants, among others, have added their voices to the debate. Sir Patrick Nairne (Reading 3.5) reflects ruefully that, while the fundamentals remain unchanged, the mutual confidences essential to a successful partnership between ministers and civil servants can no longer be taken for granted. He provides a useful restatement of those fundamentals. Nairne, incidentally, is one of the few top mandarins to receive plaudits from Barbara Castle, both in her diaries and in her memoirs. He was Permanent Secretary at the Department of Health and Social Security between 1975 and 1981. He was succeeded in that post by Sir Kenneth Stowe. Stowe poses the important question: what is good governance? (Reading 3.6.) He is no longer entirely confident about the capacity even of the British bureaucracy to resist the temptations of political expediency. He puts his faith in the machinery of Parliamentary scrutiny and in mechanisms for the redress of grievances. The traditional assumptions of neutrality and impartiality, at least as fundamental touchstones, are challenged by William Plowden (Reading 3.7). In this short extract, he calls (reluctantly) for a rejection of the tradition of the dispassionate administrator, which he dismisses as a 'psychological nonsense'.

Finally, two of the senior academics pitch in. Anthony King (Reading 3.8) examines some of the consequences of the rise of the career politician. It is tempting to ask whether the careerism to which he refers is in part responsible for the isolation experienced by the likes of Barbara Castle. King shows how the advent of career politicians has also had consequences for senior officials, not least by their proclivity for constant change and innovation. Nearly every one of King's observations holds up a decade and a half after this piece was written, save for his reference to the decline of consensual politics. Richard Rose (Reading 3.9) takes a cool look at the many and complex variables both of minister–civil servant relationships and of their respective and combined inputs to government. He concludes that there is more need for change at the political than at the official level.

3.1 | *Barbara Castle*

Mandarin power

The danger of the British civil service to our democracy lies in its excellence. I have often thought, not only between 1964 and 1970 but looking back, that if only you civil servants could have managed to be a little more corrupt or inefficient or stupid we would have done better. But you are not, and therefore I have no doubt that the civil service is a state within a state to an extent that the trade union movement could never aspire to be.

The civil service is also highly aware of its own excellence. It is extremely status-conscious. In fact if any government in this country really tried to undermine that status we should certainly see a thing or two. The jealousy of the train drivers about their rights would be absolutely nothing on what you boys would produce then.

So I think there is a crying need for the civil service to be trained and retrained and re-re-re-trained in two things. The first is in accepting the supremacy of the political function in a democracy over the administrative function. And the second is in getting into the mind of a minister.

What the civil service has not taken on board and what politicians do not take on board until they become ministers is the extent to which, from the moment a minister walks out of the Cabinet room at No. 10 Downing Street, having been asked by the Prime Minister to take on such and such a job, the civil service takes over his life.

Now you imagine. Put yourself in the place I was at in October 1964. Twenty-two years as a back-bench MP – a good one as a matter of fact – party activist, constituency member, the whole of whose political life up to then had been given meaning by representing quite deliberately a certain section of society and expressing its aspirations. Coming out of the Cabinet room very excited, I was charged with a responsibility, the new Ministry for Overseas Development.

How instantly the forces of the civil service move in. It isn't only the 'bureaucratic embrace', to use Dick Crossman's words, it is the companionable embrace. From that moment, the Minister is cut off from every sort of political activity that has given her life meaning and expression. Political activity continues only to the extent that it is authorized by the management of the minister's life. Just out of the door and they say 'Oh Minister, your permanent secretary is waiting' and your permanent secretary is either waiting for you there or in your office. Or, 'Oh, I'm so sorry Minister, your permanent secretary is out of the country or out of London at the moment but he will call on you at the weekend'. Your permanent secretary moves in on you and you suddenly realize that here is a machine which has prepared for this moment and is all too perfectly able to cope with it and digest it.

Ministry of Overseas Development, October 1964; permanent secretary, shamefully not in London for that great moment of the act of appointment, comes pedalling down to the country cottage. He is there on tap, filling the horizon. One goes into the office, the first morning. 'Oh Minister, we had prepared for the fact that there might be a Ministry of Overseas Development. Here is the whole thing worked out.' Two documents, worked out during the general election campaign – one if they win, one if the other lot win. There it is, waiting for you to take on board. Civil servants have been working away at it in the three idle weeks when you have been battling for your political life.

Ministry of Transport, December 1965, barely thirteen months later. I am suddenly moved into an atmosphere of ill-concealed hostility. Apart from anything else, if you are a woman minister, you have to move so many men out of their lavatory: you have to clear an entire floor – but that to the side, I must say they took it with very great surface courtesy. But the force was there, entrenched.

In that particular field my party had not worked out a policy as it had done in Overseas Development. It took me several months to get my civil servants even able to mouth the words 'integrated transport policy'. There they had all been, you see, in the Marples and Beeching tradition for the past four or five years, and they did not believe in an integrated transport policy. All my Question Time notes used to come up with notes for my supplementaries. My back-benchers would ask: 'When are we going to have an integrated transport policy?' Supplementary, faithfully written out by the civil servant: 'We do not believe in integrated transport policy.'

I took this for a bit, but finally wrote across the official memorandum: 'Pardon me, we do', in large letters; I crossed out the 'not'. After that, my view faithfully appeared in every supplementary: 'We do believe in an integrated transport policy.' But does anyone really believe that an attitude of mind has changed? How could it have changed as suddenly as all that?

My third experience. First Secretary and Secretary of State for the Department of Employment and Productivity. Harold Wilson got me off a night-sleeper in my nightgown to negotiate this appointment on the telephone. I was on my way to Blackburn. I duly came back on another sleeper, having been inducted, or whatever the word is – and the Civil Service was waiting, superbly. There it was on the platform as I came off the sleeper, my private secretary and my chief information officer.

You walk off a sleeper from your constituency where the raw material of politics lives and there they are waiting – the car, the men. They come to the flat. My husband is sitting up in bed. I say: 'Darling, here's my private secretary and my chief information officer' and he talks to them and makes them a cup of tea, bleary-eyed, while I have my bath. They have taken over my life and they do it superbly, charmingly, irresistibly.

The pattern of the minister's day is fixed by the private office and the gulf with the outside world begins. The minister is alone: the loneliness of the short-distance runner. We will not be there very long and Heaven knows what new minister will very shortly be greeted in the same charming, efficient and no doubt very genuine way. But the minister is the one person who cannot afford to be cut off from the political lifeline which got her there in the first place and which is going to sustain her in the next job.

And therefore I begin by putting this to you. You must, if you are to understand your proper role, first and foremost put yourself in the place of the minister and take on board the size of your own power. I don't think you have any inkling of it. You control every single ten minutes of the day and night. I would have to plead with my private office to get half an hour with my constituency secretary.

The demands of the department must always be paramount – that seems to be the good private secretary's tenet. 'Constituency secretary? Oh, we might push her in in the lunch hour if you are prepared to eat a sandwich.' 'Go to your constituency? Don't you know, Minister, you have got to go to visit Southampton Docks?' For me to say: 'Look, it really is not the CBI who put me where I am, it really is the voters of Blackburn', was bringing a Batman cartoon touch to what should have been a discussion within the bounds of administrative decency. I even had to lie to my private secretary to get a walk across St James's Park to try to keep fit. Lie like a trooper.

In my innocence when I went into Cabinet government in October 1964, I still believed that governments worked this way: that Cabinets were groups of politicians who met together and said, these are the policies we are elected on, now what will be our political priorities? And they would reach certain political decisions and then they would refer these decisions to an official committee to work out the administrative implications of what they had decided.

I was soon disabused of that. Apart from anything else, civil servants have the best spying organization I have ever known. I used to leave Cabinet meetings, perhaps after a departmental battle. I would ring up my private secretary or walk into my private office, three minutes later. I'd say 'We've won.' 'Oh yes I know, Minister', my secretary would reply. All round the village before the minister got home. The bush telegraph wasn't a patch on the civil service system.

The official net is terrific, the political net is non-existent. I wonder if you realize.

I suddenly discovered that I was never allowed to take anything to Cabinet unless it had been processed by the Official Committee. In the Official Committee the departments had all had their inter-departmental battle, and probably made their concessions to each other. The departments did the horse-trading and having struck their bargains at official level they then briefed their ministers on it, and so at Cabinet meetings I suddenly found I wasn't in a political caucus at all. I was faced by departmental enemies.

There never is political unity, as things are organized at present. I have seen what I thought were political colleagues transformed into departmental enemies. The minister is alone, except for the departmental briefings that officials may have prepared for her on this particular subject or on that. So one of the simple reforms which I think is necessary, if you believe the political role should be supreme, is for ministerial committees to meet before and not after the official one. This simple radical change in democratic government is necessary because my premise, which you may not share, is the desperate need to strengthen the political role.

There is a lot of talk about how we could do it in other ways. Bring in outside advisers, people say. Well, we brought in a lot. I brought in as many as anybody, perhaps more. Whether at ODM, Transport or the Department of Employment. But it really is no answer in itself because unless the civil service is prepared to adapt its machinery to incorporate the outside adviser, then the outside adviser will remain a specialist appendage to the administrator and not to the minister. And in that situation the administrator will always win for the simple reason that he knows the ropes.

He knows the survival syndrome in which ministers work. He knows what happens at the House of Commons: he knows that if you suddenly get a Private Notice Parliamentary Question you must have your supplementaries all ready and thought out; he knows that at a Cabinet committee your papers must be there and in the form that your colleagues will digest.

It's no good specialists panting – it's happened to me dozens of times – panting up the stairs at the last minute saying: 'We've just seen something. Look, there's a paper here. We think this is terrible.' I had to say: 'Too late, old chap, you've missed the bus! This is going through Cabinet committee or Cabinet this morning, you've missed the bus.'

I've seen more outsiders miss the administrative bus than I've seen catch it, because they are not trained in the art of servicing a minister in the rough arena of parliamentary politics which is so much part of your training. Ministers don't want to know that somebody has produced a marvellous economic report on something or other. They want the answer to the thing being shot at them at that particular time.

Experts and specialist advisers are just amateurs in this game. The specialist advisers were never integrated into the Labour Government's machinery effectively because, although they might ask for independent access to the minister, they weren't part of the minister's permanent and immediate entourage.

Never underestimate the power of the intellectual entourage. The Jesuits used to say: 'Give me the child for the first five years and I will have him for life.' I'll tell you what the civil servant says: 'Give me the minister in an administrative meeting and you can talk to her as much as you like any other time. You can talk to her on the train just as long as you like but if it's not in the crucial meeting, preparing for a crucial Cabinet discussion, she can wring her hands afterwards but it won't make any difference.'

. . .

It is imperative that we should begin consciously to introduce a counter-weight to administrative supremacy. So I think what we need for the health of British democracy is more of the short-term and less of the long-term. The current theory is that you civil servants are the custodians of the long-term and that's really where the public interest lies. I think this is wrong. I think the impact of the short-term change is imperative. When I look back on our period of government one old phrase runs through my mind – 'Nobody told us we could do that.' I thought, looking back at the Labour Government, how effectively the civil servants impeded us by saying we could not do some of the things our successors are now doing with remarkable facility. Floating the pound: something we were told would bring total disaster but which Mr Anthony Barber is getting away with almost frivolously. Tax reform: we were told we couldn't have a wealth tax, the Inland Revenue wouldn't stand any more changes in the lifetime of one government – we've now got the unified tax system.

. . .

The favourite nostrum now is more interchange between civil servants and private industry. I don't think this is any answer to the imbalance of the civil service. It would be more help if you were seconded to a union; or a voluntary organization, like Shelter, or perhaps even to the research department of the political parties. Then you might begin to be more in touch with the sort of pressures to which the minister is subjected.

But that isn't the only answer. I think we've got to face the fact – you know what I'm leading up to – that a minister must have political support inside the department. The loneliness of the shorter distance runner must be alleviated by a political 'cabinet'. There must be a politician in the private office. But it will not work, none of it will work, unless the civil servants are prepared to take that on board. Therefore I think the initiative must start with you. Are you prepared to sit down now yourselves and work out the answer as to how the outside adviser, not only the specialist adviser but the political adviser, can be integrated into your structure? Only you can do it because I am under no doubt that we would be very silly to underestimate your power of dissidence. You might not 'go slow', but I think you would be experts at another industrial tactic which is called 'working without enthusiasm'.

Junior ministers are not enough. The minister doesn't choose them. The Prime Minister does that. He does it under considerations that may not be the same as yours. He has to think of whether he's got somebody from Wales, or from Yorkshire, or from this or that union.

It can sometimes work and when it does work it is helpful. At the Ministry of Transport I happened to have, in Stephen Swingler and John Morris, two people who could not have fitted better if I had chosen them myself. We worked as a political team. Even then, I might say, we had embarrassments when we insisted on meeting alone without a private secretary present. You have to be prepared to offend somebody before you can even do that, which you should not have to do, especially when it is someone like a private secretary of whom you are fond and on whom you depend and for whom you have respect.

I do not believe I could have got the Transport Act through – through the department, that is, not the House of Commons – if I had not had a political team with the same interventionist approach, ready to do battle with the very *laissez-faire* approach that I inherited. But is it fair or sensible that a minister should have to go through such an expenditure of personal nervous energy to get a radical change in policy?

I don't know how many of those vast meetings we used to have on transport policy. It was uphill, uphill, uphill all the way. Quantity licensing – I might have been proposing publicly financed sin or something. The whole instinctive reaction of the department was against three-quarters of that Act. I'm not saying anybody sabotaged it. I'm only saying I'm the one who needed moral support, by people who had gone in with my approach to transport, instead of having to win over my civil servants.

I think we won a lot of them over in the end by sheer expenditure of nervous and physical energy. But the government as a whole needs political reminders all the time. They need all the time to remember their roots.

. . .

I don't think you have a clue to the kind of pressures and strains under which a minister lives alone, with her own parliamentary cohorts behind her, complaining and pressurizing, and her civil servants in front. Even at ODM where we had a very clear policy, I remember Andy Cohen, the Permanent Secretary, trying to wear me down. He used to come in on policy points and things like appointments. He would be in my office about seven times a day saying: 'Minister, I know the ultimate decision is yours but I would be failing in my duty if I didn't tell you how unhappy your decision makes me.' Seven times a day. One person against the vast department.

Recently, as Opposition spokesman, I've been going to meetings of the British Association of Social Workers and all sorts of other organizations, mixing with the rank and file. I've told them: 'Look, this is your chance, because if and when in 18 months' time I become Secretary of State for the Social Services you won't get anywhere near me. You know that and I know that, and if I ever come to *your* conference, I'll see the top brass and I've had it.'

It is simply that the whole status thing comes into operation. To counteract it, the minister has to have somebody close to her, feeding reality back. It may seem artificial but if you get your political contacts wrong you come a cropper. We did on several issues because of that.

I think this major problem is one for you people to argue out. I believe that you have the absolute power as a civil service, because of your excellence, to make life impossible for any government which radically tries to alter the civil service. We are talking about government by consent. This is what the current democratic argument is about and your consent above all is necessary. So it is a question first of all of getting you to accept that there is now an imbalance in government between the political and the administrative and that the political must be strengthened. Then, if you will accept the loneliness and isolation of the politician in government today, I think it is for you to sit down to work out the solution.

Unless you are prepared to do that and to say in what form you think it could be best introduced, then I think we are in trouble because I think you have the largest negative power; you can work without enthusiasm. Nobody is saying – I'm not saying it anyway – that the civil service is crudely political, sabotaging Labour governments. I'm saying that by definition there are certain jobs you cannot do and you should not attempt to do, in order to do the jobs you do well; and that you need political men to help you.

Abridged from B. Castle (1973) 'Mandarin Power', *Sunday Times*, 10 June. Reproduced with the permission of Times Newspapers Ltd and the Rt Hon Baroness Castle of Blackburn.

Where there's a will

Someone must direct policy: the department will invariably have its own existing policy which, if ministers have no ideas of their own, will naturally continue to prevent a vacuum. Decisions have to be taken: if a minister cannot make up his mind, his officials may in despair try to help the process even to the point, if need be, of making it up for him. I would never belittle this process. It carries many a department through periods of indifferent political direction. Of course, such direction could hardly happen under a colleague of my own party, but there are always others!

I freely admit to the moments where the pure gold of the perceptive permanent secretary shone through. I have as many faults as the next man but I can, by and large, take decisions. Sometimes, however, your powers fail. You are tired. It is late. The issue is of secondary importance, only half understood, and you know in your heart that you have lost control of that meeting of civil servants waiting for the firm hand of government. You ramble, hesitate and suddenly the voice at your elbow takes over: 'I think that's most helpful Secretary of State. We'll proceed as you have outlined which, if I follow your argument correctly, I would summarize as follows . . .' And the permanent secretary pours out a string of elegant phrases and concise instructions as tears of gratitude well up within you. And private secretaries – the permanent secretaries of tomorrow – make no mean fist of the same process.

A hazard for the junior minister is the private office, the small private fiefdom which, I was earnestly assured when I arrived green at the Ministry of Transport in 1970, was there to serve me. In the world outside I had run my own business and was naturally surrounded by the best and most senior people in the company.

At the Ministry I quickly found, to my considerable resentment, that while I was cutting my teeth as a parliamentary secretary my private office was staffed by young civil servants cutting their teeth on me. It was a training ground where the totally inexperienced were sent to find out what the world was all about.

Private secretaries came and went with a bewildering rush, and as soon as they began to know their job and became familiar, perhaps even friendly, with the minister they were promoted. From the minister's point of view this is a near-disaster, because he is totally reliant on his private secretary as his eyes and ears within the department.

. . .

The essential first lesson for a newly appointed secretary of state, as I had learnt, was to know what one wanted and how to get it. The other lesson well learnt was of the constantly moving private secretaries, so the first requirement . . . was that I would interview the brightest candidates in the appropriate grade and that once I had chosen a private secretary he would stay with me to the day I left the department.

Again I was lucky. David Edmonds, who remained with me as long as I remained in the Department of the Environment and then left to run the Housing Corporation, was an outstanding official and one of those with whom I worked closely who bred in me a profound admiration for the talent and loyalty of the best civil servants and a contempt for those who belittle them. In the Ministry of Defence I inherited from John Nott another quite exceptional civil servant, Richard Mottram, who survived me in the private office but moved on promotion after a few months to take charge of the budgeting controls he had helped me to undertstand.

Of the words I had written on [an] envelope for Sir John Garlick, perhaps the most challenging were: 'Staff. Reduce level. Freeze on recruitment.' They were part of a revolution in Whitehall which has by no means run its course.

The Government had come to power pledged and determined to reduce the number of civil servants, which had reached its highest level since the war. I was fortunate in having as a Minister of State Irwin Bellow, now Lord Bellwin, who had been an outstanding civic leader in Leeds. He told me that he had managed to reduce the numbers of municipal employees there only by taking over responsibility for recruitment himself. This was an affront to the orthodoxy that ministers determine but civil servants execute. It turned out also to be a priceless piece of advice.

The Government was embarked on an exercise in staff reductions. It was agreed by the Cabinet that each of us would go back to his department and examine options for securing reductions over a period of years of 2.5 per cent, 5 per cent and 7.5 per cent.

In each department the immediate assumption when this news was received was that any shedding of staff must mean shedding of responsibilities. Nobody was prepared to concede that just by squeezing numbers it would be possible to make economies and still do the same tasks. After all, there were staff inspection schemes to ensure that there was no over-manning.

This immediate and universal assumption was in time revealed to be wholly unwarranted; but it was the point of departure for the briefing of ministers on the reduction of numbers which then ensued.

The preparation of option papers gave civil servants a field day. They took the parts of prosecuting and defending counsel, of judge and of jury. I cannot now recall the exact words in which I was told the facts of life, but I will never forget the general tone and sense.

. . .

I later learnt that Labour had asked for similar manpower reductions a year or two before. No doubt the former option papers (known in Whitehall as 'horror comics') had been dusted off for me. No doubt the eloquent speech had been rehearsed with my predecessor.

The political menace behind the advice would not have been lost on the most naïve of Secretaries of State, but I was fresh from the hustings and my heart was bold. 'Go on'. I said. 'Let us consider the 5 per cent options.'

'Secretary of State, may I first say to you' – it was one of the senior civil servants speaking – 'that we consider ourselves extremely fortunate to have you, obviously one of the more determined, ambitious and talented members of this Government, in our department. Our responsibility is to protect you, Secretary of State, to ensure that all that you want for yourself is advanced, together with the interests of this department.

'Of course, if you insist upon urging us to recommend to you the 5 per cent staff reductions, we are not saying there are no options that could be considered. For example, we have considered the methods we use for monitoring pollution of waterways. If you are prepared to see increased levels of untreated sewage pumped into the rivers, then further economies could be found.' A harrowing catalogue was recited. At the end, not daunted, I asked for the 7.5 per cent options.

'Secretary of State', my principal adviser said, 'can I be quite honest with you? We have had conversations with some of our colleagues in other government departments. We know how much you care about the commitment of this Government and how determined you are to carry it out. We have been making some inquiries about the resolve of your colleagues. Secretary of State, none of your colleagues is going to consider the 7.5 per cent option. Do you think it wise, so soon in your political career and at such an early stage in this Government's fortunes, when the future is uncertain and your colleagues' resolve untested, to be out there alone, taking risks, sacrificing standards, abandoning the fruits of decades of social improvement?'

In twenty offices in Whitehall similar conversations were being held. I remembered Irwin Bellow's advice and put one last question: 'How many people are allowed to recruit to this department?' Notice was understandably required, but soon the reply came back: fifty-seven. There was only one decision to make, and I made it. I gave instructions that only one person would in future recruit to the department. That burden would be mine.

Four years later the DoE was 29 per cent smaller, employed 15,000 fewer people and remained in my view one of the most impressive and creative departments in Whitehall. I heard no more about the impossibility of a 7.5 per cent reduction in manpower.

After my crude but necessary decision officials from the personnel department paid me occasional visits to report on vacancies as they arose, and I approved or disapproved of their being filled. It was not scientific and my priorities must often have been wrong, but it was the only way to make the inroads into numbers which I intended. It was also the only way for me to find out the realities of our manpower requirements as against the superficialities which stared at me from the official briefing papers.

The threatened reduction of standards soon turned out to be one messenger lost here, one secretary there, one merging of two offices where work had previously been duplicated. It soon became plain that people were leaving the department at a rate of about 10 per cent a year. Some retired, some were fed up, but the rate of natural wastage was consistent. In the normal course of events that happens in most organizations. It also seemed clear, after a month or two, that on average only four out of every ten of the resultant vacancies needed to be filled. Gaps could be closed by moving the existing staff. After six months, with the department already 3 per cent smaller, I handed the work on to two very capable civil servants with instructions to keep up the pressure and to refer to me only when they were worried about safety or security.

Looking back, it seems incredible that a department which was supposed to be efficiently managed could lose a quarter of its manpower and still in other respects be the same department. The only possible explanation was deeply disturbing: that the system of management was nowhere near equal to the task; and that the system of scrutinizing Whitehall, the painstaking work done by the Comptroller and Auditor-General and his staff and by the Commons Public Accounts Committee, was defective.

I now decided that I must find out what was happening in my department and who was responsible for making it happen; who had set the targets, what the targets were and whether they were being monitored. Nobody could answer these questions for me. Nobody could recall them being asked before. Nobody had even the means of gathering the information. Frequently, the information did not exist.

My simple decision was to identify every person who would be able to answer my questions because he was familiar with the office or depot or laboratory where things were being done. Each such person, in private sector language, was a profit centre; and each was asked to analyse his responsibility, his activities, his authority, his manpower and his costs.

Abridged from M. Heseltine (1987) *Where There's a Will*, London, Hutchinson (Arrow Books, 1990), pp. 11–20. Reproduced with the permission of the Peters Fraser & Dunlop Group Ltd.

3.3 | *David Faulkner*

Policy making in the Home Office

The Government's change of direction in its policies on crime and criminal justice is probably the most sudden and the most radical which has ever taken place in this area of public policy.

Until a year ago, these policies had evolved gradually, through a process which took account of public feeling but which was largely driven by consultation with professionals, practitioners, academics and representatives of informed opinion. Some ideas were adopted and later discarded (sometimes more than once) but there was a sense of continuity over quite long periods of time.

Similar issues have dominated the debate for much of the period since the Second World War: rising crime, especially among young people; court procedures and especially access to jury trial; the credibility of community-based sentences; the organization of the Prison Service, chronic overcrowding and the threat of disorder in prisons. During the second half of the 1980s the Government built up, gradually and painstakingly, a programme which was meant to provide an integrated, balanced and, as far as possible, stable set of policies for tackling these issues. The Criminal Justice Act 1991 and the White Paper *Custody, Care and Justice* (which followed the Woolf report on prisons) were central features of this programme, but its scope was much wider and more comprehensive.

Within a period of less than 12 months, much of the programme has been politically discredited and seems to have been largely abandoned.

Overwhelming emphasis is now being placed on criminalization, detection, conviction and punishment as the means of dealing not only with violence and other forms of serious crime, but also with what has previously been regarded (not always universally) as anti-social behaviour, for example squatting or interference with fox hunting.

The fact is that there is now a serious void at the centre of the criminal justice system. There is no clearly understood set of purposes which it is meant to achieve or principles which it is meant to observe, and no effective and acceptable system of accountability for its operation. The police are unsure whether their main task is simply to detect and arrest criminals – the view of the old 'canteen culture' which so much had been done to correct – or whether they have a wider purpose of maintaining social stability and confidence, in tackling crime by other means, or in protecting individual rights and civil liberties. It is ironic that the (little noticed) publication of the Crown Prosecution Service's statement of purposes and values, with its emphasis on quality and satisfactory outcomes, was followed by vehement criticism of the service, which showed a deep misunderstanding of what it was trying to achieve.

The Prison Service is unclear whether it is meant to implement the programme set out in the Woolf Report and the Government's own White Paper, or concentrate on containing a much enlarged prison population and on developing more austere regimes.

The confusion is perhaps greatest for the courts, whose purpose is vague and subject to individual interpretation. This includes preventing crime, establishing the truth, punishing or trying to reform offenders and satisfying victims. Many of these are likely to conflict. It must now be unclear to the courts whether they should resolve these conflicts in favour of conviction and custodial sentences, as the Government appears to intend, or whether their independence requires a separately formulated set of purposes and principles and, if so, how this formulation could be achieved.

There is also the much wider problem of deciding the part which the criminal law and its enforcement can realistically play in tackling crime and social disorder. Other measures may be more effective, providing incentives and opportunities rather than exclusion and punishment. Controls might be less formal, perhaps relying on the civil rather than the criminal law – with different sanctions and different standards of proof – both for their enforcement and for the protection of those against whom action is taken.

For the criminal justice services, accountability seems to be interpreted as the means by which greater efficiency can be achieved in respect of a set of Government-imposed performance indicators, rather than a means of maintaining integrity, a collective sense of direction and purpose and a responsibility to those using the service.

The Citizen's Charter places emphasis on responsiveness to customers or users, but it is unclear how far the Citizen's Charter approach can be applicable to criminal justice or whether it is intended to provide a new form of accountability. There has been little discussion of accountability in relation to the judiciary and the court services, where the argument has concentrated on preserving judicial independence.

The means of reconciling independence with accountability, for example through open and structured decision-making, have been discussed only superficially, if at all.

It could fairly be said that these issues should have been more explicitly addressed while the Government's policies were being developed during the 1980s and there has been some disappointment that they were not addressed by the Royal Commission. But the issues are too complex and sensitive to be addressed coherently through the political or parliamentary process, and the Royal Commission felt constrained by its terms of reference.

The task at this stage is to consider not the terms in which new statements of purpose might be drafted, but the structures and procedures by which the issues could be addressed and a sense of purpose established. Possible proposals might include a judicial college or 'think tank', based on the existing Judicial Studies Board but able to operate more generally as a deliberate and advisory body for the judiciary as a whole; a criminal justice institute providing a similar function for the criminal justice system as a whole and working more closely with central government; the development of the Criminal Justice Consultative Council and its area committees, on a statutory basis, to provide national and local forums for consultation and planning; and a long-term strategic plan, annually updated, which would be open to public criticism.

Present policies give the impression of being hastily conceived and precarious in their application. Apart from the obvious threat to stability in prisons, they depend on the skill, integrity and commitment of thousands of men and women in all parts of the system. Many of them now feel confused and unsure of what is expected of them, politically, professionally and, perhaps, morally. Without a greater sense of purpose and direction, the prospect is one of increasing frustration and anger, a spiral of rising crime, increasing severity of punishment and the alienation of a growing section of the community.

D. Faulkner (1993) 'All flaws and disorder', *The Guardian*, 11 November. © *The Guardian*. Reproduced with the permission of Guardian Newspapers Ltd.

| *Lord Callaghan*

Whitehall under one party rule

Chairman [Giles Radice]

585. Lord Callaghan, we are very grateful that you have agreed to come to give evidence to us. Would you like to say anything at the beginning, before we start?

(Lord Callaghan of Cardiff) Yes, if I may. I have just come back from a long aircraft journey and my hearing is severely impaired, so I will ask for your indulgence. Other than that, I shall try to follow the committee wherever they want to take me.

586. You do not want to say anything to begin with, then. In December 1992 you said: 'Because the Government has been in power so long, I fear that the civil service is no longer the buffer that it was between the public and ministers.' You went on: 'I fear that we are getting to the stage where the Government has been there so long that they are regarding the civil service as part of their private fiefdom'. What evidence do you have of that?

(Lord Callaghan of Cardiff) General experience, I think, that first of all in the case of Northern Ireland, where there was one party in power for 40 years, there was no doubt that the civil service was completely the fiefdom of ministers in the Northern Ireland Government. Secondly, I remember Lord Armstrong commenting on the Gaullist Government in France which had been in power for many years, where he had formed the opinion – which was not very definite – that civil servants had certainly accepted the general ethos of ministers. Thirdly, when you have a government like the government we had in the 1980s, which emanates a very strong flavour, the civil service picks up the scent. Some are repelled by it, some are attracted by it, and I think the civil service has become more politicized as a consequence of this. I also think, incidentally, that it is one of the underlying reasons for leaks, because some of

these civil servants were repelled by this very strong scent – and I am not commenting on whether leaks should take place. I think they happen with any government – which a government gives off. So although I do not believe for one moment that senior officials were appointed because of their political views, if one takes the case of the Head of the Civil Service and the Secretary of the Cabinet, there was any one of three or four people who might have emerged. I drew up my own short list at the time, and one of those was appointed. It could have been one of three or four. I do not think there is any attempt to politicize the civil service. When you have people who are together for a long time, especially when they work as a team – and this only affects the top of the civil service – feelings of intimacy grow up, feelings of common cause that if you embark on a piece of policy you want to make it a success. If it fails, you feel slightly downcast in the private office: if it succeeds, if your minister comes back from the Cabinet with a triumph, then you all feel better and morale is improved. To that extent I think there has not been any conscious arrogance by the Government or by ministers. I do not mean that at all. What I mean is that because of the length of time by which they have been there, the civil service at the top level has unconsciously accepted, or in some cases been repelled by, the general – I use the word – 'flavour', and that is what we have had.

587.   What is the answer to that, then?

(Lord Callaghan of Cardiff) A change of government. I am quite serious about this; it is not a party point. It always happens. This feeling of intimacy grows up between ministers and their civil servants. It is inevitable. It is something which I always encouraged when I was a minister, whatever office I held, because one could not work on one's own, one wanted to work as a team. Having read all your evidence and having listened to some of it, I think that perhaps you are being over-influenced, in both your questioning and your assumptions, by the fact that it is unusual – indeed, it is probably for the first time since party politics was invented – that you have had a government in power for 14 years and which is likely to be in power for 18 years. When you had a strong government, as we had, say, in 1945 to 1951, which gave off an equally strong flavour as the Thatcher one did, it was replaced in 1951 and so the other lot came in. There was not the same continuation over a generation, or more than one generation, of civil servants at the top level. If you have the alternation of governments, I do not think this thing happens. That is why I would urge you, in reaching your conclusions, not to take too much from the fact that we have had one government for such a long period. We have an unwritten constitution. Prime ministers change, as we have seen. Attitudes change. There has been some evidence given, I notice, almost on the basis as though the administrative system in the civil service these days is always going to continue. It will not. Agencies are the flavour of the month, and so are all these other things which are going on. Market testing is another thing. That can be upset if there is a change of government very quickly, and will be. So I think that there is a certain amount of the questioning which has been going on which may well find itself in two or three years totally changed. Forgive me if I am going on too long, but the one consequence which I do see which *is* serious

is that the civil service has passed through a revolution in the last few years. It is something which has not happened for over a century. I am more worried about the civil service than I have ever been in the 60-odd years from when I first joined it and have been associated with it. I shall leave it there.

588. No, explain that remark.

(Lord Callaghan of Cardiff) My explanation would be this. A reforming government or a radical government, whatever you call the Thatcher government, it was a very radical government which made tremendous changes. All reformers believe that the things which they change are going to improve, and perhaps they do improve, but they also assume that the things they do not intend to change are going to remain as they were. That does not necessarily follow, because reforms and changes always have their impact not only on the things you are changing but on the things you do not change. This has been the impact on the civil service. I think the tremendous revolutionary changes (I use the word) which are being made and have been made in the civil service have had an impact on the things which we take for granted. By 'the things which we take for granted' I mean impartiality, I mean integrity, I mean incorruptibility, either actual or potential. This to me is the serious point, that I think it has left the civil service – and this is where I think this committee can do a very useful job – uncertain about what its role is in these new circumstances in which the values to which it had attached itself for over a century (and we know what they are, they have been explained many times) are being replaced by a new set of values. I am not saying whether those values are worse or better, but they are values such as what is cost-efficiency and all the rest of these things. We know what is important, but having been close to them, I do not think the Government have sufficiently defined what they want from the civil service and what they expect its role to be. This is where I believe you can help and where I believe that a code of ethics would be a very useful addition.

. . .

Sir Thomas Arnold

621. On the role of civil servants being asked to undertake activities which are too overtly political, what is your comment?

(Lord Callaghan of Cardiff) I think the ethos of the civil service, which has again evolved through a long period and a long tradition, would prevent that normally from happening. This is one of my concerns about the position of the civil service today: that because of these great changes which have been brought about in the civil service I think that a number of them certainly are uncertain, as has been shown in evidence given to you, about what it is they ought to be doing and where they ought to be going. That is why I welcome a new code of ethics. If the civil service is becoming much less homogeneous than it was, and as it most certainly is with the growth of the agencies, then the kind of atmosphere which I grew up with as a young man will not be present if people are moving in and out of the civil service. Again, I am not saying it is

right or wrong, I am saying it is a modern development that now we are told that young people do not look to the civil service for a career any longer. In my young days when I was 16 and took the exam, because of the experience of the post-war period my mother said to me, 'The major thing you've got to do is to make sure you get a job with a pension.' Fancy saying that to a boy of 16! Of course, I naturally listened, I took the exam and was fortunate enough to pass. Those days have gone now, and young people do not look at it in that way. The result for me was that I was imbued from the very first day of my service into a tradition which was almost unbreakable. I do not think I am departing from your question here if I say that on my second day in the Maidstone tax office I was led before a bearded gentleman in the local solicitor's office who was a commissioner of oaths and a general commissioner of income tax, and I swore a most solemn oath. I cannot exactly remember what it was, but I know that as a young man I was deeply intimidated by this gentleman looking at me over his glasses and making me swear an oath in my name for the first time in my life. That tradition in the civil service has broken up. That tradition in the civil service which affected me straightaway then is not going to affect people today, so I think there is more need for a code now to be set down not only to tell people where they are expected to go, but also because it will restore some of the sense of unity in the service which I think has partially been broken.

622. Do you feel, then, in your heart of hearts, that the recent Conservative governments have been prejudiced against the civil service?

(Lord Callaghan of Cardiff) Not in my heart of hearts. I feel that in the early 1980s there was deep hostility to the civil service, and that, I think, affected its morale at the time. I do not think that that hostility exists today, but what has happened is that on top of that early hostility there is the breaking up of the civil service. It really is a bulwark of the constitution. One has only to go to any other country and to see what happens when the civil service is not a bulwark, when it does not have the traditions of our civil service. One has only to see the consequences for society to say that any government has to consider not only whether it is efficient, not only whether it is getting most value for money, but it also has to consider the general ethos of our service and the incorruptibility of our service, the impartiality of our service. All these things are to my mind equally important with getting the maximum efficiency and the maximum value out of every last penny.

Rt Hon Lord Callaghan of Cardiff – oral evidence to the Treasury and Civil Service Committee, 25 May 1993. Extract from *Sixth Report, 1992–93: the Role of the Civil Service, Interim Report, Vol. II – Minutes of Evidence and Appendices*, HC 390–II. Reprinted in accordance with HMSO's guidelines for the reproduction of Crown and Parliamentary copyright.

Sir Patrick Nairne

Mandarins and ministers: a former official's view

Under the leadership of an innovative Head of the Civil Service, Sir William Armstrong, the principal recommendations of the Fulton Report, and the role of the new Civil Service Department, led to valuable improvements in the structure, training, and managerial standards of the service. The priority given to managerial reform by the Conservative Government since 1979 has added weight and speed to the process. But an incidental effect of significance has been to bring many departmental ministers into a functional field which had previously been the almost exclusive province of the civil service. And there have been other new and wider factors which have affected ministerial relations and the attitudes of those within the service.

When the level of inflation rose sharply, as in the 1970s, index-linked pensions for the service proved politically awkward. As unemployment grew, the job security of civil servants became a target of envy and challenge. The image of the service was damaged when its unions proved as ready to strike as other public sector unions. As government policies sought to promote the benefits of a market economy, the civil service was exposed to the charge of being a costly institution that contributed little or nothing to the productive wealth of the nation. The political objective of rolling back the frontiers of the state has tended to devalue the vocational dedication of public servants. Many of the best young men and women in the universities have come to see a career in the City as more personally satisfying as well as more financially rewarding.

All these factors have contributed to disenchantment in Whitehall, to lower morale in the service as a whole, to resignations by some of the ablest civil servants, and to an occasional sense of alienation from ministers or, at least, to more precarious relations between ministers and their officials – in short, to the more adverse political and social environment mentioned earlier.

But, while the Northcote-Trevelyan heritage is significantly changed for those who will be entering the Administrative Group of the Civil Service in the last decade of the century, the central, and most important, feature of the 1854 reforms has been maintained. The Administration Group (which replaced the Administrative Class) is still almost entirely composed of men and women who have been recruited by the independent Civil Service Commission for a career for life in the public service. Britain remains one of the few democratic countries in the world in which, while governments and ministers change as a result of the country's vote in general elections, civil servants from top to bottom of government departments do not change; and ministers can look to men and women who are professionals in the business of government and politically neutral in its discharge, to provide an invaluable commodity – the continuity of administration to balance the discontinuity of politics. It is a crucial feature of the Whitehall system which has increased in value as the complexity of government and its range of functions have grown. Although in recent years the potential advantages of some politicization of the civil service at the top has been aired, the case for it has not gathered strength and the principle of political neutrality (qualified in some limited respects) has been maintained. As Lord Bancroft put it, in a speech in 1983:

> Conviction politicians, certainly: conviction civil servants, no.

But abstinence from political convictions must continue to be complemented by vigorous commitment to policies designed to promote the political aims of the government in power. This is another aspect of the relations between ministers and civil servants that has been exposed to attack in recent years. A former Conservative minister, Lord Peyton, expressed it simply:

> At the end of the day, senior civil servants only did what they wanted to do, even if they dressed it up as the will of ministers.

Mr Anthony Benn argued in his book, *Arguments for Democracy*, that:

> It would be a mistake to suppose – as some socialists have suggested – that the senior ranks of the Civil Service are active conservatives posing as impartial administrators. The issue is not their personal political views, nor their preferences for particular governments, though as citizens they are perfectly entitled to hold such views and to vote accordingly. The problem arises from the fact that the Civil Service sees itself as being above the party battle, with a political position of its own to defend against all-comers, including incoming governments armed with their philosophy and programmes.

Mr Brian Sedgemore, a former Parliamentary Private Secretary to Mr Benn, put the matter much more strongly in a minority report to a Parliamentary select committee report of the 1970s. He claimed that civil servants had invented for themselves the role of 'governing the country':

> they [civil servants] see themselves, to the detriment of democracy, as politicians writ large. And of course, as politicians writ large, they seek to govern the country according to their own narrow, well defined interest, taste, education and background, none of which fit them on the whole to

govern a modern technological, industrialised, pluralist and urbanised society.

But more than one prime minister and several senior ministers are on the record with contrary views, based on the simple proposition expressed by Mr Denis Healey in a BBC Radio inquiry:

> I think that a minister who complains that his civil servants are too powerful is either a weak minister or an incompetent one.

It may be enough to quote from the memoirs of Lord Carrington, with 30 years of ministerial experience behind him, who refers to caricatures in which:

> the Civil Servant is determined to frustrate the will of ministers, by courteous, ingenious and constitutionally proper means, if the ministerial will or policy threatens the cosy and established civil service consensus, the bureaucratic inertia, the status quo.
>
> All this is great fun, and there is something in it sometimes, but it is, nevertheless, a distortion. I have almost always found British Civil Servants, anywhere in the higher reaches of the profession, to be models of what such men and women should be – intelligent, selfless, knowledgeable and fair minded. Of course they are in the job of making government function smoothly . . . But in all this they preserve, from my observation, both integrity and loyalty despite what must frequently be trying circumstances; and every Cabinet owes them a great deal.

From these conflicting views what emerges is significant in that the commitment of civil servants to ministers has become the subject of public debate, and that the mutual confidence essential to a partnership of trust can no longer be taken for granted – as it was in the past when Lord Vansittart, one of the outstanding public servants of 50 years ago, could trenchantly remark of the Foreign Office that 'the soul of our Service is the loyalty with which we execute ordained error'.

The civil service partnership at work

But, while the civil service partnership has to be exercised in a changed political environment, there has been no fundamental change in what civil servants expect of ministers and ministers expect of civil servants. The essential practical roles within the partnership remain the same.

First, ministers need to know their own mind – that is, to know what they want to achieve in their department in the light of their particular political and ministerial responsibilities. That sounds obvious, but in practice the transformation of a short and general text in an election manifesto into, say, a detailed basis for negotiation with a foreign government or as a brief for the Parliamentary draftsmen can often be a slow and arduous process. As a first step, civil servants have to analyse broad political aims, and to define policy options as precisely as possible. They frequently follow lengthy discussions with ministers – who may have been only a few days or weeks in charge of their departments. Civil servants depend on guidance in order to perform effectively as partners. As Mr Anthony Benn fancifully described them in a radio programme, they are 'a clockwork motor that has to be wound up all the time'. They must look to their secretary of state to know what will secure the agreement of Cabinet colleagues; what will have the support of the government's back-benchers; and what will be acceptable to the press and the public. The whole process reflects a basic doctrine which remains as valid as when Sir John Anderson, as he then was, expressed it many years ago:

> The personal responsibility of each minister to Parliament to matters within his competence is a basic principle of the constitution – a principle as fundamental as the rule of law or the sovereignty of Parliament.

Secondly, officials look to their secretary of state to argue the departmental case effectively with Cabinet colleagues. Inter-departmental discussions between civil servants may prepare the ground, but ministers may often have an exacting task in persuading their colleagues, particularly when expenditure proposals have to be agreed with Treasury ministers or when there is a clash of interests, such as in the Westland Affair, between powerful departments. It can be demoralizing for a department if the secretary of state and officials, working in partnership, fail to get Cabinet agreement for what they are seeking to do, primarily as a result of the secretary of state's own failure to judge what is needed to secure the support of the Prime Minister and ministerial colleagues.

Thirdly, a departmental minister must be effective in his dealings with Parliament. Here again the supporting role of civil servants is crucial in preparing Parliamentary answers and in briefing on a Bill. And, more generally, if officials fail to ensure that they are quickly told about any aspect of departmental policy or activity which has aroused local political criticism or caught the media headlines, ministers may be caught unawares and unbriefed. As Admiral Lord Fisher put it at the beginning of the century:

> The secret of successful administration is the intelligent anticipation of agitation.

Ministers, for their part, must know, in a way that civil servants often cannot know, how best to present a difficult political case in public, or to defend a severe attack in the House of Commons. Those outside Whitehall who criticize the failure of government to operate more efficiently, or to pursue a more consistent and coherent long-term strategy, do not fully appreciate the relentless impact of Parliament. It is hardly surprising that ministers react so drastically to embarrassing press leaks when the waves of challenge and criticism from the Parliamentary Opposition break ceaselessly on departmental shores.

Finally, the secretary of state has to be successfully 'up front' in presenting his departmental policies to the media and the country. Civil servants cannot play at party politics in disguise, but it is up to them to acquire a sensitive understanding of the political approach and tactics of their own ministers, to study Hansard and be alert to matters that are causing concern in Parliament. They have been helped in this by the employment of special advisers, appointed personally by ministers to their private offices. No minister can be immune to sudden emergencies in their departmental field or to unexpected crises outside Whitehall. They will be handled best when there is a close rapport between the secretary of state and his senior officials. When Mr Harold Macmillan, as he then was, was asked what worried him most as Prime Minister, he replied with the single word 'Events'; it was he who posted in the Private Office at No. 10 the lines from Gilbert and Sullivan's *The Gondoliers*:

Quiet, calm deliberation disentangles every knot.

Thus a good working partnership between ministers and civil servants depends upon firm political control and clear leadership by the secretary of state. Mr Edward Heath summed it up when he gave evidence in 1977 to the House of Commons Expenditure Committee and said:

I believe that civil servants like to be under ministerial control. There is nothing they dislike more than to have a minister whom they feel is weak, who does not know his mind and who wants to leave it to them. That is not their mentality or their approach. On the occasions when I have seen it happen they disliked it intensely and quite obviously disliked it. What they like is to have a minister who knows a policy he wants to pursue, who will take advice on the consequences of it, and how it can be implemented, who will carry sufficient weight in Cabinet to see it through and who will have sufficient influence with the Chancellor of the Exchequer to get it financed.

What do ministers expect in return of their senior civil servants, and in particular of the permanent secretary?

First of all, to ensure as far as possible that the department, as a whole, however large it may be, is responsive to the political direction of ministers. The diaries of Mr Richard Crossman and Mrs Barbara Castle show that is not always as easy as it may sound, particularly in the early days of a new government. There will always be a large range of departmental work of which ministers will scarcely be aware, even if a management information system (MINIS) is in operation. The permanent secretary, so far from seeking to stifle or delay the policies of new ministers, is acutely concerned to ensure that it does not take too long for the change in political attitudes or style, as well as the fresh political initiatives, to be understood in all parts, and at all levels, of the department. The thrust of Parliamentary questions, and of the constant flow of letters from Members of Parliament, and the scope and character of critical media articles and programmes, can be an invaluable indication of how the policies and performances of their departments are regarded outside Whitehall. But the views of their own ministers are the essential guidance for officials. The extension of the 'Next Steps' policy to further agencies – agencies, for example, in which executive action in individual cases needs to reflect Whitehall guidelines as closely as possible – may present a communication problem in the future when governments change.

Secondly, ministers must be able to rely on the permanent secretary and senior officials for candid, clear and rapid advice on policy proposals and plans. This is at the heart of the civil service partnership, and ministers can sometimes take a different view of what they want. Some may look to the permanent secretary to see that the department's recommendations are thoroughly prepared in considerable detail before they reach the minister's desk; and in some circumstances there may be only one course which is administratively and politically practicable. A former head of the Foreign and Commonwealth Office, Lord Strang, has expressed the view that 'the Minister's task is difficult and delicate enough without the dissemination of possibly divergent opinions from within his own house'. On the other hand, there are ministers – Mr Denis Healey and Mr Anthony Crosland are examples – who have preferred to have all reasonable options presented to them, and to listen themselves to different views among officials if there are justifiable divergencies of opinion.

The permanent secretary has a key role. He should never be a bottleneck delaying submissions to ministers, but he should be aware of, and in broad step with, all major submissions from his colleagues and be ready, when necessary, to add his own advice. The secretary of state should be able to look to him personally for support in ensuring that all relevant aspects of a difficult policy issue are exposed and discussed round the ministerial table; for frank and constructive advice in private on any issue on which there is a significant difference of view between him and his officials; and for overseeing a regular review both of progress in pursuing and implementing policy objectives, and also of measures or activities of the department which may be causing, or leading to, external challenge or criticism.

The Whitehall system of continuity may enable a minister to know his permanent secretary before he arrives as secretary of state of a department. That can help to promote mutual confidence more quickly in a working partnership that has little time to spare for informal social contact. The comment of one former permanent secretary, Sir Idwal Pugh, is quoted in Susan Crosland's biography of Mr Anthony Crosland:

> The ideal relationship between a permanent secretary and a minister is where you meet late in the evening over a whisky or a cup of tea and talk about this and that.

But, in the crowded day of a minister, there is rarely time for that; and some ministers (Anthony Crosland was evidently one) have no disposition for it. There is a crucial role for the principal private secretary. A close rapport needs to be developed, as it often is, between him and the secretary of state; and this can enable him to keep the permanent secretary in touch with the minister's current anxieties or latest ideas. Lord Beveridge compared the relations of minister and permanent secretary to that of a husband and wife in a Victorian household. It is an instructive analogy, but more applicable today, especially in the large departments, to the principal private secretary.

The permanent secretary is, however, the principal housekeeper of the department, and that is an important part of what Beveridge had in mind. Although they concern themselves more closely than in the past with departmental management, ministers cannot hope to do more than preside over managerial strategy, while relying on the permanent secretary and senior officials to consult him on major policy proposals affecting the running of the department, the regular reviews of staff numbers and all the recommendations for senior appointments. Departmental management, especially perhaps appointments and promotions, is a substantial, and inescapable, commitment for the permanent secretary, however capable his senior personnel manager (or establishments officer). In addition to his involvement in wider management policies, he must – contrary to some of the myths about the character of his role – personally oversee career planning of senior staff and concern himself with organizational changes or staff moves required for dealing with fresh tasks, such as a Parliamentary Bill or an entirely new policy initiative. All governments aim to control and, if possible, reduce civil service numbers, and only the permanent secretary can advise the ministers on the more difficult competing claims of his professional and administrative colleagues. Over the last ten years ministers have depended on their permanent secretaries to ensure that their departments effectively fulfilled the management reforms based on the 'Rayner scrutinies', the FMI (Financial Management Initiative) and other measures emerging from the Whitehall Efficiency Unit.

Finally, the secretary of state must look to his permanent secretary, together with the principal finance officer, for the proper supervision of the department's expenditure and financial management. The civil service partnership is especially close, as Mrs Barbara Castle's diary illustrates, in the annual policy and tactical discussions of the financial bids of the department for its share of the government's public expenditure programme. More personally exacting for the permanent secretary is his responsibility as the department's accounting officer (or senior accounting officer), usually involving several lengthy appearances each year before Parliament's pre-eminent committee, the Public Accounts Committee. That committee is a formidable body, well briefed by the Comptroller and Auditor-General, and a permanent secretary may find himself devoting, in all, some 20 per cent of his time to preparing for the detailed grilling he can expect. Critical questions may sometimes focus on ministerial policies, and the permanent secretary must try and foresee them and clear the answers he proposes to give with his secretary of state. Although he is personally called to account by Parliament, his primary responsibility remains to his departmental minister.

Abridged from Sir Patrick Nairne (1990) 'The civil service "mandarins and ministers"',
Wroxton Papers in Politics, Series A, Paper A6, Barnstable, Phillip Charles Media, pp. 4–11.
Reproduced with the permission of Wroxton College.

| *Sir Kenneth Stowe*

Good piano won't play bad music

Good governance

Why is the issue of good governance relevant now? The prospectus for the British Council seminar set out the reasons in late 1989:

> The need for reform of central and local government is confronting governments world-wide, in developed as much as in developing countries, and in many different political contexts. Excessive costs, poor service to the public and failure to achieve the aims of policy are a common experience – poor performance, waste, and low morale feeding a downward spiral of inefficiency. Economic constraints, demographic change, rising public expectations and media exposure of failure have combined to make reform urgent.
>
> (The British Council 1991)

I think that these claims are still valid but administrative reform is about means, not ends. It has taken a long time for international institutions and national governments to open up the issue about ends. What is the point of good public administration if it does not support good governance? What, indeed, is good governance? There was no reference to it in the UN Handbook. The first authoritative reference I know was in 1989, in a World Bank report on Sub-Saharan Africa which defined it as 'a public service that is efficient, a judicial system that is reliable and an administration that is accountable to the public'.

I think that there is more to it than that. I also think that it is highly dangerous to suppose that the prescription was appropriate only for Africa or the Third World. Falling short of goodness in government is a common experience in any and all nations, not excluding the UK. Indeed, in the UK, rather than having 'a judicial system that is reliable' what *we* have had is a spectacular series of miscarriages of justice, involving both the police and the judiciary and a Royal Commission has been set up to deal with a massive scandal.

I suggest that we have here in Britain the same need as elsewhere to define and clarify what we mean by good governance, and then test our own performance; and I set out six desiderata for this:

1 political freedom, including free speech and a freely elected Parliament, assembly or legislature;
2 constitutional and judicial protection for the rights of the individual;
3 the maintenance of the rule of law by an independent judiciary;
4 the maintenance of a stable currency, the essential underpinning of economic and social development;
5 development of society as a whole by education and health care; and finally
6 executive accountability to a freely elected legislature.

Note that I do not include the World Bank's 'public service that is efficient' in my desiderata of good government.

. . .

An efficient public service cannot of itself secure good governance: it can indeed be used *against* good government. What the World Bank was saying, I believe, was that you cannot have good governance without it, and that I subscribe to.

Administrative reform

The UK civil service has been engaged in administrative reform more or less continuously since the Fulton committee reported in 1968. There were, of course, reform initiatives before that, notably the re-training of civil servants in The Conduct of Public Business, which followed the Crichel Down fiasco. However, for much of that time these reforms were not crowned with much success, if success is measured by better performance in public services.

Nevertheless we are credited in the UK with having a better civil service than we had twenty-five years ago and, even more importantly, we are credited with a civil service that has been a material factor in the transformation of the UK economic and social scene in the 1980s. You can choose for yourself whether the transformation is for better or worse, but the credit is certainly there. We are repeatedly asked by other governments – how is it done? My response to that, in my role as a UK government adviser, boils down now to asking three further questions of them – and giving them UK-based answers as a starting point for their consideration. These questions are: (a) what is a civil service for; (b) what is a civil service in a plural democracy; and (c) how can a professional civil service be created?

What is a civil service **for**?

This question seems to me to be straightforward. The answer I gave a new democracy and its new, and very young, Prime Minister, who asked for our help in creating for his country a 'British' civil service, was that the function of a professional civil service in a multi-party or plural democracy is:

1 To *inform* ministers and Parliament – with complete and accurate data, presented objectively and in time.
2 To *advise* ministers – by analyses of data and appraisal of options in which they can have confidence.
3 To *implement* ministerial decisions and to administer the resultant legislation.
4 To *account* to ministers and Parliament for their actions (or inaction) – with particular reference to the safeguarding of public funds and ensuring effective value-for-money.

What *is* a civil service in a plural democracy?

This is a more testing question, and reveals a very real problem in emerging democracies when a single party state moves towards political plurality and democracy and the civil service has to lose its party identity and serve a national, not partial interest.

The best answer I can offer is that a professional civil service has five key attributes:

1 It is based on the merit principle.
2 It guarantees financial probity.
3 It respects political neutrality and impartiality under the law.
4 It is committed to serve any government well.
5 It is accountable at all levels.

All these attributes sound easy to achieve, but none is easy to achieve in the adverse conditions common to the new democracies. Thus, in one such country the constitution calls for a 'balanced civil service', i.e. balanced as between racial groups. Is this to be made compatible with the merit principle? How can financial probity be consistent with the starvation wages paid to civil servants in some countries? If basic human rights are ignored, can a civil service profess to be totally neutral and impartial? Should a professional civil service serve with commitment if government declines into tyranny? How can a civil service be accountable if there is no democratic and effective government and legislature to account to? When it comes to defining a professional civil service, we are fortunate in the UK – since we have had a long time in which to evolve our answer.

How to create a professional civil service?

I now confront an even more difficult question. In the UK we have been developing a professional civil service for nearly one hundred and forty years, since the Northcote-Trevelyan reforms of 1854, through a process of administrative direction and convention. We are currently putting it through the mincing machine of 'agency' development, which a World Bank official described as 'a revolution in Civil Service management'. What should Hungary or Bulgaria do? Or Namibia, Poland and Laos, when they want what we take for granted and need it tomorrow? What useful answer can we in the UK give? One answer is to send a copy of Estacode, the Civil Service Orders-in-Council and videos of all the *Yes, Minister* series (each of these has been seriously proposed). Another, all too familiar, answer is to send in the experts. One country had received 43 experts and had accumulated a debt of several million US dollars over seven years to pay for them when I went there with a colleague in response to a request for advice. I confess I have no simple answer as to how a new democracy grows its own UK style civil service.

One of our former Prime Ministers, Arthur James Balfour, pointed out that British institutions could not be assumed to work elsewhere in the absence of the 'British humour'. So, a becoming modesty and disarming simplicity might be especially relevant. This brings me to the Caribbean calypso in my title, which was part of an attempt on my part to by-pass the constraint of 'British humour' and convey a simple practical message to a foreign government aspiring to administrative reform in our image.

Good piano don't play bad music

I have tried to distil guidance on administrative reform into four simple precepts. The UK reader will recognize the first two from our domestic experiences:

1 *If it ain't broke don't fix it; if it is broke, don't polish it* – attributed to Mrs Thatcher, but I confess to adding the last bit myself.
2 *Don't make it perfect, make it Tuesday* – frequently quoted by Lord Rayner in his path-breaking role as Mrs Thatcher's Efficiency Adviser.
3 *Ownership is vital* – administrative reform cannot be created by an external presence, no matter how authoritative. It has to belong to those working with it, and should be firmly embossed 'country of origin is country of application'. The first chapter of the Fulton Committee Report is a perfect example in our own UK experience of how to destroy a good case: by stridently anathematizing the existing civil service managers at the highest levels, it alienated them and they never were committed to reforms which were really needed.
4 *Good piano don't play bad music* – I confess to authorship of this.

I hope that the point I am making in this last precept is obvious. A public service is not, in a proper sense, efficient, no matter how capable and well-tuned, if it is serving ends which are wrong by ministerial design or incompetence. Examples are legion around the world. I invented my calypso because I wanted to impress the point on a prime minister who aimed for a good public service but had plenty of bad music about.

Let me give four examples of bad music in this sense:

1 Publicly financed housing which is allocated not by need but by tribe, or party, or religion.
2 Surplus public land and property expected to be sold to political friends at below market price.

3 Public policy established on the suppression of information which would invalidate it.
4 Public assets allowed to rot by deliberate oversight (or simple unawareness of the fact that neglect costs money).

If ministers do these things, or condone them, or ignore them, what is the value of administrative reform?

You might by now have guessed that I would choose examples like these not from the Third World, but from the UK. I am referring to the allocation of council houses in Northern Ireland in the 1960s; to the sale of surplus hospital land in London in the 1980s; to the concealment of the true costs of nuclear power generation until the City flushed it out in the course of privatization; and to the deliberate neglect of the maintenance of the public estate since the Second World War. If we can do these things in the UK – and we did – we must surely be careful in what we say to the Third World and Eastern Europe about good governance and administrative reform.

The question with which I wish to end – and the most difficult question of all – is one that goes to the heart of good government: where is the safeguard against bad music? Can the good piano, the efficient and well-tuned public service, really refuse to play it? Will it refuse? On the evidence, no it won't always, not even in the UK.

Occasionally, the individual civil servant can, quite properly, prevent bad government. The accounting officer can refuse to go along with letting the political friend have a below-market price. The Head of the Statistical Service can refuse to leave publishable data concealed. There are other examples of a similar kind known to me in the UK. But it is easier to take that kind of stand in our, well-established, service with its strong conventions. In the new democracies, something more is needed. Here I pin my hopes on what may prove to be the most important administrative reform in the UK since the Second World War: the new public audit machinery. This consists first and foremost of the National Audit Office (NAO) and the Audit Commission. Their wide powers of investigation and their wide remit to go into value for money as well as probity are crucially important. Even more important is the backing of a Public Accounts Committee. I also include in the new audit machinery the Parliamentary Commissioner for Administration and the Health Services Commissioner, with their wide powers of investigation, and their Select Committees.

This may seem a surprising conclusion to be put forward by a former accounting officer – the victim, as it commonly seems, of a hostile and pressing Public Accounts Committee of the House of Commons. But the reality is that this accountability of the accounting officer to the Public Accounts Committee is his principal weapon against political expediency. As an adviser on administrative reform to several governments in very different situations, I see real difficulty in offering as a standard model our own civil service structure and practice; there is too much convention and sophistication. The principles are sound and worthy of implanting in an alien context, but only as a basis for domestic development. The Public Accounts Committee and the National Audit Office, on the other hand, are already well established in an international context. If their counterparts are functioning, there is hope of improvement; but if they are not, there is little hope. An effective public audit system also answers the third part of the World Bank definition of good governance, that the public service is accountable to the public.

References

British Council (1991) 'Towards better government: the management of administrative reform', prospectus for seminar held at Eynsham Hall, Oxford, 27 June.

Abridged from Sir Kenneth Stowe (1992) 'Good piano won't play bad music: administrative reform and good governance', *Public Administration* Vol. 70, pp. 387–94. Reproduced with the permission of Blackwell Publishers.

| *William Plowden*

Politicizing the civil service

It is not at all obvious that practices in Whitehall have in fact changed greatly in the past decade. Some of those most closely involved argue that for years determined ministers have successfully influenced at least key appointments. But, in a curious conspiracy of double-bluff, others prefer to pretend that although the formal rules acknowledge the possibility of ministerial influence none is actually exercised. This, they say, is quite right: acknowledging ministerial influence in this context would mean abandoning a tradition justified by years of practice, whereby impartial officials offer neutral advice to ministers of any persuasion and carry out, with unemotional efficiency, the instructions which they receive.

The straw man of the US federal civil service is fetched out and vigorously pummelled yet again. A recent public talk by the Secretary of the Cabinet contained not only a reference to the USA but also the dire words: 'There is an overall pattern and logic about the (constitutional and administrative) system as a whole; and it would be difficult to change particular conventions without putting the stability of other parts of the framework at risk' (Armstrong 1985).

Others argue, rather differently, that in the absence of a British Bill of Rights or constitutional court the civil service is our best available check on arbitrary behaviour by ministers (RIPA 1984).

My own belief is that recent events are indeed a portent of a long-term trend towards greater political control – using that phrase very loosely to cover both the strong and the weak senses outlined above – of the civil service. I also believe that such a trend is necessary and desirable. What C.H. Sisson called the 'non-entity of the administrator' seems to me a psychological nonsense (Sisson 1966). That is to say, I do not believe that thoughtful individuals, with their own established practices and values, can, in fact, support with equal enthusiasm governments with totally dissimilar ideologies; or that they can prevent the relative intensity of their enthusiasms from influencing their behaviour. Alternatively, an intolerable strain can be placed on conscientious officials compelled to implement policies with which they personally disagree. Whatever the theoretical right of civil servants to ask to be moved if they find themselves in this unhappy situation, the actual conventions are pretty clear: you get on with the job. The individual who successfully insists on a move is likely to be marked down as unsound. What is needed is a system, and a change of attitudes, which would make it relatively normal for individual officials to be moved, at their own request or at their minister's, out of (and into) sensitive jobs without loss of face.

Many jobs, of course, are not affected by changes in government complexion; there is no need for wholesale politicization of the civil service and there are strong arguments against this. I am thinking of the relatively few posts whose responsibilities closely touch the ideology of the governing party, or which bring them into close personal contact with ministers.

My reasons for arguing this are partly pragmatic. The relationship between politicians and bureaucrats is always liable to be problematic; I believe that in Whitehall it has for long been unsatisfactory, and that it is deteriorating. It is partly a question of the balance between politicians and officials. This may be more a psychological than a managerial issue. I suspect that some ministers' aggressive attitude towards officials derives from their feeling of insecurity when faced with these serried ranks who may not be on their side. They believe that only the brutal approach will carry them through; or, more moderately, that it is prudent not to consult the mandarins for fear of becoming engulfed in a treacly consensus. Whatever the explanations, it is no use civil servants claiming that the traditional relationship works well if politicians feel that it does not. Some account must be taken of the facts of life.

I am also uneasy at the line which seems to be gaining currency in the present government, that all these problems can be avoided if the proper distinctions are made between policy and administration (or implementation): the former should be reserved for elected politicians and political advisers, and the latter left to civil servants. Attempts to enforce this kind of distinction can do only harm. If ministers do not trust their officials' involvement in policy, they would do better to change at least some of their officials.

I am unmoved by the plausible counter-argument that if ministers are served and advised by sympathizers they will never hear the frank dissent which from time to time they need. Plain speaking is surely much more likely – and likely to be acceptable – between people who believe that they are on the same side.

Finally, the claim that a neutral civil service is the best guarantee of an Englishman's liberty seems to me a wholly undesirable argument for an increasingly undemocratic status quo. Politicians in power should be able to carry out the policies to which they are pledged, and then judged by their electorate on the effectiveness or ineffectiveness of these. They should not be obstructed by unaccountable permanent officials guided by some inexplicit private conception of the national interest.

The case in terms of effective policies can be supported by that in terms of effective *process*. The difficulties of modernizing central government are immensely increased by the system's tendency, as Lord Curzon put it, to 'throttle every reform'. The would-be reformer is always liable to be asked, as by Sir Robert Armstrong, whether he really wants to run the *risk* of endangering the *stability* of the rest of the governmental system (the italics are mine). Some people, discounting the artfully alarmist language, are indeed prepared to admit wanting to do just that. But they, and any government seriously interested in comprehensively improving its own processes, may well need to put into key positions people who share their views about the kinds of changes needed. They must also neutralize people who do not. This may mean moving, demoting or prematurely retiring (firmly though without dishonour) those incapable of accepting or adjusting to a new approach.

I suggest that we should now reject, reluctantly maybe, the myth of the totally dispassionate, totally effective administrator, as we have done other comforting but outmoded myths – such as the incorruptibility of the police, the self-governability of financial institutions or the unique tolerance of the British. Instead of instinctively resisting in principle any increase in political control of the civil service, we ought now to start thinking about how to bring this about in a controlled and constructive way.

This kind of change should be reinforced by a general relaxation of the rigid career patterns in the civil service. I would like to see much more movement in and out, temporary or permanent, at all levels of the civil service. The community as a whole does not lose if skills developed in government service are transferred elsewhere; there will always be people outside government whose skills and expertise can be better exploited inside. It is essential to leaven the present dense mass of career people with some with different experiences, insights and values. There might be a more formal and more radical change in the system of tenure of senior posts. For a start, why not publicly advertise them all? And perhaps they should all be held on short-term contract – say, five years, renewable. Mobility, or the possibility of mobility, would become part of the career expectation of senior officials.

More thoughtful and more systematic use of outsiders as temporary policy advisers could also help. This device could hardly be described as an experiment, but it is taking a very long time to develop. The major contributions of policy advisers, specialist or political, are that they help ministers to feel less isolated in face of their departments; and that they can greatly extend the number and range of the minister's effective contacts with his department. They thus improve communication in both directions and, I believe, ministerial effectiveness.

All that is easy to say, though anathema to many. But if we are to go down that road, we must do so knowingly and openly. We must understand and accept the possible consequences of modifying present career patterns. The process would need to be controlled if we were to prevent either corruption or the repeated managerial chaos of Washington, DC. Civil servants must not be demotivated by the belief that the best jobs would always be creamed off by 'outsiders'. If very high salaries were needed to attract outsiders, it might be necessary to rethink the rates offered to career officials for doing the same job. Rules and conditions would need to be defined, and known to all concerned – outside as well as inside. It is clear to me that the whole process of senior appointments – even as it is at present – ought to be much more subject to outside scrutiny. There is a task here for the Select Committees of the House of Commons, which seems to me admirably complementary to their greater concern with the efficiency and effectiveness of departments.

. . .

References

Armstrong, Sir Robert (1985) *Address to the CIPFA Annual Conference*, 18 June.
RIPA (1984) Ministers and officials: towards new constitutional arrangements, *RIPA Report*, 5(4), pp. 11–12.
Sisson, C.H. (1966) *The Spirit of British Administration and Some European Comparisons*, London, Faber and Faber.

Abridged from W. Plowden (1985) 'What prospects for the civil service?', *Public Administration*, Vol. 63, pp. 393–414. Reproduced with the permission of Blackwell Publishers.

Anthony King

The consequences of the career politician

Some possible consequences

The consequences of the rise of the career politicians have been subtle and complex. Moreover, there is no way of following them through with any degree of precision. One cannot draw a causal arrow from the rise of the career politician to some other political phenomenon and say with absolute confidence, 'The one caused the other'. The changes described in this paper are only one element in a much larger pattern of political change. Nevertheless, a number of quite important consequences can be identified, however tentatively.

The rise of the career politician in Britain means that it is even harder than it used to be for someone completely without political experience to reach high office. The British system has always been one that emphasized the importance of experience, with aspiring politicians expected to rise slowly through the ranks, from backbench Member of Parliament, through parliamentary private secretary, through junior government minister, to cabinet minister. The typical member of the British Cabinet has always been someone of substantial Parliamentary and governmental experience. Even so, it was always open to a Prime Minister to appoint someone, or indeed several people, from outside. Lloyd George did this during the First World War, Chamberlain and Churchill during the Second World War, Harold Wilson as recently as 1964 (not, it must be said, with very happy results). The rise of the career politician, however, and the increasing burdens of political life in general, make it unlikely that many such outside appointments will be made in the future. Britain's future political leaders may not have undergone professional training, but they will certainly have served a rigorous apprenticeship.

There is, however, a price to be paid. The career politician commits himself to politics. In so doing, he is unlikely to have the time or energy to commit himself to anything else. He can practise at the bar in the mornings, or write articles for the newspapers, or act as a consultant to business firms; but he cannot gain much in the way of executive experience or rise to the top of a large corporation or trade union. If politics as a career has become more demanding, so have most other walks of life. The serious politician cannot combine politics with a demanding job outside; a man or woman who enters politics at the age of between 30 and 45 is unlikely to have had time to become managing director of a large industrial firm or general secretary of an important trade union. Bevin in the 1945 Labour Cabinet had been the leader of the Transport and General Workers' Union; Cripps had been one of the outstanding barristers of his generation. The 1974–9 Labour Cabinet contained no one of comparable extra-political experience. The transition has been less abrupt on the Conservative side, because Conservative politicians have greater opportunities to acquire and maintain business contacts. Even so, the post-1979 Thatcher Cabinet contained no one with business experience on the scale of a Lyttelton or a Woolton. The professionalization of politics in Britain – and here one can use the term – means increasingly that politicians without a great deal of first-hand experience of the world outside politics are running the country, including the economy, in conjunction with senior civil servants who similarly lack first-hand experience of the world outside politics. One does not have to be a Cassandra to be worried, or at least faintly perplexed, by this development.

The rise of the career politician has probably also had the effect of intensifying a phenomenon that in any case is to be observed in governmental circles and legislative assemblies throughout the world: the tendency of politicians and civil servants to develop a private language, private quarrels, their own interests, priorities and preoccupations – what a perceptive Frenchman has called *la politique politicienne*.[1] This is to a large extent inevitable, of course: every calling and institution tends to wrap its own world around it. But circumstances may conspire to cause the politician, even in a democracy, 'to live almost entirely in an atmosphere of politics':

> It is true of course that many enjoy this type of life with its incessant stress on influence, rivalry, ambition and frustration – it sharpens political wits and has a brilliance of its own. It does, however, strengthen and even overdevelop the political orientation of men who have already entered voluntarily upon such a career. By political orientation is meant that exclusive preoccupation with political events to the point where every human activity becomes evaluated not in terms of its intrinsic value but in terms of its political significance.[2]

The person who wrote this was referring to Washington in the early 1950s, but his remarks clearly bear on the Britain of the 1980s.

With the rise of the career politician, there has also occurred a rise in the incidence of political ambition. Ambition in this context is usually taken to mean ambition for office, and it usually does mean exactly that; but it may mean other things as well. An ambitious person, even an ambitious politician, need not be ambitious only for office. He may be 'hungry', as the Americans say, in all kinds of ways. Herbert Morrison was enormously ambitious for office; he desperately wanted to be leader of the Labour Party and Prime

Minister. But, when he was accused of being ambitious, he replied: 'My ambition is to do the job I am doing as well as I can, and if another job comes, to do that also. It is to do things, not to be something, that is the worthier ambition.'[3] There was an element of humbug in this, of course; but Morrison was probably speaking the truth when he said that ambition in him was partially satisfied by the satisfaction of a job well done.

By the same token, most career politicians are undoubtedly ambitious for office; but they are probably also ambitious to express themselves politically – to influence the course of events, to have a say in the formulation of policy, to be in a position effectively to challenge the executive. For this reason, a legislature containing a high proportion of career politicians is likely to be a restless, assertive institution. It is not too much of an exaggeration to say that Parliament in Britain at one time comprised a minority of career politicians – people who wanted to get ahead, people who wanted to make their mark – and a majority of members who were altogether more relaxed about politics, who were content to be pretty much spectators: 'A hundred years or so ago most plain backbenchers knew their limitations and were not ashamed to be inconspicuous. They were so confident in their social and financial status that they felt it unnecessary continually to prove how important they were. There was not so much urge to leap up for those who were prodigiously up already.'[4] The advent of larger numbers of career politicians has wrought a substantial change. More back-bench MPs want office, but there are not nearly enough offices to go round. So, frustrated, they seek other outlets for their energies and self-assertiveness.

They have found three such outlets so far, all of them important. In the first place, Members of Parliament have become much more assiduous than they used to be in attending to the needs and wants of their constituents. The 'good constituency Member' was once sufficiently rare as to be the subject of comment. Now there are so many good constituency Members that only MPs who conspicuously neglect their constituencies attract much notice. In the second place, the last few years have seen the rise of the House of Commons select committee. Select committees in the British system consist entirely of back-benchers; they cannot examine the details of legislation, but they do have the power to investigate and report on almost everything else. After years of agitation on the part of back-benchers, a new structure of select committees was established in 1979, with one of the new committees to shadow each of the major government departments. These committees have been far more assertive than anyone expected. They have criticized ministers, they have criticized civil servants, they have attacked government policy, they have threatened to bring in Bills of their own. The select committees are, needless to say, largely manned by career politicians. Thirdly, the rise of the career politician has undoubtedly been responsible in large part for the sharp decline in party cohesion in the British House of Commons that has occurred in recent years. Career politicians may be ambitious for office; but many of them are also much too proud and wilful to be content to serve as mere lobby fodder.

It is just conceivable that the ambition – the restlessness, the activisim – of the career politician has had even more widespread consequences. The career politician takes his work seriously. If he has a job to do, he wants to do it well.

Suppose that a career politician becomes Secretary of State for the Environment or Secretary of State for the Social Services. Until very recently, confronted with such a challenge, a new minister, whatever his political views, was likely to look at the work that his department was currently doing and to begin at once to consider what else needed doing. And of course there was always something. Should more money not be spent on roads and cleaning up derelict land? Should more money not be spent on renovating old houses? Should the emission of pollutants into rivers and streams not be controlled more tightly? Should not better social provision be made for the physically handicapped? Public expenditure has increased as a proportion of gross national product in almost all liberal democracies; the volume of government regulation has also increased. Many reasons have been advanced to account for this phenomenon: the difficulty of going back on general commitments to expenditure once they have been made, the tendency for costs to rise faster in the public sector than in the private, rising public expectations, election promises and so on. But an additional explanation almost certainly lies in the self-image, in the desire for positive accomplishment, of the career politician. Activist government may be in part a consequence of activist politicians.

It does not follow, however, that the career politician need always be a force making for big government. Rather, he is likely to be a force making for change – of whatever form. In his study of state legislators in Connecticut, James David Barber emphasizes the important role played by a type of politician he labels 'the Lawmaker'. He writes: 'The Lawmaker asks more of his legislative environment than a chance to be active. Successful action, the completion of desired projects, is required for his satisfaction. In legislative terms this means that the Lawmaker is generally found pressing for new action, for innovations that will move society in directions he desires.'[5] The Lawmaker and the career politician clearly have much in common; and, while the innovations that both desire could involve an extension of government activity, they could also involve a reduction in government expenditure, a reduction in government regulation, a reduction in government intervention in industry and so on. A striking feature of British politics over the past decade has been the radicalism, the desire for change, of both major political parties, not just the Labour Party. Not only have both of the parties become more radical; so have successive governments. As a result, changes in public policy have become much more common than in the past. Again, it seems reasonable to link these changes at least in part with the rise of the career politician.

Ambition thus manifests itself in many ways apart from the desire for office; but the desire for office remains important and, if anything, has become even more important as career politicians have grown more numerous. Not all career politicians are ambitious; some of them – Prime Ministers and ex-Prime Ministers, for example – have already achieved the summit of their ambition, and some MPs and ministers remain devoted to the life of politics even though they know, perhaps because they are old or because they have recently been passed over, that they are unlikely to advance further. Still, the vast majority of career politicians are ambitious in the generally understood sense as well as in the additional ways just referred to. They are eager for office and promotion and, if they are offered them, will accept with alacrity.

One result of the increased incidence of ambition in this more conventional sense has probably been to reduce somewhat the collegial character of decision making at the top of British politics, among leaders of the opposition parties as well as in the Cabinet and its committees. Cabinets and Shadow Cabinets have, of course, always been riven by policy differences and personal animosities; the saying that there is no friendship at the top is hardly new. But there now seems to be even less friendship, even less willingness on the part of groups of ministers and shadow ministers to band together for political purposes, than there used to be. Each of those who might participate in such action is busy defending his own corner; each is looking over his shoulder at the others. Hence, for example, the surprise in the summer of 1980 when three former Labour Cabinet ministers – the 'gang of three' – agreed to be joint signatories of an open letter to a national newspaper dealing with the party's future.[6]

All this said, there remains something of a puzzle about the rise of the career politician. The puzzle is connected with the fact that the career politician – the man or woman committed to politics as a way of life – might be expected to adopt one or other of two quite different political stances. On the one hand, the career politician might be expected to don the garb of James Q. Wilson's political professional: cool, non-ideological, a trifle cynical, concerned with personal advancement, above all a vote-maximizer, far more interested in victory for its own sake than in the substance of issues. On the other hand, it is equally plausible to expect the career politician to combine a commitment to politics with a strong commitment to a political cause – just as the career priest is usually committed to a particular view of religion, and the career political scientist to a particular view of the way in which political science should be carried on. In other words, the rise of the career politician might plausibly have been expected to lead either to a highly competitive but otherwise rather low-key politics or else to a politics that was equally competitive but was also highly ideological, taken up with the clash of abstract ideas of the public good and marked by high levels of tension both within and between the parties.

Not surprisingly, signs of both developments can be seen in the British politics of the past two decades. The desire to get ahead in politics, the desire to remain in politics, have undoubtedly served to increase the power of those in the political system with the capacity to punish or reward. The non-career politician is not going to be too worried about what the party leader thinks of him or about his relations with his party supporters in the constituency. Politics? In the end, he can take it or leave it. But the career politician is likely to be torn quite often between his professional, self-assertive desire to speak his mind and his awareness of the fact that his political fate rests in the hands of somebody else: the leader, the Chief Whip, possibly the Parliamentary Labour Party, certainly his constituency party or association.

The increase in the number of ambitious politicians has clearly augmented the power of the Conservative leader, who has more leeway than her Labour opposite number in determining the composition not merely of her cabinet but also of her shadow administration. On the Labour side, the increase in the number of ambitious politicians has had the effect of increasing the power of the extra-parliamentary Labour Party in general and of constituency party activists in particular. A Labour MP may hold moderate or centrist views; he may be very worried about the left-wing drift in the party. But, if a majority of his constituency general management committee hold strong left-wing views, he is unlikely to say very much in public. It is hard on any other basis to account for the discrepancy between the well-known private views of many Labour MPs and their public silence. In both parties, it is probably no accident that a disproportionate number of those who have been willing to stand out against their party in recent years – Sir Edward Boyle on capital punishment, Roy Jenkins on Europe, Robert Carr on the admission into Britain of Ugandan Asians, James Prior on the reform of trade unions – have been less than totally committed to a political career.

Yet it seems equally clear that the rise of the career politician in the last few years has been associated, not with a lowering of the political temperature, a move away from ideological politics to a single-minded preoccupation with vote-maximizing, but rather with the reverse. By any measure, British politics from the late 1960s onwards have been more heated, more ideological and less consensual than for a long time past. The radicalism of governments of both major parties has already been remarked on. The Conservatives under both Edward Heath and Margaret Thatcher have been going through a highly doctrinaire phase; Labour has taken to adopting, almost wilfully, policies that seem all but certain to alienate the electorate. The main explanation for this phenomenon probably lies in the fact that British politics in recent years has been almost overwhelmed by the problems posed by an ailing economy; desperate problems have seemed to require desperate remedies. But a contributory factor has probably also been the rise of the career politician, who, in Britain at least, has turned out to be a much more dogmatic, much more issue-oriented person than James Q. Wilson seems ever to have imagined possible. In addition, the recent high level of vehemence in British politics is almost certainly associated with the fact that many more British politicians than in the past are now recruited from the ranks of journalism, public relations and teaching. It has been remarked elsewhere that such persons are likely to import into politics habits of disputation, generalization and abstract thought acquired in these other professions.[7]

Summary and envoi

This paper has argued that, even among politicians, some are more committed to politics as an occupation, a vocation, a calling, than others; that those who are deeply committed to politics as a way of life should be called 'career politicians' rather than 'professional politicians'; and that such career politicians have in recent years loomed larger and larger in the British House of Commons and the British Cabinet. The paper has also argued that this change in the personnel of British politics has brought certain consequences in its train. The system has changed because the people who work it have changed. On the one hand, Britain's politicians have become more politically experienced, harder working, more assertive and less in thrall to the party whips. On the other, they have had less experience of the world outside politics than their predecessors, and they show signs of being more partisan, more doctrinaire and less in touch with the mass electorate. The ambition of the career politician has led not to vote-maximizing but to the confident assertion of fundamentally different points of view, leading to far more frequent changes in public policy than were known in the past. Large events like the rise of the career politician do not necessarily have large causes. They may reasonably be expected, however, to have large consequences. It is hard to escape the conclusion that the demise of the non-career politician has led to a certain loss of experience, moderation, detachment, balance, ballast even, in the British political system.

Still, there never was a golden age, and it would be inappropriate to end on a lugubrious note. Career politicians can have their own form of detachment. One evening early in 1975, a junior minister in the then Labour Government was acting as host at an official reception. Among the guests were a Conservative Member of Parliament and his wife. The Conservative Party was at that time in the midst of the leadership struggle that eventually led to the election of Margaret Thatcher. The wife of the Conservative MP was appalled at the thought that anyone should want to be leader of one of the major political parties. 'It's awful', she said. 'Think of what it would be like – the endless television interviews, the reporters outside your house, what it would do to your family, the lack of privacy. It's a *disease*, wanting to be leader of your party, a *disease*.' She looked almost distraught. The Labour minister listened politely until she had finished, then said, 'Yes, you're right: wanting to lead your party is a disease. You're talking to a terminal case.'

References

1 Douglas Hurd attributes the phrase to the Mayor of Tours in *An End to Promises: Sketch of a Government 1970–74*, London, Collins (1979), p. 148.
2 Edward A. Shils (1959) 'Resentments and hostilities of legislators: sources, objects, consequences', in John C. Wahlke and Heinz Eulau (eds) *Legislative Behaviour: a Reader in Theory and Research*, Glencoe, IL, Free Press, p. 349.
3 Bernard Donoughue and G.W. Jones (1973) *Herbert Morrison: Portrait of a Politician*, London, Weidenfeld and Nicolson, p. 176.
4 Woodrow Wyatt (1973) *Turn Again, Westminster*, London, Andre Deutsch, p. 27.
5 David Barber (1965) *The Lawmakers: Recruitment and Adaptation to Legislative Life*, New Haven, CT, Yale University Press, p. 207.
6 *Guardian*, 1 August 1980.
7 See Anthony King (1972) 'The changing Tories', in John D. Lees and Richard Kimber (eds) *Political Parties in Modern Britain: an Organizational and Functional Guide*, London, Routledge and Kegan Paul, esp. pp. 134–5.

Abridged from A. King (1981) 'The rise of the career politician in Britain – and its consequences', *British Journal of Political Science*, Vol. 11, pp. 249–85. Reproduced with the permission of Cambridge University Press and Professor Anthony King.

3.9 | *Richard Rose*

Steering the ship of state

The metaphorical ship of state has one tiller but two pairs of hands that can give it direction, one belonging to party politicians and the other to higher civil servants. Nearly every study of the subject, from the classic works of Weber to contemporary social science writings, recognizes that the two groups, notwith-standing their differences, are jointly implicated in government. In democratic systems of government, elected office holders can claim the legitimate authority to give direction to government. But higher civil servants may have the technical knowledge of government programmes necessary for effective policy-making. These differing qualities, according to Aberbach and Rockman, create a dilemma: 'How can a satisfactory balance between democratic decision-making and effective policy be reached?'[1] . . . The conclusion is that the problem is not so much that of civil servants as of politicians, who need to improve their capacity to analyse policies if they are to be successful policy entrepreneurs rather than passengers on the ship of state.

. . .

In order to evaluate politicians and civil servants, we must pay attention to the sea as well as the ship. Here, the sea is a metaphor for the policy environment, that is, *all* the forces outside the government that affect what can and cannot be achieved. If willpower were everything, then the wants of the governing party (and by implication, of the electorate) could easily be realized, for 'wanting would make it so'. If the policy environment determined everything, then elected officials need not worry themselves about policies, for their actions would be of no avail.

The problem that politicians have in giving direction to government is not that of identifying goals: politicians reckon to know what government *ought* to do. The big problem is achieving goals that they have identified. A party newly installed in office finds that all the problems that confronted its predecessor are still in place: the only change is in the name of the politicians in office. Since political achievements are uncertain, the probability of success in achieving political goals can be indicated along a continuum ranging from very high to very low. Political will is also variable, for the strength of a politician's commitment to a goal can range from high to low.

. . .

Ministers are subject to conflicting pressures. To rely upon an inflexible will risks a political crash, for governors thereby exclude the warning signals fed back from higher civil servants. Yet for politicians to concentrate solely upon warning signals from civil servants, threatening abandonment of partisan goals, risks dissension within the party. Committed partisans may prefer to believe that their leaders have 'sold out' to higher civil servants than that the party's goals are impossible to achieve. From this can follow demands to increase the influence of the extra-governmental wing of the party upon its 'weak-willed' leaders in Cabinet. This was the reason behind changes in the Labour Party Constitution introduced by strong-willed Labour activists dissatisfied with the actions of the 1964–70 and 1974–9 Labour Governments.

The probability of achieving a political goal varies according to the object of political will, and the policy instrument employed by government, as well as by the intensity with which a goal is affirmed by politicians. Putting a man or woman on the moon is easier than solving the problems of America's inner cities. Reducing inflation or unemployment is more likely to be achieved by some policy instruments than by others.

. . .

When government action is seen as a calculation in two dimensions, involving both political will and the probability of achieving a goal that is willed, the interaction of politicians and civil servants can be viewed as a mutually beneficial exchange. Once a politician has indicated a goal, expert higher civil servants can identify a range of policy options, from those that are furthest from the goal but most likely of achievement to those approaching closest to the goal, but unlikely to achieve success.

. . .

Studies of the growth of government emphasize that there are many forces beyond the control of the government of the day, and certainly beyond easy manipulation by particular office holders at a given moment. Upon entering office, a governing party is not offered a *tabula rasa* on which it can inscribe any goals that it would like. It finds that nearly all the major activities of government are 'pre-programmed'. Politicians inherit a manifold of pro-grammes sustained by statutory commitments, established organizations and public employees, financed by substantial tax revenues, and supported by the political expectations and statutory entitlements of client groups. The inertia of big government is that of a set of programmes in motion; it is not static.[2]

If the ship of state is steered by an automatic pilot, then politicians are only passengers. Politicians do not need to make fine calculations relating their political will to the probability of success. They are bound by their oath of office to uphold existing laws that mandate a great repertoire of continuing programmes. But a deterministic political environment is not a prescription for doing nothing. Even if policy-makers feel that 'the system' is stronger than they are, they cannot ignore its effects, when rising unemployment or inner-city riots result. Negatively, politicians can avoid endorsing goals doomed to failure because they are not already pre-programmed within the machine of government. Politicians wanting to claim credit for positive achievements[3] can endorse what is already determined to take place.

The position of civil servants in such circumstances is ambiguous. When outcomes are determined by exogenous forces in the policy environment, higher civil servants are not in a position to alter the direction of government. They are no more than stewards, serving impersonal forces stronger than themselves, or the volition of politicians. But as experts in government, civil servants are able to predict the direction of public policies, and to understand why government must bow to the force of events. Even if civil servants are weak against the force of events, these stewards of the inevitable appear formidable to politicians who do not understand why they cannot do what they would like. Thus, a model of predetermination may appear as if it were proof of bureaucratic dominance.[4]

. . .

One explanation that politicians can adopt for failing to achieve their wants is that they do not know how to manage the people who count, that is, higher civil servants. An alternative explanation is that they do not know specific policies. The two explanations are not mutually exclusive. If politicians are to learn how to achieve more in government, they may need to know how to exercise their political will *vis-à-vis* higher civil servants, and how to analyse policies so as not to attempt that which is impossible to achieve.

. . .

In this political contest, the competitors are not equal. Ministers are usually portrayed as inadequate in confrontation with their nominal subordinates, whose ironical 'Yes, Minister' phrases mean 'Yes, we will do it our way.' The greater expertise of higher civil servants in the procedures and programmes of government, their greater number and their much longer experience of office are assumed to allow higher civil servants to dominate transitory, amateur and isolated party politicians. When action is required, higher civil servants who have 'captured' their ministers can recommend what they regard as the appropriate action to take in the name of the party in office. When politicians go along and achievements are as expected, then there is the appearance of politicians achieving what they will. But the reality is that the politicians who take the credit are not the persons whose hands are on the tiller.

. . .

Any measures intended to strengthen the hand of politicians on the tiller must start by asking what roles politicians are actually capable of fulfilling within government. An MP can take many roles that have little to do with the direction of government. But politicians, and especially ministers, cannot deny

Programme capacity

		High	Low
	High	**Policy entrepreneurs**	**Zealots**
Political will			
	Low	**Management technicians**	**Passengers**

Figure 3   Alternative role definitions for politicians

that they should also have a role within government. A schematic representation of roles can be developed from the foregoing, based on programme
capacity, that is, the ability to identify and evaluate policies in terms of their
probability of achievement; and the strength of political will, high or low.[5]

Politicians who can act as policy entrepreneurs, that is, office-holders who
have a well-defined political will *and* a capacity to examine programmes, are
best able to give direction to government. If a politician can only enunciate
goals without knowing how they are to be attained, such zealotry may win
popular votes or a party following, but it will not mislead higher civil servants
into believing that their vague goals constitute a programme for action. If
politicians lack both will and knowledge they will simply be passengers on a
mystery tour directed by higher civil servants (see Figure 3). Conventionally,
higher civil servants are defined as management technicians, high in their
capacity to understand programmes, but weak in preferences for programme
goals. Politicians who abandon an interest in political goals in order to become
expert in the mechanics of how programmes work may thereby gain the
esteem of higher civil servants for 'really' understanding government – but
they do so at the price of forgetting what politics is about.[6]

The incapacity of politicians need not prevent the achievement of effective
programmes – if higher civil servants are legitimately allowed to fill the gap
created by the default of elected representatives. This can happen in political
systems in which civil servants are allowed to act as policy advocates, or at least
participate in advocacy as members of issue networks involving elected
politicians and interest-group representatives, as well as themselves. Such
networks can be found in places as distant as Tokyo and Washington.[7] An
alternative and more open route is for a policy entrepreneur to leave a civil
service post to become a policy advocate, or to participate in party politics as
advocate and office-holder. France is a familiar example in which civil
servants, persons with a high degree of programme capacity, can carry forward
their ideas by being appointed a minister.[8]

Britain is an example of a political system in which the incapacity of politicians
to act as policy entrepreneurs appears substantial. The Continental practice of
allowing civil servants to participate in party politics or go on leave to enter
Parliament or serve as a minister is inconsistent with the present British
constitutional arrangements. It is significant, and entirely characteristic, that the

leaks to the press by civil servants in the Thatcher administration have been designed to *prevent* politicians (*qua* zealots, in the eyes of civil servants) from pursuing goals of which the 'leaking' civil servant disapproves. British civil servants have neither sought nor been given a mandate to act as policy entrepreneurs, individuals committed to programmes and matching their wills publicly and controversially with elected politicians. If anything, the Thatcher period has sought to promote management technicians in Whitehall, encouraging civil servants to become more effective programme managers, while leaving to ministers (zealots or entrepreneurs – and, sometimes, the one masquerading as the other) the task of identifying programme goals.

Comparative analysis suggests a variety of measures that could increase the supply of policy entrepreneurs in British government. Assuming that politicians have no shortage of political will, this would require strengthening the programme capacity of ministers. Since British (and even more, American) ministers spend only two or three years in a given office on average, an immediate step would be to have British ministers spend a longer time in one office. Such a decision by a Prime Minister would not require legislation; it would, however, restrict playing 'musical Cabinet chairs' as a technique of party management. A longer stay in office would give ministers a better chance to learn more about the programmes for which they are notionally responsible. A year or more must be invested in learning the specifics of a ministry. The prospect of a move – promotion or removal from Cabinet by the Prime Minister, or ejection by the electorate – reduces a politician's incentive to promote major policies directed at achieving long-term political goals. Political incentives direct a British politician away from the substance of his department's programmes.[9]

Given that three-quarters or more of ministers are *not* specialists in the work of the ministry to which they are appointed,[10] there is substantial scope to increase the programme capacity of a politician before (or as a condition of) appointment to office. But this would involve substantial changes in Parliamentary customs and conventions, for the activities that help an aspiring parliamentarian become a minister are related to the promotion of his career, and not to policy entrepreneurship *per se*.[11] The conventions of collective Cabinet responsibility and official secrecy preclude many Government backbench MPs, as well as Opposition front-bench MPs, from gaining substantial insight into the problems of making effective policies.[12] It would be unrealistic to expect constituency parties to give special priority to the nomination of programme specialists. Hence, a Prime Minister would have to draw more specialists from the existing House of Lords, or a Lords enlarged by the appointment of more peers with special knowledge of government programmes, plus the talents and inclinations requisite in a minister.

The logical alternative – introducing more civil servants as government ministers – faces many obstacles in a British setting. First of all, MPs would oppose people who have not served their time in party and Parliament breaking their monopoly claim to the status of Cabinet minister. Secondly, there is little or nothing in the experience of a British higher civil servant that cultivates skill in the public advocacy of policies in the face of partisan criticism. The polite words used by the Sir Humphreys of this world would be as inadequate in partisan debate in the Commons as the mandarin evasions of Sir Robert Armstrong were inadequate in a Sydney courtroom. Thirdly, and most important, higher civil servants have shown no evidence of wanting to become public politicians. Although an occasional junior civil servant has become an MP, a higher civil servant, after resignation or retirement, normally goes to a well-paid post in the profit-making sector, or an important post in the non-profit sector. While a Prime Minister could find dozens of ex-civil servants who might run a ministry better than the average MP, talking such a person into returning to Whitehall as a minister would not be easy. Whereas Washington cultivates the role of in-and-outer, a higher civil servant who goes out of Whitehall usually chooses to stay out.[13]

Ultimately, changes in the steering capacity of politicians must occur within individual politicians. A programme zealot lacks the cognitive capacity or the desire to be informed about the obstacles in the way of achieving his political will. Willpower is sufficient to keep a zealot advocating political goals without regard to the probability of achievement.

Most politicians, and particularly those who reach ministerial office, are not blind zealots. They can weigh the importance of competing arguments, not least where these may promote success in their own political career. However, the relative scarcity of politicians with strong political wills *and* a capacity to deal with programmes suggests that the disincentives to policy entrepreneurship are greater than the incentives.

The first disincentive is time. A politician spends very little time as a minister, compared to the years spent in Parliament, or the decades spent in party activities prior to entering office. In countries where higher civil servants *can* transfer to government, there is, exceptionally, the possibility of enjoying a lifetime career in public policy. In so far as the *cursus honorum* that leads to a ministerial post is now regarded as a profession requiring many years of apprenticeship, there may be a rising proportion of politicians with a little more time for learning about the problems of office. But most of their effort must be invested in activities designed to reach the threshold of office; not so much is invested in anticipating what can be done once in office.

The second disincentive is prudential: to learn about the difficulties of achieving partisan goals is bad news in a strictly partisan context. A party, and particularly a party in opposition, does not want to be told that the problems of government are not easily remedied by throwing the rascals out, and putting its own leaders in. Anyone who appears as a 'no can do' politician, concerned with keeping afloat rather than with going somewhere, may not be given the opportunity of steering the ship of state. Others, more optimistic, more ignorant, or better at concealing their scepticism, may end up with their hand on the tiller.

The American Presidency demonstrates that politicians in government may have something more important to do than worry about the problems of government. They can 'go public', a term that Samuel Kernell has taken from White House strategists; it describes the tendency for a President to be increasingly concerned with cultivating his public image and standing in opinion polls.[14] In a mass-media age in which winning the Presidential nomination requires formidable campaign skills, this is what a Presidential candidate must be good at. Ronald Reagan's inclinations have been to maximize the attention given to public relations – including the enunciation of Utopian political goals which have no probability of achievement – and to minimize involvement with the programmes of government. The result, named after a non-stick frying pan, is the 'Teflon Presidency'.

Since politicians are meant to be the masters of government, rules cannot force them to learn what they do not want to know. If the promise of success fails to motivate politicians to take more interest in steering government, then perhaps the threat of failure can. In the United States, 'Irangate' illustrates that a popular President who does not know (or control) what his staff are doing can suffer failures of policy, and lose personal popularity as well. The problems confronting the Labour Party in the 1980s reflected the creation of expectations within the party of what a Labour Government could achieve by willpower, expectations that were dashed when Labour ministers were confronted with 'some things stronger than parties'.[15] Even more, the collapse of the Heath Government in 1974 provides a dramatic example of Oakeshott's epigram, 'To try to do something which is inherently impossible is always a corrupting enterprise'.[16]

References

1 Joel D. Aberbach and Bert A. Rockman, *The Administrative State in Industrialized Democracies* (Washington, DC, American Political Science Association, 1986), p. 7. For a classic discussion, see 'Politics as a vocation' and 'Bureaucracy' in H.H. Gerth and C.W. Mills (eds) *From Max Weber* (London, Routledge and Kegan Paul, 1948).
2 See Richard Rose and Terence Karran, 'Inertia or incrementalism?' in A. Groth and L.L. Wade (eds) *Comparative Resource Allocation* (Beverly Hills, CA, Sage Publications, 1984), pp. 43–71; and Richard Rose and Terence Karran, *Taxation by Political Inertia* (London, George Allen & Unwin, 1987).
3 David Mayhew, *Congress: the Electoral Connection* (New Haven, CT, Yale University Press, 1974), pp. 49 ff.
4 For a good discussion of the differences between the two, see B. Guy Peters, *The Relationship between Civil Servants and Political Executives* (Glasgow, University of Strathclyde Studies in Public Policy No. 153, 1986), pp. 10 ff.
5 The typology is derived from that developed by Theodore R. Marmor, with Philip Fellman, 'Policy entrepreneurship in government', *Journal of Public Policy*, 6 (1986), Table 1. It differs in substituting a more general term, programme capacity, for his narrower term, managerial skills, and in the labelling of some alternatives. For example, in the Washington context Marmor sees people who have been career bureaucrats as the most likely policy entrepreneurs, a position that might also be congenial to French graduates of ENA, especially those who become ministers.
6 On the extent to which the distribution of roles differs as between national political systems, see Peters, *The Relationship between Civil Servants and Political Executives*, pp. 15 ff, and Aberbach and Rockman, *The Administrative State in Industrialized Democracies, passim.*
7 Cf. Marmor, 'Policy entrepreneurship in government'; Hugh Heclo, 'Issue networks and the executive establishment', in Anthony King (ed.) *The New American Political System* (Washington, DC, American Enterprise Institute, 1978), pp. 87–124; and T.J. Pempel, 'Organizing for efficiency: the higher civil service in Japan', in E. Suleiman (ed.) *Bureaucrats and Policy Making* (New York, Holmes and Meier, 1984), pp. 72–106.

8 See, for example, Ezra Suleiman, 'Presidential government in France', in R. Rose and E . Suleiman (eds) *Presidents and Prime Ministers* (Washington, DC, American Enterprise Institute, 1980), pp. 94–138; F. de Baecque and J.-L. Quermonne, *Administration et politiques sous la Ve République* (Paris, Presses de la Fondation Nationale des Sciences Politiques, 1981).

9 See Richard Rose, *Ministers and Ministries: a Functional Analysis* (Oxford: Clarendon Press, 1987), especially Chap. 4.

10 See, for example, Jean Blondel, *Government Ministers in the Contemporary World* (London, Sage Publications, 1985), Appendix II; and Bruce W. Headey, *British Cabinet Ministers* (London, George Allen & Unwin, 1974).

11 See Richard Rose, 'The Making of Cabinet Ministers', *British Journal of Political Science*, 1 (1971), 393–414.

12 It is arguable that in a hung Parliament, policy-making would become more open, conceivably giving Commons' committees substantial importance (see Ian Marsh, *Policy Making in a Three Party System* (London: Methuen, 1986)). But it can also be argued that the inter-party deliberations of a coalition government are more likely to encourage horse-trading and log-rolling for votes, as in the United States Congress, rather than the development of programme capacity.

13 The comparison is further flawed by the fact that the American in-and-outer starts out as a politician, typically entering the executive branch at a junior but strategically significant post when young, going out of government to acquire additional skills and resources for later use when he comes back into government at a higher level. The analogy, if there be one, is with British ministers, albeit that a British MP spends time out of executive office in the purgatory of the Opposition benches of the House of Commons.

14 See Samuel Kernell, *Going Public: New Strategies of Presidential Leadership* (Washington, DC, Congressional Quarterly Press, 1986); and Richard Rose, 'Learning to govern or learning to campaign?', in Michael Nelson and Alexander Heard (eds) *Presidential Selection* (Durham, NC, Duke University Press, 1987), pp. 53–73.

15 Richard Rose, *Do Parties Make a Difference?* (London, Macmillan, 2nd edn, 1984).

16 M. Oakeshott, *Political Education* (Cambridge, Bowes and Bowes, 1951), p. 11.

Abridged from R. Rose (1987) 'Steering the ship of state: one tiller but two pairs of hands', *British Journal of Political Science*, Vol. 17, pp. 409–33. Reproduced with the permission of Cambridge University Press and Professor Richard Rose.

4

Loyalties, responsibilities and ethics

Some of the issues alluded to in Chapter 3 are brought centre stage here. The question of loyalty is the main focus of the Armstrong Memorandum. It was first issued in 1985 in the wake of the trial of Clive Ponting. It emphasizes that the duty of the civil servant is to the minister and the government of which the minister is a member. Notwithstanding possible conflict between minister and government, it rests four-square alongside the High Court judge whose direction the jury declined to follow by granting Ponting's acquittal. The Memorandum is now incorporated into the Civil Service Management Code from which Reading 4.1 is drawn. At the moment it remains the only authoritative official statement on the subject. This has not mollified the critics. Ponting himself has continued to claim for civil servants a higher duty than simply the routine loyalty to a departmental minister. The piece included here (Reading 4.2) is his written evidence to the Treasury and Civil Service Committee enquiry that was prompted partly by his trial.

If there is no such higher duty, or if government refuses either to believe that there is or to allow expression of any alternative to strict loyalty to its own interests, then what are the consequences? Is it simply a loss of good governance for as long as such disposition prevails? Or is there some more fundamental matter of principle at stake? And, if so, is there something which, if lost, may never be recaptured? Is it the fault of this or that government? Are civil servants themselves partly to blame, or is there an underlying, secular momentum? In dealing with these and other questions, Barry O'Toole draws inspiration from T.H. Green, one of the political philosophers of the nineteenth century (Reading 4.3). He suggests the loss of motivating ideals about the 'common good' as a vehicle for a moral uplift and mutual realizations in public affairs. These are being superseded by the utilitarian calculus of costs and benefits, of a self-centred, nose to the ground, fissiparous new managerialism. The result, he says, is a threat to the public service ethic.

For a quarter of a century the First Division Association (FDA) has wrestled with the question of a code of ethics. In 1986, dissatisfied with the Armstrong Memorandum, it produced a prototype code. Eventually it succeeded in its campaign to persuade government to accept the need for a formal code. This it did with the help of the Treasury and Civil Service Committee (TCSC), which in November 1994 published a draft code of conduct (Reading 4.4). The TCSC recommendation was accepted by the Major Government with relatively few and only minor amendments. At the time of writing it is not clear whether it will replace or rest alongside the Armstrong Memorandum. Not everyone agrees about the need for a code of ethics. A former top civil servant, Sir Geoffrey Chipperfield, dismisses the case for a formal, written code (Reading 4.5). He believes that any such code will 'reduce the pressure on an individual to take responsibility for his own actions'. He is little more favourably disposed to the Armstrong Memorandum. He demurs, not as to an opportunity missed, but as to the attempt to chase a constitutional 'will-o'-the-wisp' whose very apprehension could also be its source of destruction.

All this leaves unresolved the dilemmas about conflicting loyalties, if and when they arise; about the proper order of priority in any such conflict; and about the precise circumstances in which different orders of loyalty should come into play. Peter Jay (Reading 4.6) sketches some of the considerations involved. He tries to lay bare and disentangle the threads. He concludes that the *prima facie* duty of the civil servant is to the minister, but that this is neither an absolute nor an unconditional loyalty. He thinks it may, in some circumstances, be almost impossible to reconcile the ethics of a non-political service with the duties imposed upon the modern official. He suggests a mild form of American-style partisan appointments.

Cabinet Office

The Armstrong
Memorandum

Note by the Head of the Home Civil Service

In February 1985, with the consent of the Prime Minister, I issued a note of guidance restating the general duties and responsibilities of civil servants in relation to ministers. That note was reproduced in a Written Answer by the Prime Minister to a Parliamentary Question on 26 February 1985 (OR 26 February 1985, columns 130 to 132). In the light of the subsequent discussion, including observations of the Treasury and Civil Service Select Committee and the Defence Committee of the House of Commons and comments from the Council of Civil Service Unions, I have expanded the note of guidance, and a revised version is now issued. As previously, the note is issued after consultation with permanent secretaries in charge of departments and with their agreement. As with the earlier version, this revised version is issued with the consent of the Prime Minister, and will be reported by her to the House of Commons.

2. This note is concerned with the duties and responsibilities of civil servants in relation to ministers. It should be read in the wider context of ministers' own responsibilities, which were set out in the Government's reply to the Seventh Report from the Treasury and Civil Service Committee (Cmnd 9841):

> The Government believes that Ministers are well aware of the principles that should govern their duties and responsibilities in relation to Parliament and in relation to civil servants. It goes without saying that these include the obligations of integrity. They include the duty to give Parliament and the public as full information as possible about the policies, decisions and actions of the Government, and not to deceive or mislead Parliament or the public. In relation to civil servants, they include the duty to give fair consideration and due weight to informed and impartial advice from civil servants, as well as to other considerations

and advice, in reaching policy decisions; the duty to refrain from asking or instructing civil servants to do things which they should not do; the duty to ensure that influence over appointments is not abused for partisan purposes; and the duty to observe the obligations of a good employer with regard to terms and conditions of service and the treatment of those who serve them.

3. Civil servants are servants of the Crown. For all practical purposes the Crown in this context means and is represented by the Government of the day. There are special cases in which certain functions are conferred by law upon particular members or groups of members of the public service; but in general the executive powers of the Crown are exercised by and on the advice of Her Majesty's ministers, who are in turn answerable to Parliament. The Civil Service as such has no constitutional personality or responsibility separate from the duly constituted Government of the day. It is there to provide the Government of the day with advice on the formulation of the policies of the Government, to assist in carrying out the decisions of the Government, and to manage and deliver the services for which the Government is responsible. Some civil servants are also involved, as a proper part of their duties, in the processes of presentation of Government policies and decisions.

4. The Civil Service serves the Government of the day as a whole, that is to say Her Majesty's ministers collectively, and the Prime Minister is the Minister for the Civil Service. The duty of the individual civil servant is first and foremost to the Minister of the Crown who is in charge of the department in which he or she is serving. The basic principles of accountability of Ministers and civil servants are as set out in the Government's response (Cmnd 9916) to the Defence Committee's Fourth Report of 1985–6:

- Each minister is responsible to Parliament for the conduct of his department, and for the actions carried out by his department in pursuit of Government policies or in the discharge of responsibilities laid upon him as a minister.
- A minister is accountable to Parliament, in the sense that he has a duty to explain in Parliament the exercise of his powers and duties and to give an account to Parliament of what is done by him in his capacity as a minister or by his department.
- Civil servants are responsible to their ministers for their actions and conduct.

5. It is the duty of civil servants to serve their ministers with integrity and to the best of their ability. In their dealings with the public, civil servants should always bear in mind that people have a right to expect that their affairs will be dealt with sympathetically, efficiently and promptly.

6. The British civil service is a non-political and professional career service subject to a code of rules and disciplines. Civil servants are required to serve the duly constituted Government of the day, of whatever political complexion. It is of the first importance that civil servants should conduct themselves in such a way as to deserve and retain the confidence of ministers, and to be able to establish the same relationship with those whom they may be required to serve in some future administration. That confidence is the indispensable foundation of a good relationship between ministers and civil servants. The conduct of civil servants should at all times be such that ministers and potential future ministers can be sure that that confidence can be freely given, and that the civil service will at all times conscientiously fulfil its duties and obligations to, and impartially assist, advise and carry out the policies of, the duly constituted Government of the day.

7. The determination of policy is the responsibility of the minister (within the convention of collective responsibility of the whole Government for the decisions and actions of every member of it). In the determination of policy the civil servant has no constitutional responsibility or role distinct from that of the minister. Subject to the conventions limiting the access of ministers to papers of previous administrations, it is the duty of the civil servant to make available to the minister all the information and experience at his or her disposal which may have a bearing on the policy decisions to which the minister is committed or which he is preparing to make, and to give to the minister honest and impartial advice, without fear or favour, and whether the advice accords with the minister's view or not. Civil servants are in breach of their duty, and damage their integrity as servants of the Crown, if they deliberately withhold relevant information from their minister, or if they give their minister other advice than the best they believe they can give, or if they seek to obstruct or delay a decision simply because they do not agree with it. When, having been given all the relevant information and advice, the minister has taken a decision, it is the duty of civil servants loyally to carry out that decision with precisely the same energy and good will, whether they agree with it or not.

8. Civil servants are under an obligation to keep the confidences to which they become privy in the course of their work; not only the maintenance of the trust between ministers and civil servants but also the efficiency of government depend on their doing so. There is and must be a general duty upon every civil servant, serving or retired, not without authority to make disclosures which breach that obligation. This duty applies to any document or information or knowledge of the course of business, which has come to a civil servant in confidence in the course of duty. Any such unauthorized disclosures, whether for political or personal motives, or for pecuniary gain, and quite apart from liability to prosecution under the Official Secrets Acts, result in the civil servant concerned forfeiting the trust that is put in him or her as an employee and making him or her liable to disciplinary action including the possibility of dismissal, or to civil law proceedings. He or she also undermines the confidence that ought to subsist between ministers and civil servants and thus damages colleagues and the service as well as him or herself.

9. Civil servants often find themselves in situations where they are required or expected to give information to a Parliamentary select committee, to the media or to individuals. In doing so they should be guided by the policy of the Government on evidence to select committees, as set out in memoranda of guidance issued from time to time, and on the disclosure of information, by any specifically departmental policies in relation to departmental information and by the requirements of security and confidentiality. In this respect, however, as in other respects, the civil servant's first duty is to his or her minister. Thus, when a civil servant gives evidence to a select committee on the policies or actions of his or her department, he or she does so as the representative of the minister in charge of the department and subject to the minister's instructions,[1] and is accountable to the minister for the evidence which he or she gives. As explained in paragraph 2, the ultimate responsibility lies with ministers, and not with civil servants, to decide what information should be made available, and how and when it should be released, whether it is to Parliament, to select committees, to the media or to individuals. It is not acceptable for a serving or former civil servant to seek to frustrate policies or decisions of ministers by the disclosure outside the Government of information to which he or she has had access as a civil servant.

10. The previous paragraphs have set out the basic principles which govern the relations between ministers and civil servants. The rest of this note deals with particular aspects of conduct which derive from them, where it may be felt that more detailed guidance would be helpful.

11. A civil servant should not be required to do anything unlawful. In the very unlikely event of a civil servant being asked to do something which he or she believes would put him or her in clear breach of the law, the matter should be reported to a senior officer or to the principal establishment officer, who should if necessary seek the advice of the legal adviser to the department. If legal advice confirms that the action would be likely to be held to be unlawful, the matter should be reported in writing to the permanent head of the department.

12. There may exceptionally be circumstances in which a civil servant considers that he or she is being asked to act in a manner which appears to him or her to be improper, unethical or in breach of constitutional conventions, or to involve possible maladministration, or to be otherwise inconsistent with the standards of conduct prescribed in this memorandum and in the relevant civil service codes and guides. In such an event the matter should be reported to a senior officer, and if appropriate to the permanent head of the department.

13. Civil servants should always recall that it is ministers, and not they, who bear political responsibility. A civil servant should not decline to take, or abstain from taking, an action because to do so would conflict with his or her alternative or competing objectives and benefits; he or she should consider the possibility of declining only if taking or abstaining from the personal opinions on matters of political choice or judgement between action in question is felt to be directly contrary to deeply held personal conviction on a fundamental issue of conscience.

14. A civil servant who feels that to act or to abstain from acting in a particular way, or to acquiesce in a particular decision or course of action, would raise for him or her a fundamental issue of conscience, or is so profoundly opposed to a policy as to feel unable conscientiously to administer it in accordance with the standards described in this note, should consult a senior officer. If necessary, and if the problem cannot be resolved by any other means, the civil servant may take the matter up with the permanent head of the department and also has a right, in the last resort, to have the matter referred to the Head of the Home Civil Service through the permanent head of the department; detailed provisions for such appeals are included in the Civil

Service Pay and Conditions of Service Code.[2] If the matter still cannot be resolved on a basis which the civil servant concerned is able to accept, he or she must either carry out his or her instructions or resign from the public service – though even after resignation he or she will still be bound to keep the confidences to which he or she has become privy as a civil servant.

Notes

1 A permanent head of a department giving evidence to the Committee of Public Accounts does so by virtue of his duties and responsibilities as an accounting officer as defined in the Treasury Memorandum on the Responsibilities of an Accounting Officer; but this is without prejudice to the minister's responsibility and accountability to Parliament in respect of the policies, actions and conduct of his department.
2 Superseded by the Civil Service Management Code.

Extract from the *Civil Service Management Code*, Issue 1, February 1993. Crown copyright is reproduced with the permission of the Controller of HMSO.

A higher duty?

The 'Armstrong Memorandum' was issued following my acquittal at the Old Bailey on 11 February this year but it does not really address itself to the issue raised at the trial. Part of my defence was that in certain, albeit limited, circumstances the civil servant can have a duty over and above his normal duty to ministers. The 'Armstrong Memorandum' does not accept that any real conflict can exist and that at all times the civil servant must have total loyalty to ministers. This doctrine no longer has widespread support. As Lord Scarman said in his address to the Royal Institute of Public Administration Conference in September 1984, 'A doctrine of accountability going beyond mere service to the Crown is now seen by the public to be what they require.' Sir Robert, at his press conference introducing the memorandum, admitted that he would have been unable to advise what a civil servant should do if he is asked to mislead Parliament. What is required is a code of ethics, agreed by the civil service and the Government, setting out the duties and rights of the civil servant and providing an independent route of appeal in difficult cases.

The civil service is employed by the Crown and not by ministers. Ministers have no power to either hire or fire civil servants. But the Crown is not solely a prerogative instrument, it draws many of its powers from Parliament. Any Government must have a majority in the House of Commons to survive and also requires Parliamentary consent to legislation and finance. The Crown therefore exists in conjunction with Parliament and not in a vacuum. The civil service can be seen as employed by the 'Crown in Parliament'.

This role is already recognized in the position of the permanent secretary as accounting officer. In this latter capacity he has specific obligations to Parliament for the expenditure of public money. These obligations, it is agreed, override his duty to his minister and if the latter orders him to do something that conflicts with these obligations the permanent secretary may require the minister to give him a specific order.

The civil service does not have a duty to come to any collective view about the long-term interests of the country. It is, however, naive to assume that civil servants do not have views and that departments do not come to conclusions about the correct way to deal with certain issues of direct interest to the department. It must be for ministers to make the final decision. But the civil service, as the one continuing institution in government, does see itself as the guardian of the way in which British government should work and as holding this in trust whilst the temporary occupants, the politicians, are in power. This is seen in the rule that a government may not see the papers of its predecessor and also in the document 'Questions of Procedure for Ministers', which is handed to all new ministers on taking up office. This document enshrines the accepted doctrine of how British government should work and the civil service works on the assumption that all governments will conform to this pattern.

As the one continuing part of British government the position of the civil service must be a subject of concern to all political parties. In practice nobody is responsible for this subject. Although there is a Head of the Home Civil Service he is in the end responsible, under the 'Armstrong Memorandum', solely to the Prime Minister and must do what is required by the government of the day. In the present circumstances it is difficult to see how this job can be combined with that of Secretary to the Cabinet on grounds of workload alone.

The civil service is being put increasingly in the position of the advocate of government policy in public. This is obviously the case for those civil servants working with the media, particularly at the very top of the Whitehall machine. But civil servants are also expected to defend government policies during appearances at select committee. If these trends continue, combined with a style of government that values commitment above objectivity, then there must be real questions about the future structure of the top civil service. The worst solution would be to carry on with the current arrangements whilst leaving it to the government of the day to promote those civil servants it found sympathetic. That would be politicization via the back door. It would be preferable to consider a fundamental change in the organization of the top civil service, perhaps involving more outside appointments, not just political ones, that would break the grip of the administrative class on the top echelons of Whitehall. If this is to be a lasting reform then there ought to be some element of consensus between the parties over the new settlement.

It is one of the comforting myths of the British constitution that a minister is responsible for every action of his department. Obviously this is not true, yet it is also a comforting myth for the civil service because it avoids the need for them to accept responsibility openly. There can be little doubt that ministerial responsibility is incompatible with any attempt to fundamentally increase the responsibility of individual civil servants. The government's efficiency strategy will not make any real progress until this fundamental question is tackled.

If ministers reject the advice of a civil servant and embark on a series of impracticable policies then the civil servant must accept that decision. The submission of advice to ministers is a subtle process. Few civil servants will deliberately put advice to a minister that is clearly against the known policy of the government. Once a minister has made his views known then advice tends to get shaded in that direction; certain options are not discussed and policy is presented in a way that is known to be in line with the minister's wishes. Unless civil servants are regarded as automatons then it will be more difficult for them to carry out policies with which they disagree.

Although my trial did not change the Official Secrets Act it is in practice not enforced. Paragraph 6 of the 'Armstrong Memorandum' attempts to re-emphasize the civil service code of behaviour about confidentiality at all times. A minister can always order a civil servant to release information in the same way as ministers regularly brief the media about Cabinet meetings and other parts of the working of government. All such releases are regarded as 'authorized' under Section 2 of the Official Secrets Act.

What is now required is a code of ethics for the civil service. Most other professional bodies have such codes but in this case it would have to be agreed by the government if it is to have any force. The code should cover what a civil servant is expected to do and what actions should not be undertaken even if ordered by ministers. The First Division Association has already undertaken some preliminary work on a code and this was discussed at the 1985 Conference. If a civil servant is asked to do something that is a breach of this code then there must be a mechanism for resolving the conflict. It is not adequate, as Sir Robert Armstrong suggests, for the civil servant to be expected to resign his job, lose his career and still not reveal the reasons behind his resignation for fear of the Official Secrets Act. If the matter cannot be resolved within the department then the civil servant should be able to appeal to an outside body. This could be either the Ombudsman, a select committee of the House of Commons or some independent tribunal set up for this purpose. Whatever body is established they would need to be able to protect the position of the civil servant who had complained. The Civil Service Reform Act in the United States might provide a model.

October 1985

Written evidence to the Treasury and Civil Service Committee – *Seventh Report, 1985–86: Civil Servants and Ministers: Duties and Responsibilities, Vol. II – Annexes, Minutes of Evidence and Appendices*, HC 92–II, pp. 104–5. Reprinted in accordance with HMSO's guidelines for the reproduction of Crown and Parliamentary Copyright material.

| *Barry O'Toole*

T.H. Green and the ethics of senior officials

The aim of this article is not to present a definitive account of the ideas of Thomas Hill Green. Such accounts already exist (see, for example, Milne 1962; Richter 1964; Chapman 1965, 1966; Vincent and Plant 1984). Nor is the aim to undertake a comprehensive review of all the literature on ethics from a comparative public sector management perspective. That task would be huge and almost certainly of little value. It would be of little value because, although there are similarities between one administrative system and another, there are also wide differences, especially in administrative culture. Such differences would make the quest for generalizations applicable in all circumstances almost impossible. The aim instead is to raise questions and stimulate debate about British administrative practice in central government from a particular perspective: to examine current practice in the light of observations made by T.H. Green. In the words of Melvin Richter, 'few, if any, other philosophers exerted a greater influence upon public thought and policy than did T.H. Green'. He 'converted Philosophical Idealism . . . into something close to a practical programme for the left wing of the Liberal Party'. His tutelage led to a 'stream of serious young men dedicated to reform in politics, social work and the Civil Service' (Richter 1964: 13). In his references Richter gives long lists of people directly influenced by Green, including Bernard Bosanquet, A.C. Bradley, Edward Caird, H.S. Holland, R.L. Nettleship, D.G. Ritchie and Arnold Toynbee. These people in turn influenced others and Richter lists Lord Haldane and Sir Ernest Barker as being among these. Many others could be included in such lists and many occupied senior positions in the civil service in the first part of the present century (see also Vincent and Plant 1984: 1–5).

Whether or not Green still exerts an influence in the senior ranks of the British civil service is not the question here. What can be said in passing is that just as Northcote and Trevelyan may be seen as having laid the foundations for the structure of the present civil service so Green may be seen as being responsible (in a more indirect sense) for part at least of the philosophical and ethical outlook of the people in the service, at least in the first part of this century. If that is accepted, then it can be further argued that, through the process of socialization, so often referred to by students of the British civil service, Green still exerted an influence *at least* until the recent onset of managerialism inspired by the present government.

Be that as it may, this article seeks to raise questions about whether Green's philosophy, in particular his ideas about ethics and about the 'common good', *ought* to guide public servants in the present administrative climate. In other words, just as questions should be raised about the potentially revolutionary changes in the structure of the civil service, so this article seeks to raise questions about the ethics of civil servants. The two are linked because the attempts at inculcating so-called 'managerialism', in line with structural changes, will almost certainly have an effect on administrative ethics. Few people seem to be addressing themselves adequately to the implications of any of these changes for our system of government.

Ethics are concerned with the application of moral standards. They are, it could be argued, concerned with ranking moral values. T.H. Green suggested that morality is 'the disinterested performance of self-imposed duties' (Green 1931: 39–40). For Green the end of the institutions of civil life, namely government, was that of enabling the individual 'to give reality to the capacity [of] will: they enable him to realise his reason, i.e. his idea of self-perfection, by acting as a member of a social organisation' (Green 1931: 32–3). In other words there is a 'common good' in social organization without which an individual would not be able to realize himself. The practical question then arises as to what is this 'common good'? Further, who is to be judge and what are the sanctions of the transgressions of the 'common good'?

Green's argument is as follows. Man is conscious of himself as an end in himself. He constantly seeks personal satisfaction, in the sense of moral fulfilment or 'self-realization'. However, 'self-realization' is dependent upon relations with other members of society. Green argued that man 'cannot contemplate himself as in a better state or on the way to the best, without contemplating others, not merely as a means to that better state, but as sharing it with him' (Green 1969: 210). Thus:

> Having found his pleasures and pains dependent upon the pleasures and pains of others, he must be able, in the contemplation of a possible satisfaction of himself, to include the satisfaction of those others, and . . . a satisfaction of them as ends in themselves and not as means to his pleasure. He must, in short, be capable of conceiving and seeking a permanent well-being in which the permanent well-being of others is included.
> (Green 1969: 212; see also Richter 1964: 191–221, especially 212–15)

In other words, man's nature is to be part of society, and anything which contributes to the creation, well-being or harmony of society is to be encouraged.

The 'common good' then is the mutual harmony of all in society, brought about by each seeking his own 'self-realization' which includes the self-realization of others. Such a notion may be contrasted with Utilitarian ideas about the relationship of the individual to society.

In the Utilitarian scheme of things:

> It is in vain to talk of the interest of the community without understanding what is the interest of the individual. A thing is said to promote the interest, or to be *for* the interest, of an individual, when it tends to add to the sum total of his pleasures: or, what comes to the same thing, to diminish the sum total of his pains.
>
> (Bentham 1948: 3)

. . .

The argument so far is as follows: first, morality is the disinterested performance of self-imposed duties. These duties are performed with the intention of self-realization. Self-realization involves not just the satisfaction of self, but satisfaction of self in a society which includes others who are also concerned with their own self-realization. Thus, the ultimate end of morality is the mutual harmony of all in society, or to use Green's phrase the 'common good'. An act is moral in so far as it contributes to this 'common good', though it must have as its motive the 'common good' to be counted as being a moral act. That is, motive is important in determining the morality or otherwise of an act. Government exists to promote the 'common good' by maintaining the conditions in which morality shall be possible: it does this by removing the hindrances to the achievement of self-realization, which is the realization of self in a society which includes others.

Although all people are called upon to lead a moral life, there is one group of people upon which it is particularly incumbent to act with these moral principles in mind: the governors, both politicians and officials. Government is, after all, called upon to create the conditions in which morality shall be possible. However, it has already been noted that the prevailing moral climate, a moral climate set in particular by politicians, is Utilitarian in nature. It may even be argued that politicians, no matter what their political party, are quite incapable of acting in any other way than with Utilitarian principles in mind. This then leaves officials as being the keepers of the 'common good', or to use a phrase they might be more at home with, the 'public interest'. Or does it? The questions now become, why should we see officials as the keepers of the public interest? What indeed is the public interest from the perspective of the world as the official might *actually* perceive it? And might a code of ethics, that is to say a means of ranking moral values, help these keepers of the public interest (if indeed they can be regarded as such) in the performance of their duties?

The first problem is that it must be borne in mind that civil servants are precisely that: they are the servants of the civil institutions of society. More particularly they are the servants of ministers. Ministers, it should be remembered, are the representatives of the public in the departments of government. They are, moreover, the political heads of their respective departments and as such are accountable to Parliament, in particular to the directly elected House of Commons. Although not directly elected to their high offices as ministers, nevertheless they do have the legitimacy derived, first from (usually) having been elected to represent a particular parliamentary constituency, and secondly, of having the sanction of Parliament, in particular the House of Commons, in the performance of these duties as ministers. The constitutional convention which governs the performance of these duties as ministers is known as ministerial responsibility, of which there are two aspects: first, that the ministers collectively accept responsibility for *all* of the acts of the government as a whole, thus enabling the House of Commons, if it so wishes, to dismiss the government as a whole in a vote of censure; secondly, and more importantly, that ministers are individually responsible to Parliament for *all* the official acts of all civil servants within their particular individual departments. That is to say that it is ministers, and only ministers, as politicians and representatives of the public in departments, who are responsible and answerable for all the activities of their departments and who can face the sanction of dismissal from their office if Parliament does not approve of the actions of any of the officials within departments. Thus, no civil servant, when acting on the behalf of his department, has a constitutional personality of his own. He is always acting in the minister's name. This doctrine, the doctrine of individual ministerial responsibility to Parliament, must surely raise the question of whether it is ministers, both individually and collectively, who should be seen as the keepers of the public interest.

The problem is complicated by the fact that the convention of ministerial responsibility is derived from two higher constitutional doctrines: these are what the famous constitutional lawyer A.V. Dicey referred to as 'the twin pillars of the Constitution' – the sovereignty of Parliament and the rule of law. For present purposes the rule of law means simply this, that nobody, including ministers of the Crown, is above the law. The law has two main sources, the common law, which is essentially a system of precedents built up over the centuries by the judges, and the statute law, which is the accumulation of Acts of Parliament. The sovereignty of Parliament means essentially that no body or institution has precedence over the constitutional entity known as the Queen in Parliament. That is to say that Parliament can make and unmake any law – including codifying the common law – and that the laws that it makes are binding upon the judges and take precedence over common law.

For civil servants this constitutional position raises numerous dilemmas, most notably, where there is conflict between Parliament and the government, the question as to where the civil servant's primary loyalty must lie. Is it to the Queen's ministers? Or is it to the Queen's Parliament? Or is it to neither? Should the civil servant's loyalty be solely to the 'public interest'? This is the point at which civil servants, managers in British central government, might be called upon to make judgements about the 'public interest', and in so doing to make moral judgements in line with Green's definition of morality as 'the disinterested performance of self-imposed duties'. The duty is to the public interest. It is disinterested in the sense that personal considerations, perhaps the possibility of being dismissed or even of prosecution, ought not to play a part in the decisions made. Indeed, the personal good, which properly understood is part of the common good in Idealist philosophy, does not take into account personal considerations (Milne 1962: 105–6).

The Clive Ponting and Westland affairs illustrate this point admirably (Ponting 1985; Fry 1985; Drewry 1987; Hennessy 1986; Oliver and Austin 1987; Chapman 1986), as do the recent débâcles over the government's handling of water privatization and the Lockerbie air disaster. These episodes, and others, indicate that ministers behave politically: that is to say that their judgements are affected by party political or Parliamentary advantage considerations. Although not universally true, it is fair to say that such considerations are essentially selfish, or on the behalf of particular interests, and although they may on occasion coincide with 'the public interest', they are not primarily concerned with 'the public interest'. In Green's philosophy, a moral act is one which not only enhances the 'common good' but also has as its intention that enhancement. It is motivation which makes a good act a moral act. Moreover, any act must be considered to be a good act in itself before it can be considered a moral act, in the sense of enhancing the common good. From this it can be argued that ministers often behave in ways which make them quite unfit to be the keepers of the public interest.

If ministers are often unfit, and leaving aside civil servants for the time being, what about Parliament? Dealing first with the House of Commons it is true that in a strictly constitutional sense Members of Parliament are the representatives of their constituents. That is to say, following Edmund Burke, that they exercise their judgement on behalf of their constituents, bearing no other factor in mind except the merits of the issues before them. This, of course, is a fallacy. MPs belong to political parties. They are chosen in a majority of cases not by their local electorates but by their local constituency parties. This stems from the type of electoral system we have in this country, the so-called 'first-past-the-post' system of simple plurality which allows political parties to amass concentrations of votes making the majority of constituencies 'safe' for one party or another. If the conscience of MPs somehow survives this problem, the second problem is one of ambition and advancement once in Parliament. Most MPs seek ministerial office, and this means supporting the current leadership of their particular party in the hope of being visited by the patronage held in the hands of that leadership. Even if this is an unfair characterization it is none the less true that the vast majority of MPs belong to a political party. Whether or not an MP genuinely regards those beliefs and values as being in the national or public interest, the fact remains that such is not necessarily the case.

Turning from the Commons to the Lords. Can their noble lordships be regarded as the keepers of the public interest? They are, after all, dependent on nobody for their positions, and it is true that their deliberations are often far more sensible and reflective than those of the lower house. However, the question must be raised here as to the legitimacy of that august body the House of Lords. Many peers are hereditary: they take part in the legislative process merely because of the privilege of their birth. Of the rest, most are there because of services rendered, many because of party political services rendered. Thus, while the House of Lords may aspire to act as the only effective opposition to the present government, this lack of political legitimacy renders it incapable of acting as the keeper of the public interest.

This, then, leaves the civil service, in particular those grades which have senior and middle management roles, from permanent secretary to principal. The first objection which might be raised to thinking of civil servants as keepers of the public interest is the fact of their own lack of legitimacy. In the sense that civil servants are not elected this observation cannot be refuted. However, legitimacy may have other sources than election and may be other than party political in character.

The classic source of ideas on this matter are the writings of Max Weber, on bureaucracy, authority and legitimacy (Gerth and Wright Mills 1948: Introduction and 77–128 and 196–244). Authority for Weber was the legitimate exercise of power. Legitimacy had three possible sources, what he referred to as the Charismatic, Traditional and Legal-Rational types of authority. Granted that these are ideas and that sources of authority can be multiple, the House of Commons is primarily based on a Charismatic form of authority (expressed through the electoral process), the House of Lords on a Traditional form of authority and the civil service on a Legal-Rational form of authority. The Legal-Rational form of authority was, for Weber, the basis upon which bureaucracy, which was the 'technically superior' means of administering large and complex organizations, was built and from which it derived its legitimacy. Essentially such legitimacy depended upon knowledge and ability and strict impartiality or objectivity. And since the British civil service must be acknowledged as something approaching the extreme and delimiting case of Weber's 'Ideal Type' bureaucracy, it is in the light of these ideas that the legitimacy of the civil service can be discussed. In the first place, all civil servants are appointed according to publicly known criteria. The basis of appointment to 'apprentice' positions for senior management, the grade of Administration Trainee (AT), is first of all the possession of at least a good honours degree, supplemented by rigorous examination according to criteria designed by the Civil Service Commission. The commission was set up as a body independent of both ministers and the civil service which is charged with the responsibility of certifying that candidates have the necessary prerequisites for employment in the civil service and that they are capable of carrying out whatever duties may be assigned to them. Promotion within the service is based on merit, and only at the very top of the service, the grades of under secretary, deputy secretary and permanent secretary, is there any ministerial involvement in appointments. By the time aspiring permanent secretaries have reached the grade of assistant secretary, they have proven themselves in the arts of administration. Moreover, in the process of acquiring these arts, and partly deriving from their backgrounds and educations, they have lost (probably never even had) any vestiges of party political bias. The civil service has always prided itself on its party political neutrality and thus on the acceptability of its work on the part of all governments of whichever political party. All civil servants become 'socialized' into this atmosphere of party political neutrality and were recruited in the knowledge that they could succumb to such 'socialization'. In other words, people who have strong party political views would not normally be appointed. Indeed, it is unlikely that people with strong party political views would present themselves for consideration for appointment in the civil service (Chapman 1968).

In essence, the British civil service possesses many of the prerequisites for assuming the legitimacy deriving from Legal-Rational authority: it is recruited according to publicly known stringent criteria; promotion within it is based on merit, that is on acknowledged ability within, and specialist knowledge of, the 'political environment'; and it is strictly impartial, both as between political parties and in dealing with the public.

The question now is, does it also possess some of the possible dysfunctions of bureaucracy, most notably the insularity and self-serving tendencies identified with bureaucratic organizations? If it does, then it cannot act as the keeper of the public interest, as which, by default of other institutions of civil life, it might be called upon to act. If morality consists in the performance of acts from the motive of enhancing the 'common good' through the process of self-realization, and must also be compatible with the self-realization of others in society, then any civil servant who acts in such a way that it is the bureaucracy's interests which are being served cannot be considered to be acting for the 'common good', or more practically, 'the public interest'.

. . .

Perhaps most important of all, however, is the inability in any society, but especially in a democratic society, to get away from politics. Green does not really address himself to this question; but it is a question which needs at least to be raised here. For, as noted above, civil servants *are* servants; it is politicians as ministers who are the masters, and this is as it should be in a democratic society. However, politicians, by definition, behave politically, and political acts are not necessarily acts geared towards the 'common good' or the 'public interest'. Perhaps the question could be settled simply by asserting that there is an *acceptable* area of political controversy and political debate bounded by a perimeter of *propriety* labelled the 'public interest' or the 'common good'. When that perimeter is breached then it is the duty of *all* concerned, not just civil servants, but other politicians and citizens more widely, to act to defend that breach. But when is this perimeter to be set up? Who is to guard it or to judge whether it has been breached?

The answer to this question lies in the nature of the system of government. In most societies the system of government is established and controlled by a single, sovereign document, the constitution. In this society, however, no such document exists. And, as Richard Chapman points out in his sharp and provocative inaugural lecture, it is the highly regarded traditions of public sector management which provide one of the bases for the stability of the state (Chapman 1988b: 16–17). Or at least *provided*. Those traditions are under threat from developments apparently aimed at cutting the cost of government. As Chapman states:

> These developments seem to represent such a significant change of emphasis and ultimately of direction, that even if welcomed on the grounds of cost cutting and rolling back the frontiers of the state, they seem out of character with the highly regarded traditions, standards and expectations of public sector management in this country. It may seem premature to issue dire warnings of the dangers of corruption, but if the sorts of safeguards that worked so well in the past are removed – safeguards involving regular posting of staff, recruitment on the basis of

open competitions with the objective assessment of applicants, and socialisation which encourages the highest standards of integrity and public service as the most desirable qualities in public sector management – if these safeguards no longer exist, then it may be necessary to ask if alternative measures should be introduced to ensure that high standards of public sector management are still achievable.

(Chapman 1988b: 16–17)

In other cultures, Chapman writes, there are different safeguards against the dangers he outlines: ombudsmen, *droit administratif,* written constitutions and enforceable codes of ethics. And it is at this point that the question raised earlier may be raised again. The question is whether in the circumstances outlined a 'code of ethics' is of any practical use. Will a code of ethics help civil servants determine when the perimeter of propriety has been overstepped and give an indication of what action to take in consequence? True, in this current context it can state what the constitutional position is; it can lay down where, for most practical purposes, a civil servant's everyday duty should lie; it can establish procedures of appeal against the unfair treatment of civil servants. What it cannot do is lay down the criteria, except in the most general terms, of what it is to be 'good', or what the word 'ought' means in its ethical sense. That is to say it cannot lay down what morality is or what a moral act is in any given circumstances. This, in the end, is for the personal judgement of all individuals who must make their decisions in the light of all the evidence available to them. That is to say that ethical theory has simply this as its basis: it can lay down the criteria for what *sort* of questions an individual should raise with himself over particular situations; but it cannot lay down the questions themselves. Nor does it provide any of the answers.

And this is where T.H. Green may once again be considered. For Green, as Milne points out, a theory of morality can be of help only to the man who is trying to be moral (Milne 1962: 110–20). The question is: what are the sources of the ideas which govern that man's actions, and, of course, their morality or otherwise? For civil servants it is those very traditions which Chapman sees as being under threat from the current developments in public sector management. In the past civil servants would have had as one of their primary considerations in carrying out their work the 'public interest', in the sense of the community coming before the individual (Chapman 1988a: 313–14; 1968, 1970; O'Toole 1989). However, the prevailing moral climate is Utilitarian, and has been for at least a decade, and probably longer. Civil servants have, almost inevitably, become increasingly concerned with their own interests (O'Toole 1989; Chapman 1988a: 312–14; 1988b: 15–16). The traditions of public service, of disinterestedness and of impartiality are under threat. What really is needed now is a thoroughgoing review of the position of the civil service in government and society, perhaps a royal commission, which can raise some of the questions raised here; and provide some answers. And perhaps such a review could look to T.H. Green and his concern with the 'common good' as its inspiration. What can be said is that, in the past, civil servants could have been regarded as keepers of the 'public interest'. Today, such a proposition would be questionable. Where, then, does society turn?

References

Bentham, J. (1789) *The Principles of Morals and Legislation*, New York, Haffner (1948 edition).

Chapman, R.A. (1965) 'Thomas Hill Green, 1836–1882', *Review of Politics*, 27, 516–31.

Chapman, R.A. (1966) 'The basis of T.H. Green's philosophy', *International Review of History and Political Science*, 3, 72–88.

Chapman, R.A. (1968) 'Profile of a profession', memorandum 2 in vol. 3, no. 2 of *The Civil Service*, Fulton Committee, Cmnd 3638, London, HMSO.

Chapman, R.A. (1970) *The Higher Civil Service in Britain*, London, Constable.

Chapman, R.A. (1986) 'Whitehall and Westminster: issues for education and public debate', *Parliamentary Affairs*, 40, 133–5.

Chapman, R.A. (1988a) *Ethics in the British Civil Service*, London, Routledge.

Chapman, R.A. (1988b) *The Art of Darkness*, University of Durham.

Civil Service Commission (1988) *Annual Report*, Basingstoke, CSC.

Drewry, G. (1987) 'The Defence Committee on Westland', *Political Quarterly*, 58, 82–7.

Fry, G.K. (1985) 'Government and the civil service: a review of recent developments', *Parliamentary Affairs*, 39, 267–83.

Gerth, H.H. and Wright Mills, C. (eds) (1948) *From Max Weber*, London, Routledge and Kegan Paul.

Green, T.H. (1879) *Lectures on the Principles of Political Obligation*, London, Longmans Green and Co. (1931 edition).

Green, T.H. (1883) *Prolegomena to Ethics*, New York, Thomas Y. Cromwell. (1969 edition).

Hennessy, P. (1986) 'Michael Heseltine, Mottram's Law and the efficiency of cabinet government, *Political Quarterly*, 57, 137–43.

Milne, A.J.M. (1962) *The Social Philosophy of English Idealism*, London, George Allen and Unwin.

Oliver, D. and Austin, R. (1987) 'Political and constitutional aspects of the Westland Affair', *Parliamentary Affairs*, 40, 20–40.

O'Toole, B.J. (1989) *Private Gain and Public Service: the Association of First Division Civil Servants*, London, Routledge.

Ponting, C. (1985) *The Right to Know: the Inside Story of the Belgrano Affair*, London, Sphere Books.

Richter, M. (1964) *The Politics of Conscience: T.H. Green and His Age*, London, Weidenfeld and Nicolson.

Vincent, A. and Plant, R. (1984) *Philosophy, Politics and Citizenship: the Life and Thought of the British Idealists*, Oxford, Basil Blackwell.

Abridged from B.J. O'Toole (1990) 'T.H. Green and the ethics of senior officials in British central government', *Public Administration*, Vol. 68, pp. 337–52. Reproduced with the permission of Blackwell Publishers.

A Civil Service Code

1. The constitutional and practical role of the civil service is, with integrity, honesty, impartiality and objectivity, to assist the duly constituted Government, of whatever political complexion, in formulating policies of the Government, carrying out decisions of the Government and administering services for which the Government is responsible in the interests of the public.

2. Civil servants are servants of the Crown. Constitutionally the Crown acts on the advice of ministers and, subject to the provisions of this Code, civil servants owe their loyalty to the duly constituted Government.

3. Civil servants should serve the duly constituted.Government in accordance with the principles set out in this Code and recognizing

- the duty of all public officers to discharge their public functions reasonably and according to law;
- the duty to respect, comply with and obey the law of the land, international law and the provisions of international treaties to which the United Kingdom is a party and not to imperil the due administration of justice;
- those duties which may arise as members of professions.

4. This Code should be seen in the context of the duties and responsibilities of ministers set out in Questions of Procedure for Ministers which include:

- the duty to give Parliament and the public as full information as possible about the policies, decisions and actions of the Government, and not to deceive or mislead Parliament and the public;
- the duty to give fair consideration and due weight to informed and impartial advice from civil servants, as well as to other considerations and advice, in reaching policy decisions; and
- the duty to comply with the law of the land;

together with the duty to familiarize themselves with the contents of this Code and not to ask civil servants to act in breach of it.

5. Civil servants should conduct themselves with integrity, fairness and honesty in their dealings with ministers, Parliament and the public. They should make all information and advice relevant to a decision available to ministers. They should not deceive or mislead ministers, Parliament or the public.

6. Civil servants should endeavour to deal with the affairs of the public efficiently, and without maladministration.

7. Civil servants should endeavour to ensure the proper, effective and efficient use of public money within their control.

8. Civil servants should not make use of their official position or information acquired in the course of their official duties to further private interests. They should not receive benefits of any kind from a third party which might reasonably be seen to compromise their personal judgement or integrity.

9. Civil servants should conduct themselves in such a way as to deserve and retain the confidence of ministers, and to be able to establish the same relationship with those whom they may be required to serve in some future administration. The conduct of civil servants should be such that ministers and potential future ministers can be sure that that confidence can be freely given, and that the civil service will conscientiously fulfil its duties and obligations to, and impartially assist, advise and carry out the policies of the duly constituted Government.

10. Civil servants should not misuse information which they acquire in the course of their duties or seek to frustrate the policies, decisions or actions of Government by the unauthorized, improper or premature disclosure outside the Government of any confidential information to which they have had access as civil servants.

11. Where a civil servant believes he or she is being required to act in breach of this Code or in a way which is illegal, improper, or in breach of constitutional conventions or which may involve possible maladministration, he or she should first report the matter in accordance with procedures laid down in Government guidance or rules of conduct.

12. Where a civil servant has reported a matter in accordance with procedures laid down in Government guidance or rules of conduct and believes that the response does not represent a reasonable response to the grounds of his or her reporting of the matter, he or she may report the matter in writing to the Civil Service Commissioners.

13. Civil servants should not seek to frustrate the policies, decisions or actions of Government by declining to take, or abstaining from taking, action which flows from clearly recorded ministerial decisions. Where a matter cannot be resolved by the procedures set out in paragraphs 11 and 12 above on a basis which the civil servant concerned is able to accept, he or she should either carry out ministerial instructions or resign from the civil service.

From the Treasury and Civil Service Committee, *Fifth Report, 1993–94: the Role of the Civil Service – Vol. 1*, HC 27–I, Annex 1. Reprinted in accordance with HMSO's guidelines for the reproduction of Crown and Parliamentary Copyright material.

| *Sir Geoffrey Chipperfield*

The civil servant's duty

I have . . . identified three different sets of duties which are relevant in the civil service context – the duty to set and live by one's own standards; the duty to one's minister and the wider duty to the system of government under which we live. I have said why I think that the two latter duties would only very rarely conflict. But if they do and the official concerned cannot persuade his hierarchical seniors and minister that he is right, then he, depending on the seriousness of the matter, should either seek to be moved to another post, or leave the service. It is analogous to the position of a barrister whose client asks him to act in a manner which he considers incompatible with his duty to the court.

Perhaps more difficult is the duty to set and to maintain one's own standards. This is shorthand for the responsibility to refer every one of the myriad of practical decisions which have to be taken at every moment of the working life to one's own code of conduct and ethics. These decisions range from the trivial, such as, should I stay late at work to get something up to the minister to give him more time to read it (although the probability is that he will not look at it at all)?; through the more important, such as, ought I to include a particular argument in a brief which I think irrelevant but which might influence the minister if he saw it; to the fundamental, such as, what you are asking me to do is dishonest but perhaps dishonesty is essential (e.g. denying that the devaluation of sterling is being considered). I have already said that I regard it as an overriding duty to think about these duties and decide upon their priority; and so I regard it as imperative for every individual to consider and make decisions themselves on issues such as these. Unless he can do this he can have no self respect and – apart from any psychological need he may have for possessing self respect – lack of it means that no one else will respect him. If an official does not have a respect for his own ethical values he will never be able to establish the relationship with ministers which I regard as essential. Do not think these decisions are easy – they are not. They frequently have to be taken in a rush, and with insufficient knowledge. We do not live in an ideal world: compromises are necessary if anything is to be achieved. Judging what is the necessary compromise is a fine and delicate art, and no two people will ever come to the same decisions on all points. So one thing more is necessary – there has to be respect for the decisions of others, when they differ from one's own. The only qualification is that they must be real decisions; not simply a repetition of views put forward by others.

Discussion of ethics could be endless, but all I really wish to say has been better said by Sir Michael Quinlan in his essay *Ethics and the Public Sector* published by the First Division Association. I do not agree with everything he says, but his analysis of the interaction between a civil servant's ethical principles and his activities is outstanding. He sees no conflict between the two, provided the civil servant properly understands his role: this view I share. But the proper understanding of this role is crucial. It is not one of the expert at large; the assistant to the legislature; the servant of the public; the helper of the academic or the media.

There is one practical consequence which follows from this emphasis on the need for the individual to make up his own mind and take responsibility for his actions. It is the danger of introducing a code of conduct. I think the existence of any such code would reduce the pressure on an individual to take responsibility for his own actions. There will always be a temptation, if such a code is in place, for him to look to the code to tell him what to do, rather than to take the decision himself. The argument that such a code might make it easier for people to act in accordance with their consciences might well, unfortunately, be true. Their consciences would be less exercised and weaker, and therefore easier to obey. Nor, digressing slightly, do I believe that a code is necessary because the hierarchy is itself corrupted. If corruption is being used to mean indifference to ethical values – for example, whether to tell the truth – I simply do not believe this to be true. I suspect the word is being used to mean disagreement about the job description – for example, whether a particular piece of work falls within the description of work that a civil servant does because it is of advantage to a political party. There can be genuine differences of view about the interpretation of the rules governing such matters and to call those who disagree with you 'corrupt' is to misuse the word.

I have been discussing the duties of a civil servant very much from the point of view of the 'administrative class' civil servant who works closely with ministers in a well-defined tradition of government. I believe that this tradition has great strengths of economy, democratic responsiveness and efficiency. That is not to say that it cannot be improved – but beware of throwing out the baby with the bathwater. I welcome many of the managerial changes being introduced into the service, but the question should be put, each time a change is contemplated, what the effect of it on this tradition will be. There are, in particular, two changes which could impinge significantly on it. The first is the increasing use of contract, as opposed to career, staff in the senior ranks of the service, and the second is the development of executive agencies.

. . .

One cannot, of course, discuss the duties and responsibilities of civil servants in relation to ministers without looking at the so-called Armstrong Memorandum of the same title, now enshrined in the Conditions of Service of Civil Servants. Does this document discuss these duties adequately? And, if not, why not?

The answer to the first question is, in my view, no. The memorandum is full of references to duty but the meaning of the word shifts. Sometimes it refers to an implied contract of employment – e.g. you are to do what you are told – and sometimes it describes the standards of service you should give – e.g. 'It is the duty of civil servants to serve their ministers . . . to the best of their ability.' But there is also a third usage which could be read into the document – an implication that the duty to one's minister is a superior form of duty to other duties. This is not explicit, except perhaps in the sentence, 'It is of the first importance that civil servants conduct themselves in such a way as to deserve and retain the confidence of ministers.' Someone familiar with the culture would not, perhaps, read this sentence in that way but I suggest that the whole minatory and exhortatory approach of the memorandum, and the lapidary phraseology which encapsulates it, lends itself to that interpretation. The authors of the document were, I feel, insufficiently careful that many of its readers could so read it.

The comments on duty as related to standards of service – 'It is the duty of civil servants to serve ministers . . . to the best of their ability' – are unhelpful. High flown sentiments such as these not only get us nowhere – except to inspire a vague feeling of guilt – but actually stand in the way of good management. The public sector has consistently failed – although there have recently been heroic efforts to improve – to get precise objectives for its staff, and to match performance to them. You have the obligation under any contract of employment to do your job to the standard required for that job. Your employer should set that standard for you: it may be above or below 'the best of your ability'. If it is above, then you should be moved or sacked; if it is below, you have no obligation to do more than match the standard required. What you do with the rest of your ability is your affair. But to talk of doing one's job to 'the best of one's ability' simply allows the employer to slide out of the difficult task of telling you what standard he wants, and monitoring your performance against it.

But it is the first usage – the contract of employment usage – where I find the memorandum out of kilter with my experience of how the system works. Although there are a number of references to collective government, the basic text is, 'The duty of the individual civil servant is first and foremost to the minister of the Crown who is in charge of the department in which he or she is working' – presumably because he is the paymaster and employer. But if we took this concept of duty literally we would have no collective Cabinet government, but a collection of warring ministerial baronies; not a rationally constructed bureaucracy, but individuals and groups each entitled to claim direct instructions and guidance from their minister without any recognition that there were other departments or ministers who had a right to understand and influence whatever actions were in progress. Now civil servants and ministers do not work like this. Civil servants across Whitehall work with each other because the culture is that policies are collective, and that all those who may be affected – which invariably includes the central departments – must be consulted. They feel a duty and responsibility to their colleagues in other departments to see that this is done. This feeling is based on their belief that one of their duties is to keep 'the system' – which I have earlier said includes a commitment to one unified government – going.

Now it is easy to be unfair to the Armstrong Memorandum and many have been. We must remember, however, the circumstances under which it was issued. Clive Ponting had been acquitted, and it was necessary for the Head of the Civil Service to make it clear to civil servants that behaviour such as Ponting's – the leakage of confidential information – could not be tolerated if the relationship between ministers and civil servants was to continue in its present form. It was not a philosophic treatise, nor an all-embracing manifesto designed to deal with all individual difficulties and problems. Criticism that it is restrictive and negative fails to understand its particular purpose; indeed, a more valid criticism might be that it goes beyond its particular purpose, and tangles with wider issues than it need. I am not suggesting that it was inadequate in its time and in its context. But it does not provide a comprehensive guide to the duties of a civil servant in relation to ministers and is of little help to the civil servant grappling with his day-to-day problems.

So my second question is, could it have provided a more comprehensive and helpful guide? The answer is, alas, probably no. Constitutional practice is, as anyone who has ever read a constitutional textbook should know, ever at variance with constitutional theory. To try to codify that practice – to obtain agreement that it is not only the way the system works but ought to work – would probably destroy the practice. If, as I believe, the practice is beneficial, don't risk such destruction. Let the misleading theory remain the public doctrine. Hypocrisy is, perhaps, a necessary part of good government. I doubt if any formulation of the practices which I have described could have been found which would not have raised anguished cries about the sovereignty of Parliament and the independence of ministers. Lord Armstrong may have been wise not to attempt to do so. But the result has been confusion within and without the civil service about how the system works and the motivation which guides many civil servants in their work. For some civil servants it has raised doubts about how they are supposed to work.

So I conclude by setting out the sort of guidance which I would give a young fast stream civil servant who would be likely to be engaged in policy work, in an attempt to describe to him what his job would be and what his personal responsibility should be in responding to it. It would run something like this.

'As a civil servant advising ministers on policy issues you are part of the central machinery of UK government. Your role is to act in the way best calculated to make that machinery work effectively. The machinery is subtle, complex and has evolved over many years. It is an integral part of the system of Parliamentary democracy which exists in this country. You are not here to reshape that system, whatever you may think of it, but to help it to work.

'You can accomplish this task only by remembering the limits within which you operate. You are part of a team across Whitehall which must work together in an atmosphere of trust if it is to work effectively in taking forward collective

Government decisions. But you are an official working for a particular minister who must be the principal means by which your work is carried forward. Your main function must therefore be to serve him, and you must make your relationship with him one in which he listens to – even if he does not follow – your advice; respects your expertise, your knowledge, your official (as opposed to your personal) commitment to his policies; and acknowledges your independence of mind and views.

'None of this will be easy because much will depend on your own judgements of how and when matters should be pursued and there can be tensions between the demands of individual ministers and the working of the collective system; or, if you prefer it, between your employment as an employee of the minister, and your role as a professional with the wider remit of making the system work. Fortunately these tensions do not often arise because the obligations you have as a professional will, most often, coincide with those of an employee. These obligations cover not only knowledge of your subject, but also confidentiality about matters you learn about in your job, and the development of trust and respect in those above, below and about you. Your peers, who know the pressures you are under, will judge your success but you will also have the benefit of a hierarchy who will seek to produce order and to deliver instructions but, at the same time, to guide and maintain professional standards and to buttress independence.

'Do not, however, expect explicit guidance and instruction on how to perform the many activities which will involve decisions on what to do, or to say, to whom, and when, and how to do it. You will be faced, as in all human activities, with conflicts of priorities which you will have to decide yourself in accordance with your own ethical views. It is in the highest degree unlikely that your ministers will ask you to act contrary to those views, and if they do, help through the hierarchy is at hand.

'Both ministers and your seniors will expect you to have thought out your ethical position in relation to the posts you hold and the positions you occupy. You cannot, and should not, rely on any code of conduct which others, either as masters or colleagues, may purport to draw up. To do so would be to resign your duty to take decisions for yourself and to condemn yourself to losing the respect of others. You may still lose that respect if your decisions are ill thought out, but that is a risk you will have to take. To refuse to take such a risk on the grounds that others can decide matters better than you is incompatible with the work that you have been employed to do.'

Abridged from G. Chipperfield (1994) 'The civil servant's duty', *Essex Papers in Politics and Government No. 95*, Colchester, University of Essex. Reproduced with the permission of the Department of Government, University of Essex.

Peter Jay

Public duty and public interest

In Western liberal democracies it is fundamental that we do not accept the automatic equivalence of all and any government's behaviour with the public interest, whatever Judge McCowan may have supposed to the contrary. That, after all, is what most of us understand Nuremburg, the Eichmann trial and a thousand other similar, though lesser, precedents to have been all about. We cannot therefore seriously accept the simple notion that a public servant's sole duty is one of overriding and absolute loyalty to the government no matter what it and its individual members do or propose to do.

It follows that we cannot escape the need then to examine the somewhat intricate issues which arise when we begin to try to draw the line which defines the point where a public servant's first and normal duty of loyalty as an employee of the government stops and begins to be outweighed by other, perhaps higher, duties to the public interest, duties to which he is subject as a citizen in a liberal democracy and as a man in a culture which rightly regards individual conscience as the highest moral authority of all.

So let me begin by asking some rather basic questions about the nature of the animal – the public or civil servant – whose duties I am trying to define.

. . .

What may we conclude about what is meant by 'a civil servant'? Clearly, some of the terms used to describe him are intended to include other people too, although at the same time they tell us some pertinent things about how civil servants are thought of or supposed to be, since civil servants are included in those categories.

Making allowance for this, we may decide that the following notions are included in the concept of a civil servant:

(a) that he serves and owes a duty;
(b) that he is a civilian and a citizen;

(c) that he belongs to a disciplined service with a command structure;
(d) that it is part of his role, at times, to represent and act as the agent of or in the name of either the state or the government or both;
(e) that he is – and has the rights and duties of – an employee;
(f) that he gives advice; and
(g) that the entity in relation to which he is and does all these things is variously, perhaps confusedly, ministers, the government, the state, the Crown and the public.

Can we distil all this into a single description? Only at the price of doing violence to the complexity of the concept of a civil servant in common usage. But for simplicity we can perhaps say that a civil servant is:

- a human being;
- a citizen and a civilian;
- an adviser to ministers;
- an employee of government;
- an officer of the Crown;
- an official of the state;
- a servant of the public.

What, then, are his human and citizen obligations?

Our starting point must be that a civil servant, like anyone else in a specific position whose professional ethics are to be judged, is first and foremost a human being. This reflects the fundamental ethical axiom that it is as people that we have moral duties and that those sub-sets of special duties which arise from finding ourselves in particular situations (e.g. a doctor subscribing to the Hippocratic oath, a priest preserving the secrecy of the confessional or a soldier carrying out an order) are just that, namely sub-sets of the general moral obligations of man, derived from them and therefore logically incapable of overriding the premises from which they derive.

This does not, of course, mean that a man subject to a professional ethic may not find himself morally obliged to act too differently from how he would act if he were not subject to that special ethic. A journalist may feel duty-bound to protect a source, even when legally ordered to disclose it, where a shop-keeper in possession of the same information from the same source would not feel so constrained. A doctor may feel obliged to save the life of some evil monster whom the ordinary citizen would feel justified in leaving to nature's mercies. An airman may feel duty-bound to drop a bomb where a civilian might recoil from such a deed.

But it is vital to recognize that these differences arise, not because there is some completely independent and different ethical code for those in professional or functional positions, but because the very fact that professional people are in the positions that they are in itself changes the context and means that somewhat different obligations flow from the same basic ethical premises that apply to all mankind. The first of those premises may be that everyone is morally accountable, at least to himself, for all the reasonably foreseeable consequences of his free actions. That being so, allowance has to be made for the fact that different consequences may flow from a professional person acting in a certain way from those that would follow if an ordinary citizen did so. A journalist who makes free with his sources, a doctor who violates his oath, an airman who disobeys a lawful command, all thereby call into question public confidence in the behaviour and reliability of those who are designated members of such professions. Moreover, it may not just be that the public's confidence in the predictable behaviour of people in such positions will be eroded. It may also be that quite specific undertakings given by the person in that position are broken, for example by the journalist who discloses a source to whom he has promised absolute confidentiality as a condition of being given the information in question.

. . .

But – and this too is vital – those obligations are not absolutely overriding. If after taking account of all the reasonably foreseeable consequences of his actions – *including* the precedent-setting and confidence-damaging effects described above – a professional person is convinced that he would be wrong to act in the way his professional ethic appears to constrain him to act, because this would conflict with his higher duties as a citizen and as a human being, then he will be convinced that he would be wrong so to act; and others must respect that. It does not follow that he is necessarily entitled to legal protection for his act of conscience. Nor does it follow that others must agree with his reasoning as to where his duty lies. But it does mean that he is entitled to be upheld morally for insisting that his obligations as a human being are ultimately superior to any merely professional obligations which he believes, after careful reflection, to be irreconcilable with his human duty.

. . .

This, of course, does not mean that any old duty of a citizen or a human being overrides every professional duty. Clearly people in responsible positions are excused certain duties of the ordinary citizen precisely in order that they can perform their professional roles. Doctors, by and large, are permitted to park more freely than other citizens. A soldier obviously cannot duck his military duties, which may include shooting to kill, simply on the grounds that a civilian citizen would not be expected to do such a thing – or even forgiven if he did. People in general are encouraged on moral grounds to be truthful, candid and forthcoming. But it is not always the duty of the civil servant, the diplomat or the banker, for example, to follow these precepts. Sometimes, indeed, it is their duty not to.

So, the duty of a civil servant to override his professional obligations with his duties as a citizen and human being only applies in the sense of his obligation to consider all the reasonably foreseeable consequences of his actions. Such consideration will take into account the fact that it is often necessary and beneficial for people in specific roles to be expected to behave and actually to behave differently from how they would if they were just ordinary citizens. It is only if, after that has been fully taken into account together with the precedent-setting and confidence-eroding effects of violating his professional duty, it still appears that the future sum of welfare of mankind will be worse if he follows his professional duty than if he defies it, that he is morally entitled, indeed obliged, so to defy it.

What are his official obligations?

Let me recall that previously I concluded that a civil servant could be accurately described as, in addition to human being, citizen and civilian: an adviser to ministers; an employee of government; an officer of the Crown; an official of the state; and a servant of the public.

What does this entail? The First Division Association's 'Possible code of ethics for civil servants' tackles this in its opening paragraph in the following words:

> Civil servants in the United Kingdom are servants of the Queen in Parliament. Executive government as a function of the crown is carried out by Ministers who are accountable to Parliament. Civil servants therefore owe to Ministers the duty to serve them loyally and to the best of their ability.

This formulation, though masterly in its blurring of all the tricky issues, simply will not do as a premise from which to reason about the professional ethics of civil servants. It will not do because it is itself incoherent. If civil servants are servants of the Queen in Parliament, whatever that is, then it does not logically follow that they have a duty of any kind to ministers as the agents of the Crown in carrying on the executive government. Clerks of the House of Commons are presumably servants of the Queen in Parliament; but they owe no duty to ministers, except in their role as members of Parliament.

The Crown is not, in this context, a subordinate arm of something called the Queen in Parliament. The Crown is the Crown, i.e. the monarch or the authority vested in the monarch. The Crown by itself cannot make laws. That is the prerogative of the Queen in Parliament. But the Crown can carry out the function of executive government; and it alone can do so, although what it can and cannot do in that role is limited by law and by the practical need to command a majority in the House of Commons in order to be able to vote supply and to pass necessary legislation, including the budget.

Moreover, civil servants, if they were servants of the Queen in Parliament and owed to ministers a duty to serve them loyally etc., would face a chronic conflict of duties, since ministers, as the agents of executive government, are constantly in conflict with Parliament, to which indeed, as the 'possible code' says, they are accountable for their stewardship of the function of executive government. What Parliament – and perhaps the Queen in Parliament, whatever that may be – wants, expects and needs of its loyal servants may frequently be in conflict with what ministers want, expect and need of theirs.

Far from a duty to the one following from a duty to the other, the two are incompatible, notwithstanding the fact that conflicts between ministers and Parliament are resolved by mechanisms – proceedings and votes in Parliament – which do not directly involve civil servants as such. Indeed, the FDA preamble is about as helpful as if it said, 'Men are creatures of God. Evil, as part of God's total creation, is carried out by Mammon. Men, therefore, owe to Mammon the duty to serve him loyally and to the best of their ability'.

Civil servants manifestly work for the executive government, not for Parliament and not for the Queen in any of her roles other than that of the Crown as the embodiment of executive authority. Equally clearly the conduct of the executive government is vested in ministers, which is why the prime minister is correctly described as head of government.

It is for this reason that civil servants – under all the descriptions as 'advisers to ministers', 'employees of the government', 'officers of the Crown' and 'officials of the state' – owe to ministers the duty to serve them loyally and to the best of civil servants' abilities. The FDA's initial conclusion is right, so far as it goes, but not its premise or its reasoning.

However, it is important to be clear that it is to ministers in their role as those in whom the conduct of executive government is vested that civil servants owe their duty, not to ministers as the people who occupy the post of minister, whatever they may do.

. . .

Some conclusions about civil servants

The conclusions must, I think, be that a civil servant owes a very heavy primary duty of loyalty and best endeavour to the national government which, to them as advisers to ministers, employees of the government, officers of the crown and officials of the state, is their employer, master, commander-in-chief and lawful superior. But this duty is prima facie, not absolute; and it cannot override all other considerations.

We have already dealt with the possibility that a civil servant's duty as a human being or as a citizen may in prescribed circumstances override his professional duty and loyalty. We have also seen that a duty to ministers is not a duty to the people who are ministers, only to those people acting as ministers. If they act improperly as ministers, the civil servant's correct response will depend on circumstances. If the impropriety is illegal, he almost certainly has a citizen's duty to report it, in the first instance to his departmental superiors and, conceivably, if they fail to act without good reason, to the law enforcement agencies direct.

If the act is unlawful, it may or may not be a particular civil servant's business. If it is not, he may judge that it is not incumbent upon him to do or say anything, though again circumstances could arise in which he felt he was in effect being drawn into complicity in the unlawful act, in which case again the first line of defence must be to report it to his departmental superiors.

He will also be right to refuse to take any positive act which he believes, if necessary after taking legal advice, would involve him in unlawful complicity. If again his superiors take no action – and even appear to condone the unlawful act – he may feel that the remedy for anyone who is affected by this act is in the courts. But cases may arise where the damage is diffused among so many people, perhaps the whole population, or where the chain of cause and effect between improper deed and dire consequences for the public is so long and complex, that it is unlikely that any member of the public will be aware of the specific act and its effects on him. In this case the choice may lie between, on the one hand, deciding that he has done all that he can properly do as a civil servant and, on the other, resigning. Even if he resigns, he will have to decide whether to expose the wrong-doing in violation maybe of his continuing obligations under the Official Secrets Act (if it has not been replaced by a saner law which does not have the effect of protecting from public gaze the perpetration of unlawful acts). In that event he will have to go back to his basic moral obligations as a citizen and as a human being and decide where the balance of duty lies, though this may or may not help him if and when legal proceedings are brought against him.

If the action is neither illegal nor unlawful, but simply improper, then again the civil servant will have to go through a sort of logic-tree to decide how he should act. First, is the minister purporting to act as a minister and thereby to make the action in some sense an act of the government to which the civil servant owes his duty of loyalty? If not, then on the face of it it may be none of the civil servant's business, though he may need to be careful not to act in such a way as to appear to become implicated in the improper private or party act in a way which would bring him and his service into disrepute or damaging controversy. If it is none of the civil servant's business officially or legally, he may still have to consult his human and citizen obligations; and, if the impropriety was so gross as to justify effective action against it, then again he must so act.

If, on the other hand, the impropriety is one where the minister is indeed purporting to act as a minister, then again it is likely to be the civil servant's duty in the first instance so to advise the minister, secondly to raise the matter with his superiors in his department and, if all that fails to answer, then again to consider the options of resignation and/or effective, though disloyal, action to frustrate or expose the impropriety.

. . .

Lastly, we come to the question of how far should a civil servant go in assisting his minister in achieving party political objectives. It is all very well to say that he should not and that, for example, the private office must leave it to the party headquarters to arrange transport to and maybe from events (but what if the next event is a government event?). This is not really the issue. When it comes to the substance of policies and the public presentation of them, it becomes very hard to distinguish the partisan from the governmental.

. . .

The key here is that 'non-political' does not mean 'unconnected with politics' in any broad sense of politics which includes the whole process of government. The process of government is precisely what all civil servants are concerned with all the time, unlike even politicians. 'Non-political' when applied to civil servants, perhaps also when applied in other contexts such as the campaigning activities of charities, must mean 'not motivated by a wish to secure an electoral advantage for one party or another'. The Chancellor's budget etc. may try to do just that; and the civil servants may of necessity do 99 per cent of the work in preparing it. But so long as the partisan skew was supplied by the Chancellor and the civil servants were not motivated by the wish to impart it, then their behaviour is not improper.

If, none the less, they feel so strongly that the policy is wrong as a policy – not because it is illegal, unlawful or improper, but just wrong – then their right course must either be to grin and bear it or to resign and argue their point of view, though in this case without there being any justification for damaging indiscretions based on what they learnt from their official position.

There may be some positions in government where it becomes next to impossible for the ethics of a non-political service to be reconciled with the official duties imposed upon a civil servant. For example, while I make no personal criticism at all, least of all of impropriety, I cannot persuade myself that the job of chief press officer at 10 Downing Street can ever again be reconciled with anyone's honest conception of a permanent civil servant's political neutrality. The idea that Mr Ingham – or indeed some of his predecessors – were indifferent to and inactive in trying to bring about the result of the last, or indeed many previous, general elections is just plain nonsense.

This suggests a broader point on which to conclude, namely that it may be becoming progressively more necessary candidly to recognize that a very much larger band of sensitive Whitehall jobs, mainly concerned with policy formation and public presentation of the Government's case, need to be redefined as 'political', especially now that it seems no longer to be assumed that ministers can be relied upon to put over the case unaided by troops of weird 'advisers' and now that sincere belief in the government's mission to save the nation by its own unique set of policies has become such an emotionally demanded quality.

This does not mean that these sensitive posts will get filled by party hacks, as the American experience graphically proves. Indeed, this route of so-called 'political' appointment is almost invariably responsible for the highest talent and expertise in the American administration. But it does mean that people who among other things – maybe a long way second to their specialist expertise – have vague partisan loyalties can be used in the kind of sensitive positions mentioned without creating the moral dilemma that such jobs pose for the non-political permanent civil servant.

Abridged from P. Jay (1985) 'Pontius or Ponting: public duty and public interest in secrecy and disclosure', in Royal Institute of Public Administration, *Politics, Ethics and Public Service*, London, RIPA, pp. 69–92 (based upon the Shell Lecture delivered in Glasgow, 22 May 1985). Reproduced with the permission of Touche Ross and Co., liquidators for the RIPA; Shell UK Ltd; and Peter Jay.

5

Reforming Whitehall I: hopes, visions and landmarks

Debate and controversy surround the 'new managerialism'. There is disagreement as to whether it is a force for good or ill; about how and under what conditions its potential (if any) can be harnessed to the imperatives of the British system of government; and as to where it is leading. There are disputes no less as to what exactly constitutes this new managerialism and as to how it emerged within Whitehall and how extensively it has been adopted. Whatever its genesis, most would agree that the 1980s saw a change of gear – at least in the outer manifestation of new or refashioned initiatives, if not also in administrative culture. Most, too, would agree that the 1990s have seen a consolidation of these initiatives, perhaps with some potentially crucial further shifts of emphasis.

Included in this section are two extracts from addresses given by Sir Robin Butler. In the first (Reading 5.1) he acknowledges the expression 'new public management' to describe the changes taking place. He summarizes the main forces which came together to produce the necessary momentum. Here he was giving the Frank Stacey Memorial Lecture to the annual conference of the Joint University Council Public Administration Committee in September 1992.

As Head of the Home Civil Service, Butler has views that may be taken to represent if not quite the government position then at least the 'official' position, inasmuch as there is one. Other official publications have done so in more detail. As a scene-setting document few now doubt the significance of what quickly became known as the Ibbs Report. Strictly speaking, this was a report to the Prime Minister by the PM's Efficiency Unit, rather than a statement of government policy. It nevertheless received swift endorsement. The part of the report reproduced here (Reading 5.2) sets out the main findings of the enquiry undertaken by the Efficiency Unit and the conclusions drawn from those findings. In some ways, Ibbs was an echo of Fulton. This was evident in the attempt to engineer a division of labour between policy and management operations; in its penchant for more transparently accountable management; and in its recommendations for hiving work off into semi-independent agencies. Note, though, the loss of faith in a unified career service, a signal departure from the thinking twenty years earlier. What has surprised some people is the speed and the extent to which executive agencies have become an established feature.

Two further initiatives have been conspicuous in the attempt to maintain the momentum: the Citizen's Charter and market testing. With the launch of the Citizen's Charter the government claimed 'the most comprehensive pro-gramme ever to raise quality, increase choice, secure better value, and extend accountability'. Few would deny that, in principle and at face value, this is indeed an ambitious undertaking. Exactly how ambitious can be judged by the introductory section to the White Paper, issued in July 1991 (Reading 5.3). The same reading also contains the declaration of principles of public service, as revised in The Citizen's Charter Second Report: 1994 (Cm 2540). Hard on the heels of the Citizen's Charter came market testing – the process by which areas of government activity would be examined (i.e. tested) to ascertain their suitability for transfer or contracting out to the private sector. This, the government said, was a logical extension of the deliberations involved in conferring executive agency status under the Next Steps programme. Market testing was announced under the guise of 'competing for quality', the title of the White Paper published in November 1991 (Reading 5.4).

One may ask where all this is leading. Where, indeed, *does* it leave the civil service? What vision, if any, do government ministers and others involved have as to the ultimate goal, or at least as to the broad direction? In the piece introduced above (Reading 5.1), Sir Robin Butler made reference to the work of David Osborne and Ted Gaebler. Their book, *Reinventing Government*, provoked intense and widespread interest, first in America and then in Britain, when it was published in 1992. As Butler implies, and as most academics know, such treatises are rarely the inspiration for reform in British public adminis-tration. But the central thesis of their book (Reading 5.5) expresses much not only of what certain outsiders think but also of what the British Government seems to think it is doing. And in the second of his addresses included here – this one to the FDA – Sir Robin Butler offers his vision for the future (Reading 5.6). As a civil servant, he eschews naked prescriptions. He knows that tomorrow or the day after he may find himself serving another political master. He contents himself with an exposition as to where, from his perspective, current policies are leading as distinct from other policies which might or should have been adopted or as to where existing policies ought to be directed. This task he leaves to the politicians. In a paper published in February 1993, William Waldegrave provided the synoptic vision (Reading 5.7). Waldegrave was at that time Minister for Public Service and Science. Within eighteen months he had moved to another cabinet post, perhaps justifying Sir Robin Butler in his earlier caution. Waldegrave's exposition nevertheless holds as far as the Major Government is concerned.

This chapter concentrates, then, predominantly on initiatives as seen from the perspective of the government and of those who operate in its slipstream. It is as well fully to understand the ideas and stated intentions associated with official policies. It is only right, in a democracy, that the Government's voice be heard. This is sometimes overlooked. But the critics also should be heard. They can sometimes better express the unstated assumptions, the subtexts and the possible consequences of official policies. To these aspects they can often alert us more readily than perhaps the government is able or willing to contemplate. In answering the question, 'where is it all leading?' the critics have tended to differ as much from themselves as from government. In the next chapter the critics will therefore have their say.

5.1	Sir Robin Butler

The new public management

It came as something of a surprise for some of us to find that those of you studying our goldfish bowl – still more like a goldfish bowl to those inside, I suspect, than those outside it – have identified that we are now swimming about in something called 'the new public management'.

But I think that the label – while exotic – is quite helpful in drawing attention to both the evolutionary and revolutionary changes in public management that we have experienced in the last two decades. At least, it is helpful provided that it is treated in the way that Christopher Hood described in his inaugural lecture at the LSE: 'a convenient if somewhat loose shorthand'. We have not embraced a doctrine but do respect some of the articles of faith.

I do not propose to replay here Christopher Hood's summary of what he calls the 'familiar litany of new management principles'. But I do want to pick up two of the points which he makes in that address: first, that the genesis for many of the ideas came from the private sector and consultancy, rather than from academics; secondly, that new public management is no mere flash in the pan.

Genesis

Observed from where I sit, the structural and management changes that we have seen in the recent past – and not just in this country but around the developed world – have been the result of a whole series of forces and influences. These combined to produce the momentum for the changes which are taking place. Let me pick out a few.

First, the demand for public services targeted to the needs of each individual, together with the availability of more and more techniques for meeting those needs, have put the resources available to the providers under immense strain. In the United Kingdom, the National Health Service is the most obvious example, but this is true of the public services generally. It is not surprising that the providers of such services, at their wits' end in their effort to cope, have been tempted to put considerate treatment of the consumer low down that scale of priorities, particularly if they were monopoly providers and the customers could not go elsewhere.

Secondly, the hopes that effective means of coping would come from 'economies of scale' – the watchwords of the 1960s and early 1970s – have faded. People realized the downside of scale: the loss of control and loss of personal responsibility and ownership that scale can sometimes bring. They were looking for units of a human not a superhuman scale. Rovers, not British Leylands, were on the agenda again.

Thirdly, it followed that efforts to cope within available resources concentrated on cutting out overheads and getting rid of hierarchies in both the public and the private sectors. The speed at which modern life moves and responses are required points in the same direction. Hence the pressure for delegation of decisions to a level as close to the point of delivery as possible. That in turn requires greater definition of the general standards to be observed.

In government, this has put under intolerable strain the myth of omnipotent personal ministerial responsibility for every detail of the activity of a government department – Herbert Morrison's dictum that 'The Minister is responsible for every stamp stuck on an envelope'. Personally I am glad to see that myth go, because it was a dangerous myth. If the minister is responsible in theory but not in practice, who is responsible? This has in turn led to a distinction between responsibility, which can be delegated, and accountability, which remains with the minister.

Fourthly, greater exposure to, and interchange with, the private sector and greater activity on the part of private sector consultants and management studies writers were bringing in thinking from other quarters. They were highlighting trends and fashions in management thinking which struck a chord with those in the public sector grappling with what seemed like similar problems. So Marks and Spencer have become better known in the civil service than Marx and Engels; and Peters and Waterman, or now Osborne and Gaebler, more widely quoted than Heclo and Wildavsky, Dunsire and Hood, or even Gray and Jenkins.

Moreover, Peters and Waterman had the priceless advantage as ex-consultants that they were used to working from concrete examples and accepted the concept of 'the executive summary'. Their common sense examples, as well as their language, struck home. Their boiled down thesis – one page containing the eight attributes of excellence – stuck in the memory. So thousands of managers who never read *In Search of Excellence* but photocopied the principles got the basic messages: bias for action, close to the customer, stick to the knitting, and so on. Just a glance at those principles compared with what has happened since in both the public and private sectors suggests to me the power of their contribution. In fact, their message has survived longer than some of the companies they praised.

Fifthly, government departments, like the private sector, have learned that it is more economical to get things right first time. There have always been awkwardnesses for us here, for our customers are often being both *served* and *regulated*. (Are they bringing in only their duty free allowances? Are they entitled to take out British Citizenship? Are they entitled to benefit? Are they intending to break out of prison?) Moreover, they are entitled – quite rightly – to pursue grievances through political means as well as directly with the providers.

In all this work – and partly thanks to the contribution of some outsiders who helped us like Lord Rayner and Sir Robin Ibbs – a great emphasis was put on releasing the insights and energies of those within the organization. Derek Rayner said that he did not know what all our problems were or the answers to them. But he knew someone who did: our own staff.

So his efficiency scrutinies used people from within our own ranks to get to the root of areas causing us concern. They looked at the problems on the ground, and asked the key questions. Why was something being done at all? Who was responsible? Could it be done better another way? What did it cost? Was that value for money?

Similarly, within the Next Steps initiative, the emphasis has been on releasing the initiative and energies of middle managers and staff. Managers have been given clearer strategic direction but more freedom to achieve quality results in ways they know will work for their customers in their business.

So Companies House now accepts credit cards and has cut the time for a premium search service from an hour to twenty minutes. The Driving Standards Agency now explains faults to failed candidates. The Historic Royal Palaces Agency has installed videos to be watched by those in unavoidable queues. The Benefits Agency and the Employment Services Agency have introduced more flexible opening hours. The Vehicle Inspectorate has introduced Saturday testing.

Of course, these changes could have occurred before new public management thinking caught on – but they didn't. Of course, these changes could have been inspired by some of the contributions from academics working in the fields concerned – in New Zealand, for example, the 'public choice' economists were widely quoted by the Treasury. But on the whole, here in the UK I think they were not. They have come from the pressures on the public services, from the consultants we called in to help, from comparison with the private sector, and from our own people themselves. In that context – and not only because of the ill-informed and mischievous allegations about the reasons for his departure a month or so ago – I want to pay tribute to the inspired leadership which Sir Peter Kemp gave to the Next Steps initiative over 4½ years. He and his team have made a lastingly beneficial change in the management of the Civil Service.

Flash in the pan

For I do not believe that the changes we have seen are a flash in the pan, a ritual bow to the latest managerial fashions and buzz words. Certainly, we have seen fashions before in planning and measurement, and in centralization and decentralization. We can expect pendulums to swing over the years, and we will see new gurus with mantras to sell.

But we have not undertaken our restructuring and managerial changes purely in the spirit of badge engineering. We have not just been applying fresh paint and new logos. We have been designing organizations better suited to the tasks they have to undertake and the needs and aspirations of the people who work in them and the people they serve. The evidence from staff, managers and customers is that they would not want to go back to the old structures and the old ways.

Abridged from R. Butler (1992) 'The new public management: the contribution of Whitehall and academia', *Public Policy and Administration*, Vol. 7, No. 3. Crown copyright is reproduced with the permission of the Controller of HMSO. This abridgement is reproduced with the permission also of the Joint University Council and of Sir Robin Butler.

Efficiency Unit

The Next Steps

Findings

2. As part of this scrutiny we have spent three months in discussions with people in the civil service throughout the country. We have also reviewed the evidence from other scrutinies in the central programme since 1979 and looked at earlier reports on the management of the civil service. The themes which have emerged during the scrutiny have followed a broadly consistent pattern, whether in discussions in a small local benefit office or in a minister's room. Some are also common themes in earlier scrutinies and in reports on the civil service . . . There are seven main findings.

3. First, the management and staff concerned with the delivery of government services (some 95 per cent of the civil service) are generally convinced that the developments towards more clearly defined and budgeted management are positive and helpful. The manager of a small local office in the north east said that for the first time in 20 years he felt that he could have an effect on the conditions under which his staff worked and therefore on the results they produced. But this kind of enthusiasm is tempered by frustration at constraints. Although there is a general acceptance of the importance of delegating meaningful authority down to the most effective level, diffused responsibility still flourishes, especially in offices away from the sharp end of delivery of services to the public. Middle managers in particular feel that their authority is seriously circumscribed both by unnecessary controls and by the intervention of ministers and senior officials in relatively minor issues. People who had recently resigned from the civil service told us that frustration at the lack of genuine responsibility for achieving results was a significant factor in encouraging them to move to jobs outside.

4. Second, most civil servants are very conscious that senior management is dominated by people whose skills are in policy formulation and who have relatively little experience of managing or working where services are actually being delivered. In any large organization senior appointments are watched with close attention. For the civil service the present signals are, as one senior Grade 2 told us, that 'the golden route to the top is through policy not through management'. This is reflected in the early experience and training of fast-stream recruits. This kind of signal affects the unwritten priorities of a whole organization, whatever the formal policy may be.

5. Managing large organizations involves skills which depend a great deal on experience; without experience senior managers lack confidence in their own ability to manage. Although, at the most senior levels, civil servants are responsible for both policy and service delivery, they give a greater priority to policy, not only because it demands immediate attention but because that is the area in which they are on familiar ground and where their skills lie, and where ministerial attention is focused. A proper balance between policy and delivery is hard to achieve within the present framework, even though tax-payers are becoming increasingly conscious of what they should expect from public expenditure on health, education and other services and hold ministers to blame for their deficiencies.

6. Third, senior civil servants inevitably and rightly respond to the priorities set by their ministers which tend to be dominated by the demands of Parliament and communicating government policies. In this situation it is easy for the task of improving performance to get overlooked, especially where there is, as we observed, confusion between ministers and permanent secretaries over their respective responsibilities for the management of service delivery. This confusion is made worse when short-term pressure becomes acute. Nevertheless, the ability of ministers supported by their senior officials to handle politics and political sensitivities effectively is a crucial part of any government's credibility. Changes in the management process should therefore aim to increase rather than diminish this crucial skill.

7. Fourth, the greater diversity and complexity of work in many departments, together with demands from Parliament, the media and the public for more information, has added to ministerial overload. Because of other pressures on ministers, and because for most of them management is not their forte and they don't see it as their function, better management and the achievement of improved performance is something that the civil service has to work out largely for itself. It is unrealistic to expect ministers to do more than give a broad lead. Most ministers who are worried about overload are of the view that while changes in management that reduced the ministerial load would be welcomed, provided they entailed no major political risks, ministers themselves do not have the time or the experience needed to develop such changes.

8. Fifth, the pressures on departments are mainly on expenditure and activities; there is still too little attention paid to the results to be achieved with the resources. The public expenditure system is the most powerful central influence on departmental management. It is still overwhelmingly dominated by the need to keep within the levels of money available rather than by the effectiveness with which that money is used.

9. Sixth, there are relatively few external pressures demanding improvement in performance. The Prime Minister has given a valuable lead and holds seminars to discuss value for money in individual departments. Her Adviser on Efficiency and Effectiveness has annual discussions with ministers about their priorities for getting better value for money. These are useful but occasional rather than continuous pressures. Pressure from Parliament, the Public Accounts Committee and the media tends to concentrate on alleged impropriety or incompetence, and making political points, rather than on demanding evidence of steadily improving efficiency and effectiveness. This encourages a cautious and defensive response which feeds through into management. On the positive side, the Treasury and the National Audit Office (NAO) are developing work on value for money. But the process of searching for improvement is still neither rigorous nor sustained; it is not yet part of the basic institution of government.

10.   Seventh, the civil service is too big and too diverse to manage as a single entity. With 600,000 employees it is an enormous organization compared with any private sector company and most public sector organizations. A single organization of this size which attempts to provide a detailed structure within which to carry out functions as diverse as driver licensing, fisheries protection, the catching of drug smugglers and the processing of Parliamentary Questions is bound to develop in a way which fits no single operation effectively.

11.   At present the freedom of an individual manager to manage effectively and responsibly in the civil service is severely circumscribed. There are controls not only on resources and objectives, as there should be in any effective system, but also on the way in which resources can be managed. Recruitment, dismissal, choice of staff, promotion, pay, hours of work, accommodation, grading, organization of work, the use of IT equipment, are all outside the control of most civil service managers at any level. The main decisions on rules and regulations are taken by the centre of the civil service. This tends to mean that they are structured to fit everything in general and nothing in particular. The rules are therefore seen primarily as a constraint rather than as a support; and in no sense as a pressure on managers to manage effectively. Moreover, the task of changing the rules is often seen as too great for one unit or one manager or indeed one department and is therefore assumed to be impossible.

12.   In our discussions it was clear that the advantages which a unified civil service are intended to bring are seen as outweighed by the practical disadvantages, particularly beyond Whitehall itself. We were told that the advantages of an all-embracing pay structure are breaking down, that the uniformity of grading frequently inhibits effective management and that the concept of a career in a unified civil service has little relevance for most civil servants, whose horizons are bounded by their local office, or, at most, by their department.

Conclusions

13.   The main themes which have emerged from our discussions in the course of the scrutiny suggest that the changes of the last seven years have been important in beginning to shift the focus of attention away from process towards results. The development of management systems, particularly those which cover programme as well as administrative areas, forces senior and

junior management to define the results they wish to achieve. But this also produces frustrations because of the lack of freedom to vary the factors on which results depend. The new systems are demonstrating how far attitudes and institutions have to change if the real benefits of the management reforms, in the form of improvement in the way government delivers its services, are to come through. It was striking that in our discussions with civil servants at all levels there was a strong sense that radical change in the freedom to manage is needed urgently if substantially better results are to be achieved.

14. Five main issues have emerged from the scrutiny. *First*, a lack of clear and accountable management responsibility, and the self confidence that goes with it particularly among the higher ranks in departments. *Second*, the need for greater precision about the results expected of people and of organizations. *Third*, a need to focus attention on outputs as well as inputs. *Fourth*, the handicap of imposing a uniform system in an organization of the size and diversity of the present civil service. *Fifth*, a need for a sustained pressure for improvement.

15. These are serious problems which need leadership, and commitment to change, from ministers and the senior civil service if they are to be dealt with. Our conclusions are that to begin the process of change three main priorities are necessary:

First: The work of each department must be organized in a way which focuses on the job to be done; the systems and structures must enhance the effective delivery of policies and services.

Second: The management of each department must ensure that their staff have the relevant experience and skills needed to do the tasks that are essential to effective government.

Third: There must be a real and sustained pressure on and within each department for continuous improvement in the value for money obtained in the delivery of policies and services.

These three priorities apply equally to all aspects of government. In our recommendations we apply them to the delivery of services, the tasks of departments and the centre of Whitehall. Simultaneous action is needed on all three.

16. It is important to recognize that the changes implied by these conclusions, although straightforward, are quite fundamental in the overall impact they will have if carried forward as we suggest. Some fairly radical decisions and a tightly knit timetable will be required if the necessary momentum for change is to be built up. But the process, although it must be quite rapid to maintain that momentum, will need to be evolutionary so as to gain full advantage from the favourable climate we observed, and to build on moves of the right kind already taking place in some departments. It will also need to be tightly managed so that the acute problems of transition are properly handled, and so that the drive for more positive management and more freedom for local decision is not undermined by vested interests or lack of confidence.

Abridged from *Improving Management in Government: the Next Steps. Report to the Prime Minister*, London, HMSO, 1988, pp. 3–8. Crown copyright is reproduced with the permission of the Controller of HMSO.

The Citizen's Charter

All public services are paid for by individual citizens, either directly or through their taxes. They are entitled to expect high quality services, responsive to their needs, provided efficiently at a reasonable cost. Where the state is engaged in regulating, taxing or administering justice, these functions too must be carried out fairly, effectively and courteously.

This Government continues to uphold the central principle that essential services – such as education and health – must be available to all, irrespective of means. And its consistent aim has been to increase choice, extend competition and thereby improve quality in all services.

In a free market, competing firms must strive to satisfy their customers, or they will not prosper. Where choice and competition are limited, consumers cannot as easily or effectively make their views count. In many public services, therefore, we need to increase both choice and competition where we can; but we also need to develop other ways of ensuring good standards of service.

Many of Britain's key industries and public services have been privatized in the last decade. This has been done in a way which promotes direct competition between providers as far as possible. Where elements of monopoly remain, regulation protects the consumer.

Choice can also be extended within the public sector. When the public sector remains responsible for a function it can introduce competition and pressure for efficiency by contracting with the private sector for its provision.

Finally, choice can be restored by introducing alternative forms of provision, and creating a wider range of options wherever that is cost-effective. This has been a key objective, for example, of reforms in housing and education.

Through the Citizen's Charter the Government is now determined to drive reforms further into the core of the public services, extending the benefits of choice, competition and commitment to service more widely.

The Citizen's Charter is the most comprehensive programme ever to raise quality, increase choice, secure better value, and extend accountability. We believe that it will set a pattern, not only for Britain, but for other countries of the world.

The Charter programme will be pursued in a number of ways. The approach will vary from service to service in different parts of the United Kingdom. The Citizen's Charter is not a blueprint which imposes a drab and uniform pattern on every service. It is a toolkit of initiatives and ideas to raise standards in the way most appropriate to each service.

The Charter programme will be at the heart of government policy in the 1990s. Quality of service to the public, and the new pride that it will give to the public servants who provide it, will be a central theme.

. . .

The principles of public service

Standards

Setting, monitoring and publication of explicit standards for the services that individual users can reasonably expect. Publication of actual performance against these standards.

Information and openness

Full, accurate information readily available in plain language about how public services are run, what they cost, how well they perform and who is in charge.

Choice and consultation

The public sector should provide choice wherever practicable. There should be regular and systematic consultation with those who use services. Users' views about services, and their priorities for improving them, to be taken into account in final decisions on standards.

Courtesy and helpfulness

Courteous and helpful service from public servants who will normally wear name badges. Services available equally to all who are entitled to them and run to suit their convenience.

Putting things right

If things go wrong, an apology, a full explanation and a swift and effective remedy. Well publicized and easy to use complaints procedures with in-dependent review wherever possible.

Value for money

Efficient and economical delivery of public services within the resources the nation can afford. And independent validation of performance against standards.

Extracts from *The Citizen's Charter: Raising the Standard* (Cm 1599), London, HMSO, July 1991; and from *The Citizen's Charter Second Report: 1994* (Cm 2540), London, HMSO, March 1994. Crown copyright reproduced with the permission of the Controller of HMSO.

HM Treasury

Competing for Quality

The Citizen's Charter sets out a comprehensive programme to improve the quality of public services. Central to this programme is the setting of rigorous standards for each service, and the development of ever better methods of delivering those standards. Where the Government takes the citizen's money through taxation, and buys services on the citizen's behalf, there is a heavy obligation to ensure that the services provide the highest quality and the best value that can be bought with that money.

Competition is the best guarantee of quality and value for money. In the 1980s, the Government's policy of increasing competition gave a new dynamism to the British economy. We mean to extend those policies in the 1990s. We will expand the frontiers of competition outwards, bringing new benefits to all those who use or work in public services.

Some services will always be provided in the public sector. None of the proposals in this White Paper will change that. Competition is as important for such services as it is for services which could be provided by either the private sector or the public sector.

In recent years, private sector businesses have increasingly chosen to concentrate on their core business. They stick with what they know best. And they buy in specialist contractors to provide new ideas, more flexibility, and a higher level of expertise than could exist in a purely in-house operation. Public sector bodies are increasingly doing the same.

Competition does not mean invariably choosing the cheapest service: it means finding the best combination of quality and price which reflects the priority of the service.

The potential benefits of competition are great, but delivering them requires imagination, realism, commitment and skill on the part of the purchaser. Managers in central and local government, and in the NHS, have to account for their performance against financial and quality targets. This responsibility requires them to look for the best deal for the users of their services, whether the task is done in-house or bought in from outside. These managers have come a long way since 1979. The best of public sector management now rank alongside the best of private sector management. And like all good managers, they welcome the stimulus of competition.

. . .

Since 1979 the Government has steadily opened more central government work to competition, both through its market testing programme, and through withdrawing from activities, such as construction, where it is not normally sensible to maintain an in-house operation.

Better budget and target setting and other improvements are enabling managers to do their job better. Testing the market makes good sense. It gives managers the opportunity to harness all the resources available to them, public and private, in order to give better service to the customer and better value for money.

We now propose to give a new impetus to this.

Encouragement

The Government's proposals are:

- Departments and executive agencies will in future set targets for testing new areas of activity in the market, to see if alternative sources give better service and value for money. The first targets will be published next year. In subsequent years, they will be accompanied by the previous year's results.
- These targets will be informed by studies undertaken with private sector help to determine the most promising new areas for market testing and contracting out. They will cover the activities of departments, executive agencies and non-departmental public bodies. These studies will identify the priorities for action in the first year, and areas to be explored in a rolling programme in later years.
- Departments which achieve savings through market testing and contracting out will be able to apply these savings for the benefit of their programmes.
- There will be a new Public Competition and Purchasing Unit, based in the Treasury, which will promote the programme set out in this White Paper as well as continuing the work of the Treasury's existing Unit.
- The Chancellor will appoint a part-time chairman to lead the unit and to advise on the extension of competition in the provision of public services. The chairman of the unit will also be a member of the Citizen's Charter Panel of Advisers.
- The Public Competition and Purchasing Unit will be able to advise would-be tenderers who are concerned about tendering procedures, or other aspects of the market testing programme.
- Departments will welcome suggestions from private companies on areas

which might be suitable for contracting out and on ways of improving contracting out procedures.

Expertise

Departments and executive agencies already need purchasing and supply skills. But the expansion of competition into more complex areas means that these skills need to be further developed. This will mean:

- more and better training of managers in purchasing and supply skills;
- mobilizing the expertise of others, including the private sector, for example by seeking secondments and exchanges in these skills, or by buying in services;
- sharing experience of contracting out between departments and executive agencies, and in particular drawing on the contracting and purchasing expertise of the Government's own purchasing agencies such as CCTA, HMSO, COI, and TBA.

Transparency of in-house costs

For competition to be possible, managers need to know the full cost of providing services in-house. Often overhead costs fall on central budgets and appear to be free to the user.

Where a market testing exercise is undertaken, evaluation procedures already take account of all in-house costs but these can take time to establish, delaying the process. And where some relevant costs fall outside managers' budgets there may be less incentive for them to seek savings.

Managers are increasingly being given delegated responsibility for budgets and the Government is making changes to ensure that their budgets include all costs. In particular:

- the Government is working on proposals to charge all accruing superannuation costs to departmental budgets from 1 April 1993; and
- departments are developing capital assets information systems which will enable costs to be reflected more accurately.

Where a manager's budget is fully charged for all the goods and services used, the incentive to increase efficiency is maximized for costs and savings directly affect the budget. Increasingly, services provided by one department to another are being charged for. Departments now providing services on payment terms include HMSO, CCTA, COI, the Valuation Office, the Treasury Solicitor, Property Holdings and PSA Services. Charging for the payroll service provided by Chessington Computer Centre will be introduced from 1 April 1993.

The Government is also encouraging charging for services supplied within departments. We expect this approach to be extended throughout central government. DTI is already in the process of creating an internal market in central services worth £40 million a year.

Streamlining procedures

Market testing is at present a lengthy process, in some cases taking years from start to finish. We will shorten the process by cutting out unnecessary bureaucracy and delay.

Contracting out for strategic/policy reasons

There has always been a wide area of activity where the Government has decided to contract out for policy or management reasons. Examples include:

- transfer of training and enterprise schemes to TECs;
- use of contracts with private sector suppliers for major IT projects in the DSS;
- the policy for privatizing PSA Services and contracting out of property, design and project management services;
- delivery of the Enterprise Initiative by private sector contractors;
- contracting out ground maintenance work in the Royal Parks.

In these cases the Government has taken a strategic decision not to continue as a direct provider, and such cases will continue to arise. For example, a department may conclude that in-house provision of a service detracts from its ability to concentrate on core functions. Or there may be areas where the private sector will be better equipped to provide a particular activity because it has a better understanding of market needs or specialist expertise. In such cases testing the market against in-house provision will not be necessary, although competitive tendering among contractors will generally apply to ensure value for money.

Market testing of existing services

For other activities currently carried out by departments, market testing procedures continue to be necessary to secure value for money. Hitherto the majority of contracts subjected to market testing have been won by the private sector.

In future, market testing procedures will be streamlined to ensure that savings are delivered without delay. Under existing arrangements, the procedure has often involved a prolonged exercise to bring the in-house operation to maximum efficiency before competitive tendering can begin. After a decade of efficiency reform there should no longer be a need to delay in this way.

In future, the process should move rapidly to competitive tendering. The in-house staff should have the opportunity to put forward a firm bid on the same basis and timescale as the private sector: they should be free to suggest new flexibilities and simpler procedures. Thus the scope for greater efficiency in the in-house operation will be identified in the in-house bid. If successful, in-house staff, like outside suppliers, must be held rigorously to the operational budget they have bid. In some cases more formal arrangements involving a management buy out may be appropriate. Government agencies providing services to departments should be treated on the same basis as private sector contractors. The interests of staff will be protected as now through consultation.

New services

In the case of entirely new services, where there is no in-house operation, the Government believes there should be a general presumption in favour of contracting out, subject to management or policy requirements and relative value for money. For some new services, however, contracting out may not be appropriate.

Technical redundancy

In some circumstances, a transfer of work to the private sector may be a relevant transfer for the purposes of the Transfer of Undertakings (Protection of Employment) Regulations 1981. Under present law there is room for uncertainty whether civil servants' redundancy rights are transferred in such cases. As a result, it has been the practice to legislate specifically to exclude any possible entitlement to redundancy compensation where civil servants are transferred to the private sector to do the same job, and on the same terms and conditions.

The Citizen's Charter gave a commitment to legislate to solve this problem on a permanent basis. Legislation will be introduced to ensure that a civil servant can have no entitlement to redundancy compensation where his employment is transferred under the 1981 Regulations. This will remove any disincentive to contracting out associated with the need in some cases to legislate to avoid unjustified redundancy payments.

New areas for market testing and contracting out

Market testing so far has been largely concentrated on traditional support services. The Government wishes to build on this by opening up to competition new areas, closer to the heart of government. Departments, executive agencies and non-departmental public bodies need to test the scope for a greater private sector contribution to the delivery of, for example, clerical and executive operations, specialist and professional skills, and a wide range of facilities management approaches. These are just some areas where the private sector should be able to offer new ideas and expertise.

There is a clear need to consider whether contracts should be for part or all of the task. In some markets where competition is intense among small firms, smaller contracts may offer better value. Where larger contracts are appropriate there may need to be provision for components or sub-contract work to be put out to tender.

Abridged from HM Treasury (1991) *Competing for Quality: Buying Better Public Services* (Cm 1730), London, HMSO, November. Crown copyright is reproduced with the permission of the Controller of HMSO.

David Osborne and Ted Gaebler

Reinventing government

The bankruptcy of bureaucracy

It is hard to imagine today, but 100 years ago the word *bureaucracy* meant something positive. It connoted a rational, efficient method of organization – something to take the place of the arbitrary exercise of power by authoritarian regimes. Bureaucracies brought the same logic to government work that the assembly line brought to the factory. With their hierarchical authority and functional specialization, they made possible the efficient undertaking of large, complex tasks. Max Weber, the great German sociologist, described them using words no modern American would dream of applying:

> The decisive reason for the advance of bureaucratic organization has always been its purely technical superiority over any other form of organization . . .
> Precision, speed, unambiguity . . . reduction of friction and of material and personal costs – these are raised to the optimum point in the strictly bureaucratic administration.

In the United States, the emergence of bureaucratic government was given a particular twist by its turn-of-the-century setting. A century ago, our cities were growing at breakneck speed, bulging with immigrants come to labour in the factories thrown up by our industrial revolution. Boss Tweed and his contemporaries ran these cities like personal fiefdoms: in exchange for immigrant votes, they dispensed jobs, favours, and informal services. With one hand they robbed the public blind; with the other they made sure those who delivered blocs of loyal votes were amply rewarded. Meanwhile, they ignored many of the new problems of industrial America – its slums, its sweatshops, its desperate need for a new infrastructure of sewers and water and public transit.

Young Progressives like Theodore Roosevelt, Woodrow Wilson and Louis

Brandeis watched the machines until they could stomach it no more. In the 1890s, they went to war. Over the next 30 years, the Progressive movement transformed government in America. To end the use of government jobs as patronage, the Progressives created civil service systems, with written exams, lockstep pay scales and protection from arbitrary hiring or dismissal. To keep major construction projects like bridges and tunnels out of the reach of politicians, they created independent public authorities. To limit the power of political bosses, they split up management functions, took appointments to important offices away from mayors and governors, created separately elected clerks, judges, even sheriffs. To keep the administration of public services untainted by the influence of politicians, they created a profession of city managers – professionals, insulated from politics, who would run the bureaucracy in an efficient, businesslike manner.

Thanks to Boss Tweed and his contemporaries, in other words, American society embarked on a gigantic effort to *control* what went on inside government – to keep the politicians and bureaucrats from doing anything that might endanger the public interest or purse. This cleaned up many of our governments, but in solving one set of problems it created another. In making it difficult to steal the public's money, we made it virtually impossible to *manage* the public's money. In adopting written tests scored to the third decimal point to hire our clerks and police officers and fire fighters, we built mediocrity into our work force. In making it impossible to fire people who did not perform, we turned mediocrity into deadwood. In attempting to control virtually everything, we became so obsessed with dictating *how* things should be done – regulating the process, controlling the inputs – that we ignored the outcomes, the *results*.

The product was government with a distinct ethos: slow, inefficient, impersonal. This is the mental image the word *government* invokes today; it is what most Americans assume to be the very essence of government. Even government buildings constructed during the industrial era reflect this ethos: they are immense structures, with high ceilings, large hallways and ornate architecture, all designed to impress upon the visitor the impersonal authority and immovable weight of the institution.

For a long time, the bureaucratic model worked – not because it was efficient, but because it solved the basic problems people wanted solved. It provided security – from unemployment, during old age. It provided stability, a particularly important quality after the Depression. It provided a basic sense of fairness and equity. (Bureaucracies, as Weber pointed out, are designed to treat everyone alike.) It provided jobs. And it delivered the basic, no-frills, one-size-fits-all services people needed and expected during the industrial era: roads, highways, sewers, schools.

. . .

Today all that has been swept away. We live in an era of breathtaking change. We live in a global marketplace, which puts enormous competitive pressure on our economic institutions. We live in an information society, in which people get access to information almost as fast as their leaders do. We live in a knowledge-based economy, in which educated workers bridle at commands and demand autonomy. We live in an age of niche markets, in which customers have become accustomed to high quality and extensive choice.

. . .

Over the past five years, as we have journeyed through the landscape of governmental change, we have sought constantly to understand the underlying trends. We have asked ourselves: what do these innovative, entrepreneurial organizations have in common? What incentives have they changed, to create such different behaviour? What have they done which, if other governments did the same, would make entrepreneurship the norm and bureaucracy the exception?

The common threads were not hard to find. Most entrepreneurial governments promote *competition* between service providers. They *empower* citizens by pushing control out of the bureaucracy, into the community. They measure the performance of their agencies, focusing not on inputs but on *outcomes*. They are driven by their goals – their *missions* – not by their rules and regulations. They redefine their clients as *customers* and offer them choices – between schools, between training programmes, between housing options. They *prevent* problems before they emerge, rather than simply offering services afterwards. They put their energies into *earning* money, not simply spending it. They *decentralize* authority, embracing participatory management. They prefer *market* mechanisms to bureaucratic mechanisms. And they focus not simply on providing public services, but on *catalysing* all sectors – public, private and voluntary – into action to solve their community's problems.

We believe that these ten principles . . . are the fundamental principles behind this new form of government we see emerging: the spokes that hold together this new wheel. Together they form a coherent whole, a new model of government. They will not solve all of our problems. But if the experience of organizations that have embraced them is any guide, they will solve the major problems we experience with bureaucratic government.

Why government can't be 'run like a business'

Many people, who believe government should simply be 'run like a business', may assume this is what we mean. It is not.

Government and business are fundamentally different institutions. Business leaders are driven by the profit motive; government leaders are driven by the desire to get re-elected. Businesses get most of their money from their customers; governments get most of their money from taxpayers. Businesses are usually driven by competition; governments usually use monopolies.

Differences such as these create fundamentally different incentives in the public sector. For example, in government the ultimate test for managers is not whether they produce a product or profit – it is whether they please the elected politicians. Because politicians tend to be driven by interest groups, public managers – unlike their private counterparts – must factor interest groups into every equation.

Governments also extract their income primarily through taxation, whereas businesses earn their income when customers buy products or services of their own free will. This is one reason why the public focuses so intensely on the cost of government services, exercising a constant impulse to *control* – to dictate how much the bureaucrats spend on every item, so they cannot possibly waste, misuse or steal the taxpayers' money.

All these factors combine to produce an environment in which public employees view risks and rewards very differently than do private employees. 'In government all of the incentive is in the direction of not making mistakes,' explains Lou Winnick of the Ford Foundation. 'You can have 99 successes and nobody notices, and one mistake and you're dead.' Standard business methods to motivate employees don't work very well in this kind of environment.

There are many other differences. Government is democratic and open; hence it moves more slowly than business, whose managers can make quick decisions behind closed doors. Government's fundamental mission is to 'do good', not to make money; hence cost–benefit calculations in business turn into moral absolutes in the public sector. Government must often serve everyone equally, regardless of their ability to pay or their demand for a service; hence it cannot achieve the same market efficiencies as business. One could write an entire book about the differences between business and government. Indeed, James Q. Wilson, the eminent political scientist, already has. It is called *Bureaucracy: What Government Agencies Do and Why They Do It*.

These differences add up to one conclusion: government cannot be run like a business. There are certainly many similarities. Indeed, we believe that our ten principles underlie success for *any* institution in today's world – public, private or non-profit. And we have learned a great deal from business management theorists such as Peter Drucker, W. Edwards Deming, Tom Peters and Robert Waterman. But in government, business theory is not enough.

Consider Deming's aproach, known as total quality management. Increasingly popular in the public sector, it drives public institutions to focus on five of our principles: results, customers, decentralization, prevention and a market (or systems) approach. But precisely because Deming developed his ideas for private businesses, his approach ignores the other five. For example, most businesses can take competition for granted, so total quality management ignores the problem of monopoly – which is at the heart of government's troubles. Most businesses are already driven by their missions (to make profits), so Deming does not help public leaders create mission-driven organizations. And few businesses have to be told to earn money rather than simply spending it.

The fact that government cannot be run just like a business does not mean it cannot become more *entrepreneurial*, of course. Any institution, public or private, can be entrepreneurial, just as any institution, public or private, can be bureaucratic. Few Americans would really want government to act just like a business – making quick decisions behind closed doors for private profit. If it did, democracy would be the first casualty. But most Americans would like government to be less bureaucratic. There is a vast continuum between bureaucratic behaviour and entrepreneurial behaviour, and government can surely shift its position on that spectrum.

A third choice

Most of our leaders still tell us that there are only two ways out of our repeated public crises: we can raise taxes, or we can cut spending. For almost two decades, we have asked for a third choice. We do not want less education, fewer roads, less health care. Nor do we want higher taxes. We want better education, better roads and better health care, for the same tax dollar.

Unfortunately, we do not know how to get what we want. Most of our leaders assume that the only way to cut spending is to eliminate programmes, agencies and employees. Ronald Reagan talked as if we could simply go into the bureaucracy with a scalpel and cut out pockets of waste, fraud and abuse.

But waste in government does not come tied up in neat packages. It is marbled throughout our bureaucracies. It is embedded in the very way we do business. It is employees on idle, working at half speed – or barely working at all. It is people working hard at tasks that aren't worth doing, following regulations that should never have been written, filling out forms that should never have been printed. It is the *$100 billion* a year that Bob Stone estimates the Department of Defence wastes with its foolish over-regulation.

Waste in government is staggering, but we cannot get at it by wading through budgets and cutting line items. As one observer put it, our governments are like fat people who must lose weight. They need to eat less and exercise more; instead, when money is tight they cut off a few fingers and toes.

To melt the fat, we must change the basic incentives that drive our governments. We must turn bureaucratic institutions into entrepreneurial institutions, ready to kill off obsolete initiatives, willing to do more with less, eager to absorb new ideas.

The lessons are there: our more entrepreneurial governments have shown us the way. Yet few of our leaders are listening. Too busy climbing the rungs to their next office, they don't have time to stop and look anew. So they remain trapped in old ways of looking at our problems, blind to solutions that lie right in front of them. This is perhaps our greatest stumbling block: the power of outdated ideas. As the great economist John Maynard Keynes once noted, the difficulty lies not so much in developing new ideas as in escaping from old ones.

The old ideas still embraced by most public leaders and political reporters assume that the important question is *how much* government we have – not *what kind* of government. Most of our leaders take the old model as a given, and either advocate more of it (liberal Democrats), or less of it (Reagan Republicans), or less of one programme but more of another (moderates of both parties).

But our fundamental problem today is not too much government or too little government. We have debated that issue endlessly since the tax revolt of 1978, and it has not solved our problems. Our fundamental problem is that we have *the wrong kind of government*. We do not need more government or less government, we need *better* government. To be more precise, we need better *governance*.

Governance is the process by which we collectively solve our problems and meet our society's needs. Government is the instrument we use. The instrument is outdated, and the process of reinvention has begun. We do not need another New Deal, nor another Reagan Revolution. We need an American *perestroika*.

Abridged from D. Osborne and T. Gaebler (1992) *Reinventing Government: How the Entrepreneurial Spirit is Transforming the Public Sector*, Reading, MA, Addison-Wesley, pp. 12–24. Reproduced with the permission of Addison-Wesley Publishing Company Inc.

Sir Robin Butler

The future of the civil service

If you ask me where the civil service ought to be in 10 or 20 years' time, the answer must be 'where the political and economic environment of the time requires us to be'.

For one thing so much will depend on the development of the European Community, on which David Williamson, the Secretary General of the European Commission, advanced some interesting ideas in the 1991 annual Redcliffe-Maud Memorial Lecture. That will certainly demand a more outward-looking civil service, with greater ability to work with our European partners, to deal in their languages, to have the feel for their cultures, to understand their aspirations and their administrative methods.

But other matters will depend on political decision. It is not for me to determine whether we have a bigger or a smaller civil service, whether we have this function or that, even whether we are selected for appointment by commissioners or political patronage. I hope that people do recognize the arguments for, and value of, a continuing non-political civil service able to serve governments of whatever colour. But I do not claim that the civil service has any right to that role. If Parliament wanted to change it tomorrow they could do so.

Such change will not take place so long as public opinion generally, and as a result the people's representatives in Parliament, have confidence in a non-political civil service and want it to continue. They will only have that confidence if they feel that the civil service does its job properly.

That in my view is the test which must be applied to any changes in the civil service: in today's world, and in tomorrow's so far as we can see it, will the changes enable us to do our job better? And even if they will, can we be sure that characteristics of the service which will have continuing value are not being lost? So the first question which we have to ask is 'what is the job of today's and tomorrow's civil service?' That was the principle with which the

Fulton Committee started – concentrate on the job to be done and then consider how it can best be done.

Let us start with what the civil service is not. It is not – whatever it may have been once – a small Whitehall coterie, of the sort portrayed in *Yes, Minister* or *The Men from the Ministry*.

It is not homogeneous. It is involved in a very wide range of very disparate activities – from collecting revenues, to paying benefits, to running courts, to making nuclear bombs, to testing medicines, to selling coins, to guarding the coasts.

Successive governments have caused these activities to grow enormously in their range and complexity in the course of this century in ways which have brought a very large number of civil servants into direct contact with the public.

The quality of life of the people of this country is cumulatively affected to a major extent by the efficiency and the humanity with which the services are provided. Some have a direct impact on our fellow citizens and others have an indirect impact through their effect on the economic activity of the country and hence on its prosperity.

Although the activities are so disparate, they have one thing in common – they are all accountable through ministers to Parliament, so that they are in the realm of politics.

And they have another thing in common. They are provided for an employer who cannot go out of business so that, although it may be possible to create a surrogate for market forces for some of them, the final sanction of the market – that the employer will have to close his doors – does not apply to them.

In looking ahead I do make some assumptions.

One is that, whatever the size or range of functions of the civil service, it will continue to provide a wide range of services which involve direct contact with the public, and not just with ministers and Parliament.

A second is that the tension between the demand for public services and the limits of acceptable taxation or charges by government – which during my career has thrown greater and greater emphasis on getting more and more out of the resources which can be devoted to public programmes – will continue.

A third is that the complexity of the services provided and of managing their provision will require the application of the right combination of technical and administrative skills at all levels of management.

A fourth is that the old career patterns of people joining a profession at the start of their working life and working through it until the end in a paternalist atmosphere in which they simply accept the decisions of their employer with very little say of their own on the direction of their career have gone: we must provide more flexible career patterns, more responsive to our employees' own wishes, and in particular responsive to the need to provide equal opportunities to all those with the necessary qualities.

A fifth assumption is that the revolution in information technology and communications will provide new ways of working, and in particular will allow a much greater geographical dispersal allowing us to take the back-up work to where the available labour is rather than bringing the labour to the work, which has contributed so much to congestion and excessive demand for skills in London and the South East of the country.

I could offer some other assumptions but that is perhaps enough to be going on with.

What implications does all this have for the future of the civil service? Let me start with organization and then come on to people.

I do not want to push a corporate analogy too far because I would be the first to acknowledge that there are many differences between the job of the civil service and that of a private sector business.

But it is, I suggest, fair to say that the civil service with the range and scale of activities which I have described cannot be effectively organized and run as if it was a small family company with all decisions of any significance referred to the board of directors.

Nor if we are to get best value out of the resources which the taxpayer provides for the civil service is it sensible to suggest that pay and grading structures must be uniform, however disparate the task to be performed, however different the labour markets in which they compete, whatever the traditions of management in the particular activity.

I note in passing that far more decisions to disperse civil service activities from London and the South East have been taken since it was left to the managers of services to decide for themselves how they could most effectively use their tightly controlled running costs for service provision than when campaigns for dispersal were pressures applied from the centre.

So I do conclude that we are much more likely to achieve effective delivery of services if decisions on how best to provide them are delegated to as close a level as possible to the point of the provision, if managers are given flexibility to make decisions about the ways in which they can organize and motivate their staff as effectively as possible and, above all, if their own sense of responsibility for the delivery of services is not dulled by the constant sense that their initiative is not welcome or highly regarded.

In saying this I make three caveats which, in my view, are absolutely essential. One is that, whatever the level of delegation, the line of accountability up through the chain through ministers to Parliament remains unbroken.

That does not mean that ministers have to take all the decisions: indeed, that is manifestly impossible. But it does mean that, in the last resort, if satisfaction cannot be achieved at lower levels, ministers can be challenged about any action of the civil service.

Contrary to what was argued in the otherwise excellent recent pamphlet on the civil service by the Institute for Public Policy Research, I believe that this line of accountability has to go through ministers because in a democracy the ultimate sanction on a government is that they are not re-elected; and ministers are the only people in a government who are subject to that sanction. Apart from the courts there is no other protection for the citizen.

That is, of course, a different thing from saying that ministers must take the blame for every wrong decision of their subordinates. They cannot and should not take the blame for decisions of which they know nothing or could be expected to know nothing.

But they should be responsible, if a wrong is brought to their attention, for taking action to provide redress and to ensure that mistakes do not recur. And it is wise, as well as being in the interests of good management, to ensure that their civil servants and the public know what is the borderline between what civil servants are expected to decide for themselves and what they are expected to refer to ministers. That is the purpose of the framework agreements under the Next Steps initiative.

The second caveat is that managers operate within firm and clear budgetary constraints which they have personal responsibility for observing. That will not be the only constraint under which they have to operate. There will have to be other central rules – I hope not too many because people's own good sense is usually better than any number of rules – concerning political impartiality and the means to ensure integrity, for example.

But firm budgetary limits are essential in any well-run organization.

Parliament and successive governments have with difficulty established effective safeguards against the government's overspending its budget; and it is essential, in my view, that greater delegation of responsibility does not weaken the effectiveness of those controls.

The third caveat follows from the second. The effectiveness of controls requires some sanction to enforce them. If responsibilities are delegated and the minister is not blamed for wrong decisions which he does not take, someone else must be. The delegation of responsibility, if ministers and Treasury are to be asked to make it with confidence, needs in my view to be supported by not only rewards for success but penalties for failure.

I am anxious not to be misunderstood about this. I am emphatically not one who believes that good performance can only be achieved by carrots for success and sticks for failure.

On the contrary, I believe that a far more valuable guarantee of good service is the spirit of altruistic public service which has been, and remains, such a feature of our civil service – the spirit which is demonstrated by those, for example, who work long hours through the nights and weekends in getting a Bill through Parliament for no other reward than the importance and intellectual challenge of the job or the many thousands who make a particular effort to serve and help the public by putting themselves out to be courteous, helpful and imaginative. If anybody wants to see any examples of that, I hope that they will look at the results of this year's 'Service to the customer' competition in the next edition of *Management Matters*.

That is something very precious and it must not be endangered. That is why it is so important that civil servants and the civil service should feel esteemed and valued, as in my view they deserve to be. None the less, ministers and the public are more likely to accept the delegation of responsibility which seems to me an essential element in running public services today if the delegation is buttressed by a knowledge on the part of those to whom such responsibility is delegated that their personal success or failure is in a very direct sense dependent on the way in which they exercise those responsibilities.

But there is a fly in this amber. It is now very widely asked whether, if delegation takes place in this way and different operations of the civil service are allowed to go their own way in devising terms and conditions for their own operations, anything will be left which is recognizably a single service? Is the service in the process of disintegrating and, if so, does it matter? Can we live up in practice to the manifesto which I and others issued when Next Steps was launched, that the service would remain unified though not uniform?

This is a serious question because, if I may return to my analogy with a corporate organization, it is less easy to see the tangible unifying factor in the case of the civil service once common terms and conditions and strongly centralized management give way to greater variety and delegation. Someone working in the paint division of ICI may be doing a very different job from someone in the pharmaceutical division, yet at least they are both contributing to the bottom line of ICI. There is no single bottom line for the civil service.

None the less I think that there is a glue which holds the civil service together. The political context in which the civil service operates, the public accountability through ministers to Parliament, the special need which that accountability imposes for even-handedness and integrity, the requirement for political impartiality, the safeguards against jobbery in appointment and promotion, the expectation that we will set a good example, for instance in the treatment of women and minorities, the public expenditure controls and conventions, all those give special characteristics which run across the whole of the civil service and do not apply in the same form to other professions.

But people have more practical considerations in mind when they raise anxieties about the fragmentation of the civil service. They wonder whether the advantages which derive from working for a large employer will continue to apply, in particular whether they will be able to move from one part of a department to another or from one part of the service to another to advance their career, widen their experience or because it suits them for other personal or domestic reasons.

These considerations apply to some extent at all levels. For reasons which I will go on to describe, they apply more strongly at senior levels than at junior levels. At junior levels people have perhaps always seen their career more in terms of their job centre or their tax office than of the civil service as a whole, and they may in practice stay in the same office in the same locality throughout their career. But even at junior levels I believe that people value the wider range of opportunities which the breadth of the civil service gives them, particularly in regional locations where opportunities for promotion may be limited in the outposts of a single department and people need to be able to compete for senior posts in other departments if they are qualified for them. As the civil service becomes more dispersed this is likely to be a more, rather than less, important factor.

So I think that the opportunity for movement will continue to be important, and I see no reason why a diversity of terms and conditions should prevent it. It will continue to be the case that once people have been recruited they can move anywhere within the civil service without the need for further formality – they are within the fence.

Since we shall no more be pursuing diversity for its own sake than uniformity, I have no doubt that there will be areas where unified conditions of service across departments continue to make sense.

And where there develop different regimes, I should be surprised if we find it beyond our wits to devise means by which people moving from one organization can be given their due place in the pay and grading structure of another.

. . .

One of the most important roles for those in the centre of departments and in central departments is to see that there are adequate mechanisms to enable people with talent to emerge and the necessary training facilities available to help them develop.

And it will also fall to management to provide the opportunities for them to develop their careers and for those who will eventually fill the most senior posts to get a wide experience both of policy posts and of agencies.

I should be surprised if there were any need for conditions of service to diverge between those who work in the cores of the various departments in a way which would create obstacles to movement between them. As I said earlier, where there are, as there will be, differing pay regimes in agencies or in other parts of departments, it should not be beyond our wits to devise arrangements for people to move between them. It will certainly be necessary to do so.

It is true that the greater independence of agencies, the tendency to fill appointments by competition open to outsiders and insiders instead of simply by management decision, has reduced to some extent the ability of senior management to determine and control people's careers.

A senior colleague recently consulted me on whether he should put in for a post or wait for one coming up a little later. Previously I could have advised him which one he was likely to get and played a large part in determining it. Now, since both posts were the subject of open competition, I could no longer do so. It was, of course, possible that he would fail to get either post, although in the event he succeeded in getting the first of them.

But even before the greater prevalence of open competitions, the old paternalist days of running the civil service had long since passed. Having served as a principal establishment officer, I know that people are no longer willing simply to accept the direction of their managers. They have much to say about the direction in which they want their careers to go.

Opening senior posts to competition matches opportunity with those aspirations. And I do not regret that because I believe that the vitality which comes from giving people more opportunity to shape their own careers, more chance to select themselves, more scope to determine the training and development they need, is well worth a bit more difficulty and unpredictability for the management.

Equally, I think that the civil service has much to gain and individual civil servants have little to lose, by making the profession much more open to recruitment from outside the service at all stages of career than it used to be a few years ago. I have said before that, in fair competition, a good insider is always likely to have the edge over a good outsider; and the number of those who leave the senior open structure to take jobs outside exceeds those who come into the civil service at those levels. This movement in and out is valuable in my view and the vitality of the civil service is greatly increased by an infusion of those who come in with outside experience and perspectives, just as outside organizations benefit from the services of those who have built up in government a wide knowledge of administration and public affairs.

I can well understand that, at a time when there is such a large pool of talented civil servants who are justifiably looking for promotion to the senior open structure – and who see the number of posts static or declining and many having been promoted into them young – opening a large number of senior posts to people from outside as well as inside the service must be unwelcome.

To such people I would like to repeat that I do regard it as part of the responsibility of management to ensure that even in times when the service is contracting the opportunities are created for talented people to break through and that the necessary support is available, whether in the form of training or in the form of a sufficiently wide range of postings to enable them to develop or in the form of attractive exit policies so that people at the top are willing to make room for those coming up from below. We are challenging individuals to do more to shape their own careers: the challenge to management is to ensure that they are helped to do so.

I have tried to argue that the civil service of the future will be more heterogeneous because that in fact represents the very varied range of things we have to do; that it will offer more delegation, more individual responsibility, more internal opportunities and more control over one's own career; and that hence it will be more challenging, exciting and rewarding.

Finally, I should like to say this. As I made clear at the outset, I am not offering these remarks as a blueprint of where the civil service ought to go, still less a prescription of where I will be trying to make it go. What I hope that I am offering is an analysis of where I think that it is going in response to the nature of the civil service's job and the world in which we work. I believe that the contribution of the FDA and other trade unions to these matters has been a very constructive and open-minded one.

That is important because, in the spirit of what I have said, the development of these ideas will take place not through imposition from the top but through all of us participating in working them out. I believe that Next Steps has been successful so far because it goes in a direction which civil servants themselves want.

Abridged from R. Butler (1992) 'The future of the civil service', *Public Policy and Administration*, Vol. 7, No. 2, pp. 1–10, based upon a lecture given to the Association of First Division Civil Servants on 15 October 1991, an edited version of which appeared in *FDA News*, November 1991. Crown copyright is reproduced with the permission of the Controller of HMSO. This abridgement is reproduced also with the permission of the Joint University Council and of Sir Robin Butler.

William Waldegrave

The new public service

The materials out of which we are building the necessary new structure of public service consist of five key concepts. The first is the separation of the purchaser of a public service from the provider of that service, a doctrine first introduced to government in 1971 by the late Lord Rothschild in relation to the procurement of applied research by government departments;[1] second and third are privatization and the Next Steps programme, both developed by Lady Thatcher in the 1980s. The fourth is the extension of competition by market testing, and the fifth the introduction of the Citizen's Charter – both added by John Major. All of these fit with a coherent strategy for achieving better the proper purposes of a modern public sector. These concepts can be deployed in a hierarchy to test, first, whether the public sector should be involved in a function and, if it should, to show how public provision can be organized in such a way as to achieve fairness and accountability without losing creativity, responsiveness and sharpness in the avoidance of waste.

Reappraising the role of government

The first step in the hierarchy should involve nothing less than a fundamental reappraisal of the role of government itself. We should establish what the government really needs to do – and make sure that it does it and does no more. If we can identify functions that government no longer needs to discharge, we need to end its involvement. The implementation of this policy has helped to bring about a radical reduction in the size of the state sector. In 1979, as Stephen Dorrell recently reminded us,[2] the Government was an oil producer, a car maker and a steel manufacturer – roles for which it was clearly unsuited. In subsequent years, we have managed to reduce the state sector to a smaller – and much more sensible – size.

Our policy has been driven simply by a combination of scepticism and experience: a healthy scepticism about the capabilities of politicians and civil servants as managers, and a wealth of experience about the benefits of transferring businesses from the public to the private sector. We have learnt that where there are monopolies or oligopolies, instead of attempting to run industries, we can control them to the necessary degree much more effectively while restricting ourselves to their arm's length regulation. This both avoids mixing up industrial investment with public spending decisions, and it also generates better management and frees Whitehall from the deadly embrace of privileged industrial lobbyists masquerading as 'sponsor' departments. Even so, as Stephen Dorrell has pointed out, the public sector is still surprisingly large – even after almost fourteen years of Conservative Government. In addition to industries and services such as British Coal and British Rail, central government owns over £100 billion worth of tangible assets – and local government more than another £200 billion. This reminds us of the scale of the public sector which remains.

Much of it, of course, *should* remain. There are disciplined services such as the armed forces and police, which must always answer directly to the Crown. There are policy functions which are the essence of Government, such as financial, economic and foreign and security policy. There are social functions, such as the provision of health care, education and support for those who are in need, to which modern Conservatives judge there must be equal access for all at a satisfactory level.

There is a range of functions derived from the setting of sensible boundaries to the free market in land use planning, environmental control and consumer protection. There are some functions where the timescale of investment or the 'free rider' problem make it uneconomic for the market to provide goods which most people agree are needed, like science and some patronage of the arts. There is an always unquiet frontier between public and private in the area of support for industry and trade to match the alleged state interventions of trading rivals.

There is no doubt that the most radical of campaigners for minimal government must accept that a substantial public sector goes with modern democracy. That is why, after privatizing all we should, we must have practical methods for preventing the remaining public sector reinfecting itself with the old ills of inefficiency, insensitivity and waste – a disease that American writer Jonathan Rauch has dubbed 'demosclerosis'.[3] So we take the next steps in the hierarchy of choice, and introduce *competition* into the public sector, made real by the separation of the purchaser from the provider, by asking the immensely productive question: 'granted that we need to ensure this provision, *do we, the public sector, need to do the providing ourselves?*' From pursuing this question relentlessly comes the necessary injection of competition into the supply of goods and services by the public sector.

. . .

Extending the purchaser/provider split

The introduction of competition into public provision cannot, however, properly be done without one key organizational reform, namely the separation of purchaser from provider in the public sector. Those whose duty is to spend public money on behalf of the citizen to buy public services must be quite free of pressure to provide work for whatever provider bureaucracy may happen historically to exist. They must get out into as wide a market as they can find (and help to create) – public and private – to buy on behalf of those they represent – sick people, children in school, people who want their dustbins emptied, people who want public transport. The bugbear of old-style public provision was the confusion of these two roles, and the capture of the purchaser – the proxy for the citizen – by the self-interested provider. Only if the purchaser can compare competitive bids – competitive in quality and costs – from real alternative suppliers will he have a chance of escaping provider capture. Instead, there will be clear and healthy separation of responsibilities between government – which will act as the purchaser of services – and public and private contractors, who will be responsible for their actual provision.

In this way, the purchaser/provider split, most fully developed in the NHS, will gradually come to characterize the public services as a whole. As John Willman has written, this separation of responsibilities has three virtuous consequences.[4] First, it ends potential conflicts of interests and allows the purchaser – health authority, council, local education authority or whatever – to become the advocate of the consumer, rather than the defender of the producer. Second, it gives public purchasers a means of access to private sector resources and expertise; and, third, it forces both sides to define the nature of the service and the standards of quality which are to be provided.

The system of management by contract is introducing specific and enforceable standards of outputs into the public services – often for the first time. It is also, as Stephen Dorrell has said, helping to redefine the phrase 'mixed economy'.[5] In future, the distinction between public and private provision will dwindle in significance; what will really matter is that managers should have the freedom to choose between a number of competing service providers. That, I believe, will greatly increase both the efficiency and the effectiveness of public services, right across the board: it may also, I believe, do something to diminish and blur ancient English class distinctions embedded in a perceived difference between those who use 'private' or 'public' services.

The purchaser/provider division is an immensely powerful force for good in that it releases government to fight for the citizen, and frees it from having management as its main focus. It also forces government to be clear and open about what it requires from providers in the service contract it agrees with them. This is a gain for accountability and openness (I will return to this point) but above all it puts the public service back on the high moral ground, where the 'public service ethic' becomes again what it should be in the public mind – namely, an expression of the highest ideal of service on behalf of the common good, and not, as has sometimes seemed too much the case in the past, a self-interested doctrine, defensive of inadequate standards of provision.

Many providers will be in the private sector. Many others, however, will remain in the ownership of the public sector. Here too, however, management by contract and the purchaser/provider split is just as powerful. The principal mechanism for separating out these functions in the central government sector has been the Next Steps agency, described in the following section.

'Agencification': improving accountability

It was, I believe, Winston Churchill who said that short words were the best words – but that *old* short words were even better still. On that basis, 'agencification' fails on both counts. In this case, however, a long, new-fangled and essentially unattractive word hides a concept that is simplicity itself.

The process of agencification involves the separation of the civil service into a number of smaller, increasingly specialized units known as Next Steps agencies, which operate at arm's length from Whitehall. Each agency is set a number of specific performance targets, or outputs, in a service contract called a 'framework agreement'. The most suitable man or woman is recruited for the job of its chief executive – usually through open competition (which, in itself, is unusual by past civil service standards). They are then given the freedom to get on with the job – and rewarded according to their results.

The Next Steps system, introduced in the late 1980s, has already proved its worth – for both service users and providers alike. Managers have been freed from unnecessary Whitehall regulations and controls and, as a result, users have benefited from services that are more closely tailored to their individual needs. As Colin Hughes, of *The Independent*, has written: 'The devolution of executive responsibility means that decisions are being taken much closer to the customer.' Agencies, he added, 'represent, in fact, a real transfer of power away from central government departments to staff further along the line.'[6] In this, they are part of the Government's campaign to devolve decision-taking nearer to users. NHS Trusts and grant-maintained schools show the extent to which we have been willing to reorder the organization of service delivery in this way – devolving power down, closer to patients and parents, rather than up, towards Westminster and Whitehall.

The benefits of agencification are perhaps best demonstrated by the turn-around in the performance of two organizations which, in the past, seemed determined to drag the public services into disrepute. In years gone by, the delays that people experienced in obtaining passports and in booking driving tests appeared to demonstrate that public sector efficiency was something of a lost cause. Now, however, after only a few years of Next Steps status, both the Passport Agency and the DVLA have greatly improved their performance. The time taken to process passport applications has been cut from an average of three and a half weeks to just seven days, and the average wait for driving tests has been more than halved. Indeed, the most recent figures show that agencies are meeting, or exceeding, three-quarters of the targets that have been set for their economy, efficiency and effectiveness.[7]

A number of independent observers have now recognized the true radicalism of the Next Steps programme. Vernon Bogdanor has described the reforms as 'the most radical the Civil Service has seen since the Northcote-Trevelyan Report of 1853'.[8] Similarly, in Peter Hennessy's view, they represent 'the most profound change to the Civil Service this century'; their introduction was, he added, 'a long-delayed recognition that the nature of state provision had changed. Government departments before the Next Steps programme were essentially 1830s technology'.[9] What we must address next is the way in which, while modernizing the technology, we can ensure that what was good in the old is protected. Two broad issues dominate: accountability, and the ethos of public service.

Accountability, the Citizen's Charter and the spirit of public service

A smaller public sector, managed by open service agreement, with purchasers spending the citizen's money on the citizen's behalf, seeking and finding value for money, responsiveness to the user, innovation and quality by means of competitive bids; fostering variety and plurality of suppliers; guarding against the old diseases of provider capture and top-down arrogance: this is how to deliver the true ideals of public service while avoiding the dangers we ran into in the forty years after the war. But all these are means towards the end – revitalized public service. By bringing forward the Citizen's Charter, John Major put right into the forefront what we – and I think most people – mean by the true spirit of public service we are re-establishing. What the Citizen's Charter expresses – carried through into the individual charters tailored to each service – are the standards which we should expect and the ideals which we should cherish in our public service.

First, we want to make a reality of the all-too-often theoretical concepts of accountability in the public service. The old myth of personal ministerial responsibility for every action undertaken by each government department was, in Herbert Morrison's words, 'The Minister is responsible for every stamp stuck on an envelope'; or, as Nye Bevan more colourfully had it, 'If a bed pan is dropped, the Minister will hear of it.' As Sir Robin Butler (the Head of the Home Civil Service) has said, this was not only a myth – it was a dangerous myth. In reality, no minister can check the stamps and the bedpans. And if the minister is responsible in theory, but not practice, who is actually responsible for the action in question?[10] What we have done is to make clear the distinction between responsibility, which can be delegated, and accountability, which remains firmly with the minister. The minister is properly accountable for the policies he settles, and the service his department purchases or for which it contracts; those who have agreed to provide services are quite properly responsible for their provision. Thus, far from impairing accountability, I believe that the purchaser/provider separation, executive agencies and management by contract have helped to make a reality of it. Clear targets are set, performance is monitored and published, and success or failure is rewarded or penalized. Agencies, in Sir Robin's view, represent 'a lastingly beneficial change in the management of the Civil Service'.[11] I would not dissent from that judgement; but the principle of clear devolution of management against agreed targets underlies the whole reform, from the NHS to the management of defence research.

Thus the first principle of the Charter is that explicit standards of service should not only be set, but published and then prominently displayed at the point of delivery. The purpose of this is to empower users, by providing them with the information they need to bring pressure to bear on the provider directly, or by bringing pressure to bear on the responsible purchaser, or, where possible, by introducing real choice so that the user can change to a better service. John Patten has spoken eloquently about this in his CPC lecture of 4 February 1993.[12]

Where possible, choice should be in the hands of the citizens directly, using the improved information, as it is in the hands of higher education students or, within the inevitable limits, of parents choosing schools. In health, the most sophisticated of the internal market systems increasingly makes the general practitioner the proxy purchaser for the citizen – and capitation payments to the GP make it worthwhile for him to seek to please his patients. The system genuinely devolves power right down. In other cases, where there is unavoidable monopoly, the customer's preference can only be set out in published targets after full consultation with him – and failure or success in delivery must be rewarded by the establishment of performance pay in the provider organization and, where appropriate, effective pressure from above from the government department and below by independent and open inspectorates, with lay representation, which will together stand proxy for the citizen by means of establishing and then monitoring the service contract with the supplier. Rail franchising will be a useful new mechanism for bringing agreed standards directly to bear on providers of train services on behalf of passengers: it is likely to be far more effective than the old system of confrontational departmental negotiation with a monolithic British Rail Board.

. . .

The public service of the future

These reforms will leave us with a smaller, less centralized and more customer-conscious public service. By the end of this decade, or at the start of the next, both at the centre and in local government, it is likely to consist of a comparatively small core and a series of devolved delivery organizations – many of which will be as large as, or larger than, the core. At the centre, Next Steps agencies and the contracting out of services will generate this outcome; local government is already well on the way. As Howard Davies has said, our reforms, and the new management systems that they will introduce, amount to 'a revolution leaving few parts of the public sector untouched'.[13]

References

1 *A Framework for Government Research and Development* (Cmnd. 4814), November 1971.
2 'Redefining the mixed economy', speech to the Centre for Policy Studies, 23 November 1992.
3 *National Journal*, 9 May 1992, p. 1998.
4 *Fabian Review*, November 1992.
5 See note 2 above.

6 *The Independent*, 2 April 1992.
7 See *The Next Steps Agencies: Review 1992* (Cm 2111), December 1992.
8 *The Guardian*, 29 August 1992.
9 *FDA News*, January 1993.
10 *Public Service in a Changing World*, The Frank Stacey Memorial Lecture by Sir Robin Butler, 7 September 1992.
11 See note 10 above.
12 'The home front in a new century', CPC lecture, 4 February 1993.
13 *The Times*, 7 July 1992.

Abridged from W. Waldegrave (1993) *Public Service and the Future: Reforming Britain's Bureaucracies*, London, Conservative Political Centre, pp. 13–23. Reproduced with the permission of the Conservative Political Centre.

6

Reforming Whitehall II: the critics have their say

The civil service has always had its critics. Until the past few years many of the criticisms emanating from the academic community were aimed at the status quo. Various shortcomings were identified. The bureaucracy was unduly powerful, threatening to pervert the democratic process. It was the incarnation of an elitist society. Or it was simply inefficient – inadequate to its task in the contemporary world. *Ergo*, whatever were its characteristics, new ones should be sought. The reforms of the past decade or so have, however, changed things around – more because the world has changed than because academics have voluntarily changed their minds. When seemingly encrusted traditions remain undisturbed, critics are apt to chime out their shortcomings: when these traditions are placed in jeopardy, the critics (not always the same ones) now trumpet their virtues. Some of the traditional values of the civil service are worth having, after all. They should be protected amidst the headlong rush towards the new managerialism. Efficiency has its price. The old public sector bureaucracy – slow, cumbersome and clay-footed – could at least usually be relied upon to bend its knee to the altar of justice, accountability and equity of treatment. Besides, perhaps it was not too inefficient anyway – or not so seriously flawed as to be beyond redemption without the need for major upheaval and consequent threat to its mainstay values. Such, in summary, may be said of the views of at least one body of critics.

Richard Chapman (Reading 6.1) reminds us that the values and singular characteristics of the British civil service emerged piecemeal over a long period of time. They were not the product of any monumental blueprint or 'big idea'. As such, it is easy for would-be reformers to misunderstand its nature, to strike unwittingly at its very soul in a misguided attempt to attend to some manifest bodily ailment. He thinks that the new managerialism has had some destructive and unwelcome consequences. He fears that the civil service no longer exists as a distinct institution with certain characteristics. What exactly has been lost? Fred Inglis (Reading 6.2) believes that the civil service has lost the tradition of high-minded public morality bequeathed by the grandees of the nineteenth century. He thinks that top mandarins, such as Sir Robin Butler, have been almost willing accomplices in the process by which the Thatcher and Major Governments have hijacked the state apparatus. He is dismissive of Sir Robin's Frank Stacey Memorial lecture (see Reading 5.1). At a different level Vernon Bogdanor (Reading 6.3) questions the attempt to separate service delivery from policy work, a cornerstone of the Ibbs Report and of much of the new managerialism. Specifically, Bogdanor takes issue with the assumption that such separation can secure both greater efficiency and enhanced accountability. In asserting that apparently narrow operational matters may turn out to have political and electoral significance, he restates one of the traditional principles of British public administration theory. Patricia Greer provides some empirical evidence to support the traditional position (Reading 6.4). This she does by examining the working of one of the framework agreements, the documents which specify how each Next Steps agency is to operate.

In a broader sense, Grant Jordan (Reading 6.5) questions the logic and many of the assumptions by which the new managerialism has been decorated with 'vision'. He offers a critique of Osborne and Gaebler's *Reinventing Government* (Reading 5.5). He dissects the central arguments of their best-selling volume and finds many of them wanting, not least as practical guides. He does not quite sing a hymn of praise to the traditional, rule-bound bureaucracy. But he thinks that it has sometimes been misunderstood, especially by Osborne and Gaebler. Bureaucratic failures, Jordan suggests, may be more acceptable than the failures of the now preferred entrepreneurial, enterprise style of public administration.

By no means all the critics see greater virtue in the traditional values than in the entrepreneurship of the new managerialism. Some, on the contrary, direct their critiques not to the principles associated with the initiatives of recent years, but to what they see as either the lack of vision or the faint-heartedness with which they have been put to practice. Ironically, one such critic is himself a former practitioner. Sir Peter Kemp was, between 1988 and 1992, the Next Steps Project Manager. Claims and counter-claims have been made about the precise reasons for his enforced early retirement. His enthusiasm for reform, perhaps part of the problem, has since shown no sign of abating. In a widely publicized monograph (Reading 6.6) he offers both an analysis and an agenda for reform. He questions the existence of a single 'public service ethos'. He opposes a code of conduct. He identifies what he sees as sources of resistance to change, urging a bolder thrust in the direction of the new managerialism. Norman Lewis is another friendly critic of the recent changes, though one with a difference. For one thing, he is an academic. For another, he advocates further reforms, not all of which would be welcome even to the most ardent supporter of the present Conservative Government. The piece reproduced here (Reading 6.7) is from his booklet *How to Reinvent Government*. With obvious reference to Osborne and Gaebler, he poses some of the bigger questions. There is a need, he says, for more strategic vision, for a redefinition of the public sector. He favours the contractual approach but stresses the need for more fundamental readjustments if worthwhile benefits are to accrue to the citizen.

Richard Chapman

The end of the civil service?

Until recently, the British civil service was generally thought, by those who served in it, to be the best in the world. Citizens, too, in so far as they knew anything about the institutions of British public administration, tended to be proud of it. Anyone who doubted this confidence had only to compare British experience with other countries and/or talk to many foreigners who came to Britain to study it and consider how some of its best features could be copied. By comparison, in other countries there was often corruption; political influence; a lack of ethical standards; no tradition of public service; and all sorts of inefficiency, especially in connection with recruitment and the management of public finance.

In Britain the civil service was recruited on the basis of publicly known criteria, by open competitions, administered by a Civil Service Commission, under commissioners whose independence was ensured because they were directly appointed by the Queen. The service was, for many years, politically neutral in a partisan sense: officials did not change with governments. Over a considerable period of time, they developed a professional pride, with ethical standards that were generally learned not from formal training sessions or from codes or statements that had the status of law, but from socialization and learning from experience. They were sensitive to the constraints of the political environment in which they worked but, whatever their personal ideologies, they believed in the values of a public service which put the interests of citizens before their own or those of political parties. They also received personal satisfaction from the management techniques they pioneered and developed and from providing services that gave citizens generally, and not just customers of particular services, good value for the taxes and other revenues raised by government.

There were a number of practical reasons why this civil service was so respected. The absence of corruption and political influence in the executive operations of government was thought to be consistent with the highest aspirations of democratic government, and especially well suited to the British political and administrative culture. The ethical standards put the interests of citizens foremost and did not result in personal glory or financial benefits to particular officials; instead the officials remained anonymous in a system which made politicians publicly accountable. The civil service was seen as a highly developed organization containing many outstandingly able people whose achievements justly earned admiration and praise, especially in comparison with the lesser achievements and significant failures of comparable work in business or industry.

Many of these good qualities were achieved piecemeal, over long periods of time. They were not the result of major statutes or great constitutional landmarks. Indeed, the civil service has never even been precisely and authoritatively defined, but this may be entirely consistent with other features of a system of government that does not have a single written document known as a constitution. The Tomlin and Priestley Royal Commissions on the Civil Service said that civil servants were 'those servants of the Crown, other than holders of political or judicial offices, who are employed in a civil capacity, and whose remuneration is paid wholly and directly out of monies voted by Parliament'.[1] For all practical purposes, it was generally known that civil servants were civilians who worked in government departments, but who did not work for local authorities or public corporations. Nowadays, however, with the majority of civil servants working in agencies, some of which are Trading Funds[2] and therefore not entirely dependent on monies voted by Parliament, many people who are said to be part of the civil service do not meet the remuneration requirement in the Tomlin definition, and this makes it difficult to apply the basic test of who civil servants are.

The piecemeal development of the high standards achieved by the British civil service was largely the result of pressures for efficiency in the nineteenth century and early years of this century. This is well illustrated in the reports of commissions and committees of inquiry, including the Northcote-Trevelyan Report of 1854,[3] the Playfair Report of 1875,[4] the Ridley Report of 1888,[5] the MacDonnell Report of 1914.[6] Together, the implemented recommendations from these and other internal Treasury reports resulted in effective Treasury control over civil establishments and high standards of management within government departments. These were thought to be necessary but not sufficient features of a good civil service. The service also developed in other, less tangible, ways.

Perhaps the most important characteristic of the British civil service developed in this century was its sense of unity. As Sir Warren Fisher told the Tomlin Royal Commission:

> Until relatively recent years the expression 'Civil Service' did not correspond either to the spirit or to the facts of the organisation so described. There was a series of Departments with conditions of service which in quite important respects differed materially. Departments did not really think of themselves as merely units of a complete and correlated whole . . . Such departmentalism is, of course, the antithesis

of a 'Service' ... Status, remuneration, prestige and organisation throughout the Departments have been assimilated. There is an ever-growing team sense in all ranks; it pervades the whole conduct of public business . . . [and] if the country is to go on getting in requisite measure the service it needs from the civil establishments of the Crown, the ideal of a Service must be fostered and supported in all ways possible and thereby traditions and experience be broader and deeper based.[7]

Fisher could look on these aspects of the British civil service with pride, for he did much to foster the team spirit he thought so essential. He set personal standards which he fearlessly defended and expected in others. He taught these standards by example, and largely through informal contacts. He developed the Civil Service Sports Council, whose Vice-Chairman (the executive position in the Council) Fisher reckoned to have 'done more to make the civil service realise that it is not a lot of disjointed parochial Departments than the whole of the rest of us put together'.[8]

Much, however, has altered in the civil service in the past ten years or so, and it may now be doubted whether Britain still has a civil service in the sense outlined above. Indeed, in the ways Fisher and his immediate successors saw it, as the fourth service of the Crown, the civil service as an entity no longer exists. Four closely related important changes illustrate why this is so, each of which is worth further examination and might, indeed, be dealt with as undergraduate dissertation topics.

First are the methods of selection for the civil service. One of the significant reforms of the nineteenth century was to introduce open competitive examination on a service-wide basis with the recruitment responsibilities in the hands of the Civil Service Commission. Now, from 1991,[9] we no longer have a Civil Service Commission. Instead there is an agency called Recruitment and Assessment Services, which contracts to do recruitment for departments (though last year it made a significant deficit because departments preferred to do their own recruitment)[10] and a small Office of the Civil Service Commissioners. The Office of the Civil Service Commissioners consists of twenty people based in Basingstoke plus two in London.[11] Among their duties the Commissioners monitor, in a 'light-handed and economical way',[12] the now more than 3,000 devolved units of recruitment, known as 'accountable units', to ensure that they are recruiting according to the principles laid down by the minister for fair and open competition. It is too early yet to assess the effectiveness of the Commissioners in this task, but the new arrangements undoubtedly mean the end of the common system of recruitment. Furthermore, it seems unlikely that the numerous recruitment agencies will be able to maintain the high standards previously expected and achieved by the Civil Service Commission, and so much admired in other countries.

Secondly, there is now no real sense of unity in the civil service. Sir Robin Butler, the present Head of the Civil Service, has said that we now have a civil service that is unified but not uniform,[13] but the sense of unity he believes still exists is largely undermined by the fact that about half the civil service now works in agencies or other organizations operating on Next Steps lines, which are being positively encouraged to develop their own team spirit and loyalties.

Staff, we are told, now often think of themselves as belonging to a particular department or agency, not to a wider civil service. They work in units that, far from displaying a team spirit with a common ethos, compete with each other, issue contracts to each other, and in so doing charge what are thought to be business-like rates for their services. In some respects the agencies are not completely independent entities, especially as they have been created by executive decisions and no legislation has been required, but conscious efforts are now made to stimulate feelings of enterprise and initiative in them and there can be no doubt that these have resulted in a fundamental change from an ethos that was previously admired, and which contributed to the identity of the civil service.

Thirdly, the emphasis on enterprise, initiative and a more business-like style of management, illustrated in the Thatcher years by preference in promotion or appointment of staff who were thought to be 'can do' types,[14] seems oddly at variance with the expectations of officials working in a bureaucracy. The dangers in adopting these preferred qualities is well illustrated by examples like Crichel Down (where the enthusiasm of officials for creating model farms was a factor in a situation that led to a ministerial resignation) and the dismissal of Sir Christopher Bullock (whose enthusiasm for his work as permanent secretary in the 1930s led to errors of judgement).[15]

Fourthly, since the important written statement from the Chancellor of the Exchequer on the day the House of Commons adjourned for its 1991 summer recess,[16] departments have been given much greater freedom to introduce flexible staff structures and pay systems. This means that there is now much less opportunity to transfer between departments and much less expectation that there are similar conditions of service in different departments. Indeed, the trade unions now refer to 'employment ghettoes'. Furthermore, as a result of legislation now being considered by Parliament, known as the Civil Service (Management Functions) Bill, there is to be increased scope for delegation of functions according to what appear to be quite extraordinary powers to be given to ministers to delegate functions to 'a servant of the Crown of such description as he may specify' and 'subject to such conditions as he thinks fit'. In the House of Lords, where this controversial Bill was introduced, Earl Russell said that these powers amount to saying that 'the Secretary of State may do whatever he likes'.[17]

The lesson seems to be that the British civil service, as a distinct institution of the public service, identifiable primarily through certain characteristics or qualities rather than through an authoritative and/or legal definition, no longer exists. If others claim that it does, can they reasonably point to unifying characteristics to sustain that claim? How can such an institution be so identified if it has flexible methods of selection of staff; or has different staff grading and pay structures; or different conditions of service for staff employed in a large number of independent or quasi-independent departments and agencies? In some cases, pay is not even dependent on moneys voted by Parliament. Moreover, throughout the system, if system it is, there is positive encouragement of staff to identify with their independent units rather than with the service as whole; and there is encouragement, too, for staff to discard their anonymity and exercise management enterprise and initiative on their own account. The new and much looser conception of public service, which sees citizens as customers, seems increasingly through the Charter Movement to be assuming precedence over Crown service. If the characteristics associated with the British civil service are no longer present, the consequences may be serious for the position of officials in an accountable democracy, for the efficient and economical management of public services within the British political system and also for the interests of individual citizens within it. Is it not a responsibility for teachers of public administration to see that these points are examined by officials working in the public sector and also by citizens at large?

References

1 Tomlin Commission: *Royal Commission on the Civil Service 1929–31, Report,* Cmd 3909, London, HMSO, 1931; Priestly Commission: *Royal Commission on the Civil Service 1953–55, Report,* Cmd 9613, London, HMSO, 1955.
2 Government Trading Funds Act 1973 (as amended, 1990).
3 Northcote-Trevelyan Report: *Report on the Organisation of the Permanent Civil Service,* London, HMSO, 1854.
4 Playfair Reports: *Reports of the Civil Service Inquiry Commission,* C. 1113 and C. 1266, London, HMSO, 1875.
5 Ridley Report: *Royal Commission on Civil Establishments of the Different Offices of State at Home and Abroad,* C. 5545, London, HMSO, 1888.
6 MacDonnell Report: *Royal Commission on the Civil Service, 1914, Fourth Report,* Cd 7338, London, HMSO, 1914.
7 Minutes of Evidence to the Tomlin Commission, p. 1267, Statement submitted by the Permanent Secretary to the Treasury, paras 3, 4, 5, 6.
8 *First and Second Report from the Committee of Public Accounts, together with the Proceedings of the Committee, Minutes of Evidence, Appendices and Index,* HC 45, 144, London, HMSO, 1936, Q. 4488.
9 *Civil Service Commissioners' Report 1990–91 and Report 1991–92,* London, Office of the Civil Service Commissioners, 1991 and 1992.
10 *The Guardian,* 7 February 1992.
11 *Civil Service Commissioners' Report,* 1991–92.
12 *Civil Service Commissioners' Report,* 1990–91.
13 Treasury and Civil Service Committee, Fifth Report, Session 1988–89, *Developments in the Next Steps Programme, together with the Proceedings of the Committee, Minutes of Evidence and Appendices,* HC 348, London, HMSO, 1989, Q. 320.
14 Report of an RIPA Working Group, *Top Jobs in Whitehall, Appointments and Promotions in the Senior Civil Service,* London, Royal Institute of Public Administration, 1987.
15 See Richard A. Chapman, *Ethics in the British Civil Service,* London, Routledge, 1988.
16 195 HC Deb., 6s, Col. *604–5* (24 July 1991).
17 538 HL Deb., 6s, Col. *1078* (7 July 1992).

From R. Chapman (1992) 'The end of the civil service?', *Teaching Public Administration,* Vol. 7, No. 2, pp. 1–5. Reproduced with the permission of IDPM, University of Manchester.

So farewell then, citizen servant!

Last autumn Public Policy and Administration published Sir Robin Butler's Stacey Lecture, given in memory of a famously discreet but unbending Vosper figure in the civil service. The occasion was the annual conference of the public administration committee of the joint universities council, which may sound arcane but which echoes to the long history of coincidences between England's governance of Britain by its ruling class, and the intellectual elite which has held its hand and dogged its footsteps.

Surprisingly enough, this is a rich and complex history which has never found its historian. Not surprisingly, Noel Annan, looking for his own parentage, long ago contributed a rather good essay on the network of rulers and advisers in the golden triangle of Oxford, Cambridge and London; but no one else has followed him up.

Such an effort would be the more timely because that same network is now become a cobweb. It is torn, forgotten and dusty; most of it was swept away by the coarse witch's broom brought so uncomprehendingly to British society by Margaret Thatcher.

At its best, the propinquity and collaboration – the sheer familiarity – of, let us say, the early Fabians and the Asquith government made for a marvellous model of what the politics of policy-making could and should look like. The high-minded legacy of Mill and the glowing aura of T.H. Green tilted and filled the minds of an idealistic generation seeking to build the institutions which would make Britain a finer, juster, more equal, dammit, a more comfortable place to live.

Morris, Mill and Green – as Mrs Humphrey Ward of all people realized in *Robert Elsmere* – are our great ancestors here, and it is more than time we put a bit more fervour into our ancestor-worship after the vicious defiling of the university sarcophagi since 1979. Such men, and a very few women, Beatrice

Webb, Mary Richmond, Margaret MacMillan and the barmy Annie Besant among them, gave form and content to the good life of the intellectual, as lived in the highly peculiar context of imperial Britain.

No doubt, according to the standards of latter-day cynicism as lived in the scrubbed-pine kitchen, there is plenty to laugh at in the lives of these worthies . . . Lockjawed Marxists for whom sanctimony has always proved easier than hard political work have also much given themselves to jeering, especially when that tradition of philanthropic and idealist intelligence founded itself in its own image at the LSE. Those eminent Victorians devised empiricism-with-a-social-purpose, and they did great good with it. The unalike and noble lives of Keynes and R.H. Tawney are proof of that. Keynes invented the Arts Council and world prosperity for a generation. Tawney begot education for all and the idea of equality.

None of us can find a picture of the good life, whether of individuals or of societies, without historical examples to admire, to criticize and – with suitably modest modifications – to follow. The lives of those academics and intellectuals I have named here are not so remote they cannot be applied today, even in the quality-assessed concentration camps of the Very Old, the Oldish, the Old-New and the New Universities.

But that tradition has suffered dreadful fractures. They have been caused quite intentionally. It was Robin Butler's business in his lecture last year to pretend that the crack of the break has been inaudible, and that the bones were not sticking through the skin of the body politic.

For it was the civil service committed to his care which, at his mistress's voice, did so much to smash the shins in question, and few people in power respond sympathetically to charges of venality, still less of treason. After all, the civil servants of the past 15 years were bustled on to the fast track from the golden triangle. The principles and methods of inquiry instilled by the Spirit of British Administration as extolled by that bleak old poet C.H. Sisson dissolved deplorably fast. The much-quoted adjustment of the unemployment figures 19 (or is it 20?) times over these years, and only once to the disadvantage of a Government which didn't give a toss about them anyway, is only the best-known of a long series of instances in which the always so very Civil Service was instructed to evade, conceal, propagandize and, ultimately, lie on behalf of the ruling political party . . .

Time after time, under its supine and conniving leadership, the Civil Service has taken an active hand in its own corruption. And what opposition has it to boast of when asked what it did in the great class war? Clive Ponting and Sarah Tisdall. The latter, shamefully exposed by our great liberal newspaper, did time. The former was only saved by the sudden return of their guts to 12 good persons and true, those guts presumably having been turned over by the then Secretary of State for Defence, and his sickening and mendacious vilification (presumably shaped by Civil Service colleagues) of Clive Ponting in the House of Commons . . .

Even worms as well trodden on as these worms may turn in the end, however. Their genteel union the First Division Association has, in a hilarity-provoking suggestion to the select committee, proposed that there be a published code of civil service ethics. In a gingerly way, this has recently given the association a chance to murmur, after clearing its throat, that its members have been writing Tory propaganda.

Such murmurings are too mild beside the plain and visible facts. A torrent of events, gross errors and plain disasters makes it clear that the sometime impartiality, careful objectivity and intelligent balancing of arguments, once the master-symbols of the service, have all been irrevocably contaminated by the conscious decisions of the Thatcher and Major Governments to close the gap between the interests of their party and the state itself. The Clinton business was the unbelievable caricature of this process.

Once upon a time, when Hobbes first thought of it, but then more comprehensively when Mill invented liberalism and its institutions, the state was conceived of as a protector of the citizen against the predictable horribleness of rulers. Thanks to the *Daily Express*, the *Sun* and *Yes, Minister*, the state has been turned into an enemy, and subsequently transformed by the Enemy Herself into an adjunct of power-without-value. Now, to their panic, the Civil Service elite has discovered that every job in the place may be sold off to tender in a desperate attempt to shave another sliver off the deficit, and this knight and that (specifically Sir Michael Partridge) are belatedly rediscovering dismal staff morale and the virtues of an educated and disinterested administration not just in it for the money.

Robin Butler has pursued this politics much as he played rugby for Oxford: cheerfully, charmingly, spoilingly, negligently; even a bit lazily. But he is only last in a chain of responsibility which has gone a long way to destroy the great canons of the Service, themselves culled from Max Weber's good bureaucrat. Efficiency, mastery of the files, impartiality towards the client, judiciousness, fairness, fidelity to the facts – the simple virtues of a humane social science – are all fearfully wounded casualties of the ideological gangsters.

These wounds, gangrenous already, run backwards into the veins of intellectual life. In science, as everybody knows, the continuities of seriously difficult research and the provision of the best recruits able to sustain such work have been utterly severed by Thatcherism (and Waldegrave's new White Paper, you may be sure, will do nothing for it). So too social science, ever since Keith Joseph's fatuous insistence that there is no such thing, has been cut off from the humane vision which it drew from its great past and without which it becomes, as they say, merely academic . . .

Something has died. Something idealistic and public spirited which brought a generation into universities after Robbins has been put out by a brief Terror. As is generally the case in our somnambulist society, the boss goes about saying nothing much is the matter and everything will soon be fine. But what is really at stake is what university teachers still with a social conscience may do for the large, blunt and disobliging names of the liberal polity: for justice, freedom, equality, truth and all that; for comfort and happiness, also. In short, what is now the point of the job?

Abridged from F. Inglis (1993) 'So farewell then, citizen servant!', *Times Higher Education Supplement*, 6 August 1993. Reproduced with the permission of Times Newspapers Ltd and of Professor Fred Inglis.

| *Vernon Bogdanor*

A threat to democracy?

The central theme of John Major's administration can be summed up in the phrase *the privatization of choice*. This, the Prime Minister has insisted, is 'the greatest and most far-reaching' privatization and 'the one to which I am most committed'.

He seeks to give the consumer the same rights in respect of public services as are already enjoyed by the shopper at Marks and Spencer or Sainsbury. To achieve this, the Government has set in motion the most radical changes in the structure of British administration since the Northcote-Trevelyan report laid the basis of the modern civil service in 1853.

These changes have been described by the minister responsible for the civil service, William Waldegrave, as a genuine revolution in Whitehall, a revolution involving the Citizen's Charter, the contracting out of public services, market testing and the devolution of functions to new executive agencies outside Whitehall.

The fundamental premise is that public services can be made both more efficient and more accountable if the two functions of policy and service delivery are separated. Policy will remain with ministers, who will continue to be advised by a core civil service; but the delivery of services is to be located outside departments and conducted, so far as possible, according to commercial criteria.

Is the delivery of public services, then – health, social security or education – merely a complex form of commercial activity?

In a democracy, those who deliver a service – the chief executive of an agency, the managers of a trust hospital, or the governors of a grant-maintained school – work under constraints which have no counterpart in the business world. They are subject to Treasury control, statutory obligations to deal with difficult 'customers' and they are, in the last resort, responsible to ministers for what they do.

But, above all, chief executives and managers remain under the authority of ministers whose political careers will depend upon the efficiency with which services are delivered.

It is this political element which makes the separation of powers between policy-making and service delivery unworkable under our present constitutional arrangements.

What is policy and how is it to be distinguished from service delivery? If someone is denied a benefit, or his or her child is denied admission to a school of first choice, is that a matter of policy or management?

What may seem a mere matter of administrative detail can have enormous political and electoral repercussions. If, for example, the social security system operates inefficiently, or small rural schools are being closed, the political standing of the government will be affected, and ministers will be pressed to intervene . . .

It was for this reason that a similar attempt to demarcate separate spheres of responsibility in relation to the nationalized industries failed so dismally.

The theory behind the public corporation was that the boards would be responsible for commercial management, while ministers would be responsible for policy. In practice, however, governments intervened on highly detailed matters in accordance with their political imperatives . . .

Why should it be any easier to devise a separation of powers in the case of the public services? If no clear line can be drawn, then devolution to agencies will serve to blur accountability, not to clarify it.

It will never be clear whether the failure to achieve a target is due to an 'operational' factor, the inefficiency of an agency or to a 'policy' factor – the interference of the minister.

What is likely is that ministers will take the credit when targets are achieved, while officials will be given the blame when things go wrong.

The principle of ministerial responsibility holds that ministers take the credit for what goes right and the blame for what goes wrong. The 'revolution' in the public services will make it easier for ministers to accept the first part of that principle.

The 'revolution in government', then, will fail, because it will be found to offend against our basic norms of accountability and democracy.

The fundamental mistake is the attempt to treat government as a form of business. A consumer can, by shifting his or her custom from Marks and Spencer to Sainsbury, use market mechanisms to secure his or her needs. A 'customer' of the Benefits Agency or a trust hospital has no such option. The only way in which the citizen can influence social security or health policy is through the political process.

The cumulative effect of the reforms is to create what Professor John Stewart has called a new magistracy of unelected and unaccountable managers. Their 'customers' will enjoy the right which was also guaranteed under the constitution of the former Soviet Union, the right to complain.

Ministers claim that their 'revolution in government' puts into practice the precepts of *Reinventing Government*, by David Osborne and Ted Gaebler, a book difficult to obtain in Britain. It is perhaps for this reason that so few seem to have noticed that its precepts point in a different direction from that taken by the government.

The prescriptions of Osborne and Gaebler are based on the experience of America. It is hardly likely that the same prescriptions will be appropriate for a country with quite the opposite characteristics.

Crucial to the whole Osborne/Gaebler argument is the principle of decentralization. Responsibility, they declare, 'should lie with the lowest level of government possible'. They would hardly regard an English funding agency which could become responsible for schools, serving a population of 40 million people, for example, as an exemplification of their principles.

For them, it is local communities, through their elected representatives, not unelected boards and agencies, which should decide upon priorities for the public services.

Sensible reform must begin with a determined attack on central government overload. That means restoring power to local authorities as representatives of their communities, together with devolution to elected regional authorities, which would be responsible for the National Health Service and other public services unsuitable for local control.

At the level of central government, we badly need to clarify the precise constitutional responsibilities of ministers and civil servants. In particular, civil servants are entitled to far better guidance than they, at present, receive as to what ministers can require them to do, and the circumstances under which they themselves must accept responsibility.

We badly need a proper code delineating not only civil service ethics, but also the proper role of ministers.

The truth is that the government's 'reform' of the public services has become a substitute for the democratization of the British state. While our partners in the European Community have been moving in the direction of devolution and decentralization, we have been moving in the opposite direction, away from the principles of citizenship and towards a system of government which reduces the ethic of public service to a form of commercialism.

It may be too late to reverse this trend; but, if we do not, we shall find that the government's public service reforms will have undermined the democratic rights of every man and woman in this country.

Abridged from V. Bogdanor (1993) 'Market must not sell democracy short', *The Times*, 7 June. Reproduced with the permission of Times Newspapers and of Vernon Bogdanor.

| *Patricia Greer*

Executive agencies and public administration theory

Working within the framework agreements

This section considers how the framework documents have been working in practice as 'contracts' by which agencies can be 'managed' at arm's length. It focuses on two areas covered by the agency framework documents: the division of responsibilities between the various parties involved in an agency agreement and the extent to which the personnel and financial freedoms delegated to agencies in the framework documents have allowed them to get on with their jobs in the most efficient and effective way. The section then considers how the framework documents are likely to develop.

The theoretical difficulties with the division of responsibilities between departmental headquarters and agencies have been well documented.[1] The main difficulty is that despite their attempts at clarity, the framework documents fail to paint a black and white divide in respective responsibilities because of the lack of a clear dividing line between 'policy' and 'day to day operational issues'. The scope for departmental headquarters to become involved in detailed agency activities by classifying them as 'policy' is highlighted by Robert Maclennan MP who, in debating the National Audit Act, stated,

> I believe that it is possible to go right through the decision making process in any Department, Authority or Body which could be subject to examination and at almost any point seek to cover the subject under investigation by the claim that it is an issue of policy . . . Policy is not determinable either as a matter of fact or as as matter of law. It can be determinable only as a matter of judgement by those called upon to distinguish it.[2]

There may be an incentive for departmental headquarters to define policy issues downwards into operational issues because ministers remain ultimately responsible for *all* of the activities of their departments and as such may be reluctant to devolve responsibility to their agencies.[3]

Classifying detailed agency activities as 'policy' provides departments with the rationale for close involvement in agency day to day affairs. This downward defining of 'policy' is more likely to happen in areas of political sensitivity such as social security. Clearly the day to day activities of the Benefits Agency are more likely to incite political interest than the activities of something like the Meteorological Office executive agency. For example, decisions about the layout of local social security offices are clearly operational but the questions are of considerable political interest. Should the wall to floor bullet-proof screens be removed to make the offices more friendly or would this put staff at risk? Should the offices have private areas or rooms where people can talk about their financial affairs out of the earshot of their neighbours? MPs all have social security staff and recipients in their constituencies, many of whom have strong feelings about such issues.

In practice it seems that these fears have been realized. Despite the Next Steps rhetoric . . . Tony Newton, when he was the Social Security Secretary of State, found that the number of managerial issues he dealt with had not reduced and he saw that the high political profile of social security meant that this was unlikely to change ('depending on the future of social security'!).

The political nature of the Social Security Benefits Agency may also explain why it was the only executive agency examined by the Treasury and Civil Service Committee in 1991 for which a departmental spokesman (a deputy secretary) accompanied the agency chief executive to the committee hearing. Indeed, Mr Montagu, the then deputy secretary who attended the hearing, was asked by the committee chairman whether he was in attendance in order to 'mind the agency'. Of course he replied that he was 'absolutely not' there to 'mind the agency'.

It does seem, therefore, that the framework documents have not been entirely successful in ensuring that the parties to an agency agreement all play their parts in ensuring the success and development of the agency. Certainly initially, some departments have been exploiting the blurred border between policy and operations in order to become more involved in agency affairs. As we have already seen, this was also the conclusion of the Prime Minister's Efficiency Unit, who undertook a study in 1991, commonly known as the Fraser Report, which examined the relationship between departmental headquarters and their agencies.[4] The main thrust of the recommendations was that departments should reduce their level of involvement in agency activities.

Personnel and financial freedoms

This section considers whether the freedoms granted in the initial agency framework documents have directly resulted in changes to existing personnel and financial management practices. Overall, the initial agency framework documents have not in general granted much in the way of personnel or financial freedoms. On the personnel side, agencies were initially contracted to stay within the overall civil service pay and grading arrangements. These arrangements did allow certain flexibilities; for example, to recruit staff directly but only up to relatively low levels (in most cases to clerical officer and in only seven cases out of the first 34 agencies, to lower middle management levels – grades 6 and 7) and to pay some staff group bonuses and individual performance bonuses.[5] Equally, with regard to the new financial arrangements, the first agency framework documents only allowed limited freedoms; for example, in the amounts that they could transfer between current and capital budgets, in how they could use any revenue they generate or efficiency savings they make or in the amounts or surplus they can carry between years.

This cautious start led to agencies experiencing some frustration and to some poor financial practices. For example, on the personnel side, Ros Hepplewhite, the chief executive of the Child Support Agency, said that the personnel constraints meant that she was limited in her ability to match skills to jobs: 'In a market place there is a free flow of labour but if I advertise a grade 7 post, I can only have grade 7 people apply even if there are other people at more junior levels more suited to the particular post'.[6]

Equally, within the Benefits Agency, the system of assessing staff's suitability for promotion and then sending them for interviews to promotion boards, without full regard to the numbers of vacancies at the more senior level available, continued throughout the early days of the agency. Again staff were not being matched to jobs. It also meant that it was difficult to keep and to motivate good staff as all the emphasis was on promotion rather than on development within a job and possibly being paid a higher salary for doing a job well.

On the financial side, there have been some examples of poor financial management resulting from the half delegation of financial freedoms. An example relates to the freedom for the Benefits Agency to carry over to the following year any underspend. At present the Benefits Agency can carry over only 0.5 per cent of its total current budget if it underspends. The incentive, contrary to the aims of Next Steps, is therefore to find ways of spending any money over and above this 0.5 per cent before the end of the financial year or it will be lost!

The initial personnel and financial freedoms as specified in the first framework documents were therefore cautious and this caution has led to some difficulties . . . However, the agencies are now in the process of negotiating with their departments and with the Treasury for additional personnel flexibilities and there are also calls for greater financial flexibilities.

Developing the framework documents

This section has shown that the framework documents have not been entirely successful in structuring the relationships between the various parties involved in an agency agreement or in ensuring that agencies have the autonomy to maximize their efficiency and effectiveness. Returning to our main theme of the division between 'policy' and 'operational' issues, the failure of the Next Steps framework documents to clearly divide the responsibilities of ministers, departments and agencies and the reluctance to address this obfuscation of responsibilities suggests that administrative theory was right and that 'policy' and 'operational' issues cannot be clearly divided.

Two possible options for the future of the framework documents have been aired . . . The Fraser Report came up with the suggestion of 'upside down' framework documents, i.e. where the documents specify everything that an agency cannot do rather than everything that an agency can do. The idea has not entirely been laid to rest but in addition to the opposition to the idea, for example, from some Department of Social Security headquarters people, there are clearly also practical difficulties in devising a list of everything that an agency cannot not do.

The second, and most probable, scenario is that the blurring of responsibilities will not be directly addressed and framework documents will increasingly fade into the background as Next Steps develops, with the agency business plans becoming more important in also setting out any changes in the environment in which an agency must operate. Certainly the Department of Social Security has decided that reviewing the framework documents every three years for the very large agencies is inappropriate: 'The Secretary of State will look at the Framework Documents every three years and see if anything needs changing but if not, the review period in which it must be revised will be much longer.'[7]

References

1 For example, see P. Greer (1992) 'The Next Steps initiatives: an examination of the agency framework documents', *Public Administration*, 70(1), 89–98.
2 R. Maclennan MP, Debate on National Audit Act, 23 March 1983.
3 P. Greer (1992), *op. cit.*
4 Efficiency Unit (1991) *Making the Most of Next Steps: the Management of Ministers' Departments and their Executive Agencies.* London, HMSO.
5 P. Greer (1992) *op. cit.*
6 Interview with Ros Hepplewhite, Chief Executive of the Child Support Agency, 12 February 1992.
7 Interview with Sir Michael Partridge, Permanent Secretary, Department of Social Security, 8 February 1993.

From P. Greer (1994) *Transforming Central Government: the Next Steps Initiative*, Buckingham, Open University Press, pp. 64–7. Reproduced with the permission of Open University Press.

Reinventing government – but will it work?

Osborne and Gaebler have maximized their popularity by, at first sight, going for a central position in the public sector/private sector debate. They argue (1992: 23), 'We do not need more government or less government, we need *better* government'. So their argument is a compromise that can appeal to all: we do not need to get rid of the public sector because we can transform it with a new culture. They argue that they are *not* proposing that government be 'run like a business' (p. 20). They suggest that, 'Few Americans would really want government to act just like a business – making quick decisions behind closed doors for private profit. If it did, democracy would be the first casualty' (p. 22). Even if the work as a whole is far more sympathetic to the 'business is best' idea than that disclaimer suggests, some of the book's appeal to those in the public sector may rest with the fact that a willingness to embrace Osborne and Gaebler's ideas might deflect even more fundamental questioning.

The ten principles

Like all management best-sellers this book has a list. The ten principles around which entrepreneurial public organizations are built are that they:

1 steer more than they row;
2 empower communities rather than simply deliver services;
3 encourage competition rather than monopoly;
4 are driven by their missions, not their rules;
5 fund outcomes rather than inputs;
6 meet the needs of the customer, not the bureaucracy;
7 concentrate on earning, not just spending;
8 invest in prevention rather than cure;
9 decentralize authority;

10 solve problems by leveraging the market place, rather than simply creating public programmes.

It is easy to agree with these propositions. Who, given the 'apple pie' nature of these features, can be against Reinventing Government? The label has already been adopted by Labour as well as government politicians. However, at issue is whether Osborne and Gaebler's prescriptions are both consistent and signposts that usefully instruct practice.

. . .

Choosing imperfections?

The authors acknowledge that in previous times Boss Tweed and his contemporaries ran (American) cities like corrupt personal fiefdoms. In reaction to this, they argue, over the next thirty years, the Progressive Movement transformed government in America by creating civil service systems with written exams, lock step pay scales, and protection from arbitrary hiring or dismissal (p. 3).

They say that

> American society embarked on a gigantic effort to control what went on inside government . . . this cleaned up many of our governments, *but in solving one set of problems, it created another*. In making it difficult to steal the public's money, we have made it virtually impossible to manage the public's money [italics added].
>
> (p. 14)

The emphasized passage signals the essence of another weakness of the book. They recognize that reforms have their 'costs', but it is not something on which they dwell. For example, in the case of a leaking steam valve they claim that the time the military takes to get the best buy on a replacement means that far more money is wasted in energy costs than is saved (p. 10). As the authors intend, one concludes that this is a silly state of affairs, but what principles does it establish? Does it say that one should not look for competitive prices – or simply that sometimes it is sensible and sometimes not. In any case, is the resource issue at Defence not about programmes that represent waste rather than waste within programmes? The issue is whether *on balance* procedures solve more problems than they create. Entrepreneurial innovation will change problems rather than eradicate them. We can only choose our problems: we cannot choose whether we have them or not.

Understanding the rationale for the past: the dilution of control?

As already implied, much of the argument of the book rests on telling illustrations. In reading their account about the success of the Expenditure Control Budget system in Visalia in California it is easy to be seduced. The community had no swimming pool. A parks and recreation official got a call from a friend in Los Angeles that the Olympic committee was selling off its training pool. The official told colleagues and they reckoned that they could save half of the $800,000 cost of a new pool. They got a second call. Two colleges wanted the pool. So a third level official raced to get a non-refundable deposit for $60,000. They quote an admiring school superintendent, 'It's something you'd find in private enterprise' (p. 4).

However, it is not enough to say that the pool was cheap and so was a good deal. Even if elected politicians want a pool in the medium term, there is no guarantee that they want it in preference to other short-term priorities. Some would argue that if the public want a pool why not let the market provide it? If the market is not interested does this mean that the running costs will be considerable? This may be more important than saving in purchase costs.

There is very little in the text on corruption and yet that is presumably the main reason for the traditional level of control. The old fashioned rules and procedures that are criticized in the book were not invented to inhibit entrepreneurial activity but were seen as a price to pay to inhibit malpractice. Osborne and Gaebler argue, 'If it costs far more to eliminate corruption than we save by doing so, is it worth the expense?' They say that to control the 5 per cent who were dishonest, the Progressives created the red tape that frustrates the other 95 per cent (p. 111). In contrast, in February 1994 Sir John Bourn gave evidence to the Treasury and Civil Service Committee that argued against the prevailing contempt for 'unnecessary red tape and bureaucracy' in the drive for change and value for money.

Local authorities are commended by Osborne and Gaebler for smart operations involving land and development, but this is precisely the sort of activity that is going to throw up conflicts of interest. Cultural change in the civil service brings disadvantages too. Osborne and Gaebler have a determined 'see no problems' attitude concerning the potential for corruption. They argue (p. 137) that, a century ago, it was relatively easy to hide corruption but, with today's information technologies, it is harder. Is it really the case that new technology has made corruption more transparent or has it given new opportunities?

How does the Osborne and Gaebler agenda deal with failure?

Osborne and Gaebler commend entrepreneurial activity, but what happens when this fails? Development deals that work are all very well but what about the consequences of a failed project? In Britain in the past decade we have seen a string of major bankruptcies among private sector developers. Why should the local authorities be more successful at this game than the private sector? Were the Crown Agents entrepreneurial? Was the hiving off of training to Astra an entrepreneurial move? Was the BCCI money borrowing/relending scheme of the Western Isles Council not a perfect example of entrepreneurial practice? What of the creative accounting of other local authorities, such as Hammersmith, that ended in the courts when losses were made? What about the taking of the student games to Sheffield? Was this a commendable piece of imagination?

It is fashionable to advocate that public sector employees be entrepreneurial but as soon as these sorts of deals go wrong we shall no doubt have the counter idea that local authorities should leave money making to the professionals. The argument here is not that when bureaucratic government fails we should label it 'entrepreneurial', but that the disadvantages of cautious, predictable, ordered administration may be more widely acceptable than the disadvantages of a more creative and risky style.

Osborne and Gaebler observe that 'entrepreneurs are people who fail many times' (p. 135). This leads Osborne and Gaebler to cite Florida's State Management Guide: 'If a department or program does not have the opportunity to do things wrong, authority is lacking to do them right' (p. 136). They write of 'creating permission to fail'. This is politically incredible. Could a politician with any hope of re-election tell his constituents, 'Sorry about the planning fiasco, but it was all in the name of experiment'? Moreover, how does this 'right to fail' sit with performance accountability? Within five pages Osborne and Gaebler are advocating replacing managers whose performance fails: so much for the authority to do things wrong.

Where is the evidence?

The Preface assumes that governments are in deep trouble. They say, 'The greatest irritant most people experience in their dealings with government is the arrogance of the bureaucracy' (p. 167). This is saloon-bar assertion. What of Goodsell's contrary survey evidence? He argues that the cases which appear in the press and are generalized into an image of an unacceptable whole are there precisely because they are unusual. He cites survey data that find far more satisfaction than otherwise with government services (Goodsell 1983: 9).

Osborne and Gaebler cite anecdotal evidence of the type, 'Federal employees we know describe colleagues who spend their days reading magazines, planning sailing trips, or buying and selling stocks. Scott Shuger . . . found that most estimated the number of "useless personnel" in their offices at 25% to 50%' (p. 127). The issue is not only the slender nature of the evidence but whether such views are peculiar to the traditional public sector. Unless such complaints also applied to the private sector was there a need for Peters and Waterman (1982)?

How does Osborne and Gaebler's case meet the sort of argument put up by Peter Blau as long ago as 1956 and mentioned in so many management and administration books since? He explained that the detailed information that offends or irritates the person from whom it is requested is exactly the requirement of the effective organization. No doubt British farmers don't like filling in returns in 1993 about their land holdings, but it is this kind of data that must be gathered if administration is to be effective.

Blau describes the consequences of Osborne and Gaebler type changes, but there is no attempt to anticipate such objections. Osborne and Gaebler commend Arkansas and Florida for removing funding from an adult education programme if 70 per cent of its graduates fail to find jobs. Didn't Blau tell us that the response will be to accept recruits to the programme on a selective basis? Osborne and Gaebler themselves quote the example of what happened when the FBI were given targets. They asked local police for lists of stolen cars that had been found – so that they could claim them as recoveries. They pursued minor felons and military deserters as they were easier to apprehend than major criminals. By the 1970s, US attorneys were declining to prosecute 60 per cent of FBI cases as they were so trivial (p. 157). In Britain in 1993 it is claimed that the new Child Support Agency has found it more cost effective to try to gain increased sums from fathers who live apart from their children but who are already making a contribution than to seek fathers who are absent and give no assistance.

As examples of the old unreformed ways, they accumulate horror stories that sound credible. The moral that they seem to want us to draw from the story is that their new menu of budgetary options will produce such advantages. One is reminded of Leslie Chapman's neglected *Your Disobedient Servant* (1978). He produced plenty of examples of poor management but prescribed better management rather than a new regime.

. . .

Competing within the public sector

As noted, the book's core argument is not that business is *always* more efficient than government. The authors claim that the important distinction is not public versus private but monopoly versus competition (p. 79). They point out that in the public sector competition is derided as 'waste and duplication', but this point only serves to remind us of the conflicting demands we have of organizations.

They admit that competition can bring out the bad as well as the good. They accept that the Defense Department use of contracting is hardly an appealing record (p. 87). They concede, 'If competition saves money only by skimping on wages and benefits, for instance, governments should question its value'.

They approve of New York Sanitation Department taking in work from other departments that were privatizing their repairs; again Britain is out of step and the British government would see this as encroaching on the private sector terrain. Osborne and Gaebler disapprove of organizing by turf rather than mission. A 'Reinvented Government' label cannot be attached to British innovations such as Next Steps agencies, which represent a move *away* from the idea of handling related problems in an integrated manner.

What is special about this time?

Osborne and Gaebler argue that zero-based budgets were a good idea in theory but in practice they have proven to be too cumbersome, too time consuming, too fraught with paperwork and too easy for managers to manipulate (p. 16). They do not convince that their own suggested reforms are going to avoid a similar fate.

It is not long since we were being told by reformers that corporate management or giant departments or reducing the number of civil service grades was the solution to inefficiency. One imagines that those who told us to set up the Management Teams might absorb Reinvented Government as uncritically as they accepted corporate management.

An alternative view to that put forward by Osborne and Gaebler might be that almost any of a wide range of arrangements *could* work if well implemented. However, the record of failure should encourage us to be sceptical of the zealots. As Downs and Larkey (1986) put it, 'The same strategies, usually renamed, are tried again and again with limited success. Rarely do proponents ask why previous attempts achieved only modest success.' Already business fashion has moved on to re-engineering rather than re-inventing (Hammer and Champy 1993).

Conclusion

If we follow the authors and accept that public bureaucracies are poor at responding to changed environments, absorb unacceptably high proportions of resources in administration, serve the interests of staff rather than the public, (and that none the less many staff find the work unsatisfying), we might still not accept Osborne and Gaebler's remedy. That neglects the fact that traditional systems had 'defects' as a consequence of delivering virtues such as reliability, fairness and probity. The issue is not why one system is a failure and needs to be abandoned, but *under what circumstances* did it or did it not produce acceptable results.

Osborne and Gaebler talk about the 36 arrows in 'government's quiver' (p. 31) but when should each be used? In Appendix A they say that once a government decides to look into the alternatives to service delivery by public employees, it faces an array of choices from 'creating legal rules and sanctions' to 'restructuring the market'. They do not help select *which* arrow is needed.

In a way which is out of step with their overall thrust that the public sector can be entrepreneurial they assert that different economic sectors (public, private, voluntary) are best suited to different tasks. Thus for economic activities, investment, profit generation, promotion of self-sufficiency, the private sector is rated as effective and the public sector is ineffective. On matters such as policy management, regulation, enforcement of equity, prevention of exploitation, promotion of social cohesion, the private sector is ineffective and the public sector is effective (p. 348). In other words Appendix A merely confirms prejudices about the nature of the three types of organizational form. Appendix B on the 'art of performance measurement' also sits uneasily with the fuller text because it acknowledges many of the problems in using indicators in a way that the core of the book neglects.

The design of government involves choosing between different packages of costs and benefits. If one chooses to remedy a specific defect one has to face up to the adverse consequences in other areas. There is much to be said for the idea that government should steer rather than row, that it should not always attempt to deliver by old-style bureaucracies. However, Osborne and Gaebler take a good case and do it a disservice by ignoring the difficulties. The trouble about the real world is that it involves trade-offs among desirable goals: we want services that are cheap to deliver but high standards; we want organizations lean but reliable; we want them flexible but predictable; we want low salaries but well-motivated staff.

Of course, perhaps it may not matter if the Osborne and Gaebler doctrines are inconsistent and poorly integrated with the massive literatures in these areas. To be an effective catalyst of change might mean that one has to evolve simple slogans that do not bear too much close scrutiny. But best if we do not believe that the slogans are enough. As Kay writes of advice on business strategy,

> Too much of what is offered as strategy consists of lists or platitudes. The value of these is not negligible . . . Platitudes are often . . . necessary reassertions of important truths . . . (but) the quack who promises relief often receives a warmer welcome than the practitioner who recognises the limitations of his own knowledge . . .
>
> (Kay 1993: 362)

The book has often been praised because it deals with concrete examples. Yet, arguably and perversely, this is the weakness of the work. In 'cherry picking' success stories the book is unrealistic; this approach *describes* successes but does not *explain* them. The major objection to Osborne and Gaebler is that it is not 'real world' enough to deal with the problems of practice.

References

Blau, P. (1956) *Bureaucracy in Modern Society*, New York, Random House.

Chapman, L. (1978) *Your Disobedient Servant*, London, Chatto and Windus.

Downs, G.W. and Larkey, P.D. (1986) *The Search for Government Efficiency*, Philadelphia, Temple.

Goodsell, C. (1983) *The Case for Bureaucracy*, Chatham, NJ, Chatham House Publishers.

Hammer, M. and Champy, R. (1993) *Re-engineering the Corporation*, Australia, Allen and Unwin.

Kay, J. (1993) *Foundations of Corporate Success*, Oxford, OUP.

Osborne, D. and Gaebler, T. (1992) *Reinventing Government*, Reading, MA; Addison-Wesley.

Peters, T. and Waterman, R. (1982) *In Search of Excellence*, New York, Harper and Row.

Abridged from G. Jordan (1994) ' "Reinventing government": but will it work?', *Public Administration*, Vol. 72, pp. 271–9. Reproduced with the permission of Blackwell Publishers.

Sir Peter Kemp

Beyond Next Steps: obstacles to fulfilment

Advising on policy, translating policy into action and delivering results is what the civil service must be all about. And that is what discussion should always primarily focus on. But in fact there is often more talk about a range of concerns which are essentially second-order questions. But they are not negligible questions, particularly during a time of change, and it is important to recognize some of the issues and concerns that have been raised and highlighted.

In examining these challenges it should be emphasized that none of them invalidate the direction in which we should be heading, indeed most underline the pressing need to undertake reform in the first place. It is also vital that all these outstanding issues be viewed in context: they are neither absolute nor universal. What suits the Treasury in Whitehall does not necessarily apply to the Coastguard in Cornwall. To think otherwise is again to risk falling back into the 'one service' trap. Here are three of the concerns that most often come up.

Accountability

The argument here is a confused one, largely because many of the commentators and critics fail to grasp the difference between an agency which lies within the civil service, and a contracted out or privatized operation which falls outside it. The latter are governed not by direct accountability to the minister but by their own statute or private contract. There may be a debate about how accountable these agencies are and over the merits of what some have dubbed 'the new magistracy' (a phrase used dismissively by those who forget how bad the old magistracy was), but there is certainly no such argument in relation to Next Steps agencies, whose chief executives remain civil servants and as such answerable to ministers and Parliament.

This point needs to be reinforced, not subsumed in some sterile argument over democratic gains and deficits. There is a substantial shift in the whole way that the civil service is organized and its services are delivered so that they are run for the benefit of the customer. This is a fundamental change and a change for the better.

That an ever greater proportion of public services are now being delivered by providers outside the civil service of course places an obligation on purchasers to build the appropriate disciplines, oversight functions and safeguards into their contracts. That these seem sometimes not to work is because civil servants have largely failed to learn how to write a sensible contract and then how to monitor it in an effective but light-handed manner. There are honourable exceptions to this; in particular the Ministry of Defence now has all its warships built and ammunition supplied under contract, and the nation remains well-defended. Other departments have to learn the same skills.

Ethics and behaviour

The question of ethics is allied to accountability and suffers from the same confusions. In fact there is no such thing as a single 'public service ethos'. Different parts of the service and different agencies and units have their own ethos which will vary according to their function in just the same way as any entity, public or private, trading or non-trading, big or small, must have a valid and appropriate set of values if it is to maintain the confidence of the public it serves.

Much has been made of the way in which 'commercialism' is supposed to have undermined standards of behaviour, the suggestion being that the existence of targets, financial or non-financial, and of a more business-like way of doing things has eroded some of the safeguards against malpractice. Yet the setting of targets is part of the monitoring process, and within the civil service that oversight function remains with the minister and Parliament. One may argue that the politicians are failing to discharge their responsibilities properly, but that is a different point. There is no such thing as a free-range manager, especially in the civil service.

. . .

Openness

Much progress has been made in increasing openness in the service in recent years, with the introduction of framework documents, reports on agencies and charters. But the recent White Paper contains one glaring omission: it fails to recognize that open government if it means anything at all is a two-way process, requiring greater participation of people in the way things are done. How much better it would be if this had been recognized, and civil servants trusted, so that they were actually encouraged to explain their actions in public. Instead there is a tendency to view openness as one-way traffic, flowing from the government to the public, and to treat it as an afterthought, part of the post-mortem, rather than as a process of opening up government.

The instinct to secrecy, to play safe, to be eternally defensive, is already so entrenched in the service that it requires little encouragement, let alone the effective endorsement of a government White Paper. A braver government would have reversed some of the present rules, so that those who spoke out would be congratulated, rather than penalized. It was after all Winston Churchill who directed that 'no officer should be penalised for lack of discretion towards the enemy'.

How to get there

The success of Next Steps and the Citizen's Charter points to a general recognition that change is necessary and possible. But the reform process hasn't yet gone far enough, nor is it so deeply rooted that a transformation of the civil service can be taken for granted. Already some are calling for a halt and the forces of darkness, to borrow Francis Maude's phrase, are gathering strength and challenging further progress. 'Concerns' are emerging to delight the complicated minds of the old school and to distract them from the straightforward task at hand.

To maintain the momentum for change it is necessary to sustain the vision of what a twenty-first century civil service should be. This requires a belief in the reforms and their purpose stemming from ministers and senior officials at the very top of the service. Unfortunately this also means placing the process in the hands of some who may not want change or believe in it.

This is the major constraint we face. As William Godwin wrote in *Political Justice* in 1793:

> There is no mistake more thoroughly to be deplored on this subject than that of persons, sitting at their ease and surrounded with all the conveniences of life, who are apt to exclaim 'We find things very well as they are'; and to inveigh bitterly against all projects of reform, as 'the romances of visionary men and the declamations of those who are never to be satisfied'.

Two hundred years on little has changed. In particular the idea that the civil service has a justification independent of the demands of society dies hard. Bureaucracies are 'built safe' — like good motor cars they veer back to the middle of the road if people try to change their course. In a democracy people tend to want more rather than less stability and changelessness in their civil service, because they know that the power that comes from free elections can be dangerous. But even if this is a correct perception it can go too far. Bureaucracies are as change-resistant as they are shrink-resistant.

Engaging the major players

What matters are the people who hold the reins. Some of them don't like what they see. Others are too busy or timid to want to go forward. This is understandable; change is uncomfortable and awkward and individuals lose out; tomorrow's winners aren't to be heard today. More profoundly, individuals in such positions have a deep belief that the machine is right as it stands and that reform can only bring disadvantage. This is particularly true when the changes start reaching their own doors, as has been happening with what some would call indecent speed, thus magnifying their fears.

Parliament

The present enquiry into the civil service is a most important one, and it may be that this paper will be some contribution to the next stage of that work. But Parliament needs to be won over more widely to the reforms, especially since one of its most important functions is, or should be, to secure and maintain a proper system of public administration.

In practice this should mean select committees taking a more active interest in the departments and agencies they watch over. We need a regular form of 'shareholders' meeting' where the appropriate committee considers the year's work of the cores and the agencies and examines the performance of those in charge. It should also assume the 'consult and advise' role for new senior appointments.

Ministers

For their part ministers need to recognize and believe in change too. They need to be vocal in their support for it. There are political gains to be had from successful reform beyond simply improving services; however, the temptation to politicize the process should be avoided. Public service reform ought not to be a matter of party political dispute since the efficient delivery of services is something every government should aspire to. Equally, any government, actual or potential, wants an effective machine to give advice and see that its policies are carried out properly.

In real life, of course, that consensus is seldom visible. Public service reform can be among the most bitterly contentious issues between opposing parties. But this need not always be the case. Next Steps succeeded in eliciting all-party support, due largely to the efforts of Giles Radice the Chairman of the TCSC sub-committee which monitored it from its inception.

Senior civil servants

Senior civil servants were on the whole fairly relaxed about the establishment of Next Steps agencies when they were far away units which usually did not come to their attention. They are now much more concerned as it becomes evident that the centre of departments and their own posts will also be affected. They are like people waging a losing war; when distant colonies and possessions fall and battles far away are lost, they are not much concerned; but when the guns can be heard from the bunker, they get very worried. The hearts and minds of these people must be won, or the individuals changed. If this is not done there is a serious risk to the present reforms, and to their future.

Staff and trade unions

More needs to be done to explain the rationale behind the reforms to individual members of the workforce and how such changes can enhance the jobs they are doing. The actual effects of market testing and privatization have seldom been negative; so called 'job losses' have almost invariably been the result of eliminating posts through natural wastage or recruitment freezes. Job security in the civil service is still better than almost anywhere else.

There is a mighty myth here, based on politics rather than fact, which might have been more easily slain if the case for reform had been handled with greater sensitivity and objectivity from the outset. In logic, all the present reforms ought to be welcome to staff and unions and it is probably not too late to start trying to win them round. Experience with the negotiation and introduction of new pay agreements from 1986 onwards, and with Next Steps itself, shows that this is possible.

Academics and other observers

Academics and similar commentators have, until recently, underestimated the reforms because most of them stayed prisoners of their own textbooks and lecture notes for too long, and it is only recently they have woken up to the extent, actual and potential, of the changes. This neglect has certainly aided the process and added to its speed since little time has been wasted on arid intellectual debate.

Now the reforms are coming under close academic scrutiny. They are being examined, analysed and pulled to bits in the way academics do. This does not mean that all such criticism is unwelcome. During the course of developing Next Steps meetings were held from time to time to explain what we were doing, leaving these experts better informed if not always wiser, and it worked. Such discussions should carry on.

The Treasury

The central departments – the Treasury and the Cabinet Office – are just that. They lie at the heart of the system, determining what does and does not happen. The division of labour between the two departments has been one of long experiment. Before 1968 the Treasury did everything. Then the CSD took over the running of the civil service, including responsibility for much of the reform process, such as it was. The CSD, in turn, was succeeded by the Management and Personnel Office (MPO), at a time when pay and other matters went back to the Treasury. After that we had the Office of the Minister for the Civil Service (OMCS), following yet another reshuffle of duties when Next Steps was launched and the responsibility for that was given to the OMCS. Now we have the Office of Public Service and Science (OPSS – will the acronyms never cease?) headed up by a full Cabinet minister with responsibilities for science, overseeing many aspects of civil service management and, crucially, public service reform.

The current arrangements are probably as good as any, provided both sides play their allotted parts properly. But they still suffer from jagged edges in some matters of managing the civil service. For instance, the Treasury claims responsibility for ensuring value for money, a role for which it is not culturally or practically suited. The prevailing attitude is summed up by a former Treasury permanent secretary who at the time of one public expenditure squeeze said that his department 'would rather have two pound notes torn up in Whitehall than three pound notes well spent'. The Treasury has to be got on side to keep reform rolling forward and, to its credit, did back Next Steps, after some initial unease. However, it cannot be expected both to exercise its banker's caution and to be vanguard of the change at the same time.

Where the Treasury can, and must, help is in those areas of the civil service which it 'owns'. It is guardedly helpful on pay delegation. But there are two other areas. First it should support changing the status of accounting officers and a more positive interpretation, or if necessary amendment, of the Exchequer and Audit Act 1866. The negotiations with the National Audit Office and the Public Accounts Committee should begin immediately.

Second, the questions of financial control, from annuality to very high short-term discount rates, which are designed to keep public spending under control year-on-year, require further thought. Little attention is paid to the longer run. This will remain the case while macro-economists and the markets continue to share this more immediate view. However, it would still be worth looking into precisely how the figures are presented and the book-keeping operated to see whether the shorter-term banker's interest can be better reconciled with longer-term managerial concerns. Practical developments such as the introduction of private money into public services, trading funds which permit circulating money outside the annual cycle and more carry over between years should be developed, as should the availability of better and more meaningful information for the public.

The role of the OPSS

It is essential to a successful partnership between the Treasury and the OPSS that there be tension between them. The OPSS must have as its distinctive task the consolidation of existing reforms and ensuring that the process of change continues. Its role is thus crucial; if it does not lead nothing will happen. Unfortunately there are ominous signs of just such a lack of leadership.

Of greatest concern has been the OPSS's failure to treat the various legs of civil service reform, the Next Steps, the Citizen's Charter and market testing, as an integrated whole. As importantly, it has failed to link issues such as reforming the selection of senior people, abolishing the fast stream, reforming the civil service commissioners and better training. The OPSS has been accused of over-intellectualization and a lack of vision, coupled with having no 'production engineers' to bring about the changes. The picture it paints is seen as blurred and piecemeal. Public service reform is a very down-to-earth sort of job with down-to-earth results, and does not require excessive elaboration. The story would be coherent, if it were allowed to get out. William Waldegrave's CPS paper *Public Service and the Future* was a good shot, but it hasn't quite worked. The perils of politicization are best illustrated by the emerging problems which market testing has encountered.

Nobody can seriously object to the thrust behind market testing, namely that public services are best carried out by the people who offer the best combination of service and cost effectiveness; and that the most appropriate way to find these people is by competitive tender. This, however, is not the way it has been handled by the Government, which has equated market testing with contracting out (it is revealing that people now use these terms interchangeably). The original intention that a level playing field be created where the best provider, in terms of value for money and all-round performance, including quality of service, would receive the contract, has been lost sight of, or at least heavily discounted.

Taken with the vagueness of what departments and agencies are asked to do, the residual confusion over matters like the transfer of undertakings and protection of employees and the way the whole operation is being treated just like another internal civil service exercise, market testing shows every sign of being a good idea which is going awry.

Abridged from P. Kemp (1993) *Beyond Next Steps: a Civil Service for the 21st Century*, London, Social Market Foundation, pp. 32–40. Reproduced with the permission of the Social Market Foundation.

6.7 Norman Lewis

How to reinvent government

It is good to watch the development of government by contract (subject to reservations), good to witness partnerships between public, private and voluntary organizations, good to see companies for estate management run by tenants who are budget holders. It is encouraging to observe competition within and between the public and other sectors, even if there has not been adequate experimentation with 'linkage' whereby contractors and others provide value-added public service provision. There is a need to repeat, none the less, that incremental, annualized, cash-limited budgeting does not help the process of reforming the delivery of public services as is advocated here. Ways need to be found of providing *longer budget cycles* which are innovative and which produce value-for-money, which advantage the public purse while rewarding cost-centres. The UK is not yet far enough down that road. Nor indeed far enough down the road to providing real choice in education, training and other services. There are too many half-way houses.

The twin requirements are *quality and choice*. There is no point in arguing for the citizen as king if programmes are simply directed at cost. This merely devastates the quality of life of the vulnerable. Of prime importance is the development of attainable standards and effective performance criteria and the avoidance of second-rate quality assurance schemes. The latter could result in neither savings nor overall improvements in the provision of public services. Alongside the development of procedures for arbitrating disputes and complaints, the inclusion of quality terms in contracts has begun to show how to protect consumers and citizens against inadequate standards. Law can play an important part in guiding providers and purchasers in the need to balance financial and quality concerns by providing a framework in which these different elements can be taken into account, standards can be set and evaluative systems can be designed and applied.

Market mechanisms alone, presently characterized by inadequate information and an emphasis on cost, are unlikely to solve the problems of producing equitable, high quality and efficient public services. The use of contract has a valuable role to play, but within a broader constitutional and legal framework which encourages a more considered and open set of *consultative practices* throughout policy and management processes. Structured competition cannot be regarded as a substitute for reasoned policy and planning. To ensure resources and objectives are properly matched, further consideration needs to be given to financial, management and information schemes. All the objectives espoused here can be significantly affected by the quality of developments in law as well as the exigencies of economics and politics.

To achieve most of these ends it will be necessary to abandon the obsession with short-term funding if long-term improvement and the encouragement of experiment is to occur. The USA is beginning to appreciate the folly of measuring returns on welfare programmes on an annual cycle. All Swedish agencies, for example, are now beginning to operate with *three year budgets*, making it possible to shift finance between years within an overall planning framework. Such a medium-term approach will also encourage concentration on policy priorities and needs. It will also reward new ideas and new ways of resolving old dilemmas. If there are sharper budgets, sharpened accounting systems and if some form of 'virement' is permitted, governments and citizens together might decide that they do not want to subsidize particular services if the alternative is increased spending on, say, health or education. Public servants will not be inventive if they are hog-tied to detailed short-term financial formulas and they will certainly not be encouraged to think strategically. Approval of the thinking behind City Challenge has already been expressed. It is most regrettable that it now appears to be in the process of being abandoned. This is the very time when such developments should be occupying the high ground.

There is an urgent need to develop a principle of constitutional *subsidiarity* to sharpen and make transparent relations between the centre and local government. Law has an important part to play here as well, but it is doubtful if the Banham Commission can carry its brief this far. Central government needs the experience of local communities to enrich policy-making in a way that cannot be matched by quangos. Local government needs reform but it needs, at the strategic level, to be strengthened so that it can engage in dialogue and partnership with its citizens and the business and voluntary community. New relationships of accountability should also be considered as between local government and local public agencies; a more open and accountable 'local state'. This is to attack the severe problems of the degradation of inner city life at the heart. Either government is serious about handing back more power to ordinary people or it is not.

There are avant-garde methods of service delivery and budget-stretching through seed-corn experiments, equity investments, the sale or leasing of property, joint ventures etc. The logic of markets, the logic of choice, extends to politics too. Local communities can, to paraphrase, represent the mother of all invention. This is one way to attempt to achieve what Vibert has elegantly sought; viz., to produce a constant response to changing customer needs, to examine alternative means of provision, to review what the market will provide and where the gaps are; to look at how the public and private sectors can best relate and to promote *competition between public and private providers* (Vibert 1992).

There is an acute need for a re-inventing of the doctrine of the *separation of powers*. Contract can assist with this by clarifying what government expects from service providers in being designed to pinpoint responsibility and thereby improve accountability. Instead of distinguishing between legislative, executive and judicial functions there is a need to concentrate on separating out purchaser and provider functions. But, as has been said, public law contracts will often have to be different from the commercial variety and to embrace constitutional values in terms of formation of terms, pricing and dispute-resolution. Public law contracts will largely need to be based on common values which are often difficult to express. In defining ways for the best form of delivery of public services there is a need to avoid the failures and the evasions of ministerial responsibility. This will require imagination but it can and must be done. Contract can be used for the pursuit of political objectives through individual rights and freedom of choice. Yet in decisions about what to produce and in efficiency in the process of supply, the commercial style contract will have to be re-examined to look for constitutional fit.

It should by now be clear that, for all the advantages of a contractual-style approach to government, it will not, of itself, empower individuals or groups regarding decisions either about the kind of public service to be provided or, for stronger reasons, about the level of public services which should be provided. This is the stuff of politics and politics needs to be reformed in the process of reinvented government. In this Osborne and Gaebler can once more be affirmed for their observation that even the most carefully structured markets are capable of creating inequitable outcomes. That is why they, quite properly, stress 'the other half of the equation' – the *empowerment of communities*.

This empowerment in short requires a revised compact between central and local government and a revised compact between all levels of government and the citizenry. Wherever possible that citizenry should be encouraged to be part of the management of public services; where that is not possible their experiences and preferences should be brought institutionally to bear on the process of the formulation of needs and ends. And collectively they should be encouraged to work with market processes for the greater prosperity of all. But when governments push ownership and control down into the community, their responsibilities are not at an end. Even if they no longer, or rarely, provide services, they remain responsible for ensuring that needs are met. And if markets are to work effectively they need the highest quality inputs they can get in terms of trained workers, research, infrastructure and accessible capital. Again to quote the original *Reinventing Government*: 'This makes government's various roles as educator, trainer, research funder, regulator, rule setter, and infrastructure operator far more important than they were 30 years ago.' Furthermore they must learn to take their budgets apart and reassemble them painstakingly to reaffirm or to alter their policies. There is no point in cutting public expenditure if it is unclear whether fat or muscle is disappearing. So also, there is no point in throwing money at failed systems, which is, after all, an almost universal temptation. The other side of marketizing services is to be good at governing; to be good at strategy; to produce policies that people want and policies that relate outputs to outcomes; policies that work.

Last, but by no means least, all this needs to be accompanied by the 'repatriation' of human rights. This is at the basis of our communal living and if it is good enough for new democracies then it is good enough for one of the oldest.

The missing vision

It is difficult to know how many of the developments outlined here were anticipated by leading political actors. It is unlikely that many saw a clear pattern; had the vision to work to a game plan. Nevertheless a pattern of sorts can now be discerned. Now is the time to respond to the emerging forms of government in a principled and imaginative fashion. Privatization, contracting out, market-mimicking, regulation and the Citizen's Charter can all be seen to be part of a piece.

What is emerging is the 'empowering' state which acts, to a greater or lesser degree, as the guardian of citizenship. So far the empowerment has been largely confined to an image of government meeting once a year to hand out the contracts. This, of course, is a caricature but the aspect of empowerment which has been accentuated is that of offloading service delivery to competitive centres. This aspect has been sufficiently aired already but it is worth repeating that it poses constitutional problems which need to be addressed. However, the movement can be justified *a priori* on the basis of choice, pricing (in order to make priority-setting more visible) and efficiency.

Empowerment in the sense of giving citizens and citizen groups a sense of ownership of the state has not, on the other hand, received the attention it deserves. The state is more than periodic elections; it is freedom of information, the opportunity to contribute to debate, to share the management of services and much more besides. This is the side of empowerment that needs to be examined far more critically than is currently the case. This, in a sense, is to bring the argument back to the necessity of re-examining policy-making arrangements to ensure that they are both effective and democratic. It would be a dreadful waste of a golden opportunity if the purchaser–provider separation became stuck in the rut of an obsession with service delivery as opposed to the creation of sensible and meaningful targets, standards, outputs and outcomes. The state needs to be empowered to do these things properly and the citizen to make a mature contribution to the process.

There are other aspects of citizenship which have not been adequately debated. The concentration on the citizen as consumer of public services is overbalanced if understandable. The citizen is entitled to better public services but is entitled to more besides. (S)he has a claim to civic rights and civic responsibilities, to freedom from want, to the now-established political rights recognized throughout the Western world and to fellowship; in short to participate fully in the community.

The British constitution is based on a combination of cultural tradition and human rights. It is the justification for the kind of developments which can be seen dimly emerging but it must not be forgotten that those developments have to be justified in terms of their meeting the larger constitutional expectations. Political and legal systems need to be reformed in order to facilitate those expectations, not least to make sure that *political* choice is made possible. Once that has been done, purely party politics, the exploration of genuine political differences, can be played out. But some of the emerging pattern of new government is above party and resides in the grain of the constitution itself. It is crucially important that no one works against that grain as the new government unfolds. Vision is required and there is much work to be done.

References

Osborne, D. and Gaebler, T. (1992) *Reinventing Government*, New York, Addison-Wesley.
Vibert, F. (1992) *Contract and Accountability, the Social Market and the Fourth Term*, Speech to the Annual Conference of the Tory Reform Group.

From N. Lewis (1993) *How to Reinvent British Government*, London, European Policy Forum, pp. 31–5. Reproduced with the permission of the European Policy Forum.

Civil servants, Parliament and the public

There has been no shortage of comment about the workings of the Parliamentary select committees that were introduced in 1979–80. Many critics believe that they are inadequate as an instrument of Parliamentary scrutiny. One reason sometimes adduced to account for this inadequacy is the Osmotherly Rules. These are the rules which govern the conduct of civil servants appearing before select committees. In December 1994 they were redrafted and issued in a document entitled *Departmental Evidence and Response to Select Committees*. The extract included here (Reading 7.1) is from that document and sets out the official position. It is, of course, a restatement of traditional principles, as commonly understood. Many of the critics think that, whatever the merits of such a position in times gone by, it is now an anachronism, an obstacle to accountability. Peter Hennessy, with support from Gavin Drewry, presented such a case in oral evidence to the Commons' Select Committee on Procedure (Reading 7.2). This extract is from a dialogue with one of the Committee members, Frank Cook, Labour back-bench MP for Stockton North. The chairman of the Committee was Sir Peter Emery, Conservative MP for Honiton. In the final analysis, the Committee was not convinced that the Osmotherly Rules had inhibited the probings of the select committees (Reading 7.3).

Clearly there are questions of political sensitivity which civil servants must bear in mind when appearing before Parliamentary committees. From the perspective of a former top official, Sir Frank Cooper explains what it is like to appear before a Parliamentary committee (Reading 7.4). Cooper was Permanent Under Secretary at the Northern Ireland Office (1973–6) and at the Ministry of Defence (1976–82). His comments are based largely, though not exclusively, on experiences with the Committee of Public Accounts. This is one of the oldest and most revered of the select committees, its origins lying in the mid-nineteenth century. Note the extensive preparations involving numerous officials within a department, not just the one or the few who appear in person before these committees.

Clearly the advent of executive agencies has been one of the most visible features of recent years. Whitehall and the entire edifice of central government has always been more fragmented, less tidy and with more loose ends than is often supposed. But the ends are now looser and there are more of them. In particular, some agency chief executives have a higher public profile than top officials in their respective core departments. Some, such as the Benefits Agency and the Prison Service, have for various reasons been at the centre of controversy. So, too, has the Child Support Agency. In a special BBC Radio 4 series, *Inside the New Civil Service*, the agency's then chief executive, Ros Hepplewhite, had an interesting exchange with the interviewer (Reading 7.5). Hepplewhite was unapologetic about her high public profile, even where this had drawn her into discussion about policy. In the same extract William Waldegrave and Sir Robin Butler give their views. Butler denies that Next Steps agencies have been responsible for any democratic deficit or that they constitute any evasion or diminution of accountability – a view challenged by Vernon Bogdanor. Whatever the case, the heat of controversy and the close association with unpopular policies proved too much for Ros Hepplewhite. She resigned her position at the Child Support Agency during the summer of 1994.

In a White Paper published in 1993, the Major administration set out its proposals for open government, including a draft code. With this it signalled its commitment to the principle of greater openness. The code came into effect in April 1994, known as the *Access to Government Code of Practice*. Reading 7.6 is an extract from this document. Note its reference to costing, a reminder that making available more information takes time and money. If the citizen wants more, the citizen will have to pay. Eschewing legislation, the government put its faith in the Parliamentary Commissioner (Ombudsman) as the fail-safe for the citizen who feels denied reasonable access. In this and in the range of exemptions or exceptions (Part 2 of the code) many critics felt that the government had already sold the public short. A former civil servant, Robert Hazell, has proposed a Freedom of Information Act. This he did at a convention jointly organized in 1991 by Charter 88 and *The Independent* (Reading 7.7). He cites the introduction of such legislation in Australia, Canada and New Zealand, fashionable exemplars for would-be reformers of the 1990s. Far more radical proposals are contained in Tony Benn's Commonwealth of Britain Bill (Reading 7.8). The extract reproduced here makes provision for the entire executive branch of government. He would abolish the monarchy, introducing instead a presidency and a council of state. All the Official Secrets Acts would be repealed and an onus placed upon ministers to request permission for the withholding of information. Needless to say, Benn's Bill did not reach the Statute Book. But if his proposals were ever to come to fruition civil servants would certainly know that they were living in a different world.

The Osmotherly Rules (Revised)

1. This memorandum gives guidance to officials from departments and their agencies who may be called upon to give evidence before, or prepare memoranda for submission to, Parliamentary select committees. It supersedes the 'Memorandum of Guidance for Officials Appearing before Select Committees' issued in March 1988.

2. In providing guidance, the memorandum attempts to summarize a number of long-standing conventions that have developed in the relationship between Parliament, in the form of its select committees, and successive Governments. As a matter of practice, Parliament has generally recognized these conventions. It is important to note, however, that this memorandum is a Government document. Although select committees will be familiar with its contents, it has no formal Parliamentary standing or approval, nor does it claim to have.

. . .

Powers of select committees

23. The powers of select committees derive from the powers of the House and from the Standing Orders containing their terms of reference. It is for the committees themselves, and ultimately for the House, to interpret these terms of reference.

24. Select committees (and their sub-committees) have power to 'send for persons, papers and records' relevant to their terms of reference. These powers can be exercised, formally, by the issue of an order for an individual to attend or to provide evidence. Enforcement of these formal powers and, in particular, the power to punish for contempt of the House, is retained by the House itself and can be exercised only by the House as a whole, not by the select committee.

. . .

Public and closed evidence sessions

30. Select committees' own deliberations are held in closed session but committees usually admit the public and the press to hearings at which they take evidence from witnesses. Departmental witnesses (and those officials who are sitting behind them in support) should bear in mind that such public proceedings may also be televised or broadcast, usually in edited form. Committees may, on request from a witness, agree to take evidence in closed session if sensitive or confidential material is likely to be discussed.

. . .

Section 3: Role of officials giving evidence to select committees

General

38. Officials who give evidence to select committees do so on behalf of their ministers and under their directions.

39. This is in accordance with the principle that it is ministers who are directly accountable to Parliament for both their own policies and for the actions of their departments. Officials are accountable to ministers and are subject to their instruction; but they are not directly accountable to Parliament in the same way. This does not mean, of course, that officials may not be called upon to give an account of Government policies or indeed of their own actions or recollections of particular events.

40. This guidance note can therefore be seen as representing standing instructions to officials appearing before select committees. These instructions may be supplemented by specific ministerial instructions on specific matters.

Summoning of named officials

41. By the same principle, it is customary for ministers to decide which official or officials should represent them. Select committees have generally accepted this position. Should a committee invite a named official to appear, and the minister concerned did not wish to be represented by that official, the minister might suggest to the committee that another official could more appropriately do so. If a committee insisted on a particular official appearing before them, they could issue a formal order for attendance, and request the House to enforce it. In such an event the official would have to appear before the committee but, in all circumstances, the official would remain subject to ministerial instruction on how to answer questions and on what information to disclose. Such an impasse is, however, unprecedented.

Agency chief executives

42. Where a select committee is investigating matters which are delegated to an agency in its framework document, evidence will normally be given by the chief executive. Like other officials, agency chief executives give evidence on behalf of the minister to whom they are accountable and are subject to that minister's instruction.

. . .

Section 4: Evidence to select committees

4A: Provision of evidence by officials: central principles

General

45. The central principle to be followed is that it is the duty of officials to be as helpful as possible to select committees, and that any withholding of information should be limited to reservations that are necessary in the public interest, including the interests of good government and of safeguarding national security. Departments should therefore be as forthcoming as they can (within the limits set out in Section 4B) in providing information, whether in writing or in oral evidence, relevant to a select committee's field of inquiry.

Accuracy of evidence

46. Officials appearing before select committees are responsible for ensuring that the evidence they give is accurate. They will therefore need to be fully briefed on the main facts of the matters on which they expect to be examined. This can be a major exercise as a committee's questions can range widely and can be expected to be testing. Should it nevertheless be discovered sub-sequently that the evidence unwittingly contained factual errors, these should be made known to the committee, usually via the clerk, at the earliest opportunity. Where appropriate, a correcting footnote will appear in the published transcript of the evidence.

Discussion of government policy

47. Officials should as far as possible confine their evidence to questions of fact and explanation relating to government policies and actions. They should be ready to explain what those policies are; the justification and objectives of those policies as the Government sees them; the extent to which those objectives have been met; and also to explain how administrative factors may have affected both the choice of policy measures and the manner of their implementation. Any comment by officials on government policies and actions should always be consistent with the principle of civil service political impartiality. Officials should as far as possible avoid being drawn into discussion of the merits of alternative policies where this is politically contentious. If official witnesses are pressed by the committee to go beyond these limits, they should suggest that the questioning should be referred to ministers.

48. A select committee may invite specialist (as opposed to administrative) officials to comment on the professional or technical issues underlying government policies or decisions. This can require careful handling where committees wish to take evidence from, for example, government economists or statisticians on issues which bear on controversial policy questions and which are also matters of controversy within the respective profession. Such specialists may find themselves in some difficulty if their own judgement on the professional issues has, or appears to have, implications that are critical of government policies. It is not generally open to such witnesses to describe or comment upon the advice which they have given to departments, or would give if asked. They should not therefore go beyond explaining the reasoning which, in the Government's judgement, supports its policy. The status of such evidence should, if necessary, be made clear to the committee. If pressed for a professional judgement on the question the witness should, if necessary, refer to the political nature of the issue and, as above, suggest that the line of questioning be referred to ministers.

. . .

Consulting ministers on evidence

52. Because officials appear on behalf of their ministers, written evidence and briefing material should be cleared with them as necessary. It may only be necessary for ministers to be consulted if there is any doubt among officials on the detail of the policy to be explained to the committee, or on what information should be disclosed. However, as ministers are ultimately accountable for deciding what information is to be given and for defending those decisions as necessary, their views should be sought if a question arises of withholding information which a committee has asked for.

. . .

4B: Limitations on the provision of information

General

60. Although the powers of select committees to send for 'persons, papers and records' relating to their field of enquiry are unqualified, there are certain long-standing conventions on the provision of information which have been observed by successive administrations on grounds of public policy.

. . .

Internal discussion and advice

66. Given that the essential function of select committees is to call ministers to account for the decisions and actions of Government, it has generally been accepted that the internal discussion and advice which has preceded ministerial decisions should not be disclosed. This is necessary to preserve both the principle of the *collective responsibility of ministers* and the principle of *confidentiality between ministers and their advisers*.

   67. Witnesses may answer questions on whether or not particular decisions were referred to and approved by ministers but should not disclose: the internal advice given to ministers or to other officials; the details of inter-departmental exchanges on policy issues; the specific level at which particular decisions were taken, which particular minister or official took the decision, or the manner in which a minister consulted colleagues.

. . .

Conduct of individual officials

80. Occasionally questions from a departmentally related select committee may appear to be directed to the conduct of individual officials, not just in the sense of establishing the facts about what occurred in making decisions or implementing Government policies, but with the implication of allocating individual criticism or blame.

81. In such circumstances, and in accordance with the principles of ministerial accountability, it is for the minister to look into the matter and if necessary to institute a formal inquiry. Such an inquiry into the conduct and behaviour of individual officials and consideration of disciplinary action is properly carried out within a department according to established procedures designed and agreed for the purpose, and with appropriate safeguards for the individual. It is then the minister's responsibility to inform the committee of what has happened, and of what has been done to put the matter right and to prevent a recurrence. Evidence to a select committee on this should be given not by the official or officials concerned, but by the minister or by a senior official designated by the minister to give such evidence on the minister's behalf. This would include the result of any disciplinary or other departmental proceedings against individual officials.

82. Select committees have agreed that it is not their task to act as disciplinary tribunals. Accordingly, if in the course of an inquiry a select committee were to discover evidence that called into question the conduct (in this sense) of individual named officials, the committee should be asked not to pursue their own investigation into the conduct of the person concerned, but to take up the matter with the minister.

83. If it is foreseen that a select committee's line of enquiry may involve questions about the conduct of named officials, it should be suggested to the committee that it would be appropriate for a minister or a senior official designated by the minister to give evidence, rather than the named officials in question. If an official giving evidence to a committee is unexpectedly asked questions which are directed at his or her individual conduct, or at the conduct of another named official, the official should indicate that he wishes to seek instructions from ministers, and the committee should be asked to allow time for this.

. . .

4C: Status and handling of evidence

Status of evidence

89. Once information has been supplied to a committee it becomes 'evidence' and, subject to any agreement with the committee on the non-publication of protectively marked information (paragraphs 93–100), it is entirely up to the committee whether or not to publish it and report it to the House. Certain rules apply to the further public use of such evidence by the Government prior to its publication by the committee. Departments should be careful to observe these rules as failure to do so could amount to a breach of Parliamentary privilege. Committees are usually helpfully flexible in applying the rules but, in cases of doubt, departments should consult the relevant committee clerk for guidance.

. . .

Providing sensitive information in confidence

93. It is to the benefit of committees in carrying out their task of scrutinizing Government activities, and to Government in explaining its actions and policies, for sensitive information, including that carrying a protective security marking, to be provided from time to time on the basis that it will not be published and will be treated in confidence. Procedures have been developed to accommodate this.

94. When this arises, the department should inform the clerk that the information in question can be made available only on this basis, explaining the reasons in general terms. Such information should not be made available until the committee has agreed to handle it appropriately, either by treating it wholly in confidence or by agreeing to publish it with a reasonable degree of *sidelining* (i.e. with the relevant passages omitted but with the location of the omissions indicated).

Handling of sensitive information in oral evidence

95. It would clearly be inappropriate for any evidence which a department wished to be treated as confidential to be given at a public session of the committee. If it appears likely, therefore, that subjects to be discussed at a forthcoming public session are such that the witnesses would only be able to give substantive answers in confidence, the department should write to the chairman or the clerk explaining why this is so. The committee may then agree to take that part of the department's evidence in closed session.

96. If, despite such an approach, a committee questions an official witness in public session on confidential matters, or if such matters are raised un-expectedly, the official should inform the committee that the questions could only be answered on a confidential basis. The committee may then decide to go into closed session or request a confidential memorandum. It is not for the witness to suggest that the committee should go into closed session as this is wholly a matter for them to decide.

97. Where confidential evidence has been given in a closed session the witness should, at the end of the session, let the clerk know which parts of the evidence these are. Pending the committee's final decision on what they will agree to omit from the published version, the clerk will instruct the shorthand writer not to send for printing the transcript of these passages but will send two copies of a full transcript to the department. One copy is for retention; the other should be returned to the clerk with those passages sidelined which contain sensitive information which, in the department's judgement, it would not be in the public interest to publish. One copy of the full transcript is also retained in the Committee Office for Members authorized to have access to it (paragraph 100).

98. Although committees usually respect such requests for sidelining they may occasionally challenge a particular request. Witnesses should therefore always be sure that their requests are justified – in terms of the definitions of the protective marking system or the exemptions in the Code of Practice on Access to Government Information.

Abridged from *Departmental Evidence and Response to Select Committees*, London, Cabinet Office, December 1994. Crown copyright is reproduced with the permission of the Controller of HMSO.

| *Peter Hennessy and Gavin Drewry*

Critics of the Osmotherly Rules

Mr Cook

657. Dr Hennessy, you said that one of your high priorities would be to change the Osmotherly Rules and both you and Dr Giddings placed great emphasis on accountability. In fact, your intriguing phrase was, I think, 'evidence-driven accountability'. To whom is the civil servant accountable?

(Dr Hennessy) This is where the Head of the Home Civil Service, who is a thoroughly good chap, will disagree with me profoundly. But I shall tell you what I think. I think the civil service in pretty well every day-to-day circumstance is responsible to the minister; because the minister, as the current position has it, quite rightly, is the embodiment of the Crown for most practical purposes most days. There is, however, a view I take of the civil service which is rather different from that of the chap who is in charge of it at the moment. It is this.

658. Can you say the last couple of phrases again?

(Dr Hennessy) I take a different view, however, from the current Head of the Home Civil Service about the civil service. I am closer to one of his predecessors, Lord Bancroft, who, in a public lecture a few years ago, said, in effect, that the civil service is not owned wholly by the particular set of ministers who find themselves in charge of it. It is a national asset. I would say that it is a piece of transferable technology. Under our system, it is a national asset which has to be capable of being transferred in a matter of hours on the Friday afternoon after a general election when power has shifted. And to do that, it has to be in a position to command the confidence of the incoming Cabinet at the drop-of-a-hat. And to do that, it has to be made quite plain, both to every member of the 600,000-strong civil service and to people outside, that it is not in the pocket of any political administration. It is a neutral force and it is a genuinely transferable piece of technology, with no permanent secretary

being sent on 'gardening leave' or retired early to encourage the others. That would be the end of the nineteenth century settlement which, like most good things in here, was invented by that chap up there, Gladstone. So, as a result of that, there is one exception to my general statement that to all intents and purposes civil servants are Crown servants answering, in effect, to ministers. And it is this. If they think they are being required to do anything that is improper – not unlawful necessarily, but improper in the sense of being partisan – they actually should have some final form of appeal beyond the head of their profession, which is where the chain of appeal stops now, to turn to. Because it is a necessary safeguard for the Opposition party, for the public and for those who think that a politicized civil service would be ruinous, that they are in fact in a position to keep themselves clean and decent, bearing on the day when they might have to be shifted to 'other ownership', as it were. In that sense, the Cabinet are the temporary owners of a permanent national asset. So, in that sense, there is one sense in which they are not accountable only to their ministers; they are accountable to a wider public interest.

659. Would you remove the kind of coverlet of their ability to say, 'My advice to my minister is privy'?

(Dr Hennessy) What I would change about the Osmotherlys, Mr Cook, I could tell you very briefly. There are a few Osmotherlys which I think are an outrage. For example, let me start by saying that the way to change it would be to change the whole philosophy of this document. The philosophy at the moment is this: that you will be able to say only a kind of residue; that once all the hot and delicate subjects have been removed, once anything to do with current policy has been removed, you can say that. If they literally stuck to this rule book, they would be able to tell you only what was in Written Answers, oral questions, White Papers – and they could confirm the day of the week and the time of the day. That is, if they literally stuck to this, as it is now written. What is needed at the beginning is a general statement – which, in fact, they have in paragraph 20 – where it says:

> The general principle to be followed is that it is the duty of officials to be as helpful as possible to committees . . .

Then they have 25 pages of exceptions and caveats. It should open with a statement that public servants are there to give to Parliament everything except in those narrowly defined areas of special sensitivity. In that sense, you would shift the whole philosophy round to one of openness except in exceptional circumstances. It is the other way round at the moment.

Chairman

660. Do you see that actually being acceptable either to ministers or to the Head of the Civil Service?

(Dr Hennessy) That is a different question. Can I give you, Chairman, one bit on which I think you could negotiate on – in fact, three bits – with considerable success? First of all, on page 11 of the Osmotherlys (and it is Rule 30) they are, if they take this literally, required to refrain from commenting in any way at all

on 'questions in the field of political controversy' – which is pretty much a blanket ban if you take it literally. This is in page 11; it is point iv of Rule 30. That, to me, is moving towards George Jones' territory; that, in effect, is really offering you a suicide note to go out of business. Or to die of boredom. The next Osmotherly which I think really does need looking at is Rule 31. Of course, you have to recognize collective Cabinet responsibility as the basis of our constitution. Even if several members of the Cabinet do not and the Prime Minister's Press Secretary every day upstairs does not, you have to, I have to, because we are all God-fearing citizens. But it strikes me here that when they rule out on that basis their capacity to answer questions in any form on any inter-departmental business, that pretty well covers anything, everything. Can you think of anything that is hot that the Treasury is not involved in, because money is involved? That makes it inter-departmental. If you take these things literally, and one has to be a literal man because it is carefully drafted, that rules out everything. You cannot even be told at the level to which discussions are taken. If you ask a civil servant, 'Has the Cabinet considered that?' – he cannot tell you. It is out of bounds. The third Osmotherly Rule is the one which I think is a real outrage. There is no question. You could perhaps argue about some of the things I have said; but this, I think, should enrage all decent parliamentarians. It is Rule 41. It says:

> While select committees should not press for internal advice to ministers to be revealed, they are less likely to accept without argument –

You see, they do expect some spirit on your behalf!:

> a refusal to reveal a report from a departmental committee containing outside members, and even less likely to accept a refusal in the case of a wholly external committee. In particular, they will be understandably reluctant to accept a refusal where the establishment of the committee in question has been announced, together with its membership and terms of reference, and where its report is known to exist. These implications need to be taken into account in deciding how much publicity should be given to the establishment of committees of this kind.

This is open government with a vengeance, is it not? This is classifying the existence of departmental committees of inquiry. Mr Chairman, I am one of those who believes –

661. There is a lovely example of that (which Mr Maxwell-Hyslop might even remind you about) in his tin inquiry where, in fact, the civil servants were actually not even allowed to give us minutes of an international committee which we finally got from Washington, under the Freedom of Information Act, although we could not get them from our own civil servants. So that we understand too well that there are nonsenses.

(Dr Hennessy) Yes. I think that sometimes you need some civil rights when it comes to this kind of thing.

662. I am glad that you are not cynical about it.

(Dr Hennessy) Not at all. I was about to say, Chairman, that the chap who wrote this or, let me put it this way, the spirit of the people who drafted this –

for it would be unfair to name Osmotherly, who, although he was sanctified with it and has his place in constitutional history through it, took over the job when this was already drafted – I sometimes think would classify *Hansard* if they thought they could get away with it.

(Professor Drewry) As far as I am concerned, the Osmotherly Rules really have the sort of baleful impact that the Official Secrets Acts have always had; namely, they are very seldom invoked but they cast a pall of gloom and unnecessary reticence over what should be essentially open proceedings. Once again, I was very attracted to some of the points that were raised by the Chairman of the Defence Committee in his memorandum where he highlighted some specific points, noting, for example, that under the financial management initiative there has been a considerable evolution of budgetary responsibilities within departments and it is important for committees to be able to establish contact with the people who are actually taking decisions at that sort of level. This links to a point which I made in my own written submission of evidence about the 'Next Steps' initiative which I think provides an added incentive to look at these rules afresh.

From Select Committee on Procedure, *Second Report, 1989–90: the Working of the Select Committee System – Vol. II, Minutes of Evidence etc.*, HC 19–II. Reprinted in accordance with HMSO's guidelines for the reproduction of Crown and Parliamentary copyright.

The working of the select committees

Relations between the departmentally related select committees and the Government: Conclusions

General

150. Over the first ten years of the new system, relations between the departmentally related select committees and the Government, with the obvious exception of the Defence Committee and the MoD, appear to have been largely free of problems. Given the potential for friction in terms of the demands placed on departments by committees, this is a pleasant surprise and one which reflects credit on both sides. We were particularly pleased that the Leader of the House, while drawing attention to occasional pressure points, did not seek to overstress the additional costs to departments of the select committee system. Indeed, it is doubtful, in our view, whether these should properly be regarded as 'additional' at all, any more than are the costs to departments of servicing public enquiries or Royal Commissions. Moreover, any serious attempt to draw up a balance sheet for select committees would need to take account of cost savings and improvements in efficiency which had resulted directly or indirectly from their recommendations.

151. Despite the generally healthy state of relations between departments and select committees, there have inevitably been one or two matters on which disagreement has occurred. The question of unfinished enquiries, first brought up by the Leader of the House, led to an exchange of memoranda between his office and the Chairman of the Treasury and Civil Service Committee. In his supplementary memorandum Mr Higgins set out in some detail the reasons why in some cases enquiries carried out by his committee had not been completed or why in others the Leader of the House had, in Mr Higgins's view, been misinformed in so describing them.

152. It is not for us to seek to act as adjudicators on this matter. We would merely observe that there are bound to be occasions when it is not possible to bring an enquiry to a conclusion – the calling of a general election being the obvious example. Similarly, as was pointed out during questioning, it may not always be clear until an enquiry has got under way that a report is, or is not, called for. Finally, and most importantly, there is the value, which we have strongly underlined, of evidence-taking in its own right as a tool of scrutiny. Provided that enquiries are not entered into lightly – and we have received no evidence that they are – these are facts of life which departments must live with, however tiresome they may be. There is therefore no need for committees to feel unduly defensive about this subject. It may be that there is a case for improved liaison between committees and departments over individual committees' intentions with regard to proposed enquiries and, in particular, as an enquiry progresses, about the likelihood and timing of a subsequent report. No doubt many committees already do this; it is therefore more a question of best practice being universally applied.

153. At the time the departmentally related select committees were established, there was much debate about the adequacy of their powers to obtain all the evidence they might need and to secure the attendance of witnesses, especially ministers. In the event, this does not appear to have been a major problem, judging by the evidence submitted to us by the committees themselves. The majority have gone so far as to describe the Government's attitude towards the provision of information as helpful and cooperative and very few have reported any specific disagreements. It is perhaps noteworthy that, with the exception of the Chairmen of the Defence and Transport Committees, the main criticism of the Government in this context came from an academic source, Professor Peter Hennessy, visiting Professor of Government at the University of Strathclyde. We deal with Professor Hennessy's principal concern – the Memorandum of Guidance, or Osmotherly Rules – later in this section of our report.

154. As regards the specific point raised by the Chairman of the Transport Committee, we have considerable sympathy with his complaint about lack of cooperation from the Treasury. While we understand its reluctance to give separate evidence to departmentally related committees about, say, the adequacy of resources available for a particular programme, we think it is much harder to defend its refusal to appear before the Transport Committee to discuss the principles underlying a set of rules governing infrastructure investment, for the content of which the Treasury alone is responsible. It was clearly not an adequate substitute in this case for the Transport Committee to have to obtain the information it needed at second-hand from Department of Transport officials. *We hope, therefore, that in future the Treasury will adopt a less restrictive and more helpful attitude towards the types of subject on which it is prepared to provide evidence directly to select committees.*

The Osmotherly Rules

155. The document which governs the conduct of departmental witnesses, the Memorandum of Guidance, was first published as an Appendix to the 1976 Procedure Committee's Report,[1] although the guidance was originally issued within the civil service in September 1972. *It is important to note that the Memorandum of Guidance has no Parliamentary status whatever.* As the Treasury and Civil Service Committee recently stated: 'The responsibility for issuing the rules falls solely upon the Government and, although Select Committees have from time to time commented upon them, they have never formally agreed to them'.[2]

156. We understand Professor Hennessy's irritation[3] with the Osmotherly Rules, of which paragraph 41(i) provides an illustration:[4]

> While select committees should not press for internal advice to ministers to be revealed, they are less likely to accept without argument a refusal to reveal a report from a departmental committee containing outside members, and even less likely to accept a refusal in the case of a wholly external committee. In particular, they will be understandably reluctant to accept a refusal where the establishment of the committee in question has been announced, together with its membership and terms of reference, and where its report is known to exist. These implications need to be taken into account in deciding how much publicity should be given to the establishment of committees of this kind.

157. Our overall approach to the Osmotherly Rules is a pragmatic one, however. We have received no evidence that their existence or current working has placed unacceptable constraints on select committees across the whole range of their scrutinizing functions. As Professor Hennessy himself pointed out,[5] the rules are in any case honoured more in the breach than the observance. (This is perhaps just as well given their scope and detail.) Above all, we are conscious of the danger, described during evidence,[6] that a wholesale review at Parliament's behest could simply result in a new set of guidelines which, while superficially less restrictive, would then be applied rigorously and to the letter. At the risk of accusations of defeatism, therefore, we believe that discretion is the sensible approach, particularly unless further experience demonstrates an urgent need for change.

158. We would, however, like to see the principle enunciated – far more prominently than a single sentence within 14 pages of the Memorandum of Guidance – that it is the duty of departmental witnesses to be as helpful as possible to select committees. This goes beyond giving direct replies to questions; it is well understood that the literally correct answer may conceal as much information as it imparts. *It should be the aim of departments to ensure that select committees are furnished with any important information which appears to be relevant to their enquiries, without waiting to be asked for it specifically. We recommend accordingly.*

159. There is no doubt that, in an ideal world, there would be no place for comprehensive rules of the sort contained in the Memorandum of Guidance. We share the view expressed by Dr Giddings of Reading University[7] that the only areas in which restrictions on the giving of information by officials can be justified, apart from security matters, or issues of great diplomatic or commercial sensitivity, are the *content* of advice to ministers and the need to preserve collective responsibility. Even the latter should be interpreted as liberally as possible. We doubt whether the fabric of constitutional government would suffer fatal injury if witnesses were more forthcoming about the level at which decisions are taken and the extent of the involvement of different departments.

160. Similarly, with very few exceptions, it is difficult to see why, without breaching the confidentiality of advice to ministers, committees cannot be told, in purely factual terms, what options are under consideration, as well as their cost implications. We regard as unsustainable the Government's argument that experienced and trained officials cannot distinguish between the *subjects* on which ministers have sought advice, on the one hand, and the *substance* of that advice, on the other. *We therefore urge the Government to review these specific aspects of its approach towards the giving of evidence to select committees with the aim of formulating a more constructive and open policy.*

The timing of enquiries

161. The timing of enquiries is likely from time to time to cause friction between departments and committees. This is especially true when a committee wishes to investigate an issue which is the subject of simultaneous consideration by ministers. In such cases, a minister is perfectly within his rights to make representations to the chairman of the relevant committee, seeking a postponement. By the same token, however, the committee, having listened to such an approach, must form its own judgement as to whether the reasons adduced by the minister are reasonable or are concerned simply with the convenience of the government. There is no contradiction here; both sides are right in their own terms. But a select committee's obligations are to the House and, ultimately, if it is not persuaded by a minister's pleas for delay, then it should proceed with its enquiry.

. . .

The case studies

164. Our case studies of two individual select committees revealed a remarkable divergence in their relations with the Government. We have devoted a significant part of our report to the problems experienced by the Defence Committee, not because they are typical – they are not – but because they illustrate what *can* happen when things go wrong. It would not be appropriate for us to appear to take sides in this argument. We can only speculate on some of the factors which led to the tension between the committee and the ministry. We suspect that traditional, ingrained Whitehall defensiveness, overlaid with an additional thick carapace of security, has played its part in fostering the committee's perception of uncooperativeness on the ministry's side. No doubt, as Mr King himself hinted, personalities may also have made their contribution.

165. There are positive signs, in any case, that both sides have realized that a continuation of their frayed relationship serves no one's interests. We welcome the conciliatory note struck by Mr King in his evidence: 'I have already spoken to the Chairman of the Defence Committee on this matter to say that I recognize that there have been some problems in the past, that we will seek to do what we can from our side and I look for a response in a similar way on his side to try and see if we can get that on a happier basis.'[8]

166. The contrast with the Home Affairs Committee is of particular interest. Neither the committee nor the Home Office drew our attention to any problems in their relationship, and liaison at all levels appears to be cordial and constructive. A relatively high percentage of the Home Affairs Committee's recommendations have been accepted or indirectly implemented, and while that is not the only, or even necessarily the main, test of effectiveness, it shows that the committee is closely in tune with the Home Office's thinking. The Chairman of the Defence Committee, speaking from his rather different experience, referred to 'the constructive tension that should exist between a department and a select committee'. We are not seeking to imply that the Home Affairs Committee and Home Office have fallen into the opposite trap. Indeed, the Home Secretary drew attention to recent enquiries by the committee which had not, initially at least, been warmly received in the department. On the other hand, the remark by the Home Office in its memorandum that it had not been 'surprised' by any subject chosen by the committee in the current Parliament might perhaps be viewed as something of a double-edged compliment.

167. *The worst fate which can befall any select committee is to be used by the department it is supposed to be monitoring.* Thankfully, there is no clear evidence that this has happened. It was the Leader of the House who most succinctly summed up the appropriate state of relations between select committees and the Government: 'I think that we still work within a framework of trust with each other. It is important that we should.'[9] *We agree; this should be the principle by which all departments and select committees operate.*

References

1 HC (1977–78) 558–I, p. 38.
2 Fifth Report ('The Civil Service Pay and Conditions of Service Code'), HC (1989–90) 260, para. 8.
3 Q. 650–670.
4 Evidence, p. 213.
5 Q. 669.
6 Q. 670.
7 Q. 672.
8 Q. 402.
9 Q. 126.

Abridged from Select Committee on Procedure, *Second Report, 1989–90: the Working of the Select Committee System – Vol. 1, Report,* HC 19–I, pp. xxxviii–xli. Reprinted in accordance with HMSO's guidelines for the reproduction of Crown and Parliamentary copyright.

Sir Frank Cooper

Select committees – a view from a witness

My first real awareness of a Parliamentary committee was of the Public Accounts Committee (PAC). At least once each year the permanent secretary was called to account before it. For him this appearance and the preparation for it took precedence over other matters.

Vast quantities of minutely detailed briefs were prepared. Extracts from relevant documents were flagged. The permanent secretary was able to answer any questions.

The normal time for appearance was 4 p.m. I recall one permanent secretary who used to prepare on the final day not by asking any last minute questions but by arriving in the office late, forgoing his lunch, having two very strong gins and then a lie on the couch in his office before setting forth for the House of Commons.

The whole subject was taken with immense seriousness. Word went round, both at Westminster and within the department, as to how well the permanent secretary had performed. How well or ill he fared affected the perception of him both among his peers and within his department.

Some years later I had an extraordinary experience. I was for a short period Director of Accounts in the then Air Ministry. Traditionally, the director of accounts accompanied the permanent secretary to his appearance in front of the PAC. I accompanied the late Sir Maurice Dean. We sat outside the committee room on a bench in the long corridor of power. After an unusually long wait the door opened, a stretcher emerged and on it lay the stalwart figure of Sir James Crombie, at that time Commissioner of Customs and Excise. He had been taken ill while appearing in front of the committee!

When in the fullness of time my own years of appearing in front of the PAC began, I was grateful for my earlier experiences. The hearings were battles of wits; there were certain golden rules.

Preparation was of the essence. Zealous departmental staff prepared tomes of paper. Briefs were needed, but facts rather than discussion – facts which, by hook or by crook, had to be put in front of the committee. The most important preparations were question and answer sessions in the department – you questioned the staff and they questioned you.

It was important to visit the scene of the alleged crime or misdemeanour. An hour or so on the site where the events which the Comptroller and Auditor-General had reported had taken place gave one an insight and an overwhelming advantage. I inaugurated the idea that members of the PAC should pay visits and, indeed, they visited the Royal Dockyard at Chatham. This did not find a great deal of favour with either the committee or the Comptroller and Auditor-General. Were they becoming less detached?

I attached great importance – though by no means all my colleagues agreed with me – to sitting *alone* on the 'front bench'. The reasons for this were two-fold. First, it was very easy to get into a pickle if too many people answered questions. 'Divide and rule' is still alive and well! Second, I felt (despite the vast size of the Ministry of Defence) that the Accounting Officer role was a very personal one.

The PAC – the doyen of Parliamentary committees – remains in my view superior to the others: its chairman is invariably a former senior minister; its membership is of very high calibre; it is not a 'political' committee; and it is genuinely concerned with the real stuff of Parliament. The Comptroller and Auditor-General and his staff are professionally competent, work full time and look at the facts.

The PAC is primarily concerned with efficiency and correctness rather than policy. The significant development of recent years is the extent to which the committee has rightly and increasingly concerned itself with 'value for money'.

Some have said that the PAC has a bad effect – that it bears responsibility for creating the 'abominable no-men' within departments. It discourages the taking of risks, and the threat of an issue going to the PAC has caused sensible actions not to be taken. In my view this attitude has diminished significantly over the past quarter of a century.

Finally, there is the position of the secretary of state in relation to the Public Accounts Committee. It remains true today that the relationship between the PAC and the department is with the accounting officer rather than with the secretary of state.

Does this cause difficulty? Rarely – secretaries of state do not involve themselves in PAC issues of propriety and facts or the policy and politics of Parliamentary select committees.

Select committees have greatly extended their role since 1979. How do they compare with the PAC? First, and foremost, select committees are dealing largely with policy issues. Hence there is a growing relationship with the secretary of state. The civil servants appear as agents of the secretary of state. Second, most ministers have tended increasingly to ensure that they carry the committee marking their department along with them. The chairmen and members of those committees have increased their influence with ministers and now acquire a good deal more official and unofficial information than they did in the past.

The select committees are less well 'staffed' than the PAC. They tend to gather together a limited number of advisers who come from academic life, from former members of the central or local bureaucracy, from former serving officers or to a lesser extent from the private sector. The quality and attitudes of these advisers vary widely. The time they can make available is limited. This position is in no way comparable in influence, status or as a career stepping-stone with 'staffers' in the United States.

Select committees are much more 'political' than is the PAC. Secretaries of state take a considerable interest in them and are also interested in what their officials say or submit as evidence. Usually memoranda are cleared inside the department with a minister, and where difficult or delicate points arise ministers may well give directions about the evidence to be given.

There are, inevitably, some sensitive and difficult areas in consequence of this background. My own judgement is that middle-ranking officials quite like to appear in front of select committees, not least because one result is to put more factual information on the table than might otherwise be the case.

Permanent secretaries are less involved with either the select committee which marks their department or with the Treasury and Civil Service Committee which has a wider remit. Permanent secretaries themselves tend not to appear frequently in front of select committees. But there are occasions, particularly when a major question about the running of the department is involved, when they would be summoned. They are more likely to be involved in internal discussions as to the nature and presentations of the evidence to be given to the select committee where politics, policies and facts may require some harmonization.

This process can on occasions, but in my own experience not very frequently, lead to difficulty within departments on the line to be taken and what can or should not be said. Over the years, due processes have been worked out. It is permissible for an official to say to a committee 'Well, that is something you will have to ask my Secretary of State', or 'My Secretary of State's view on this point is specifically that . . .' It is likely that ministerial appearances in front of select committees will grow.

Secretaries of state are particularly sensitive to the rule that the Government decides and Parliament approves or disapproves the decision. In other words, ministers are unenthusiastic about select committees carrying out parallel enquiries prior to decision taking. This is perhaps a likely area of friction between the executive and the legislature in years to come.

Have the select committees been a success? We are certainly better off with them than without them. Much more factual information is now available – though how much use is made of it is debatable. Success has inevitably been limited because of the restricted role that the committees play. There is little hostility within the civil service to the committees and, increasingly, appearing before them has been quite welcomed by officials both in its own right and as a change from the normal daily routine. At this stage select committees are a typical British compromise.

What of the future? The critical issues surely centre on the balance of power between the executive and the legislature and on the powers of the committees. From the point of view of a permanent secretary, my own judgement would be that the PAC has always been of inestimable value in assisting the permanent secretary in the management and direction of his department. The select committees have had some impact in terms of exposing issues which either the department or ministers would prefer to have left alone. There are more pluses than minuses.

From F. Cooper (1987) 'Select committees – a view from a witness', *Contemporary Record*, Vol. 1, No. 1, pp. 16–17. Reproduced with the permission of Frank Cass Publishers.

Inside the new civil service

Presenter: Ros Hepplewhite is 43. Since last April, she's been Chief Executive of the Child Support Agency, set up to implement new policy on child maintenance introduced by the Child Support Act 1991. She left her job as national director of the mental health charity, MIND, for a fixed term contract, earning over £47,000 plus an unspecified performance bonus if the CSA hits its targets, which are to save rather than spend money. She has a staff of four and a half thousand, many of them new recruits to the civil service. And Ros Hepplewhite has very clear views on the role and responsibilities of a new civil servant. Particularly in the ticklish area of policy explanation and defence.

Hepplewhite: I was recruited from outside the civil service to do this job, I do feel that the child maintenance system needs changing, I do feel that the new arrangements are an improvement on the previous arrangements, and I want my staff to feel that as well. And I feel quite comfortable about going out to my staff and saying it is important that we make these new changes work. For reasons other than security of our own jobs, but also because we believe in what we do, but it is you're quite right, it is a very real cultural shift from the civil service of ten years ago.

Interviewer: And are you finding that given this completely fresh structure and this new culture that you are bringing in, in terms of the way you are approaching the business of the agency, that you are having to defend the policy?

Hepplewhite: Yes I find that I have to defend the policy in the sense that clearly the broad thrust of the policy is something that I must feel that operationally I can deliver, and that it will be a genuine improvement to people's lives over the previous system. But in general terms, yes, I think that new civil servants, they're not just the head of Next Steps agencies, but all civil servants in these agencies, do need to have not only an understanding of policy, but a sense of driving a policy forward.

Presenter: So when the shortcomings of the new CSA legislation first manifested themselves it wasn't the Minister, Peter Lilley, who fielded hostile media questions, it was Ros Hepplewhite.

Hepplewhite: I find that I am often asked to appear on TV and radio allegedly about operations, it moves into policy areas, it will be quite irresponsible of me it seems, in my view, to say I, I am not able to comment on this at all, what I can do is I can explain the thinking behind the policy, how this works in operational terms. I am willing and ready to discuss with people what they consider their problems are in relation to certain aspects of the policy. I suppose I am unusual, even in today's civil service, in moving quite so far out into the public arena. *But* I don't feel apologetic about it, I think it's the way forward.

Presenter: Now what's the problem with this way forward? Why shouldn't chief executives of agencies get even more involved in policy making and defending? Because, say the critics, they are, as civil servants, not accountable to the citizenry. That is the role of the minister, accountable through Parliament. Once chief executives of agencies are publicly fielded to answer complaints, or enter the sensitive area of policy explanation and defence, ministers are in effect being shielded from proper interrogation. A democratic deficit is being created under the guise of open government. But the Minister responsible for the reform process, William Waldegrave, is unimpressed by that argument. It is, he avers, quite proper for Ros Hepplewhite to defend the operation of her new agency.

Waldegrave: She should defend herself against accusations that she's doing badly, and that's perfectly legitimate for her to do that. But when it comes to saying what the policy is, she must say, and this is the divide which we've sharpened I think, well that is what I've agreed to do, and here is the policy directive which instructs me to do it, which makes the service agreement able to do it, so you must ask the secretary of state about that. And I think that's much clearer than the old days of a huge hierarchical organization where we wouldn't have known that there was a Ros Hepplewhite in the mix anyway. There would have been all sorts of people and we would have had the theoretical doctrine that everything was the responsibility of the minister. Now if you have a doctrine which says that everything is the responsibility of the minister, which all common sense people know to be false, then you're really saying that the minister is in a wonderful position to say that nothing is his responsibility.

Presenter: According to William Waldegrave then, the reforms clarify and improve the line between the managerial responsibilities of chief executives, as defined in the framework contracts they sign, and the accountability of ministers. And Head of the Home Civil Service, Sir Robin Butler, isn't only happy with the effect of the reforms, he's positively sanguine about the idea of accountable ministers being offered the protective figleaf of an agency chief executive, when the circumstances are appropriate.

Butler: I think that up to a point, it's right that there should be a figleaf, because the minister in a complex society cannot be responsible for every service that's performed at every level in the department. So that, for example, the governor of a prison must be responsible for the way that prison is run and for keeping the inmates inside. The minister can't be expected to take responsibility for every detail of that. So if the new arrangement makes that clear, but does produce somebody who is directly responsible in the system, that seems to be an improvement in accountability rather than a diminution.

Presenter: And yet it has been described as a component of a democratic deficit, that's growing.

Butler: Well I don't think there is a democratic deficit in that sense. As I say, I think we've improved accountability because you identify someone in the system who is responsible for providing the service, but the matter can always be taken up with the minister. If you had situations in which the minister could not even be asked questions about such services, there would be a democratic deficit. But in the last resort if people are dissatisfied with the operation of a chief executive, they can always take it up with the minister, and the minister is ultimately accountable.

Presenter: So are you now sure that you know where the buck is going to stop? Vernon Bogdanor is not.

Bogdanor: The new system allows for tremendous buck passing, we saw with the Child Support Agency that when things went wrong it was the chief executive who was blamed and not the minister, and I fear that what is going to happen is that the minister will take the credit when things go right, but will blame officials when things go wrong, he or she will say don't blame me, it's the chief executive's fault. But when things go right, the ministers will take the credit.

Presenter: In practice we can now expect to see chief executives not only running a policy, but accepting responsibility for the policy itself in a way which the old style nameless, faceless, bureaucrats were never expected to be. But then they were not on limited period contracts, with targets to achieve and performance pay resting on successful achievement. In a few years, we've replaced facilitators of government policy with committed doers, to use John Ford's phrase, some of whom will be committed believers in the policy they've been hired to implement. It's a considerable cultural shift from the anonymous, permanent, career civil servants of the pre-reform days. And it's a shift that affects the lower civil service grades too. Most of the CSA staff were recruited from outside the civil service, like their boss, Ros Hepplewhite.

Hepplewhite: Most of the staff who have chosen to work for the Child Support Agency, and we are again unusual in central government in that staff have not been posted to us, they have volunteered and been recruited, some from within the civil service, some from outside, identify very strongly with the new arrangements and feel that this is necessary and long overdue. That, in itself, is relatively unusual in central government. Clearly, the Child Support Act, as enacted, is a very major social policy change, and it would be unusual for someone to come and work for the Child Support Agency if they felt that this major social policy change was not, in fact, the right one. Now it is not a requirement of the job, that you are signed up to the policy, but it would be very unusual if people didn't feel that what they were doing as well as paying their own mortgage, was actually something worthwhile, and we encourage that in the Agency.

From the BBC News and Current Affairs programme, *Inside the New Civil Service: Politics and Pioneers*, first broadcast on Radio 4, 20 January 1994. Reproduced with the permission of the BBC.

| *Cabinet Office*

Open government

Part I

Purpose

1. This Code of Practice supports the Government's policy under the Citizen's Charter of extending access to official information, and responding to reasonable requests for information, except where disclosure would not be in the public interest as specified in Part II of this Code.

    2. The aims of the Code are:

- to improve policy-making and the democratic process by extending access to the facts and analyses which provide the basis for the consideration of proposed policy;
- to protect the interests of individuals and companies by ensuring that reasons are given for administrative decisions, except where there is statutory authority or established convention to the contrary; and
- to support and extend the principles of public service established under the Citizen's Charter.

These aims are balanced by the need:

- to maintain high standards of care in ensuring the privacy of personal and commercially confidential information; and
- to preserve confidentiality where disclosure would not be in the public interest or would breach personal privacy or the confidences of a third party, in accordance with statutory requirements and Part II of the Code.

Information the Government will release

3. Subject to the exemptions in Part II, the Code commits departments and public bodies under the jurisdiction of the Parliamentary Commissioner for Administration (the Ombudsman):[1]

(i)   to publish the facts and analysis of the facts which the Government considers relevant and important in framing major policy proposals and decisions; such information will normally be made available when policies and decisions are announced;
(ii) to publish or otherwise make available, as soon as practicable after the Code becomes operational, explanatory material on departments' dealings with the public (including such rules, procedures, internal guidance to officials and similar administrative manuals as will assist better understanding of departmental action in dealing with the public) except where publication could prejudice any matter which should properly be kept confidential under Part II of the Code;
(iii) to give reasons for administrative decisions to those affected;[2]
(iv) to publish in accordance with the Citizen's Charter:

  ● full information about how public services are run, how much they cost, who is in charge, and what complaints and redress procedures are available;
  ● full and, where possible, comparable information about what services are being provided, what targets are set, what standards of service are expected and the results achieved.

(v)   to release, in response to specific requests, information relating to their policies, actions and decisions and other matters related to their areas of responsibility.

4. There is no commitment that pre-existing documents, as distinct from information, will be made available in response to requests. The Code does not require departments to acquire information they do not possess, to provide information which is already published, to provide material which the Government did not consider to be reliable information, or to provide information which is provided as part of an existing charge service other than through that service.

Responses to requests for information

5. Information will be provided as soon as practicable. The target for response to simple requests for information is 20 working days from the date of receipt. This target may need to be extended when significant search or collation of material is required. Where information cannot be provided under the terms of the Code, an explanation will normally be given.

Scope

6. The Code applies to those Government departments and other bodies within the jurisdiction of the Ombudsman (as listed in Schedule 2 to the Parliamentary Commissioner Act 1967).[3] The Code applies to agencies within departments and to functions carried out on behalf of a department or public body by contractors.

Charges

7. Departments, agencies and public bodies will make their own arrangements for charging. Details of charges are available from departments on request. Schemes may include a standard charge for processing simple requests for information. Where a request is complex and would require extensive searches of records or processing or collation of information, an additional charge, reflecting reasonable costs, may be notified.

. . .

Part II

Reasons for confidentiality

The following categories of information are exempt from the commitments to provide information in this Code.

References to harm or prejudice include both actual harm or prejudice and risk or reasonable expectation of harm or prejudice. In such cases it should be considered whether any harm or prejudice arising from disclosure is out-weighed by the public interest in making information available.

The exemptions will not be interpreted in a way which causes injustice to individuals.

1 Defence, security and international relations
(a) Information whose disclosure would harm national security or defence.
(b) Information whose disclosure would harm the conduct of international relations or affairs.
(c) Information received in confidence from foreign governments, foreign courts or international organizations.

2 Internal discussion and advice
Information whose disclosure would harm the frankness and candour of internal discussion, including:

- proceedings of Cabinet and Cabinet committees;
- internal opinion, advice, recommendation, consultation and deliberation;
- projections and assumptions relating to internal policy analysis; analysis of alternative policy options and information relating to rejected policy options;
- confidential communications between departments, public bodies and regulatory bodies.

3 Communications with the Royal Household
Information relating to confidential communications between Ministers and Her Majesty the Queen or other Members of the Royal Household, or relating to confidential proceedings of the Privy Council.

4 *Law enforcement and legal proceedings*
(a) Information whose disclosure would prejudice the administration of justice, including fair trial and the enforcement or proper administration of the law.
(b) Information whose disclosure would prejudice legal proceedings or the proceedings of any tribunal, public inquiry or other formal investigation (whether actual or likely) or whose disclosure is, has been or is likely to be addressed in the context of such proceedings.
(c) Information relating to proceedings which have been completed or terminated, or relating to investigations which have or might have resulted in proceedings.
(d) Information covered by legal professional privilege.
(e) Information whose disclosure would prejudice the prevention, investigation or detection of crime, the apprehension or prosecution of offenders, or the security of any building or penal institution.
(f) Information whose disclosure would harm public safety or public order.
(g) Information whose disclosure could endanger the life or physical safety of any person, or identify the source of information or assistance given in confidence for law enforcement or security purposes.
(h) Information whose disclosure would increase the likelihood of damage to the environment, or rare or endangered species and their habitats.

5 *Immigration and nationality*
Information relating to immigration, nationality, consular and entry clearance cases.

6 *Effective management of the economy and collection of tax*
(a) Information whose disclosure would harm the ability of the Government to manage the economy, prejudice the conduct of official market operations or lead to improper gain or advantage.
(b) Information whose disclosure would prejudice the assessment or collection of tax, duties or National Insurance contributions, or assist tax avoidance or evasion.

7 *Effective management and operations of the public service*
(a) Information whose disclosure could lead to improper gain or advantage or would prejudice:

  • the competitive position of a department or other public body or authority;
  • negotiations or the effective conduct of personnel management, or commercial or contractual activities;
  • the awarding of discretionary grants.

(b) Information whose disclosure would harm the proper and efficient conduct of the operations of a department or other public body or authority, including NHS organizations, or of any regulatory body.

8 Public employment, public appointments and honours
(a) Personnel records (relating to public appointments as well as employees of public authorities) including those relating to recruitment, promotion and security vetting.
(b) Information, opinions and assessments given in confidence in relation to public employment and public appointments made by ministers of the Crown, by the Crown on the advice of ministers or by statutory office holders.
(c) Information, opinions and assessments given in relation to recommendations for honours.

9 Voluminous or vexatious requests
Requests for information which are vexatious or manifestly unreasonable or are formulated in too general a manner, or which (because of the amount of information to be processed or the need to retrieve information from files not in current use) would require unreasonable diversion of resources.

10 Publication and prematurity in relation to publication
Information which is or will soon be published, or whose disclosure would be premature in relation to a planned announcement or publication.

11 Research, statistics and analysis
(a) Information relating to incomplete analysis, research or statistics, where disclosure could be misleading or deprive the holder of priority of publication or commercial value.
(b) Information held only for preparing statistics or carrying out research, or for surveillance for health and safety purposes (including food safety), and which relates to individuals, companies or products which will not be identified in reports of that research or surveillance, or in published statistics.

12 Privacy of an individual
Unwarranted disclosure to a third party of personal information about any person (including a deceased person) or any other disclosure which would constitute or could facilitate an unwarranted invasion of privacy.

13 Third party's commercial confidences
Information including commercial confidences, trade secrets or intellectual property whose unwarranted disclosure would harm the competitive position of a third party.

14 Information given in confidence
(a) Information held in consequence of having been supplied in confidence by a person who:

- gave the information under a statutory guarantee that its confidentiality would be protected; or
- was not under any legal obligation, whether actual or implied, to supply it, and has not consented to its disclosure.

(b) Information whose disclosure without the consent of the supplier would prejudice the future supply of such information.
(c) Medical information provided in confidence if disclosure to the subject would harm their physical or mental health, or should only be made by a medical practitioner:

15 Statutory and other restrictions
(a) Information whose disclosure is prohibited by or under any enactment, regulation, European Community law or international agreement.
(b) Information whose release would constitute a breach of Parliamentary Privilege.

Notes

1 In Northern Ireland, the Parliamentary Commissioner for Administration and the Commissioner for Complaints.
2 There will be a few areas where well-established convention or legal authority limits the commitment to give reasons, for example decisions on citizenship applications (see s.44(2) of the British Nationality Act 1981) or certain decisions on merger and monopoly cases or on whether to take enforcement action.
3 In Northern Ireland the Code applies to public bodies under the jurisdiction of the Northern Ireland Parliamentary Commissioner for Administration and the Commissioner for Complaints, with the exception of local government and health and personal social services bodies, for which separate arrangements are being developed as in Great Britain. Some Northern Ireland departments and bodies are expressly subject to the jurisdiction of the Parliamentary Commissioner under the 1967 Act.

Robert Hazell

Making the civil service more accountable

I spent fourteen years as a civil servant, working in the Home Office from 1975 to 1989. That experience left me with a great deal of respect for my former colleagues in Whitehall, so I begin with some rather defensive, traditional remarks about the nature of the civil service.

The civil service is very large, employing some 600,000 people. All large bureaucracies tend to be regarded as remote, and it is difficult for them to establish a close relationship with their customers. The big banks and insurance companies are also perceived as being relatively distant from their customers. They too are huge organizations, and in recent years they have looked to the public sector for new techniques in increasing their accountability; both the banks and the insurance industry have borrowed from government the device of an Ombudsman to investigate customers' complaints.

Second, it is not just in the UK that the government is perceived as being unaccountable; government departments the world over are accused of being over large and remote. What distinguishes the British government from its Western counterparts is its excessive secrecy. But here again this is not something which is peculiar to government in Britain. Des Wilson gave examples at the Manchester Convention of his accountant and his hospital doctor both refusing to allow him to see his own file. Even the voluntary sector is not immune; there are charitable trusts which refuse to disclose the identity of their trustees. Secrecy is truly the British disease. But in tackling the disease it is right that we should start at the top, with the agencies of central government.

For that we need a Freedom of Information Act. It is depressing to find that the government still maintains that freedom of information is somehow incompatible with a Westminister system of ministerial accountability to Parliament. This was the line adopted by Francis Maude in July 1991, when he claimed that freedom of information 'would undermine the traditional concepts of ministerial responsibility under the Crown and accountability to Parliament'. The experience of the freedom of information legislation in Australia, Canada and New Zealand, ten years old this year, is that freedom of information can work well in countries with a constitution on the Westminster model. Ministerial accountability is not undermined but enhanced by legislation which enables MPs and others to get more background information about government decisions. In itself it is not the panacea which some reformers seem to hope for. Nor is it an automatic guarantee of good government, nor of totally open government. But it is a useful extra check on the efficiency and fairness of the government machine, and it could symbolize an important change in attitude and principle.

The sub-title for our session at Manchester was 'How do we ensure that those who carry out public policy owe their allegiance to the public?' I believe that this is a mistaken way of expressing the present position, or indeed any future aspirations. Civil servants owe their allegiance to the Crown. If and when we have a written constitution they will owe their allegiance to the constitution. In the Institute for Public Policy Research (IPPR) draft constitution which was presented to the Manchester Convention this principle is written into Article 114.5: 'The first duty of each public service, and of every person appointed to a public service, is to the Constitution.'

This is not to say that civil servants owe no duty towards the public. They have a duty to be courteous; to be efficient; to be fair and to be truthful. They must show no favours; deal with matters as expeditiously as possible; and be as open as possible. That is essentially the agenda of the Citizen's Charter. It seems modest enough. Indeed, it need not require a radical constitutional change. But it would require a major shift in attitudes and a cultural change, particularly in the junior ranks of the civil service, who are the front line in terms of day-to-day dealing with members of the public.

It is also part of the agenda behind the hiving off of large parts of the civil service into agencies under the Next Steps initiative. The new agencies will be accountable to ministers for their performance, specified in a detailed and demanding contract; but greater management accountability need not necessarily mean lesser accountability to the public. Many of the targets set for service agencies like the Benefits Agency or the Driver and Vehicle Licensing Centre relate to the quality of the service they provide to their customers; and in some areas, like waiting times for driving tests, there have been major improvements as a result.

But treating citizens as customers is not a complete agenda. How can our *rights* as citizens be improved? There are four practical measures which I would like to see introduced, none of which requires legislation, and all of which could be implemented quickly.

Publication of departments' staff directories

These are invaluable detailed guides to who does what, giving civil servants' telephone numbers etc. In Washington DC they are freely available to journalists and the like; in London they are still classified. The Home Office staff directory is a restricted document.

Reform of departmental press offices

These represent a Maginot Line which journalists and enquirers seldom manage to get behind. I would like to encourage press officers to transfer enquiries as much as possible to the official responsible for that particular area. When I was a civil servant I used to insist on talking direct to journalists: I would prefer that the briefing came from me rather than playing a game of Chinese whispers through a press officer.

A code of conduct for the civil service

The First Division Association (FDA, the senior civil servants' trade union) have called for such a code in order to offer guidance in cases like that of Clive Ponting and others where a conflict has arisen between a civil servant's duty to ministers and his duty to the public. I would hope that such a code might also be a code of ethics, which would help to resurrect the ethic of the public service as being a serious calling, something of value, and not simply a haven for those who could not make it in the private sector.

Reasons for departmental decisions

I would like to require officials in government departments always to give reasons for their decisions. This would be an important step forward in our administrative law. It is one that has already been made in Australia and New Zealand and in some European countries. It goes to the heart of accountability: a citizen cannot challenge an official decision until he knows the reasons which lie behind it.

What about the accountability of the higher civil service, in particular for policy-making? One reason for the civil service being something of a closed world to outsiders is that the senior civil service is quite a narrow caste, which would be greatly improved by greater movement in and out. The need for this has been accepted in principle by Whitehall, and last year saw the establishment of the Whitehall and Industry Trust to help promote more secondments; but a lot more could be done. In New Zealand, for example, permanent secretaries are now on five year contracts.

Finally I return to the traditional meaning of civil service accountability, in the sense of the civil service being accountable to the government of the day. I do not subscribe to the conspiracy theory that Whitehall constantly undermines government plans and prevents any radical agenda being implemented. That represented a strong current in Labour thinking, after 1970 and even more so after 1979, with politicians like Tony Benn claiming in their memoirs that the Labour Government had been frustrated and undermined by the Whitehall mandarins. At the time the theory sounded plausible; but I believe it has been completely exploded by the experience of the Thatcher Government. In the years since 1979 Whitehall has showed itself to be a very flexible, and highly effective machine in doing the Government's bidding. Opponents of the Conservative Government may not like the result, but it is undeniable that the civil service did respond to ministerial commands and has implemented the

Conservative Government's agenda, even when many civil servants disliked that policy.

In conclusion I would say there is no quick fix or simple solution to achieve greater civil service accountability. Government departments are huge and complex organizations, and like Gulliver lying on the sands of Lilliput, they need many different lines of accountability to pin them down. These include Parliament, the press, the courts, tribunals, select committees, auditors and ombudsmen. All have an important role to play in maintaining a check on the efficiency, fairness and integrity of government, and in ensuring that the civil service is responsive both to its political masters and to the needs of the people.

From R. Hazell (1991) 'Making the civil service more accountable', *Charter 88/The Independent Constitutional Convention*, Manchester, November. Reproduced with the permission of Charter 88 Trust.

7.8 | *Tony Benn*

Commonwealth of Britain Bill

Part III   The Presidency

13.—(1) There shall be a President elected from among their number, by a two-thirds majority, by both Houses of Parliament sitting together, to serve for a three year term and to be eligible for re-election for one further three year term.

(2) If the office of President is vacant, or the President is unable to discharge the duties of the Presidency, the Speaker of the House of Commons shall act as President until the President is able to discharge the duties of the Presidency or until a new President is elected.

14.—(1)(a) The powers now exercised under Crown prerogative shall be exercised by the President, who shall act solely upon the advice of the Prime Minister, or of a resolution of the House of Commons (which shall prevail if such resolution is in conflict with the advice of the Prime Minister);

(b) The exercise of such powers shall require the assent of the House of Commons before having effect; and

(c) the powers of the President shall include power –

- to give assent to the passage of legislation;
- to dissolve Parliament;
- to invite a person to attempt to form an administration;
- to make orders for any purpose for which Orders in Council were required before the coming into force of this Act;
- to declare war;
- to order British forces into armed conflict;
- to make peace;
- to recognize foreign governments;

The President.

Presidential powers.

- to sign or ratify treaties;
- to grant pardons;
- to grant charters;
- to make appointments;
- to establish commissions of inquiry;
- to grant commissions in the armed forces;
- to issue orders; and
- to exercise other executive powers not conferred by statute.

(2) Instruments previously made by Order in the Council and which are legislative in character, after being made by the President, shall be brought in as Bills.

(3) Instruments exercising the general administrative powers of the President shall be published and laid before the House of Commons for approval by resolution of that House.

(4) Instruments exercising powers of appointment shall be published, as separate orders for each appointment, and shall be subject to annulment in pursuance of a resolution of the House of Commons.

Part IV   The Council of State

Establishment of the Council of State.

15.—(1) There shall be a Council of State consisting of twenty-four persons, of whom twelve shall be men and twelve shall be women.

(2) Half of the members of the Council of State shall be elected by the House of Commons from among its members and half by the House of the People from among its members.

(3) Each member shall serve for a period of two years.

Powers of the Council of State.

16.—(1) In the event of no government being in office, the powers of government shall be vested in the Council of State, and all decisions made by the Council of State shall be subject to confirmation by the House of Commons.

(2) The President shall preside over the Council of State and shall report its decisions to both Houses of Parliament.

Part V   The Executive

The government.

17.—(1) The House of Commons shall, by a simple majority, elect one of its members to form a government as Prime Minister, and that person shall present the government to the House of Commons for approval as a whole, by resolution, before, he or she takes office.

(2) All executive power shall be vested in the government for so long as it enjoys a majority in the House of Commons, or until the day of first meeting of a new Parliament.

(3) In the event of a government being defeated in the House of Commons on a matter of confidence, the Prime Minister shall

tender his or her resignation forthwith to the President who shall consult widely to determine who might best be able to form a new administration, and shall issue an invitation to that person to attempt to do so, and to present his or her government to the House of Commons for approval.

(4) Parliament shall be dissolved before the expiry of its term only if—

(a) no person attempting to form a government has secured the approval of the House of Commons for that government;
(b) the President recommends a dissolution; and
(c) the House of Commons votes in favour of a dissolution

and in such a case there shall be a general election to elect a new Parliament for the unexpired term of the previous Parliament.

18.—(1)(a) In the Public Records Act 1958 references to 'four years' shall be substituted for references to 'thirty years'. *Freedom of information. 1958. c. 51.*

(b) In section 5(1) of that Act the words from 'created' to the end of the subsection, and section 5(2), shall be omitted.

(2) Notwithstanding subsection 1 above, a minister may certify that a paper should remain secret, and any such certificate shall be laid before the House of Commons for approval by resolution.

(3) The Official Secrets Acts 1911, 1920, 1939 and 1989 are hereby repealed. *1911 c. 28. 1920 c. 75. 1939 c. 121. 1989 c. 6.*

(4) All official information shall be published, or made available on request, save that categories of information relating to the following subjects may be protected by order subject to approval by resolution:

(i) defence and security matters;
(ii) economic policy;
(iii) international relations; and
(iv) personal data.

(5) It shall be a criminal offence to disclose protected information, and penalties and defences shall be specified by an order under section 52 below.

19.—(1) The legal status of all the armed forces of Britain shall depend upon the passing by the House of Commons of an annual authorization order. *The armed forces.*

(2) The Chief and Vice-Chief of the Defence Staff, and the Chief of Staff of each of the three Services shall be nominated by the Government and confirmed by the Defence Committee of the House of Commons before they are appointed.

20.—(1) The security services of the Commonwealth shall be accountable to Parliament through the responsible minister or ministers, who shall make a report annually to the House of Commons containing the information set out in Schedule 3 to this Act. *The security services.*

(2) The House of Commons may make recommendations by resolution on any aspect of the work of the security services.

(3) The legal status of the security services shall depend upon the passing of an annual authorization order by the House of Commons.

(4) The head of each security service shall be nominated by the Government and confirmed by the Select Committee of the House of Commons for the time being having responsibility for matters relating to that service.

From *Commonwealth of Britain Bill*, HC 1992–93 (103). Reprinted in accordance with HMSO's guidelines for the reproduction of Crown and Parliamentary copyright.

8

Select annotated bibliography

The following is merely a selection from a vast literature on a number of aspects associated with Whitehall. As with the choice of readings, these further sources reflect some of the editor's quirks, prejudices and preferences. There is the further matter of delineation. Whitehall is part of a wider web of governmental and political institutions. The official civil service connects at many points with the world of political parties, pressure groups and other representative institutions, most notably Parliament. It has been the focus of attention among political scientists, organizational theorists, constitutional lawyers and historians – to mention only the more obvious. Whitehall comes within the purview of practitioners from all these disciplines: yet each of them also looks out beyond Whitehall. It is therefore difficult to know quite where to draw the line when talking about the literature on Whitehall. Many of the sources referred to below focus mainly if not exclusively upon the civil service, more particularly the senior civil service, as it is now officially called. Some of the sources, though, have a wider vista. The net has been cast fairly widely, for two reasons. First, because the wider perspective can often throw extra light on the more specific object, i.e. Whitehall; second, because students who are studying Whitehall may wish to follow other, connecting, pathways. So, the literature surveyed below goes rather beyond the scope of the readings in this volume. This, it is hoped, will not lead people astray. Such at least is not the intention. Quite the contrary: rather it is to offer students a number of possible directions that may be found rewarding and worthy of pursuit. It is the intention also to assist tutors in their task of guiding students.

The literature is classified under seven headings, broadly but not exactly corresponding to the substantive chapters or sections of this volume: background and general; structure and processes; civil servants and ministers; loyalties, responsibilities and ethics; the new managerialism; Whitehall, Parliament and the public; and other issues and other sources.

Background and general

There is a massive literature on the history of the British civil service, even if departmental histories are excluded. The latter is itself a specialized field which need not be explored here, save for two modern classics: Roseveare (1969) and Wright (1969). Both examine the role of the Treasury in the development of the civil service, Wright concentrating on the generation following the Northcote-Trevelyan Report. Among the more general chronological and/or thematic treatments, Cohen (1965) is old but still useful on the nineteenth-century reforms. Chester (1981) is sound but dull on the nineteenth century while Greenleaf (1983, 1987) is a monumental survey in three parts and four volumes. Hard going but worth the effort is Parris (1969), who examines the constitutional development of the civil service. Upon this topic Clark (1959) remains a seminal article, while Greenaway (1985) offers a brief but illuminating perspective. Sutherland (1972) and Cromwell (1977) are useful collections containing a wealth of ideas about government in the nineteenth century, Burk (1982) likewise on the administrative consequences of the First World War. Gowan (1987) challenges traditional assumptions about the ulterior motives of the nineteenth-century reformers. Fry (1969) traces the development of the administration elite class and (in Fry 1979) of changing ideas as well as the evolving institutional structures of central government. Tivey (1988) tries to explain what has made the whole system tick over the years, though there is little about Whitehall. Birch (1964) falls into the same category – a classic which examines context rather than institutional anatomy. Chapman and Greenaway (1980) offer an interpretation of central administrative development from the mid-nineteenth century, while Elcock (1991) is a thematic, diagnostic *tour de force* covering mainly the post-war years and looking well beyond Whitehall.

Some of the more general texts contain potted histories. Drewry and Butcher (1991) do so in what is a sound introduction. It is worth looking at the relevant chapters in Greenwood and Wilson (1989) and in Kingdom (1991). The latter also edits a comparative survey in which he contributes the chapter on Britain (Kingdom 1990). Some find the style in Hennessy (1989) too breezy, but it is a rich source, based as it is upon many years of scholarship and observation. Pyper (1991, 1995) offers brief though useful introductory volumes; McDonald (1992) raises some interesting questions and is more opinionated. Jordan (1994b) is much more than a book about Whitehall, though it covers relevant ground.

Both the interim and the final reports from the Treasury and Civil Service Committee (1993, 1994) enquiry into the role of the civil service are worth consulting. They cover quite a lot of ground and should be used to supplement the basic texts. So, too, should the two more recent and more important White Papers (Cabinet Office 1994, 1995). Of course, they present only the government's position as the government would have everyone believe it to be.

Whitehall: structure and processes

The redoubtable Chester and Willson (1968) remains the standard source on changes in the organization and structure of central government between

1914 and 1964. The famous Haldane Report (Ministry of Reconstruction 1918) is unsurpassed as an official document which tried to establish and proceed from first principles. In this it has had little subsequent competition, though the Heath government's white paper (Cabinet Office 1970) was a brave attempt to do likewise. The 1960s and 1970s were heroic years for structural upheavals. Ministries and departments were set up, abolished or merged with sometimes bewildering frequency. Clarke (1971) conveys the spirit of these times. Robertson (1971) shows that not everyone was convinced. Pollitt (1984) offers a scholarly analysis of departmental reorganizations from the Macmillan era to the early Thatcher years. This can be supplemented and updated by turning to Radcliffe (1991) or Madgwick (1991). Both are useful, the latter with a stronger emphasis upon the political executive.

There is a specialist literature on the core executive, much of it focusing on the political level and therefore going rather beyond the scope of this volume. This is not always the case. Dunleavy (1989) develops a rarefied and highly analytical approach to the 'architecture' of the British state (see Reading 2.2). This follows the earlier and equally ambitious theoretical work of Hood and Dunsire (1981) – an attempt to measure the differences (and similarities) between government departments. On a different plane and with a different focus are Hennessy (1986) and James (1992). Both are books about the Cabinet but which have quite a bit to say about its interaction with the bureaucracy. The same can be said for two volumes which concentrate upon Cabinet ministers. Headey (1974) is obviously dated but still useful, while Searing (1994) is more recently published and also useful, but with surprisingly little on the Thatcher and Major years. Theakston (1987) is the standard and indeed the only full-length volume devoted to junior ministers.

Plowden (1987) is a country-by-country collection of essays which examine the way political leaders are advised. One such adviser (Donoughue 1987) served the Wilson and Callaghan governments in the 1970s. His story is interesting and the early chapters are still valuable in explaining how the very centre of the Whitehall machine works. Jones (1976) describes the development of the Prime Minister's Private Office. Willetts (1987) is an account by a former member of the PM's Policy Unit (not to be confused with the Private Office) under Margaret Thatcher, while Seldon (1990) assesses the Cabinet Office as an instrument of coordination during the 1980s. Dickie (1992) is a readable, journalistic but serious account of the way the Foreign and Commonwealth Office (FCO) works and of how things have changed there over the past couple of decades. So, too, is Edwards (1994), based upon a television series. Needless to say, what is true of the FCO does not necessarily hold for the rest of Whitehall.

It is often said that the process by which scarce resources are allocated says much about the character of an institution. And money is usually among the scarcer resources – at least in relation to demand and potential spending commitments. This is certainly so within Whitehall. The classic account of the budgetary process from Heclo and Wildavsky (1981) forms one of the readings for this volume, as does the update of Thain and Wright (1988). The latter have produced what should become the definitive modern study of the Treasury and Whitehall (Thain and Wright 1995).

If many of the decisions about public spending are, in the final analysis, taken behind closed doors, they nevertheless reflect certain pressures and clearly have a wider resonance. The day-to-day contacts between Whitehall and various organized interests have long attracted the attention of academics. Alderman (1984) and Grant (1995) explore the world of pressure groups, including their interaction with Whitehall, the efficacy of which (for government) is questioned by Watt (1988). This interaction often takes place through what in recent years have become known as policy networks. The reading included in this volume from Wright explains about policy networks. Other examples of this approach may be found in Rhodes (1990) and in Marsh and Rhodes (1992), an edited collection. Raab (1992) and Smith (1993) demonstrate the utility of the concept and argue that it is more than simply a metaphor. Atkinson and Coleman (1992) offer a constructive critique, as does Dowding (1995), the latter being the more critical. Richardson (1990) explores changing styles of interaction between pressure groups and government.

Academic interest in networks is part of a wider preoccupation with the analysis of public policy. The specialist literature (especially American) is vast and beyond the scope of this survey. Hogwood (1995) provides a useful and up to date review: Burch and Wood (1989), Ham and Hill (1993), Hogwood (1987) and Jordan and Richardson (1987) will do for starters. Case studies of specific policies feature in Greenaway *et al.* (1992) and in Butler *et al.* (1994). The latter is a post-mortem on the poll tax, for which the authors hold top officials partly to blame. Why do certain policies fail (or succeed)? Hood (1976) and Shils (1989) identify some of the 'secular' impediments.

Civil servants and ministers

The relationship between civil servants and their ministers is a perennial topic. There are two main branches of the literature. First, there are accounts written by participants: usually ministers and often in the form of memoirs or diaries; less frequently and then with greater circumspection by civil servants. Second, there are the more analytical, detached though not necessarily impartial perspectives of academics, journalists and other informed observers.

Ministers are party political animals. No one expects them to make any pretence at impartiality. Until the Crossman diaries there was an understanding that ministers would not publicly impugn their officials. Richard Crossman (1975–7) did just that. He had been a senior member of Harold Wilson's governments between 1964 and 1970. Whitehall tried in vain to prevent the publication of his diaries. They are still worth dipping into, especially Volume 1, for a vivid impression of the official machine as seen by a frustrated minister. Others have followed the Crossman idiom. One such is Crossman's former cabinet colleague Barbara Castle (1980, 1984), whose 'mandarin power' article is reproduced in abridged form above (see Reading 3.1). Tony Benn was also one of Crossman's cabinet colleagues. Those volumes of his diaries which cover his years as a minister are also worth a look (Benn 1987–90). Elsewhere (Benn 1979) he sets out his views on Whitehall officialdom. While clearly critical of the way the permanent bureaucracy works, neither Crossman nor Castle, nor even Benn, held it primarily responsible for Labour's apparent failings in office.

Meacher (1979) and Sedgemore (1980) come closer to saying this. But not all Labour ministers have been so critical (see Royal Institute of Public Administration 1980; Dell 1991). The memoirs of Denis Healey (1989) and of Roy Jenkins (1991) also give reasonably balanced though by no means uncritical appraisals. The same can be said of two among the leading Conservative ministers from the Thatcher years: Nigel Lawson (1992) and Geoffrey Howe (1994). For insights into Whitehall – and in other respects, too – they are the pick among those who have turned to account their experiences in office during the 1980s, especially Lawson. There is an informative and readable portrait of the Whitehall village by Bruce-Gardyne (1986), based upon his time as a Treasury minister in the early 1980s. Heseltine (1990), from which one of the above readings is drawn, is more of a personal manifesto than a set of memoirs, but is still useful. Clark (1993) matches Crossman or any other Labour diarist for sheer entertainment and waspishness towards Whitehall. From an earlier generation of Conservative ministers, Boyle (1980) wrote, not long before his death, a brief but typically common-sensical survey of the respective roles of ministers and officials.

Even when they have retired or left Whitehall, permanent officials have to be discreet about what they say in public about ministers and about the relationships between ministers and civil servants. Partly for this reason, the accounts of the more critical ministers mentioned above have often passed without challenge. An exception was Richard Crossman's permanent secretary at the Ministry of Housing and Local Government (now the Department of the Environment). Dame Evelyn Sharp, the first woman to hold a top post, gave her side of the story in an interview (see Jenkins 1975). Among the former permanent officials to have published in recent years full-length accounts of their careers are Lord (Sir Eric) Roll (1985), Lord (Sir Denis) Greenhill (1993) and Sir Antony Part (1990). Roll is less discreet than the other two, perhaps reflecting the fact that he did not spend his entire career in the civil service. There are memoirs from others who have been in and out of Whitehall (MacDougall 1987; Plowden 1989), but none with experience of recent times. Sir Nicholas Henderson was British Ambassador to Washington between 1979 and 1982. His memoirs (Henderson 1994) did not pass through the Cabinet Office sieve prior to publication. His earlier volume on the private office (Henderson 1984) is also worth reading. Sir Leo Pliatzky spent most of his career in the Treasury and finished up heading the Department of Trade between 1977 and 1979. He wrote two lively treatises on public expenditure (Pliatzky 1982, 1985) and an analysis of the Treasury under Margaret Thatcher (1989). He has also reflected more specifically upon minister–civil servant relationships (Pliatzky 1984). So, too, has Sir Patrick Nairne (1982, 1990), one of Pliatzky's contemporaries. Two former heads of the home civil service made their parting shots either en route or shortly after their exit from Whitehall in the early 1980s. Sir Ian (Lord) Bancroft (1981) offered a buoyant defence of officialdom, while acknowledging the need for greater efficiency. Sir Douglas Wass (1983, 1984, 1985) also made a number of carefully crafted observations. More circumspect but attempting a useful long term analysis is Delafons (1982). Much less discreet and indeed openly hostile are the works of Clive Ponting (1986, 1989). In the wake of his famous trial (see Introductory Essay) he vented his frustrations in a number of highly readable and not unscholarly tracts. From a different but no less controversial trajectory, Bernard Ingham (1991) has a good deal to say about Whitehall during the Thatcher years. Technically a permanent official, he was much, much more than this in his capacity as Thatcher's Press Secretary. Not surprisingly, he gives a different spin from that which is presented in the 'unauthorized' biography (Harris 1990).

For different reasons both Ponting and Ingham have written about Whitehall with the lesser inhibition usually associated with those who have operated as temporary political advisers. Among the more vivid accounts from this group of people are those of Williams (1975) and Haines (1977). They are entertaining but should be approached with care. Mitchell (1978) is worth consulting, as is Donoughue (1987). Hoskyns (1983) offers an outsider's critique based upon his experiences during the early years of the Thatcher Government.

Theakston (1992) looks at the Labour Party and Whitehall. He concludes that the Party was mainly to blame for its failures in office. Theakston and Fry (1994) provide a similar but briefer analysis of the Conservatives and Whitehall, following on from those of Fry (1984) and Butcher (1991), which deal only with the Thatcher years. In a UK–USA comparison, Peters (1986) also examines the Thatcher position on the civil service, while Barberis (1994) considers the role of top officials in policy making during the 1980s. Dated but still useful as a starting point on minister–civil servant relationships is Wright (1977), as are the trilogy, based upon respective radio series, of Young and Sloman (1982, 1984) and Jenkins and Sloman (1985). Following the Ponting Trial, the Treasury and Civil Service Committee (TCSC) conducted its own enquiry into minister–civil servant relationships. Its report (1986) is worth looking at, as are the accompanying minutes of evidence. Rose (1987) fleshes out some of the themes touched upon in the reading contained in this volume, while King (1981), also included here in abridged form, still deserves to be read in full. Riddell (1993) develops some of this work on the career politician but has little to say about the civil service. Alderman and Cross (1979) and Alderman and Carter (1992) explore the phenomenon of ministerial reshuffles and their consequences within Whitehall.

Plowden (1994) provides stimulating comment on minister–civil servant relationships and upon much else besides. Aberbach and Rockman (1994) offer a brief but no less stimulating discussion about the dilemma of neutral independence versus responsiveness to democracy. This does not supplant their earlier work, which compares the roles of senior officials in Western democracies (Aberbach *et al.* 1981). Dogan (1975) is an edited volume with a similar focus in which Christoph's chapter on Britain is still worth a look. Campbell's (1988) review is also useful.

Loyalties, responsibilities and ethics

Minister–civil servant relationships have always been conducted within a framework of conventions and mutual understandings. Some think that these conventions and understandings have in recent years been placed under greater strain. This has sharpened the debate about the loyalties of officials, both in theory and in practice. A valuable collection of essays was published by the Royal Institute of Public Administration (1985). From this comes the piece by Peter Jay, included in abridged form in the present volume. Others from the RIPA collection by Fred Ridley and by Bernard Williams are particularly worthy of attention. With differing inflections Shepherd (1987), Plowden (1985) and Inglis (1993) express concern about the durability of some of the traditional precepts. Extracts from the latter two appear in this volume, as do those from O'Toole (1990) and Stowe (1992), who are worth reading in full. Sir Michael Quinlan (1993) offers some personal and anodyne views as a retired permanent under secretary. Chipperfield (1994) also takes the traditional line. Johnson (1985) assesses both the impetus and the limitations of a more managerial civil service for traditional assumptions. In one of the earliest public lectures he gave after becoming Head of the Home Civil Service, Sir Robin Butler (1988) questioned whether the new managerialism was compatible with the traditional canons of public service. His conclusion was emphatically in the affirmative. Others have been less sanguine. O'Toole (1993) thinks that there has been a loss of purity.

This raises a question about whether top officials, as an elite group, should adopt a certain detachment in order to maintain a higher ethical and moral touchstone. In Reading 4.3, O'Toole (1990) discusses T.H. Green's prescription for such a touchstone. Zentner (1994) argues the need for leadership in the administrative state, while Dobell (1986) examines the special responsibilities and dilemmas of 'the public servant as God' – especially the tensions between public service and public interest. Stoker (1992) ponders the possibility of self-interest as incorporating a conception of the public ethic – and not merely as an unintended consequence of selfish impulses. Even more optimistically, Goodin (1989) suggests that such ideals are as well served by the democratic process as are the more 'lowly' utilitarian interests.

Those who fear that there has nevertheless been a decline in public morality may take some comfort from the fact that such observations are neither recent nor confined to Britain. Arendt (1972) and Sennett (1977) are classics of their type. Neither has anything whatever to say specifically about Whitehall but both employ moral injunctions in discussing what they separately see as a widespread and more deep-seated erosion of the public realm, of the ideal of public duty and of the fall of 'public man'. From the antipodes, Parker (1989) warns about the decline of the 'official conscience', and Rohr (1991) discusses ethical issues in French public administration. *The Indian Journal of Public Administration* (Vol. 36, 1990) devoted an entire issue to administrative culture. There is a contribution by Thomas (on Britain) and brief but invigorating discussions from, among others, Sarkar, and Subramanian on India. The causes for concern in India – the alleged subjugation of intellect, integrity and independence to the search for popularity (with political leaders), contacts (with 'interests') and opportunism (for personal advancement) – have a familiar ring. On the other hand, Thompson (1992) draws attention to some of the paradoxes of 'higher' ethics.

There has been much talk about codes of ethics for civil servants. This was the principal recommendation from the eighteen-month enquiry of the

Treasury and Civil Service Committee (1993, 1994). The government accepted this recommendation (Cabinet Office 1995). Public discussion of this whole area has prompted more elaborate articulation of the traditional values that are supposed to be under threat. Thomas (1978) shows how a peculiarly British philosophy of public administration matured during the early decades of the twentieth century. In recent years there have been biographies of some of the major figures from the middle decades of the century – men who may be said to have made, developed, consolidated or at least personified the British mandarin tradition and its essential values. For most of the inter-war years Sir Warren Fisher was Permanent Secretary to the Treasury and Head of the Civil Service, Sir Maurice (Lord) Hankey was Cabinet Secretary and Thomas Jones (until 1930) was Deputy Cabinet Secretary. Each is given the full treatment by O'Halpin (1989), Naylor (1984) and Ellis (1992) respectively. Sir Robert (Lord) Vansittart was Permanent Under Secretary at the Foreign Office between 1930 and 1938. Rose (1978) tells the story of his opposition to the government's policy of appeasement towards the European dictators. For this he was duly removed from any position of central influence – a reminder of what can happen when officials allow moral passions to override their loyalty to the elected government. During the post-war years Sir Oliver (Lord) Franks toed most of the 'establishment' lines and still managed to maintain a reputation for integrity (Danchev 1993).

Sisson (1966), a near contemporary of Franks, remains the elegant and prim statement of traditional notions about the role of the permanent bureaucracy, as does Bridges (1950). Bridges was Head of the Home Civil Service between 1945 and 1956. His efforts to uphold the highest standards of conduct and probity are chronicled by Chapman (1988), who has much else to say about ethics. He also edits a collection which deals with ethical questions in a number of countries (Chapman 1993). Although based upon local government, Stewart and Clarke (1987) explain what is distinctive about the public service.

The new managerialism

As managerialism has assumed a higher profile in Whitehall, so the management literature has come to the fore. The Fulton Report (1968) is a good starting point. Some of the more notable commentators of the time are noted in the Introductory Essay. Garrett (1980) and Kellner and Crowther-Hunt (1980) are what may be regarded as half-time reports on post-Fulton developments, from the more radical fraternity. A progress report from a different pitch may be found in Fry (1981). Carey (1984) is a salvo from a former top mandarin bemoaning the low priority given to management in Whitehall. Hennessy, Fry *et al.* (1988) is an edited transcript of a symposium held twenty years after Fulton. Fry (1993) provides mature reflection upon the work of the Fulton Committee: his book is based on unpublished papers to which he was given special access.

There are a number of sound general surveys of the new managerialism in Whitehall during the 1980s and 1990s. Gray and Jenkins (1985) is dated now but is still useful on the early 1980s. Harrison and Gretton's (1987) collection is also dated but includes accounts of the Rayner scrutinies (from Collins), FMI

(Richards), performance measurement (Beeton) and an assessment of the new managerialism in the Ministry of Defence by its former permanent chief, Sir Frank Cooper. Metcalfe and Richards (1990), Flynn (1993) and Pollitt (1993a) yield fuller treatments, while Massey (1993) and Zifcak (1994) compare Whitehall with the USA and Australia respectively. McKevitt and Lawton (1994) edit a wide-ranging collection of writings, old and new.

Particular aspects of the new managerialism have their own literature. Likierman (1982) is a useful account of MINIS in the Department of the Environment, though Cooper (1986) thinks that ministers should not get heavily involved in departmental management. Thomas (1984) and Warner (1984) provide case-study approaches to the Rayner scrutinies, while Bray (1988) makes a broader assessment. Metcalfe and Richards (1984), Fry (1988) and Gray *et al.* (1991) examine the FMI. Doern (1993) describes and Goldsworthy (1994) defends the Citizen's Charter. The latter is a Cabinet Office civil servant responsible for its successful promotion. Connolly *et al.* (1994) are much more critical. Their analysis connects with two adjacent issues: performance measurement and 'user friendliness', or consumerism. Flynn (1986), Carter (1988) and Carter *et al.* (1992) consider the ramifications of performance measurement while Pollitt (1988, 1993b) highlights the difficulties of combining performance measurement with consumerism and of operationalizing and achieving 'quality' – indeed, of getting agreement as to what exactly it means.

The biggest literature is on the Next Steps. Davies and Willman (1991) are highly critical. Greer (1994) is critical but also more analytical. So too is Hogwood (1993), whose paper also contains an extensive bibliography. Elsewhere he emphasizes the *ad hoc* nature of the development of agencies (Hogwood 1994). O'Toole and Jordan (1995) edit a useful collection covering a wide range of issues associated with Next Steps. Knox and McHugh (1991) examine the impact in Northern Ireland. Sir Peter Kemp was the Next Steps Project Manager and a second permanent secretary (grade 1A) until his involuntary departure in 1992. His subsequent writings (Kemp 1993, 1994) betray a sustained impatience with the pace of change. They make interesting comparison with those of the current Head of the Home Civil Service (Butler 1993, 1994). In the latter piece Butler tries to show some correspondence between the changes taking place in Whitehall and the vision set out in *Reinventing Government* by the Americans Osborne and Gaebler (1992). Their book has achieved almost cult status among a certain fraternity, surpassing the earlier business 'handbook' of Peters and Waterman (1982). Hughes (1994) offers a friendly if not uncritical analysis but many academics remain to be convinced. Jordan (1994a), Moe (1994) and Rhodes (1994) are among the voices of scepticism. Other cool assessments as to where the new public management is leading may be found in articles by Bogdanor (1994) and Hood (1991a). This is not to imply that reforms have been driven by any grand strategy or accompanied by detailed public debate (Pinkney 1989; Painter 1991; Dunleavy and Hood 1994). Hood (1991b) explores the consequences of the new public management in the wider context of what he calls 'de-Sir Humphreyfying' the Westminster model of bureaucracy. In a mini-classic of its type, Charles Goodsell's *The Case for Bureaucracy: a Public Administration Polemic* is just that. In the third edition (Goodsell 1994) he takes on Osborne and Gaebler as part of his defence of 'traditional' public administration, American style.

There has been much talk about a new paradigm of public administration – or a shift from public administration to public management (Hood 1987; Kernaghan 1993). Its concrete manifestations include a more decentralized management style, 'freedom within boundaries' (i.e. budgets) rather than detailed central, hierarchical control and, of course, contracting out. Some have highlighted the secular trends and impulses towards operational decentralization (Sharpe 1988; Hoggett 1991); others have drawn attention to questions of coordination (Webb 1991). Hardin (1992) explores the different dimensions in local as well as in central government of what he cleverly calls *The Contracting State*; Self (1993) seriously doubts the widespread applicability to government of market economics, preferring a more active and firmly grounded notion of citizenship.

Students should cultivate the habit of consulting official publications. In recent years the Ibbs Report (Efficiency Unit 1988) is an obvious one. Efficiency Unit (1991) and Trosa (1994) are, in effect, progress reports – not uncritical – of what has happened since Ibbs. For those who want to trace the genesis of FMI as seen from Whitehall the two White Papers of the early 1980s are a useful starting point (Cabinet Office 1982, 1983). Excerpts from the White Papers on the Citizen's Charter and on market testing are contained in this volume. They are worth following up (Cabinet Office 1991 and HM Treasury 1991 respectively). Note how White Papers seemed to be getting thinner on analysis and detail while glossier in presentation – and not always white!

The Treasury and Civil Service Committee took a keen interest in the early development of the Next Steps programme. So far it has issued four main reports (TCSC 1988, 1989, 1990, 1991). The Committee of Public Accounts (PAC) has produced two reports of particular relevance to the new managerialism – one on the FMI (PAC 1987) and another on the conduct of public business (PAC 1994). The latter may sound more like a foray into ethics. In a sense it is, but on the specific question as to whether greater delegation and other streamlining management techniques have brought a loosening of financial control.

Mention has already been made of the White Papers of July 1994 and January 1995. These *were* white and in part the product of an internal enquiry headed by a Cabinet Office under secretary, John Oughton. The Oughton Report (Efficiency Unit 1993) is a published document and worth perusal for those who are interested in human resource management and related issues within Whitehall.

Whitehall, Parliament and the public

Upon their creation in 1979–80, the new select committees were seen by some as a challenge to the mores of Whitehall. Senior officials had long been accustomed to making appearances before such committees from time to time, especially permanent secretaries before the Committee of Public Accounts.

Now they and, even more so, their mid-ranking colleagues would be exposed to more frequent probings. Hawes (1993) analyses the select committees' growing influence: it is useful and more up to date but does not displace Drewry (1989), an edited collection. The Select Committee on Procedure (1990) reviewed the working of the select committee system. Reading 7.3 is an excerpt from the report, which, together with the accompanying volume of evidence, is as good as a textbook. Cooper (1987), also reprinted here, puts a Whitehall view.

The select committees have provided more published material and have brought a greater transparency to Whitehall. This has not satisfied and may even have given further stimulus to calls for more open government. The most recent White Paper (Cabinet Office 1993) sets out the official position and is an obvious starting point, together with the subsequent code, reproduced above in abridged form (Reading 7.6). Needless to say, the critics continue to express dissatisfaction. Clive Ponting (1985) wrote his own account of the Belgrano Affair and of his subsequent trial: it is a polemic for greater openness and more information. So, too, is the paper by Hennessy and Westcott (1992). Elsewhere there have been some sober discussions about the right to leak (Pyper 1985) and the right to know (Bennett 1985). Chapman and Hunt (1989) edit a useful collection. Austin (1994) makes an eloquent call for more freedom of information, while Hunt (1987) identifies some of the practical problems. Calls for more freedom of information are often linked with arguments for a Bill of Rights. Anthony (Lord) Lester (1994) is an ardent advocate for this and for a system of public law on the continental model. Implicit in this would be a written constitution of one sort or another. For this among other reasons constitutional lawyers have (again) begun to take a greater interest in Whitehall. Brazier (1991) is a good example and worth reading. Benn and Hood (1993) provide, as one would expect, a *cri de coeur* for extensive constitutional reform. They also contribute a chapter in a more varied but consistently pro-reform collection of essays (Barnett *et al.* 1993). Equally varied but with a different prevailing inflection is Vibert's (1991) edited volume. Mather, for example, justifies market testing. A collection edited by Holme and Elliott (1988) contains useful chapters, including those by William Plowden (on Whitehall and the civil service), John Grigg (on government and Parliament) and James Cornford (on official secrecy). Charter 88 and the Institute for Public Policy Research (IPPR) are among the pressure groups to have made the running in recent years for a written constitution. The IPPR (1991) has produced a blueprint, replete with commentary. Norton (1991) is the most prominent among academics who do not see a written constitution as a very good way forward, while Mount (1992), from an otherwise similar political perspective, explains why it is not possible to move backwards. Oliver (1991) takes a more rounded, erudite approach to constitutional reform. She has quite a bit to say about the civil service.

Although Britain has at present no unified written constitution it nevertheless has its own tramlines. These mostly take the form of conventions, the subject of an interesting collection by Marshall (1984). There are useful chapters on the theory of conventions and on ministerial responsibility. The convention of ministerial responsibility assumes that ministers, not civil servants, are both answerable and accountable to Parliament. Civil servants are responsible to their ministers *within* Whitehall but are not directly accountable to Parliament, except for the special responsibility of permanent secretaries to the PAC in their role as accounting officers. When appearing before Parliamentary select committees, civil servants normally act as 'representatives' of their ministers, certainly when discussing policy issues. But it has been frequently alleged that the doctrine no longer operates in the way that it used to operate or was supposed to operate. Turpin (1994) provides a very good discussion, as do Judge (1993) and Jordan (1994b). There has been much soul searching. Robinson (1987) argues that the greater delegation to civil servants arising from the new managerialism renders absurd the notion that ministers should be responsible for everything. A few pages on, Jones (1987) takes the opposite view: if the ground has shifted, then it is time to bring the reality into closer conformity with the principle.

Other issues, other sources

Brief mention may be made of a miscellany of sources under three headings: career issues; macro issues associated with the role of the state; and regular publications.

A perennial career issue has been recruitment. The Northcote-Trevelyan Report (1854) is an obvious starting point on this, as on much else concerning the nineteenth-century heritage: it is reprinted in Volume 1 of the Fulton Report (1968). Mueller (1984) provides a fascinating Anglo-Prussian comparison of recruitment reforms in the nineteenth century while Chapman (1984) studies the efforts of Sir Percival Waterfield and the creation of the Civil Service Selection Board during the earlier decades of the present century. The Office of Public Service and Science (OPSS) produced two reports in 1994, one detailing changes in responsibilities for recruitment (OPSS 1994a), the other a review of the fast stream (OPSS 1994b). Chapman (1991, 1994) has carried the battle among the critics of these changes.

Top appointments have received continued attention. The Royal Institute of Public Administration (1987) and Richards (1993) examine allegations that political considerations have been brought to bear in appointing people to top permanent posts. They find little evidence. Theakston and Fry (1989) provide a profile of top post-holders since 1900. They carry forward aspects of the earlier work of Kelsall (1955, 1974) and of Headey (1972). Armstrong (1973) is a sophisticated comparative work on administrative elites (to 1945), which tackles questions about behaviour as well as background. So too does Dowse (1987) – though more briefly and with only implicit reference to Whitehall.

Few senior civil servants are women, though this is now beginning slowly to change. The potentially emotive topic of equality is examined with commendable sanity by Brimelow (1981), by Behrens (1989) and by Watson (1992). Gosling and Netley (1990) report the findings of a research project into secondments between government and business. Christoph (1993) examines the effects upon Whitehall of civil servants' secondments to Brussels. O'Toole (1989) is the standard work on the trade union for senior officials, the Association of First Division Civil Servants. Fairbrother (1994) takes a broad and critical look at employee relations in the civil service, while Corby (1994) analyses the implications of Next Steps.

At the macro level, Page (1985), Smith (1988) and Peters (1989) offer comparative perspectives on the political control of state bureaucracies. Preston (1987), Bellone and Goerl (1992) and Wood and Waterman (1991, 1993) develop various angles on the tensions between bureaucracy and democracy; and Etzioni-Halevy (1983) reviews some of the Marxist approaches. Two of the classic modern Marxist accounts may be found in Miliband (1969, 1982), the earlier one containing a careful analysis of senior officials and of their role in the capitalist state. From the opposite end of the political spectrum, Niskanen (1971) argues that vote-seeking politicians and budget maximizing officials usually coalesce to produce excessive government. Bender and Moe (1985) and Blais and Dion (1990) offer critiques of this and of other 'New Right' public choice models of public bureaucracy, as does Dunleavy (1991). Elsewhere (Dunleavy 1982) he sketches an alternative, radical model of public administration. Hartley (1986) examines models of civil service reform, while Smith *et al.* (1993) provide a good review of the literature on government departments and pose some interesting questions. Self (1977, 1985) is discursive and no less stimulating and Judge (1993) also employs a wide sweep in his survey of the 'Parliamentary state'. In the general area of bureaucratic behaviour some of the earlier American classics should never be neglected (Downs 1967; Simon 1976; Mosher 1982; Waldo 1984). Nor should the pioneering work of Max Weber (Gerth and Wright Mills 1948). There are some useful 'modern' treatments of bureaucracy and administration (Dunsire 1973; Beetham 1987; Lane 1993).

There are a number of annual official publications which can be useful. The *Civil Service Yearbook* began publication in the early nineteenth century. (Until 1974 it was called *The British Imperial Calendar and Civil Service List.*) It lists all civil servants of note within Whitehall (and others, too) and now gives more detail as to the responsibilities of different sections within each department and agency. *Civil Service Statistics* is a valuable source, as are the annual *Civil Service Commissioners' Reports.* The latter deal with recruitment: they are glossier than they used to be, though no more informative. The Cabinet Office has begun to issue annual reviews of *Next Steps Agencies* and *The Citizen's Charter.* Under the wing of the Cabinet Office, the Office of Public Service publishes *Equal Opportunities in the Civil Service for Women* and *Equal Opportunities in the Civil Service for Ethnic Minorities.* These are, in effect, annual progress reports. *Public Bodies* is an official annual profile of QUANGOs.

Finally, a number of regular non-official 'guides' may be mentioned. *Dod's Parliamentary Companion* has been in publication since the early nineteenth century. Its main focus is upon MPs and their constituencies but it also has an extensive section on government and other public offices. From the same stable, a new production was launched in the early 1990s: *The Whitehall Companion.* This handsome (and expensive) volume has appeared annually and draws together much detail about each of the main departments and executive agencies. It also contains *Who's Who* type profiles of many senior officials. *The Times* has produced a guide to the British state (Dynes and Walker 1995). Racy and more journalistic in style, it nevertheless contains a wealth of relevant information about Whitehall. On a smaller scale there is the *Parliament and Government Pocket Book* from NTC Publications in association with the Hansard Society. PMS Publications produces a quarterly *Parliamentary Companion*. It is useful for keeping up to date with personnel changes in Whitehall and Westminster and has a section on European Union institutions. There is also *The Westminster, Whitehall and Brussels Report*. This appears ten times a year from DPR Publishing. It collects the latest information on people and events.

Bibliography

This bibliography includes sources referred to in the Introductory Essay, the Annotated Bibliography and the commentaries introducing each chapter.

Aberbach, J., Putnam, R.D. and Rockman, B.A. (1981) *Bureaucrats and Politicians in Western Democracies*, Cambridge, MA, Harvard University Press.

Aberbach, J. and Rockman, B.A. (1994) 'Civil servants and policy makers: neutral or responsive competence', *Governance*, 7, 461–9.

Alderman, G. (1984) *Pressure Groups and Government in Britain*, London, Longman.

Alderman, R.K. and Carter, N. (1992) 'The logistics of ministerial reshuffles', *Public Administration*, 70, 519–34.

Alderman, R.K. and Cross, J.A. (1979) 'Ministerial reshuffles and the civil service', *British Journal of Political Science*, 9, 41–65.

Arendt, H. (1972) *Crisis of the Republic*, New York, Harcourt Brace Jovanovich.

Armstrong, J.A. (1973) *The European Administrative Elite*, Princeton, NJ, Princeton University Press.

Armstrong, R.T. (1988) 'Taking stock of our achievements', in Peat Marwick McLintock/ Royal Institute of Public Administration, *The Future Shape of Reform in Whitehall*, London, RIPA, 11–21.

Atkinson, M.M. and Coleman, W.D. (1992) 'Policy networks, policy communities and the problems of governance', *Governance*, 5, 154–80.

Austin, R. (1994) 'Freedom of information: the constitutional impact', in J. Jowell and D. Oliver (eds) *The Changing Constitution*, Oxford, Clarendon, 393–439.

Balogh, T. (1959) 'The apotheosis of the dilettante', in H. Thomas (ed.) *The Establishment*, London, Anthony Blond, 83–126.

Bancroft, I. (1981) 'The civil service in the 1980s', *Public Administration*, 59, 139–50.

Barberis, P. (1994) 'Permanent secretaries and policy making in the 1980s', *Public Policy and Administration*, 9, 35–48.

Barnett, A., Ellis, C. and Hirst, P. (eds) (1993) *Debating the Constitution: New Perspectives on Constitutional Reform*, Cambridge, Polity Press.

Beetham, D. (1987) *Bureaucracy*, Milton Keynes, Open University Press.

Behrens, R. (1989) 'Equal opportunities for women in the British civil service', *Teaching Public Administration*, 9(2), 1–7.

Bellone, C.J. and Goerl, G.F. (1992) 'Reconciling public entrepreneurship and democracy', *Public Administration Review*, 52, 130–4.

Bender, J. and Moe, T.M. (1985) 'An adaptive model of bureaucratic politics', *American Political Science Review*, 79, 755–74.

Benn, T. (1979) *Arguments for Socialism*, London, Jonathan Cape.

Benn, T. (1987–90) *Out of the Wilderness – Diaries Vol. 1: 1963–67* (1987); *Office without Power – Diaries Vol. 2: 1968–72* (1988); *Against the Tide – Diaries Vol. 3: 1973–6* (1989); *Conflicts of Interest – Diaries Vol. 4: 1977–80* (1990), London, Hutchinson.

Benn, T. and Hood, A. (1993) *Common Sense: a New Constitution for Britain*, London, Hutchinson.

Bennett, C. (1985) 'From the dark to the light: the open government debate in Britain', *Journal of Public Policy*, 5, 187–213.

Birch, A.H. (1964) *Representative and Responsible Government: an Essay on the Constitution*, London, George Allen and Unwin.

Blackstone, T. and Plowden, W. (1988) *Inside the Think Tank: Advising the Cabinet 1971–83*, London, Heinemann.

Blais, A. and Dion, S. (1990) 'Are bureaucrats budget maximisers? The Niskanen model and its critics', *Polity*, 22, 657–74.

Bogdanor, V. (1994) 'Ministers, civil servants and the constitution', *Government and Opposition*, 29, 676–95.

Boyle, E. (Lord) (1980) 'Ministers and the administrative process', *Public Administration*, 58, 1–12.

Bray, A.J.M. (1988) 'The clandestine reformer: a study of the Rayner scrutinies', *Strathclyde Papers on Government and Politics No. 55*, Glasgow, University of Strathclyde.

Brazier, R. (1991) *Constitutional Reform: Reshaping the British Political System*, Oxford, Oxford University Press.

Bridges, E. (1950) *Portrait of a Profession: the Civil Service Tradition*, London, Cambridge University Press.

Brimelow, E. (1981) 'Women in the civil service', *Public Administration*, 59, 313–35.

Bruce-Gardyne, J. (1986) *Ministers and Mandarins: Inside the Whitehall Village*, London, Sidgwick and Jackson.

Burch, M. and Wood, B. (1989) *Public Policy in Britain*, 2nd edn, Oxford, Blackwell.

Burk, K. (ed.) (1982) *War and the State: the Transformation of British Government 1914–19*, London, George Allen and Unwin.

Butcher, T. (1991) 'The Thatcher era and the civil service: the legacy of the 1980s', *Teaching Public Administration*, 11(2), 12–21.

Butler, D., Adonis, A. and Travers, T. (1994) *Failure in British Government: the Politics of the Poll Tax*, Oxford, Oxford University Press.

Butler, R. (1988) *Government and Good Public Management – Are They Compatible?*, London, Institute of Personnel Management.

Butler, R. (1993) 'The evolution of the civil service – a progress report', *Public Administration*, 71, 395–406.

Butler, R. (1994) 'Reinventing British government', *Public Administration*, 72, 263–70.

Cabinet Office (1970) *The Reorganization of Central Government* (Cmnd 4506), London, HMSO.

Cabinet Office (1982) *Efficiency and Effectiveness in the Civil Service: Government Observations on the Third Report from the Treasury and Civil Service Committee, Session 1981–82, HC 236* (Cmnd 8616), London, HMSO.

Cabinet Office (1983) *Financial Management in Government Departments.* (Cmnd 9057), London, HMSO.

Cabinet Office (1991) *The Citizen's Charter: Raising the Standard* (Cm 1599), London, HMSO.

Cabinet Office (1993) *Open Government* (Cm 2290), London, HMSO.

Cabinet Office (1994) *The Civil Service: Continuity and Change* (Cm 2627), London, HMSO.

Cabinet Office (1995) *The Civil Service: Taking Forward Continuity and Change* (Cm 2748), London, HMSO.

Campbell, C. (1988) 'Review article: the political roles of senior government officials in advanced democracies', *British Journal of Political Science*, 18, 243–72.

Carey, P. (1984) 'Management in the civil service', *Management in Government*, 39, 81–5.

Carter, N. (1988) 'Measuring government performance', *Political Quarterly*, 59, 369–75.

Carter, N., Klein, R. and Day, P. (1992) *How Organizations Measure Success: the Use of Performance Indicators in Government*, London, Routledge.

Castle, B. (1973) 'Mandarin power', *Sunday Times*, 10 June.

Castle, B. (1980) *The Castle Diaries 1974–76*, London, Weidenfeld and Nicolson.

Castle, B. (1984) *The Castle Diaries 1964–70*, London, Weidenfeld and Nicolson.

Chapman, B. (1963) *British Government Observed*, London, George Allen and Unwin.

Chapman, R.A. (1983) 'The rise and fall of the CSD', *Policy and Politics*, 11, 41–61.

Chapman, R.A. (1984) *Leadership in the Civil Service: a Study of Sir Percival Waterfield and the Creation of the Civil Service Selection Board*, London, Croom Helm.

Chapman, R.A. (1988) *Ethics in the British Civil Service*, London, Routledge.

Chapman, R.A. (1991) 'New arrangements for recruitment to the British civil service: cause for concern', *Public Policy and Administration*, 6(3), 1–6.

Chapman, R.A. (ed.) (1993) *Ethics in Public Service*, Edinburgh, Edinburgh University Press.

Chapman, R.A. (1994) 'Change in the civil service', *Public Administration*, 72, 599–610.

Chapman, R.A. and Greenaway, J.R. (1980) *The Dynamics of Administrative Reform*, London, Croom Helm.

Chapman, R.A. and Hunt, M. (eds) (1989) *Open Government*, London, Routledge.

Chester, D.N. (1979) 'Fringe bodies, QUANGOs and all that', *Public Administration*, 57, 51–4.

Chester, D.N. (1981) *The English Administrative System 1780–1870*, Oxford, Clarendon.

Chester, D.N. and Willson, F.M.G. (1968) *The Organization of British Central Government 1914–64*, 2nd edn, London, George Allen and Unwin.

Chipperfield, G. (1994) 'The civil servant's duty', *Essex Papers in Politics and Government No. 95*, Colchester, University of Essex.

Christoph, J.B. (1993) 'The effects of Britons in Brussels: the European Community and the culture of Whitehall', *Governance*, 6, 518–37.

Clark, A. (1993) *Diaries*, London, Weidenfeld and Nicolson.

Clark, G.K. (1959) 'Statesmen in disguise: reflections on the history of the neutrality of the civil service', *Historical Journal*, 2, 19–39.

Clarke, R. (1971) *New Trends in Government*, London, HMSO.

Cockett, R. (1994) *Thinking the Unthinkable: Think Tanks and the Economic Counter-revolution 1931–83*, London, Harper Collins.

Cohen, E. (1965) *The Growth of the British Civil Service 1780–1939*, London, Frank Cass.

Committee of Public Accounts: see Public Accounts Committee.

Connolly, M., McKeown, P. and Milligan-Byrne, G. (1994) 'Making the public sector more user friendly? A critical examination of the Citizen's Charter', *Parliamentary Affairs*, 47, 23–36.

Cooper, F. (1986) 'Changing the establishment', *Political Quarterly*, 57, 267–77.

Cooper, F. (1987) 'Select committees – a view from a witness', *Contemporary Record*, 1(1), 16–17.

Corby, S. (1994) 'How big a step is "Next Steps"? Industrial relations developments in civil service executive agencies', *Human Resource Management Journal*, 4(2), 52–69.

Cromwell, V. (ed.) (1977) *Revolution or Evolution: British Government in the Nineteenth Century*, London, Longman.

Crossman, R.H.S. (1975–7) *The Diaries of a Cabinet Minister – Vols 1–3*, London, Hamish Hamilton and Jonathan Cape.

Danchev, A. (1993) *Oliver Franks: Founding Father*, Oxford, Clarendon.

Davies, A. and Willman, J. (1991) *What Next? Agencies, Departments and the Civil Service*, London, Institute of Public Policy Research.

Delafons, J. (1982) 'Working in Whitehall: changes in public administration 1952–82', *Public Administration*, 60, 253–72.

Dell, E. (1991) *A Hard Pounding: Politics and Economic Crisis 1974–76*, Oxford, Oxford University Press.

Demetriadi, S. (1921a) *Inside a Government Office*, London, Cassell.

Demetriadi, S. (1921b) *A Reform for the Civil Service*, London, Cassell.

Dickie, J. (1992) *Inside the Foreign Office*, London, Chapmans.

Dobell, A.R. (1986) 'The public servant as God: taking risks with the public', *Canadian Public Administration*, 29, 601–17.

Doern, G.B. (1993) 'The UK Citizen's Charter: origins and implementation in three agencies', *Policy and Politics*, 21, 17–29.

Dogan, M. (ed.) (1975) *The Mandarins of Western Europe: the Political Role of Top Civil Servants*, London, Sage.

Donoughue, B. (1987) *Prime Minister: the Conduct of Policy under Harold Wilson and James Callaghan*, London, Jonathan Cape.

Dowding, K. (1995) 'Model or metaphor? A critical review of the policy network approach', *Political Studies*, 43, 136–58.

Downs, A. (1967) *Inside Bureaucracy*, Boston, MA, Little Brown.

Dowse, R.E. (1987) 'Consensus among a putative elite: some empirical findings', *Political Science*, 39, 161–71.

Drewry, G. (ed.) (1989) *The New Select Committees*, 2nd edn, Oxford, Clarendon.

Drewry, G. and Butcher, T. (1991) *The Civil Service Today*, 2nd edn, Oxford, Blackwell.

Dunleavy, P. (1982) 'Is there a radical approach to public administration?', *Public Administration*, 60, 215–24.

Dunleavy, P. (1989) 'The architecture of the British central state: part I – framework for analysis: part II – empirical findings', *Public Administration*, 67, 249–75, 391–417.

Dunleavy, P. (1991) *Democracy, Bureaucracy and Public Choice*, Brighton, Harvester Wheatsheaf.

Dunleavy, P. and Hood, C. (1994) 'From old public administration to new public management', *Public Money and Management*, 14(3), 9–16.

Dunsire, A. (1973) *Administration: the Word and the Science*, London, Martin Robertson.

Dynes, M. and Walker, D. (1995) *The Times Guide to the New British State: the Government Machine in the 1990s*, London, Times Books.

Edwards, R.D. (1994) *True Brits: Inside the Foreign Office*, London, BBC.

Efficiency Unit (1988) *Improving Management in Government: the Next Steps. Report to the Prime Minister* (Ibbs Report), London, HMSO.

Efficiency Unit (1991) *Making the Most of Next Steps: the Management of Ministers' Departments and their Executive Agencies* (Fraser Report), London, HMSO.

Efficiency Unit (1993) *Career Management and Succession Planning Study* (Oughton Report), London, HMSO.

Elcock, H. (1991) *Change and Decay? Public Administration in the 1990s*, London, Longman.

Ellis, E.L. (1992) *T.J. – A Life of Thomas Jones, CB*, Cardiff, University of Wales Press.

Estimates Committee (1958) *Sixth Report, 1957–58: Treasury Control of Expenditure*, HC 254.

Estimates Committee (1965) *Sixth Report 1964–65: Recruitment to the Civil Service*, HC 308.

Etzioni-Halevy, E. (1983) *Bureaucracy and Democracy: a Political Dilemma*, London, Routledge and Kegan Paul.

Expenditure Committee (1977) *Eleventh Report 1976–77: the Civil Service* (English Report), HC 535 I, II.

Fabian Society (1964) *The Administrators: the Reform of the Civil Service* (Fabian Tract 355), London, Fabian Society.

Fairbrother, P. (1994) *Politics and the State as Employer*, London, Mansell.

Flynn, N. (1986) 'Performance measurement in public sector services', *Policy and Politics*, 14, 389–404.

Flynn, N. (1993) *Public Sector Management*, 2nd edn, Brighton, Harvester Wheatsheaf.

Fry, G.K. (1969) *Statesmen in Disguise: the Changing Role of the Administrative Class of the Home Civil Service 1853–1966*, London, Macmillan.

Fry, G.K. (1979) *The Growth of Government: the Development of Ideas about the Role of the State and the Machinery and Functions of Government in Britain since 1780*, London, Frank Cass.

Fry, G.K. (1981) *The Administrative 'Revolution' in Whitehall: a Study of the Politics of Administrative Change in British Central Government since the 1950s*, London, Croom Helm.

Fry, G.K. (1984) 'The development of the Thatcher government's "grand strategy" for the civil service: a public policy perspective', *Public Administration*, 62, 322–35.

Fry, G.K. (1986) 'The British career civil service under challenge', *Political Studies*, 34, 533–55.

Fry, G.K. (1988) 'The Thatcher government, the Financial Management Initiative and the "new civil service"', *Public Administration*, 66, 1–20.

Fry, G.K. (1993) *Reforming the Civil Service: the Fulton Committee on the British Home Civil Service 1966–68*, Edinburgh, Edinburgh University Press.

Fulton (1968) *The Civil Service, Vol. I: Report of the Committee 1966–68*, (Fulton Report) (Cmnd 3638), London, HMSO.

Garrett, J. (1980) *Managing the Civil Service*, London, Heinemann.

Gerth, H.H. and Wright Mills, C. (eds) (1948) *From Max Weber: Essays in Sociology*, London, Routledge and Kegan Paul.

Goldsworthy, D. (1994) 'Efficiency and effectiveness in public management: a UK perspective', *Administration*, 41, 137–48.

Goodin, R.E. (1989) 'Stars to steer by: the political impact of moral values', *Journal of Public Policy*, 9, 241–59.

Goodsell, C. (1994) *The Case for Bureaucracy: a Public Administration Polemic*, 3rd edn, Chatham, NJ, Chatham House.

Gosling, R. and Netley, S. (1990) *Bridging the Gap: Secondments Between Government and Business*, London, RIPA.

Gowan, P. (1987) 'The origins of the administrative elite', *New Left Review*, 162, 4–34.

Grant, W. (1995) *Pressure Groups, Politics and Democracy in Britain*, 2nd edn, Hemel Hempstead, Prentice Hall/Harvester Wheatsheaf.

Gray, A. and Jenkins, W.I. (1982) 'Policy analysis in British central government: the experience of PAR', *Public Administration*, 60, 429–50.

Gray, A. and Jenkins, W.I. (1985) *Administrative Politics in British Government*, Brighton, Harvester Wheatsheaf.

Gray, A., Jenkins, W.I., Flynn, A. and Rutherford, B. (1991) 'The management of change in Whitehall: the experience of the FMI', *Public Administration*, 69, 41–59.

Greaves, H.R.G. (1947) *The Civil Service in the Changing State*, London, George G. Harrop.

Greenaway, J.R. (1985) 'Parliamentary reform and civil service reform: a nineteenth century debate reassessed', *Parliamentary History*, 4, 157–69.

Greenaway, J.R., Smith, S. and Street, J. (1992) *Deciding Factors in British Politics: a Case-studies Approach*, London, Routledge.

Greenhill, D. (1993) *More by Accident*, 2nd edn, York, Wilton 65.

Greenleaf, W.H. (1983–7) *The British Political Tradition: Vol. 1, The Rise of Collectivism* (1983); *Vol. 2, The Ideological Heritage* (1983); *Vol. 3 (Parts I and II), A Much Governed Nation* (1987), London, Methuen.

Greenwood, J.R. and Wilson, D.J. (1989) *Public Administration in Britain Today*, 2nd edn, London, Unwin Hyman.

Greer, P. (1994) *Transforming Central Government: the Next Steps Initiative*, Buckingham, Open University Press.

Haines, J. (1977) *The Politics of Power*, London, Coronet, Hodder and Stoughton.

Ham, C. and Hill, M. (1993) *The Policy Process in the Modern Capitalist State*, 2nd edn, New York, Harvester Wheatsheaf.

Hardin, I. (1992) *The Contracting State*, Buckingham, Open University Press.

Harris, R. (1990) *Good and Faithful Servant: the Unauthorized Biography of Bernard Ingham*, London, Faber and Faber.

Harrison, A. and Gretton, J. (eds) (1987) *Reshaping Central Government*, Oxford, Policy Journals.

Hartley, K. (1986) 'Economic models of civil service reform', in Shenfield *et al.* (eds) *Managing the Bureaucracy*, London, Adam Smith Institute.

Hawes, D. (1993) *Power on the Back Benches? The Growth of Select Committee Influence*, Bristol, School of Advanced Urban Studies.

Headey, B. (1972) 'The civil service as an administrative elite in Britain and Germany', *International Review of Administrative Sciences*, 38, 41–8.

Headey, B. (1974) *British Cabinet Ministers: the Roles of Politicians in Executive Office*, London, George Allen and Unwin.

Healey, D. (1989) *The Time of My Life*, London, Michael Joseph.

Heclo, H. and Wildavsky, A. (1981) *The Private Government of Public Money: Community and Policy inside British Politics*, 2nd edn, London, Macmillan.

Henderson, N. (1984) *The Private Office: a Personal View of Five Foreign Secretaries and of Government from the Inside*, London, Weidenfeld and Nicolson.

Henderson, N. (1994) *Mandarin: the Diaries of an Ambassador 1969–82*, London, Weidenfeld and Nicolson.

Hennessy, P. (1986) *Cabinet*, Oxford, Blackwell.

Hennessy, P. (1989, 1990) *Whitehall*, London, Secker and Warburg (1990 edn, London, Fontana).

Hennessy, P., Fry, G.K. *et al.* (1988) 'Symposium. Fulton: 20 years on', *Contemporary Record*, 2(2), 44–55.

Hennessy, P. and Westcott, C. (1992) 'The last right? Open government, freedom of information and the right to know', *Strathclyde Analysis Paper No. 12*, Glasgow, University of Strathclyde.

Heseltine, M. (1990) *Where There's a Will*, London, Arrow.

HM Treasury (1961) *Control of Public Expenditure* (Plowden Report) (Cmnd 1432), London, HMSO.

HM Treasury (1991) *Competing for Quality: Buying Better Public Services* (Cm 1730), London, HMSO.

HM Treasury (1993) *Civil Service Management Code*, London, HM Treasury/Cabinet Office.

HM Treasury (1994) *Better Accounting for the Taxpayer's Money: Resource Accounting and Budgeting in Government – a Consultation Paper* (Cm 2626), London, HMSO.

Hoggett, P. (1991) 'A new management in the public sector', *Policy and Politics*, 19, 243–56.

Hogwood, B.W. (1987) *From Crisis to Complacency? Shaping Public Policy in Britain*, Oxford, Oxford University Press.

Hogwood, B.W. (1993) 'The uneven staircase: measuring up to Next Steps', *Strathclyde Papers on Government and Politics No. 92*, Glasgow, University of Strathclyde.

Hogwood, B.W. (1994) 'A reform beyond compare? The Next Steps restructuring of British central government', *Journal of European Public Policy*, 1(1), 71–94.

Hogwood, B.W. (1995) 'Public policy', *Public Administration*, 73, 59–73.

Holme, R. and Elliott, M. (1988) *1688–1988: Time for a New Constitution*, Basingstoke, Macmillan.

Hood, C. (1976) *The Limits of Administration*, London, Wiley.

Hood, C. (1987) 'British administrative trends and the public choice revolution', in J.-E. Lane (ed.) *Bureaucracy and Public Choice*, London, Sage, 145–70.

Hood, C. (1991a) 'A public management for all seasons?', *Public Administration*, 69, 3–19.

Hood, C. (1991b) 'De-Sir Humphreyfying the Westminster model of bureaucracy: a new style of government?', *Governance*, 3, 205–14.

Hood, C. and Dunsire, A. (1981) *Bureaumetrics: the Quantitative Comparison of British Central Government Agencies*, Farnborough, Gower.

Hoskyns, J. (1983) 'Whitehall and Westminster: an outsider's view', *Parliamentary Affairs*, 36, 137–47.

Howe, G. (1994) *Conflict of Loyalty*, London, Macmillan.

Hughes, O.E. (1994) *Public Management and Administration: an Introduction*, Basingstoke, Macmillan.

Hunt, M. (1987) 'The practical problems of open government', *Teaching Public Administration*, 7(1), 1–14.

Ingham, B. (1991) *Kill the Messenger*, London, Harper Collins.

Inglis, F. (1993) 'So farewell then, citizen servant', *Times Higher Education Supplement*, 6 August.

Institute for Public Policy Research (IPPR) (1991) *The Constitution of the United Kingdom*, London, IPPR.

James, S. (1992) *British Cabinet Government*, London, Routledge.

Jenkins, R. (1991) *A Life at the Centre*, London, Macmillan.

Jenkins, S. (1975) 'The Dame hits back – Evelyn Sharp interviewed by Simon Jenkins', *Sunday Times*, 5 October.

Jenkins, S. and Sloman, A. (1985) *With Respect, Ambassador: Inquiry into the Foreign Office*, London, BBC.

Johnson, N. (1985) 'Change in the civil service: retrospect and prospects', *Public Administration*, 63, 415–33.

Jones, G.W. (1976) 'Prime ministers' secretaries – politicians or administrators?', in J.A.G. Griffith (ed.) *From Policy to Administration: Essays in Honour of William Robson*, London, George Allen and Unwin, 13–38.

Jones, G.W. (1987) 'Stand up for ministerial responsibility', *Public Administration*, 65, 87–91.

Jordan, G. (1994a) 'Reinventing government: but will it work?', *Public Administration*, 72, 271–9.

Jordan, G. (1994b) *The British Administrative System: Principles Versus Practice*, London, Routledge.

Jordan, G. and Richardson, J.J. (1987) *British Politics and the Policy Process*, London, George Allen and Unwin.

Judge, D. (1993) *The Parliamentary State*, London, Sage.

Kellner, P. and Crowther-Hunt, Lord (1980) *The Civil Servants: an Inquiry into Britain's Ruling Class*, London, Macdonald.

Kelsall, R.K. (1955) *Higher Civil Servants in Britain from 1870 to the Present Day*, London, Routledge and Kegan Paul.

Kelsall, R.K. (1974) 'Recruitment to the higher civil service: how has the pattern changed?', in P. Stanworth and A. Giddens (eds) *Elites and Power in British Society*, Cambridge, Cambridge University Press, 170–84.

Kemp, P. (1993) *Beyond Next Steps: a Civil Service for the 21st Century*, London, Social Market Foundation.

Kemp, P. (1994) 'The civil service white paper: a job half finished', *Public Administration*, 72, 591–8.

Kernaghan, K. (1993) 'Reshaping government: the post-bureaucratic paradigm', *Canadian Public Administration*, 36, 636–44.

King, A. (1981) 'The rise of the career politician in Britain – and its consequences', *British Journal of Political Science*, 11, 249–85.

Kingdom, J.E. (ed.) (1990) *The Civil Service in Liberal Democracies: an Introductory Survey*, London, Routledge.

Kingdom, J.E. (1991) *Government and Politics in Britain: an Introduction*, Cambridge, Polity.

Knox, C. and McHugh, M. (1991) 'Management in government – the "Next Steps" in Northern Ireland', *Administration*, 38, 251–70.

Lane, J.-E. (1993) *The Public Sector: Concepts, Models and Approaches*, London, Sage.

Laski, H.J. (1938) *Parliamentary Government in England: a Commentary*, London, George Allen and Unwin.

Lawson, N. (1992) *The View from No. 11: Memoirs of a Tory Radical*, London, Bantam.

Lester, Lord (Anthony) (1994) 'European human rights and the British constitution', in J. Jowell and D. Oliver (eds) *The Changing Constitution*, 3rd edn, Oxford, Clarendon, 33–53.

Likierman, A. (1982) 'Management information for ministers: the MINIS system in the DoE', *Public Administration*, 60, 127–42.

Lowell, A.L. (1908) *The Government of England* (2 vols), New York, Macmillan.

McDonald, O. (1992) *The Future of Whitehall*, London, Weidenfeld and Nicolson.

MacDonnell (1912–15) *Reports of the Royal Commission on the Civil Service* (MacDonnell Commission): *First Report* (Cmd 6209/10) P.P. 1912–13, xv; *Second Report* (Cmd 6534/5) P.P. 1912–13, xv; *Third Report* (Cmd 6739/40) P.P. 1913, xviii; *Fourth Report* (Cmd 7338/9/40) P.P. 1914, xvi; *Fifth Report* (Cmd 7748) P.P. 1914–16, xi; *Sixth Report* (Cmd 7832) P.P. 1914–16, xii.

MacDougall, D. (1987) *Don and Mandarin: Memoirs of an Economist*, London, John Murray.

McKevitt, D. and Lawton, A. (eds) (1994) *Public Sector Management: Theory, Critique and Practice*, London, Sage.

Madgwick, P. (1991) *British Government: the Central Executive Territory*, Hemel Hempstead, Philip Allan.

Mallalieu, J.P.W. (1942) *'Passed to You, Please': Britain's Red-tape Machine at War*, London, Victor Gollancz.

Marsh, D. and Rhodes, R.A.W. (eds) (1992) *Policy Networks in British Government*, Oxford, Clarendon.

Marshall, G. (1984) *Constitutional Conventions: the Rules and Forms of Political Accountability*, Oxford, Clarendon.

Massey, A. (1993) *Managing the Public Sector: a Comparative Analysis of the UK and the USA*, Aldershot, Edward Elgar.

Meacher, M. (1979) 'Whitehall's short way with democracy', in K. Coates (ed.) *What Went Wrong: Explaining the Fall of the Labour Government*, Nottingham, Spokesman Books, 170–86.

Metcalfe, L. and Richards, S. (1984) 'The impact of the efficiency strategy: political clout or cultural change?', *Public Administration*, 62, 439–54.

Metcalfe, L. and Richards, S. (1990) *Improving Public Management*, 2nd edn, London, Sage.

Middlemas, K. (1986, 1990, 1991) *Power, Competition and the State: Vol. 1, 1940–61* (1986); *Vol. 2, 1961–74* (1990); *Vol. 3, Since 1974* (1991), Basingstoke, Macmillan.

Miliband, R. (1969) *The State in Capitalist Society: the Analysis of the Western System of Power*, London, Weidenfeld and Nicolson.

Miliband, R. (1982) *Capitalist Democracy in Britain*, Oxford, Oxford University Press.

Ministry of Reconstruction (1918) *Report of the Machinery of Government Committee* (Haldane Committee) (Cd 9230), London, HMSO.

Mitchell, J.E. (1978) 'Special advisers: a personal view', *Public Administration*, 56, 87–98.

Moe, R.C. (1994) 'The reinventing government exercise: misinterpreting the problem, misjudging the consequences', *Public Administration Review*, 54, 111–22.

Mosher, F.C. (1982) *Democracy and the Public Service*, 2nd edn, New York, Oxford University Press.

Mount, F. (1992) *The British Constitution Now – Recovery or Decline?*, London, Heinemann.

Mueller, H.-E. (1984) *Bureaucracy, Education and Monopoly: Civil Service Reform in Prussia and England*, Berkeley, University of California Press.

Nairne, P. (1982) 'Some reflections on change', *Management in Government*, 37, 70–82.

Nairne, P. (1990) 'The civil service "mandarins and ministers"', *Wroxton Papers in Politics – Series A, Paper A6*, Barnstable, Phillip Charles Media.

Naylor, J.F. (1984) *A Man and an Institution: Sir Maurice Hankey, the Cabinet Secretariat and the Custody of Cabinet Secrecy*, Cambridge, Cambridge University Press.

Nicholson, M. (1967) *The System: the Misgovernment of Modern Britain*, London, Hodder and Stoughton.

Niskanen, W.A. (1971) *Bureaucracy and Representative Government*, Chicago, Aldine-Atherton.

Nolan (1995) *Standards in Public Life: First Report of the Committee on Standards in Public Life* (Nolan Report), Cm 2850–I, London, HMSO.

Northcote-Trevelyan (1854) *Report of the Organisation of the Permanent Civil Service* (Cmd 1713) P.P. 1854, xxvii.

Norton, P. (1991) 'In defence of the constitution: a riposte to the radicals', in P. Norton (ed.) *New Directions in British Politics?*, Aldershot, Edward Elgar.

Office of Public Service and Science (OPSS) (1994a) *Responsibilities for Recruitment to the Civil Service*, London, HMSO.

Office of Public Service and Science (OPSS) (1994b) *Review of Fast Stream Recruitment*, London, HMSO.

O'Halpin, E.J. (1989) *Head of the Civil Service: a Study of Sir Warren Fisher*, London, Routledge.

Oliver, D. (1991) *Government in the United Kingdom: the Search for Accountability, Effectiveness and Citizenship*, Milton Keynes, Open University Press.

Osborne, D. and Gaebler, T. (1992) *Reinventing Government: How the Entrepreneurial Spirit is Transforming the Public Sector*, Reading, MA, Addison-Wesley.

O'Toole, B.J. (1989) *Private Gain and Public Service: the Association of First Division Civil Servants*, London, Routledge.

O'Toole, B.J. (1990) 'T.H. Green and the ethics of senior officials in British central government', *Public Administration*, 68, 337–52.

O'Toole, B.J. (1993) 'The loss of purity: the corruption of public services in Britain', *Public Policy and Administration*, 8(2), 1–6.

O'Toole, B.J. and Jordan, G. (eds) (1995) *Next Steps: Improving Management in Government?*, Aldershot, Dartmouth.

Page, E.C. (1985) *Political Authority and Bureaucratic Power: a Comparative Analysis*, Brighton, Harvester Wheatsheaf.

Painter, C. (1991) 'The public sector and current orthodoxies: revitalisation or decay?', *Political Quarterly*, 62, 75–89.

Parker, R.S. (1989) 'The quest for administrative leadership', *Political Science*, 41, 18–29.

Parris, H. (1969) *Constitutional Bureaucracy: the Development of British Central Administration since the Eighteenth Century*, London, George Allen and Unwin.

Parris, H. (1973) *Staff Relations in the Civil Service: Fifty Years of Whitleyism*, London, George Allen and Unwin.

Part, A. (1990) *The Making of a Mandarin*, London, Andre Deutsch.

Peters, G. (1986) 'Burning the village: the civil service under Reagan and Thatcher', *Parliamentary Affairs*, 39, 79–97.

Peters, G. (1989) *The Politics of Bureaucracy*, 3rd edn, London, Longman.

Peters, T.J. and Waterman, R.H. (1982) *In Search of Excellence: Lessons from America's Best-run Companies*, New York, Harper and Row.

Pimlott, B. (1992) *Harold Wilson*, London, Harper Collins.

Pinkney, R. (1989) 'The British civil service: political or politically neutral?', *Teaching Public Administration*, 9(2), 37–44.

Playfair (1875) *Reports of the Commission of Inquiry into the Civil Service* (Playfair Commission) (Cmd 1113) P.P. 1875, xxiii.

Pliatzky, L. (1982) *Getting and Spending: Public Expenditure, Employment and Inflation*, Oxford, Blackwell.

Pliatzky, L. (1984) 'Mandarins, ministers and the management of Britain', *Political Quarterly*, 55, 23–38.

Pliatzky, L. (1985) *Paying and Choosing: the Intelligent Person's Guide to the Mixed Economy*, Oxford, Blackwell.

Pliatzky, L. (1989) *The Treasury under Mrs Thatcher*, Oxford, Blackwell.

Plowden, E. (1989) *An Industrialist in the Treasury: the Post-war Years*, London, Andre Deutsch.

Plowden, W. (1985) 'What prospects for the civil service?', *Public Administration*, 63, 393–414.

Plowden, W. (ed.) (1987) *Advising the Rulers*, Oxford, Blackwell.

Plowden, W. (1994) *Ministers and Mandarins*, London, Institute for Public Policy Research.

Pollitt, C. (1984) *Manipulating the Machine: Changing the Pattern of Ministerial Departments 1960–83*, London, George Allen and Unwin.

Pollitt, C. (1988) 'Bringing consumers into performance measurement: concepts, consequences and constraints', *Policy and Politics*, 16, 77–87.

Pollitt, C. (1993a) *Managerialism in the Public Services*, 2nd edn, Oxford, Blackwell.

Pollitt, C. (1993b) 'The struggle for quality: the case of the NHS', *Policy and Politics*, 21, 161–70.

Ponting, C. (1985) *the Right to Know: the Inside Story of the Belgrano Affair*, London, Sphere Books.

Ponting, C. (1986) *Whitehall: Tragedy and Farce*, London, Hamish Hamilton.

Ponting, C. (1989) *Whitehall: Changing the Old Guard*, London, Unwin Hyman.

Preston, L.M. (1987) 'Freedom and bureaucracy', *American Journal of Political Science*, 31, 773–95.

Priestley (1955) *Report of the Royal Commission on the Civil Service 1953–55* (Priestley Commission) (C. 9613) P.P. 1955–56, xi.

Public Accounts Committee (PAC) (1987) *Thirteenth Report 1986–87 – the Financial Management Initiative*, HC 61.

Public Accounts Committee (PAC) (1994) *Eighth Report 1993–94 – the Proper Conduct of Public Business*, HC 154.

Pyper, R. (1985) 'Sarah Tisdall, Ian Willmore and the civil servant's "right to leak"', *Political Quarterly*, 56, 72–81.

Pyper, R. (1991) *The Evolving Civil Service*, London, Longman.

Pyper, R. (1995) *The British Civil Service*, Hemel Hempstead, Prentice Hall/Harvester Wheatsheaf.

Quinlan, M. (1993) 'Ethics in the public service', *Governance*, 6, 538–44.

Raab, C. (1992) 'Taking networks seriously: education policy in Britain', *European Journal of Political Research*, 21, 69–90.

Radcliffe, J. (1985) 'The role of politicians and administrators in departmental reorganization: the case of the DoE', *Public Administration*, 63, 201–18.

Radcliffe, J. (1991) *The Reorganization of British Central Government*, Aldershot, Dartmouth.

Rees, G. (1963) 'Amateurs and gentlemen: or the cult of incompetence', *Encounter*, 21, 20–5.

Rhodes, R.A.W. (1990) 'Policy networks: a British perspective', *Journal of Theoretical Politics*, 2, 292–316.

Rhodes, R.A.W. (1994) 'Revinventing excellence: or how best-sellers thwart the search for lessons to transform the public sector', *Public Administration*, 72, 281–9.

Richards, D. (1993) 'Appointments in the higher civil service: assessing a "Thatcher effect"', *Strathclyde Papers on Government and Politics No. 93*, Glasgow, University of Strathclyde.

Richards, S. (1987) 'The financial management initiative', in A. Harrison and J. Gretton (eds) *Reshaping Central Government*, Oxford, Policy Journals, 22–49.

Richardson, J.J. (1990) 'Government and groups in Britain: changing styles', *Strathclyde Papers on Government and Politics, No. 69*, Glasgow, University of Strathclyde.

Riddell, P. (1993) *Honest Opportunism: the Rise of the Career Politician*, London, Hamish Hamilton.

Ridley (1887–90) *Reports of the Royal Commission on Civil Establishments* (Ridley Commission): *First Report* (Cmd 5226) P.P. 1887, xix; *Second Report* (Cmd 5545) P.P. 1888, xxvii; *Third Report* (Cmd 5748) P.P. 1889, xxi; *Fourth Report* (Cmd 6172) P.P. 1890, xxvii.

Robertson, J. (1971) *The Reform of Central Government*, London, Chatto and Windus/ Charles Knight.

Robinson, A. (1987) 'What are the implications of devolved budgeting for ministerial responsibility?', *Public Administration*, 65, 62–8.

Robson, W.A. (1937) *The British Civil Servant*, London, George Allen and Unwin.

Rohr, J.A. (1991) 'Ethical issues in French public administration: a comparative study', *Public Administration Review*, 51, 283–97.

Roll, E. (1985) *Crowded Hours*, London, Faber and Faber.

Rose, N. (1978) *Vansittart: Study of a Diplomat*, London, Heinemann.

Rose, R. (1987) *Ministers and Ministries: a Functional Analysis*, Oxford, Clarendon.

Roseveare, H. (1969) *The Treasury: the Evolution of a British Institution*, London, Allen Lane.

Royal Institute of Public Administration (RIPA) (1968) 'Editorial: reforming the bureaucracy', *Public Administration*, 46, 367–74.

Royal Institute of Public Administration (RIPA) (1980) *Policy and Practice: The Experience of Government*, London, RIPA.

Royal Institute of Public Administration (RIPA) (1985) *Politics, Ethics and Public Service*, London, RIPA.

Royal Institute of Public Administration (RIPA) (1987) *Top Jobs in Whitehall: Appointments and Promotions in the Senior Civil Service. Report of an RIPA Working Group*, London, RIPA.

Searing, D.D. (1994) *Westminster's World: Understanding Political Roles*, Cambridge, MA, Harvard University Press.

Sedgemore, B. (1980) *The Secret Constitution: an Analysis of the Political Establishment*, London, Hodder and Stoughton.

Seldon, A. (1990) 'The Cabinet Office and coordination 1979–87', *Public Administration*, 68, 103–21.

Select Committee on Procedure (1990) *Second Report 1989–90: the Working of the Select Committee System*, HC 19–I, *Vol. II: Evidence*, HC 19–II.

Self, P. (1977) *Administrative Theories and Politics*, 2nd edn, London, George Allen and Unwin.

Self, P. (1985) *Political Theories of Modern Government*, London, George Allen and Unwin.

Self, P. (1993) *Government by the Market? The Politics of Public Choice*, Basingstoke, Macmillan.

Sennett, R. (1977) *The Fall of Public Man*, Cambridge, Cambridge University Press.

Sharpe, L.J. (1988) 'The growth and decentralisation of the modern democratic state', *European Journal of Political Research*, 16, 365–80.

Shepherd, R. (1987) 'Is the age of civil service neutrality over?', *Public Administration*, 65, 69–78.

Shils, E. (1989) 'The limits on the capacities of government', *Government and Opposition*, 24, 441–57.

Simon, H. (1976) *Administrative Behaviour: a Study of Decision-making Processes in Administrative Organizations*, 3rd edn, New York, Free Press.

Sisson, C.H. (1966) *The Spirit of British Administration – and Some European Comparisons*, 2nd edn, London, Faber and Faber.

Sisson, C.H. (1971) 'The great management hoax', *The Spectator*, 27 February.

Smith, B.C. (1988) *Bureaucracy and Political Power*, Brighton, Harvester Wheatsheaf.

Smith, M.J. (1993) *Pressure, Power and Policy: State Autonomy and Policy Networks in Britain and the United States*, Brighton, Harvester Wheatsheaf.

Smith, M.J., Marsh, D. and Richards, D. (1993) 'Central government departments and the policy process', *Public Administration*, 71, 567–94.

Stewart, J. and Clarke, M. (1987) 'The public service orientation: issues and dilemmas', *Public Administration*, 65, 161–77.

Stoker, L. (1992) 'Interests and ethics in politics', *American Political Science Review*, 86, 369–80.

Stowe, K. (1992) 'Good piano won't play bad music: administrative reform and good governance', *Public Administration*, 70, 387–94.

Sutherland, G. (ed.) (1972) *Studies in the Growth of Nineteenth Century Government*, London, Routledge and Kegan Paul.

Thain, C. and Wright, M. (1988) 'Public expenditure in the UK since 1976: still the "private government of public money"?', *Public Policy and Administration*, 3(1), 1–18.

Thain, C. and Wright, M. (1995) *The Treasury and Whitehall: Planning and Controlling Public Expenditure*, Oxford, Oxford University Press.

Theakston, K. (1987) *Junior Ministers in British Government*, Oxford, Blackwell.

Theakston, K. (1992) *The Labour Party and Whitehall*, London, Routledge.

Theakston, K. and Fry, G.K. (1989) 'Britain's administrative elite: permanent secretaries 1900–86', *Public Administration*, 67, 129–47.

Theakston, K. and Fry, G.K. (1994) 'The Party and the civil service', in A. Seldon and S. Ball (eds) *Conservative Century: the Conservative Party since 1900*, Oxford, Oxford University Press, 383–402.

Thomas, Ray (1984) 'A critique of the Rayner review of the Government Statistical Service', *Public Administration*, 62, 224–8.

Thomas, R. (1978) *The British Philosophy of Administration: a Comparison of British and American Ideas 1900–39*, London, Longman.

Thompson, D.F. (1992) 'Paradoxes of government ethics', *Public Administration Review*, 52, 254–9.

Tivey, L. (1988) *Interpretations of British Politics: the Image and the System*, Brighton, Harvester Wheatsheaf.

Tomlin (1931) *Report of the Royal Commission on the Civil Service 1929–31* (Tomlin Commission) (Cmd 3909) P.P. 1930–31, x.

Treasury and Civil Service Committee (TCSC) (1986) *Seventh Report 1985–86 – Civil Servants and Ministers: Duties and Responsibilities*, HC 92.

Treasury and Civil Service Committee (TCSC) (1988) *Eighth Report 1987–88 – Civil Service Management Reform: The Next Steps*, HC 494–I and II.

Treasury and Civil Service Committee (TCSC) (1989) *Fifth Report 1988–89 – Developments in the Next Steps Programme*, HC 348.

Treasury and Civil Service Committee (TCSC) (1990) *Eighth Report 1989–90 – Progress in the Next Steps Initiative*, HC 481.

Treasury and Civil Service Committee (TCSC) (1991) *Seventeenth Report 1990–91 – the Next Steps Initiative*, HC 496.

Treasury and Civil Service Committee (TCSC) (1993) *Sixth Report 1992–93 – the Role of the Civil Service: Interim Report*, HC 390–I and II.

Treasury and Civil Service Committee (TCSC) (1994) *Fifth Report 1993–94 – the Role of the Civil Service*, HC 27–I, II and III.

Trosa, S. (1994) *Next Steps: Moving On. An Examination of the Progress to Date of the Next Steps Reforms against a Background of Recommendations Made in the Fraser Report, 1991*, London, Office of Public Service and Science.

Turpin, C. (1994) 'Ministerial responsibility', in J. Jowell and D. Oliver (eds) *The Changing Constitution*, 3rd edn, Oxford, Clarendon, 109–51.

Vibert, F. (ed.) (1991) *Britain's Constitutional Future*, London, Institute of Economic Affairs.

Waldo, D. (1984) *The Administrative State: a Study of the Political Theory of American Public Administration*, 2nd edn, New York, Holmes and Meier.

Warner, N. (1984) 'Raynerism in practice: anatomy of a Rayner scrutiny', *Public Administration*, 62, 7–22.

Wass, D. (1983) 'The public service in modern society', *Public Administration*, 61, 8–20.

Wass, D. (1984) *Government and the Governed*, London, Routledge and Kegan Paul.

Wass, D. (1985) 'The civil service at the crossroads', *Political Quarterly*, 56, 227–41.

Watson, S. (1992) 'Is Sir Humphrey dead? The changing culture of the civil service', *School for Advanced Urban Studies (SAUS) Working Paper 103*, Bristol, SAUS.

Watt, D.C. (1988) 'The public interest in question: industry as clients and constituents of government departments', *Political Quarterly*, 59, 56–62.

Webb, A. (1991) 'Coordination: a problem in public sector management', *Policy and Politics*, 19, 229–41.

Willetts, D. (1987) 'The role of the Prime Minister's Policy Unit', *Public Administration*, 65, 443–54.

Williams, M. (1975) *Inside Number 10*, London, New English Library.

Wood, B.D. and Waterman, R.W. (1991) 'The dynamics of political control of the bureaucracy', *American Political Science Review*, 85, 801–28.

Wood, B.D. and Waterman, R.W. (1993) 'The dynamics of bureaucratic adaptation', *American Journal of Political Science*, 37, 497–528.

Wright, M. (1969) *Treasury Control of the Civil Service 1854–74*, Oxford, Clarendon.

Wright, M. (1977) 'Ministers and civil servants: relations and responsibilities', *Parliamentary Affairs*, 30, 293–315.

Wright, M. (1988) 'Policy community, policy network and comparative industrial policies', *Political Studies*, 36, 593–612.

Young, H. and Sloman, A. (1982) *No, Minister: an Inquiry into the Civil Service*, London, BBC.

Young, H. and Sloman, A. (1984) *But, Chancellor: an Inquiry into the Treasury*, London, BBC.

Zentner, S.J. (1994) 'Liberalism and executive power: Woodrow Wilson and the American founders', *Polity*, 26, 579–99.

Zifcak, S. (1994) *New Managerialism: Administrative Reform in Whitehall and Canberra*, Buckingham, Open University Press.

Index